BESTSELLING BOOK SERIES

DotNetNuke™ For Dummies®

Cheat Sheet

W9-AHL-669

Sneak Preview

Use the Preview button to get an idea of how a Web page will appear when you are logged out from the Administrator role. Although the Control Panel is still displayed, the skin template and the editing buttons are hidden, giving you a sneak preview of how the page will appear to others.

	Preview	Click to display the current Web page in preview mode.
	Preview	Click again to exit preview mode.

Common Task Buttons

If you use the Common Task buttons in the Control Panel, you are only a click away from these common Administrator tasks.

	Site	Takes you to the Admin⇨Site Settings page
	Users	Takes you to the Admin⇨User Accounts page
	Roles	Takes you to the Admin⇨Security Roles page
	Files	Takes you to the Admin⇨File Manager page

DotNetNuke™ For Dummies®

Common Buttons

Although the images used on these buttons may vary slightly, these buttons do the same thing throughout DotNetNuke.

	Edit	Add a new item, or edit an existing item.
	Save	Saves a new item or an item being edited.
	Delete	This button has a number of different representations, but as a rule of thumb, if a red X is displayed on a button, it's a Delete button.
	Module Settings	Go to the Module Settings page of that module.
	Help	Takes you to help on using DotNetNuke. Depending on where the help button is located, it will either bring up the offline help included with DNN, or take you to the free online help page of the DotNetNuke Web site.

Fiddling with Text

You can copy and paste text into DotNetNuke fields as you would in any word processor. Here are the shortcuts (for Macs, use ⌘ instead of Ctrl):

Ctrl+C	Copy text
Ctrl+X	Delete or cut text
Ctrl+V	Paste copied text
Ctrl+Z	Undo last command

Moving Around

Use your Tab key to move to the next field or back to the last field when editing and updating fields:

Tab	Move forwards to the next field
Shift+Tab	Move backwards to the previous field

For Dummies: Bestselling Book Series for Beginners

by Lorraine Young, Philip Beadle, Scott Willhite, and Chris Paterra

1807
WILEY
2007

Wiley Publishing, Inc.

DotNetNuke™ For Dummies®

Published by
Wiley Publishing, Inc.
111 River Street
Hoboken, NJ 07030-5774
www.wiley.com

For general information on our other products and services, please contact our Customer Care Department within the U.S. at 800-762-2974, outside the U.S. at 317-572-3993, or fax 317-572-4002.

For technical support, please visit www.wiley.com/techsupport.

Wiley also publishes its books in a variety of electronic formats. Some content that appears in print may not be available in electronic books.

Library of Congress Control Number: 2006927772

ISBN: 978-0-471-79843-9

Manufactured in the United States of America

10 9 8 7 6 5 4 3 2 1

WILEY

About the Authors

Lorraine Young is a founding member of the DotNetNuke Core Team and a member of the DNN Help Project team. Lorraine began her IT career in 1999 when she cofounded a Web development company with her coauthor and husband, Philip Beadle. When the company decided to use DNN exclusively for Web site development, Lorraine undertook the task of writing a user manual for her clients and then decided to share it with the DNN community in a bid to expose DNN to a wider audience. Lorraine continues to provide free user help by writing the DNN online help as well as through her personal Web site, www.dnnangel.com. She holds a bachelor of arts in professional writing and literature and a post-graduate degree in orientation and mobility for visually impaired adults and children. Lorraine lives in Melbourne, Australia and works as an independent consultant.

Philip Beadle is a founding member of the DotNetNuke Core Team, a member of the DNN Help Project team, and a Microsoft Certified Application Developer (MCAD). He began his IT career in 1997 developing risk analysis software for the Australian oil and gas industry. In 1999, he founded a Web development company that focused on solutions using the application of the DNN framework. He is currently employed by Readify (www.readify.net) as a consultant. Philip runs a personal Web site for .NET developers at www.philipbeadle.net and blogs regularly on an environmentally focused Web site (www.hitechandgreen.com), which he initiated in 2006.

Scott Willhite is the COO of DotNetNuke Corporation. Scott's technology pedigree is distinguished, including a bachelor of science in computer science and MBA in information systems management from Baylor University. Scott has 20 years of technology experience as senior manager and technical architect for Andersen Consulting (now Accenture), CTO and VP of Technology for 10x Labs, and program director for Safeco's Office of the CIO. He's architected, developed, and managed systems built on technologies ranging from COBOL to Java and .NET, solving all kinds of real-world business problems in industries from banking, insurance, utilities, and healthcare to faith-based applications. Among other things, he oversees the Projects initiatives at DotNetNuke, cultivating BSD licensed (unencumbered) practical applications of Microsoft technology and programming for the world. Scott currently resides in Seattle, Washington with his lovely wife Allison and son Kyle (the first and best loves of his life) and a host of crazy pets, neighbors, and friends that he wouldn't trade for gold.

Chris Paterra is a founding member of the DotNetNuke Core Team who works for a .NET development shop in Atlanta, Georgia as lead architect. He is the project leader of the popular Forum and Gallery modules for

DotNetNuke and also aids in the agile development of the DotNetNuke Core project itself. He has written magazine articles on managing the projects, coauthored the DotNetNuke Professional Portals 4.x, and is currently writing a book titled *Professional DotNetNuke Modules*. His community involvement has earned him the Microsoft MVP award in ASP.NET for 2007.

Dedication

To our loving parents and everyone who has generously given a moment of their time to support and grow the DNN community. Nice work, team!

Authors' Acknowledgments

This book has been a team effort right from the beginning — and what a fun team it's been. Thanks to Scott Willhite for envisioning this book and working with Wiley to bring it into existence. Thanks to Lorraine for stepping forward to produce the lion's share of the book and to Philip and Chris for joining in along the way when we needed a helping hand.

It's also been a fabulous experience working with the patient and supportive team at Wiley, including Katie Feltman, Linda Morris, and the entire Composition Services group. Three cheers to you all!

Publisher's Acknowledgments

We're proud of this book; please send us your comments through our online registration form located at www.dummies.com/register/.

Some of the people who helped bring this book to market include the following:

Acquisitions, Editorial, and Media Development

Project Editor: Linda Morris

Acquisitions Editor: Katie Feltman

Copy Editor: Linda Morris

Technical Editor: Steve Fabian

Editorial Manager: Jodi Jensen

Media Development Specialists: Angela Denny, Kate Jenkins, Steven Kudirka, Kit Malone

Media Development Manager: Laura VanWinkle

Editorial Assistant: Amanda Foxworth

Sr. Editorial Assistant: Cherie Case

Cartoons: Rich Tennant (www.the5thwave.com)

Composition Services

Project Coordinator: Jennifer Theriot

Layout and Graphics: Claudia Bell, Carl Byers, Stacie Brooks, Stephanie D. Jumper, Barbara Moore, Laura Pence, Alicia B. South

Proofreaders: Aptara, Todd Lothery

Indexer: Aptara

Anniversary Logo Design: Richard Pacifico

Publishing and Editorial for Technology Dummies

    Richard Swadley, Vice President and Executive Group Publisher

    Andy Cummings, Vice President and Publisher

    Mary Bednarek, Executive Acquisitions Director

    Mary C. Corder, Editorial Director

Publishing for Consumer Dummies

    Diane Graves Steele, Vice President and Publisher

    Joyce Pepple, Acquisitions Director

Composition Services

    Gerry Fahey, Vice President of Production Services

    Debbie Stailey, Director of Composition Services

Contents at a Glance

Table of Contents

Introduction

*W*elcome to the world of DotNetNuke!

DotNetNuke is not just a great piece of free (yes, free!) software: It's your key to a vibrant and ever-changing community of software users, designers, and developers. How deeply you choose to get involved with the DotNetNuke world is up to you. If you opt for little involvement, you can simply download the code or find a hosting provider who can set you up with a domain and hosting where you can build your DotNetNuke Web site. In fact, you may never visit the official DotNetNuke Web site! Alternatively, if you do catch the DotNetNuke bug, you may find yourself taking the red pill along with many other excited and dedicated community members and seeing just how deep the rabbit hole goes.

DotNetNuke (DNN) is a Content Management System (CMS) that enables you to build and maintain dynamic Web sites by using a Web browser. It's a powerful tool that can meet most business or personal Web site needs, as well as being customizable to suit specific requirements. DNN is supported by a dedicated and ever-growing community of computer users who are constantly improving the product, creating complementary add-ons and services, as well as offering their time and support to you and other DNN users.

Because it's an open-source project, there is always a lot going on in the DotNetNuke world. Companies and individuals offer help and advice, free resources are available on the DotNetNuke Web site, and helpful blogs, Web sites, and movies are everywhere!

So with so much help everywhere, why are we writing this book?

First, this book has been written to provide you with a simple entry path into using DNN. This book helps you to get familiar with the fundamental concepts of DNN, guides you through the basics of building a Web site, and points you to other Web sites where you can find more information.

Second, this book aims to plug you in to the wider world of DNN where an ever-growing range of free and commercial resources including content, content management, Web site design, and hosting services are available to enhance your DNN experience.

Foolish Assumptions

On the whole, we wrote this book for beginners who may have never built a Web site before. In this book, we do assume readers know how to find files on their own computers and have used a Web site browser to surf the Internet at least a few times.

The book does, however, include a couple of chapters in which we do assume readers know a lot more about technology. These chapters are included to give the children in your household some light reading material, but they can be a bit more challenging for adults. The information contained in these chapters is not required to build a Web site. Chapter 2 and Chapter 11 assume readers have an understanding of computer system administration such as Internet Information Server (IIS) and Internet protocols such as File Transfer Protocol (FTP). These chapters are for readers who have existing technical knowledge in these areas and want to find out how to apply it to DNN.

How To Use This Book

This book is developed to assist with the building and maintaining of Web sites by using DNN. If you read the book from start to finish, it walks you through the full DNN journey beginning with downloading the free software, installing it on your Web service, configuring the basic settings, adding pages and content to your Web site, tweaking settings, and exploring the wider DotNetNuke community. However, we realize that your own personal DNN journey may be quite different from this depending upon whether you set up your own DNN, buy it installed from a hosting company, or are provided with a DNN Web site by your company's IT department. As such, you don't need to read the book from start to finish, but begin wherever you pick up the baton.

We recommend that readers who are being introduced to DNN for the first time read Chapter 1, which outlines the fundamentals, introduces common terminology, and provides an understanding of the way the DNN community operates. From there, you are free to pick and mix your chapters as you need!

Conventions Used in This Book

To help you get the most out of this book, we follow a few simple typographical conventions. Text that you have to type appears in **boldface**. Programming code or URLs appear in a `monospaced` font. Clickable links are <u>underlined</u>.

A Note on the Different Versions of DNN

This book will be useful for readers with any DNN 3 or DNN 4 version.

Versions of DotNetNuke change rapidly. Typically, three new versions of DNN are released each year. Each new version typically contains new features, improvements to security and speed as well as takes advantage of new features in the Microsoft .NET platform.

The numbering of versions works like this: The first version of DNN was called Version 1 and is written as DNN (01.00.00). Each time a major change is made to a version, the number changes like this: DNN (1.01.00), DNN (1.02.00), DNN (1.03.00), and so on. Each time a minor change is made to a version, the number changes like this: DNN (1.00.01), DNN (1.00.02), DNN (1.00.03), and so on. Sometimes minor versioning skips a few numbers, say, from DNN (1.00.01) to DNN (1.00.03). This happens when minor version changes are made but not released for download to the public.

This book uses the fourth major release of DNN Version 4, which is DNN (04.04.00). This is the latest version available at the time of writing. Readers with an earlier or a later version of DNN will find small variations on how tasks are performed as well as different features.

How This Book Is Organized

Whether you are planning to use DNN to build a personal Web site, a single business Web site, or to manage multiple Web sites, this book guides you through all the steps required to set up and create one or more dynamic Web sites by using DNN.

Part 1: Drawing from the DotNetNuke Power Source

This section is about getting started with DNN and is written for a mixed audience.

Chapter 1 covers all the definitions and the basic foundational concepts to understand DotNetNuke. It also explains a little bit about open source and why that aspect of DNN is important to a user right now. We recommend that everyone read this chapter.

Chapter 2 covers installing DNN on a Web server for more advanced readers who intend to download the DNN software and install it themselves.

Chapter 3 covers how to configure the general settings of DNN before you begin building your Web site. If you have purchased a single Web site from a hosting company, you don't need to read this chapter.

Part II: Putting the Power of DotNetNuke to Work

This section covers the building of the Web site. It covers the main activities of the portal Administrator, including how to create pages and add content to the Web site as well as how to create registered Web site users and control which users can see which information. The section is written sequentially, with each chapter covering a slightly more complex task or tool. Mastering this Part means that you are a skilled DNN Administrator.

Part III: Jumping to Light Speed with DotNetNuke

This section kicks Web site administration up a notch. It covers the more advanced content modules that enable your Web site users to interact with the Web site by submitting their feedback, participating in forums, subscribing to newsletters and more.

Part IV: Getting Under the Hood

This section is for readers who want to delve deeper into customizing, personalizing, and improving the experience of users. It explains how to customize the wording of automated e-mail messages sent out by DNN, how to enable users to change the language of certain information, and ways to customize the registration and login experience.

This section also demonstrates how to undertake routine maintenance and support activities for your Web site.

Part V: The Part of Tens

This section has three lists of ten. The first two lists are a sampler platter of the numerous content modules that you can add to your Web site. One lists really cheap or free modules and the other lists modules that cost a bit more money. The third list is a supplement to the Forum module and lists ten fun things for forum users.

Icons Used in This Book

This icon means that we're mentioning some really nifty point or idea that you may want to keep in mind as you use DNN.

This icon lets you know something you'll want to keep in mind. If you forget it later, that's fine, but if you remember it, it will make your DotNetNuke life a little easier.

If you skip all the other icons, pay attention to this one. Why? Because ignoring it could cause something really, really bad or embarrassing to happen, like when you were sitting in your second-grade classroom waiting for the teacher to call on you to answer a question, and you noticed that you still had your pajama shirt on. We don't want that to happen to you!

This icon shows up when thing get a bit technical. You may need to seek the assistance of a .NET developer or someone with knowledge of Web site hosting.

Part I

Drawing from the DotNetNuke Power Source

In This Part . . .

This Part is about getting started with DNN. Chapter 1 covers all the definitions and the basic foundational concepts for understanding DotNetNuke. It also explains a little bit about open source and why that aspect of DNN is important. Everyone should read Chapter 1.

Chapter 2 covers installing DNN on a Web server for advanced readers who intend to download the DNN software and install it themselves. Chapter 3 covers how to configure the general settings of DNN before you begin building your Web site. If you've purchased a single Web site from a hosting company, you don't need to read Chapter 3.

Chapter 1

Maximize Your Web Potential

· ·

· ·

DotNetNuke revolutionizes common notions of consumer-oriented Web publishing by putting enormous power, affordably, into the hands of regular people. Whereas most tools for creating Web sites just let you type a little text and change a few colors and graphics, DotNetNuke makes it possible for anyone to secure private information, host interactive content, and transact real business.

One of the great things about the Internet is that it levels the playing field when it comes to competing with the big boys. Whether you are a private individual, a sole proprietor, or a small business owner, an interactive Web site that engages your audience can project an image of professionalism previously achievable only by a much larger company. However, the inverse of that statement is also true: Many Web sites of large companies, even international conglomerates, are so woefully sleep-inducing that nobody will remember where they are, much less care to return to them.

If the Internet is teaching us one thing, it's that value is vastly increased through interaction. That means that your Web site should not only share your own information, but make it possible for others who share interest in that information to expand upon it, comment on it, rate it, add to it, subscribe to it, e-mail it, and so on.

The good news is DotNetNuke.

Don't worry; despite its name, DotNetNuke won't blow up! Most computer geeks can glean a bit of understanding from the name *DotNetNuke*. However, for those of us with jobs that involve actually interacting with customers, selling goods and services, or otherwise getting out of a cubicle once in a while, don't worry, there is some rhyme and reason to it!

In its earliest incarnation, now many generations past, DotNetNuke had many features in common with some open-source applications that ran on the Linux platform. The most popular of those had names that included the term "Nuke" prefaced by some acronym or word describing aspects of the technology the solution was based on (for example, phpNuke, PostNuke, and so on). Internet applications that run on a Microsoft platform utilize a technology called .NET (pronounced "dot net"). Hence, the name DotNetNuke was born.

DotNetNuke Is More than Web Publishing

DNN offers online editing rather than push-publishing, which means it allows you to create and manage Web pages and their content by using a Web site browser. Instead of building a Web site by creating Web site pages on your computer and then uploading these pages to a Web site server, DNN allows you to build and maintain your Web site live on the Internet — simply by logging in to the Web site and adding your changes.

Throughout this book, we refer to Web sites as *portals,* and when you are logged in as the host user, you'll see that DNN refers to Web sites as portals too. The terms *portal* and *Web site* are interchangeable.

DotNetNuke is a Content Management System (CMS). The online encyclopedia Wikipedia (www.wikipedia.com) defines a CMS as "a computer software system used to assist its users in the process of content management. A CMS facilitates the organization, control, and publication of a large body of documents and other content, such as images and multimedia resources." Sounds right to us!

The main benefits of a CMS are that it helps you organize your content and gives you ideas of what you should add to your Web site. It's kind of like the difference between having built-in cupboards versus a stack of cardboard boxes. If you have a pile of boxes, everything is just crammed in together and that's that — you need time, intuition, and luck to find those red socks again. But if you have custom-built cupboards, you're likely to remember to store them in the sock drawer. With the assistance of a good CMS, you quickly find how to organize your content effectively and, more important, your Web site visitors can easily find information.

The tag line for DotNetNuke is "It's community, It's content, It's collaboration, it's the vibe of the thing," which defines the key concepts of DNN.

DNN Is Community

Historically, Web sites were viewed by many people as an easy way to access company information such as contact details or product information. A visitor would come to a Web site, look around and then leave again — a bit like an armchair tourist. However, as Web sites evolve, it has become clear that their power and popularity lie not in the "look, but don't touch" sphere of brochure Web sites, but with Web sites that connect people who have common interests and that enable people to share their thoughts and wares with each other.

At the time of writing, the latest community Web site to take the world by storm was `http://youtube.com`. YouTube members can upload and share their videos worldwide, view thousands of videos, join interest groups, vote for favorite videos, and more. YouTube enables everyone to be a movie star, and the Web site offers free content and a devoted community. The good news is that DNN enables you to build a Web site just like this — with lots of members who can communicate, join groups, upload movies or photos or documents, write content, and much more.

Of course, YouTube is just one example of a large and popular community — it doesn't necessarily reflect the kind of community you want to have accessing your DNN Web site. Perhaps you want to build a community that is restricted to the staff of your company, customers of your business, or just your family. All of this is possible with DNN because you control who can join your community, what information they can access, and how they interact with the Web site. When you manage a DNN Web site, you really are the king of your domain. You can even choose to be the only member of your Web site if you like: Be a lone ranger!

Registered users: Members and non-members of your Web site

Access to different areas of a DNN Web site can be controlled through membership and roles. This is one of the key concepts behind DNN. Two basic categories of people can access your DNN Web site:

- Non-members (also referred to as visitors or unauthenticated users) who can only look around the publicly accessible areas of your Web site.

- Members (also referred to as registered users, or authenticated users, or users) who have logged in to the Web site and can access member-only areas and tools. Members can manage their own details such as password, name, and contact details.

Authentication refers to whether a person is logged in to the Web site or not. If a person is logged in, they are called an *authenticated user;* if they are not logged in, they are called an *unauthenticated user.* An unauthenticated user may actually be a member, but, until they log in, DNN doesn't know who they are and just treats them like a stranger.

Security roles: Sorting your members into groups

After a person has become a registered user (member) of your DNN Web site, they can then access a wide range of member-only pages and content. They can join chat groups, post to members forums, subscribe to services, manage a photo gallery, share files, or any number of other things that you choose to let them do. You have full control over which members can do which things on your Web site through the creation of *security roles* (also referred to as *roles*), which permit or restrict access to view, add, edit, and delete content on your Web site.

A *role* is a member's group that you create on your Web site. You can create as many roles as you like. After you have created these roles, you add members to one or more of these roles, or you can set up your Web site to allow members to add themselves. For example, you might create two roles on your Web site, one called Friends and one called Travel Buddies. Because Sam and Grace are your friends, you add them to the Friends role. Sam is also a Travel Buddy, so you can add him to that role as well. This means that when Grace logs in to your Web, site she can not only see the publicly available pages of your Web site, but also any special pages and content that is restricted to the security role called Friends, such as your Events diary. However, when Sam logs in to your Web site, he not only can see your Events diary for the Friends role, but he can also browse through your holiday photo gallery, which is available to members of the Travel Buddies role.

Roles are not only used to control access to different areas of your Web site, but they also control what members can do in each area. Using the preceding example, say you change your mind and decide you want to allow members of both the Friends and Travel Buddies roles to view your holiday photo gallery. You have also decided that you want to let your Travel Buddies add their own holiday snapshots to the gallery. Not a problem! You just need to check and uncheck a couple of check boxes, and then your Travel Buddies will be able to add their own snapshots, as shown in Figure 1-1. Yes, it's really that easy!

To find out more on how to register members and add members to roles, see Chapter 4.

Figure 1-1:
The Security
Roles page,
where you
can view,
add, and edit
your Web
site roles.

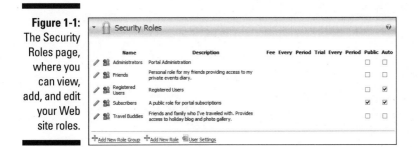

DNN Is Content

After you create your DNN Web site, you need to add something for visitors to look at or do. Web sites consist of one of more pages with either static or interactive content on each page. In DNN, Web pages are called pages and the content on those pages is maintained through building blocks called modules.

DNN Web pages

A DNN Web site consists of as many pages as you like. A page in DNN consists of a skin that controls the look and feel of the page and modules that display the content of the page. Skins and modules are covered in the next two sections, "DNN modules," and "A designer's delight." To add a new page, simply click the Add button on the left side of the Control Panel shown in Figure 1-2 and fill out the form. Your new page is now added to your Web site and you can now add modules to it to complete the page.

One of the best features of a DNN Web site is that when you add a new page, it is automatically added to the navigation menu of the Web site. If you have ever built a Web site before, you may have had the experience of the wasted time that occurs when you add a new page to a Web site and then need to also change the navigation menu on each Web page to include the new page. This manual system can cause people to avoid changing their Web site, which leads to a stagnant and boring Web site. Not so with DNN. You can add, edit, hide, and delete pages at any time and the dynamic navigation menu is always up-to-date.

DNN modules

The content of a DNN Web site is displayed on each page by using modules. A *module* is a discrete piece of functionality that you can add to a page to show content. For example, if you want to show a list of documents on your Web site, you simply select the Documents module from the drop-down list in the center of the Control Panel (refer to Figure 1-2) and click the Add button next to it. This adds the module to your page in the pane you have selected and you can now add documents to your Web site.

After a module has been added to your page, it can then be configured by Administrators and, where they have been given the necessary role access, by members. DNN ships with 27 ready-to-use modules (some of which work together to achieve a single goal). Many more are available from the DotNetNuke Marketplace (`http://marketplace.dotnetnuke.com/`) and from independent third-party vendors. Many of these modules are for sale, and most vendors also have some free modules or free versions of their commercial modules. Each module is designed to manage a particular type of content or address a particular business need. There is a module for display-ing movies or images (the Media module), a module for displaying a list of hyperlinks (the Links module), and a module that enables people to e-mail comments (the Feedback form).

The layout of your Web site is designed by adding one or more modules to a page. By combining different modules, you can create an endless number of unique pages. Modules are great because they are not tied down to a page. You can move a module to a new position on the page, move it to a new page, display it on all pages, copy it onto another page, or delete it from a page altogether and then add it back to another page later by retrieving it from the Recycle Bin.

Another benefit of modules is that they display information attractively and consistently on your Web site pages. For example, DNN comes with a Documents module that displays a list of documents. Say you want to allow all of your staff members to add new documents to your Web site. If you give your staff access to add documents to the Documents module, they can complete a simple form, click Update, and then the document is displayed on the Web site in a uniform manner. Your staff doesn't need to worry about how it will look and they don't need to know anything about how to build Web pages. The task is simple and the result is consistent and professional.

Not only is it very easy to discover how to add new documents or announcements to a module, but it's also very simple to edit existing items in the module. If the module is one that has many items in it, such as the Documents module, you can edit an existing document record by clicking the edit icon next to the record, as shown in Figure 1-3.

If the module is one that only has one record, such as the Text/HTML module, all you have to do is mouse over the Module menu and click Edit Text, as shown in Figure 1-3 on the right.

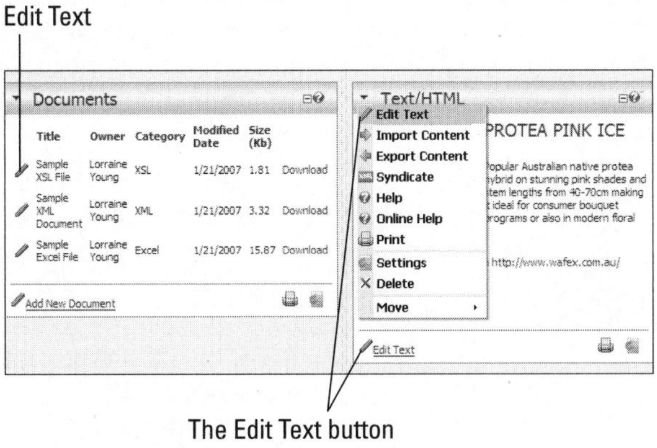

Figure 1-3:
The Documents module on the left displays a list of documents in a consistent and professional format. The Text/HTML module on the right shows how easy it is to edit the content of a module with one item.

Edit Text

The Edit Text button

A designer's delight

One of the central purposes of a good Content Management System is to keep the design of the Web site separate from the content that is added to the Web site. Achieving this separation enables the content to be changed at any time without modifying the design; likewise, you can modify the design without affecting the content. DNN is an absolute winner on this front.

If you have ever collaborated on a document, you know how difficult it can be to keep a standard look and feel. One person makes a heading large, another uses Styles to control the headings, and yet another person makes the headings bold. By the end of the process, the document can look like a dog's breakfast and any sense of professionalism or corporate branding has left the building. For this reason, separating the design from the content is the right way to go. If people cannot fiddle with the design, they will simply add their information and get back to their work. There are many examples of Web sites on the Internet that look cheap and tacky because they don't have a consistent design across the Web site.

Design in DNN is called *skinning*. When you want to add a design to your DNN Web site, you simply slip a new skin onto it, and voilà! A skin sets the layout of the page, controls the colors of the page, and controls the standard colors and sizes of text and headings on the page, as shown in Figure 1-4. A skin is made up of an HTML file, a Cascading Style Sheet (CSS), some images, and maybe a configuration file. When these files are packaged up into a skin, which comes as a compressed .ZIP file, you can install these skins onto your Web site with a few clicks. A skin package has two main elements: One or more page skins and one or more module containers. A *page skin* is the design for the whole page, and the *module container* is the design for a single module.

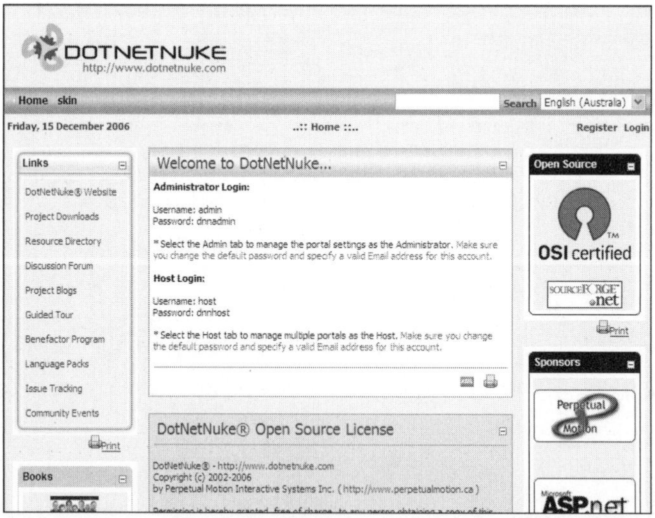

Figure 1-4:
This image shows a DNN Web site page with different module containers set on each module.

DNN skinning is completely mix and match. You can have the same page and module container design across all pages and modules on the Web site, you can have the same page design with different module container designs for each module, or you can have a different skin for every page of your Web site. It's all up to you! Because design is separate from content, you can change your design at any time. For example, if your Web site is celebrating its anniversary, you can change the module container design on the Home page to a special anniversary design, or you might like to change the design for the whole Web site. All of this is possible with only a few clicks. Here are some other features of skins:

✔ Skins have one or more panes that modules can be added to.

✔ When you are logged in as the administrator, you can view the layout of the skin, which is displayed as a gray dotted line table with the name of each pane displayed at the top of each pane, as shown in Figure 1-5.

✔ The names of the panes show up in the drop-down list of Panes in the Control Panel, as shown in the center of Figure 1-2.

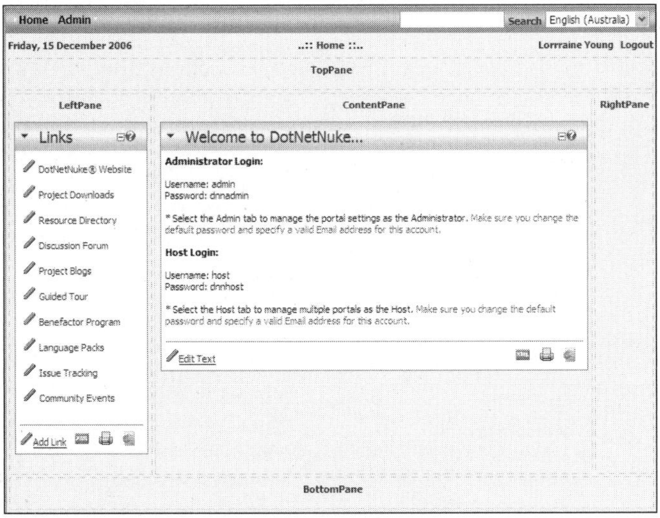

Figure 1-5: This skin has five panes available to add modules to; however, only two panes have modules added to them.

DNN Is Collaboration

In the "DNN Is Community" section earlier in this chapter, we discuss the concept of allowing members to join your Web site to create a community and how, by adding those members to one or more roles, you can control access to pages and modules.

Here's how to set permissions to a page:

1. **Log in to your Web site.**

   See "Logging in to your DNN Web site" later in this chapter.

2. **Click the Settings button or link in the Page Functions area of the Control Panel.**

   This opens the settings page for this page, which is called Page Management.

3. **Select or deselect any role in either the View Page or Edit Page columns of the Permissions section, as shown in Figure 1-6.**

   This is how easy it is to change access to pages of your Web site. Note that you cannot remove the Administrator permission; otherwise, you won't be able to manage your whole Web site.

4. **Click the Update link.**

   These new permissions are now set. See Chapter 3 for more details on working with pages and modules.

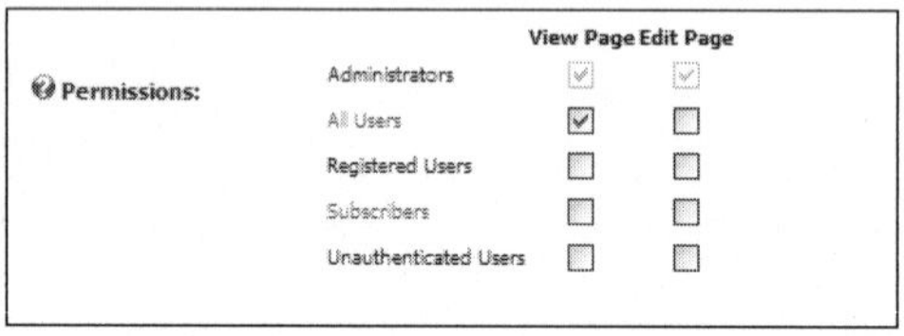

Figure 1-6:
Every page and module has a Settings page that enables you to maintain which roles are able to view or edit the page or module.

Special roles: Administrator and host roles

Roles not only control what visitors and members can see and do on your Web site, roles also provide members with access to do more powerful things on your Web site such as add new pages, manage communities, change the design of a page, or even manage the whole Web site. Roles can either provide members with just a little bit of access or a whole lot of power— and it's all up to you!

One of the special roles on your Web site is the Administrator (also known as the Portal Administrator, Site Administrator, or Admin). Most of this book is written from the perspective of the Administrator, so chances are that if you are reading this book, you may well have administration rights to a DNN Web site. Administrators have full access and absolute power to build and modify all pages of a DNN Web site. DNN Web sites are created with only one Administrator, who is then able to assign more members to the Administrator role if they choose.

As you can see in Figure 1-7, DNN offers lots of tools to help you manage all aspects of your Web site. These tools are explained in detail throughout this book, but here's a quick explanation of what each of the tools allows you to do:

- ✔ **Site Settings:** Here you can do things like change the title of your site, enter keywords and a description for search engines, change your skins, and set your default time zone.

- ✔ **Pages:** Pages lets you manage your navigation menu by moving pages around. You can also access any of your pages directly from here.

- ✔ **Security Roles:** Add, edit, and delete your user groups here. You can set whether your users can subscribe to a role and you can set the cost for a subscription.

- ✔ **User Accounts:** Here you can add, edit, and delete users on your site. You can also access the profiles of your users, manage their passwords, and look after which security roles they are members of.

- ✔ **Vendors:** DNN has a cool system for allowing you to manage advertising on your site. You do this by managing your vendors, banners, and affiliates here.

- ✔ **Site Log:** DNN records heaps of information about who is using your Web site, when they are using it, what pages they got to, and what sort of browser they are using. You can access 12 reports about the use of your site here.

- ✔ **Newsletters:** Part of managing a Web site is keeping in contact with your members. Newsletters allows you to easily send e-mails to your members with a few clicks.

- ✔ **File Manager:** Content is what your site's about! The File Manager gives you a familiar way to manage files and folders on your Web site.

- ✔ **Recycle Bin:** Whoops, didn't mean to delete that? The Recycle Bin will save the day and allow you to restore modules and pages.

- ✔ **Log Viewer:** Want to know what's going on behind the scenes on your site? The Log Viewer records 47 different events that occur on your site.

- ✔ **Skins:** Upload new designs to your site and easily apply them on the Skins page.

- ✔ **Languages:** You can change the words that describe anything on a DNN site here. If you want to change the word Cell on the registration form to Mobile Phone, this is where you do it.

- ✔ **Authentication:** If you are using DNN in an intranet, this is where you can set up Windows Authentication.

Figure 1-7:
When you log in to your DNN Web site as the Administrator, you can see all the tools that enable you to build and maintain your Web site.

If an Administrator is the queen of her Web site domain, the superuser or host is the mistress of all domains. There is only one Host Account for the whole of your DNN installation and, like the Admin, the host can add new superusers. The host can build whole new Web sites within the one DNN installation, manage files that can be shared across all Web sites, and can control what types of content and files are available on a Web site.

Figure 1-8 shows the extra tools available to superusers. These tools are explained in detail throughout this book, but here's a quick explanation of what each of the tools allows you to do:

- ✔ **Host Settings:** See Chapter 3 for a rundown on the host settings.

- ✔ **Portal:** Add new Web sites to your DNN installation and manage existing sites here.

- ✔ **Module Definitions:** See what modules are currently installed and what version they are here. You can also install new modules and get new versions of modules here.

✔ **File Manager:** This is the very similar to the File Manager in the Admin menu, except these files are for the superuser.

✔ **Vendors:** Here you can manage vendors just like under the Admin menu, except these vendors are available to every portal in your installation.

✔ **SQL:** If you know how to write SQL, you can execute it here. Be careful with SQL: It's a very powerful tool and, used wrongly, can break DNN.

✔ **Schedule:** DNN has some tasks that run in the background that look after the database for you. Here you can see how they are going by checking the History of the item.

✔ **Languages:** This is a more powerful version of the Languages tool under Admin.

✔ **Search Admin:** Manage how you want the DNN search to work and show its results.

✔ **Lists:** Many parts of DNN use lists to give you options. Here you can look after those lists of information.

✔ **Superusers Accounts:** This is a separate list of users who have access to every feature of DNN, including the host menu tools.

✔ **Skins:** Manage the skins that are available to all sites in your installation here.

Figure 1-8: When you log in to your DNN Web site as the host, you can see more of the tools that enable you to build and maintain all the sites in your installation.

Logging in to your DNN Web site

If you have a DNN Web site already installed, you can log in now and see how the look of the Web site changes based upon your role access.

1. **Click the <u>Login</u> link.**

   This link is usually located at the top of every page, usually on the right side.

2. **Enter your username into the User Name text box.**

   The out-of-the-box username for the Web site Administrator is Admin. Unless you have been given a different username, this is what you will enter here.

3. **Enter your password into the Password text box.**

   The out-of-the-box password for the Web site Administrator is dnnadmin. Unless you have been given a different username, this is what you will enter here.

4. **Click the Login button.**

   You are now logged in as the Administrator of your Web site. As the Administrator, you can build and maintain all pages, all content, and all settings for this Web site.

After you are logged in, you will see that the page has changed significantly. At the top of the page is now an Admin bar, which has frequently used tools to add pages and content. Also on the page you find small upside down triangles that display popup menus when you mouse over them. The popup menu details the features of the module. You will also see dotted lines around the panes of the skin and the names of those panes.

If you don't see these things but you know that you are logged in because the words Admin Account are visible, click the Preview button on the top left of the page to turn off Preview mode. The Preview button hides these things so you can see what the page would look like if you weren't logged in. This feature is very helpful during construction of your site.

Changing your login credentials

The first time you log in to your DNN Web site by using the default logins, you should change your password to prevent others from logging in to your Web site and adding or deleting your work. Here's how:

1. **Log in to your Web site.**

2. **Click the <u>Admin Account</u> link.**

This is located wherever the <u>Login</u> link was before you logged in. This displays the user account for the Web site Administrator.

3. **Enter your e-mail address into the E-mail Address field.**

   This enables you to receive any e-mail notifications from the DNN system, such as when you request a password reminder.

4. **Click the <u>Update</u> link.**

5. **Click the <u>Manage Password</u> link.**

6. **Enter your current password into the Current Password field.**

7. **Enter a new password into the New Password and the Confirm Password fields.**

   Note that passwords are case-sensitive.

8. **Click the <u>Change Password</u> link.**

   Your new password is now set.

If you get an error that says the e-mail couldn't be sent, go to the site and host settings pages and update the SMTP details and the e-mail addresses. See Chapter 3 for more on for this.

If you also have access to the host role, you will need to change the e-mail address and password for this account too. Follow the same steps as in the preceding list. The default host login username is host and the default password is dnnhost.

DNN serves applications, not just online brochures

With all this power to have members on your Web site, to provide different levels of access to the Web site based on roles, and to distribute the maintenance of content and the building of the Web site among many people, it's no surprise that the power of DotNetNuke goes well beyond the ability to build a five-page Web site that give basic information about your business. Depending on your goals, you can use DNN for a multitude of purposes, ranging from simple static text to robust Web-based business applications. DotNetNuke Web sites don't just sit there: They do stuff!

DNN out of the box delivers most of the functionality required to build and maintain a dynamic Web site, but you are not limited by this initial offering. As well as being able to purchase modules from third-party vendors and the DNN market place, you can also enlist the services of a DotNetNuke developer to build you a module custom designed to suit your needs. This could be a module that interacts with your existing business systems, provides an online quotation system for your products, or anything else you want. If you can dream it, DNN can deliver it!

DNN is used for many large Web sites across the world for all sorts of businesses, including national sporting Web sites (www.bigpondsport.com), transportation Web sites (http://www.transperth.wa.gov.au), corporate Web sites (www.readify.net), and small to medium businesses (www.wafex.com.au). From these examples, you can see that DNN can deliver all kinds of information to all kinds of businesses — no matter how large or small.

DNN gives you N for the price of 1

DNN is not just a tool that enables you to build a fabulous Web site — it is a tool that enables you to build 1, 2, 3, 10, 20, 30, or even 100 completely different and unique Web sites!

For developers, this means you can manage multiple portals on a single code-base, with a single IP address. For those of you with an interest in running an online Web site design business, this means you install DNN just once and build all of your customers their own Web site by using the same instance of DNN. And for those of you who have more modest aspirations, it means you can host your family Web site and your small business Web site from the same installation. Any user can create new Web sites quickly and cheaply. You can create templates from existing Web sites and use them to stamp out new Web sites. You can even export the content from a module on one Web site into a module on another Web site.

Members are unique for each portal. Joining one Web site doesn't give you access to log in to another Web site in the same installation. All settings are unique from one Web site to the next.

Plug in to Open Source

Open source means that the code used to build an application is freely available to be distributed and modified as desired within the limitations of the license. Anyone can go to the DNN Web site, download the code, and use it to build their Web site without having to ever pay one cent back to the DNN Corporation. Amazing, huh?

The philosophy behind open source is that when a large group of people come together and develop and freely share their ideas, knowledge, skills, and time with each other, the quality of the application as well as the rate at which it develops and evolves is exponentially faster than any other method of doing so. It's like having thousands of free developers working on your application day and night.

Unlike with a commercial application, which you buy or have developed for your business, the culture of open source is one of sharing, helping, and community.

DNN is developed and tested all year-round; however, the code is generally released to the public three times each year. That means that three times every year, thousands and thousands of hours of development work are neatly packaged up and available for you to download — all for free!

One common myth about open source is that it isn't secure because anyone can look at the code. People who are new to open source often have fears surrounding the security of the code. How can a Web site be safe from hackers if they can readily look through the code and find its weaknesses? Probably the most honest answer is that nothing is ever 100% secure! However, open source has many advantages over closed-source projects. Because the philosophy of open source is one of sharing and caring, it isn't typically a place where hackers go to make mischief. Instead, the golden orbs of hacking are closed proprietary code, or perhaps unethical global businesses. Hackers are generally supportive of open source and the philosophy that it represents. A hacker who is proud that she has found a security leak is more likely to use that information to help secure DNN, rather than hack into millions of DNN Web sites. Another advantage here is that the DNN community openly shares information, including any limitations. Unlike buying software from a business that wants to keep their limitations quiet for fear of losing profits, the DNN community is all about improving its wares for the greater good.

To find out more about open source, the Berkley System Distribution (BSD) license that DNN uses, some of the benefits for choosing open source, and a business case study of open source, see `http://opensource.org/index.php`.

Yes, it's free!

There are a number of different open-source licenses in existence, but DNN uses the BSD license, which is one of the most liberal licenses around. Essentially, the BSD license enables you to modify and redistribute DNN at no cost. How is it free? It is made possible by the generous license and a synergy of contributors.

Making the switch to thinking in an open-source mindset can be confusing for many businesses, especially Web development companies that ask themselves, "If it's free, how can we make money?" The answer is through building and maintaining Web sites for your customers as per usual; however, by choosing DNN, you are able to save an enormous amount of time by not having to develop it all from scratch. Instead, you have a robust and well-tested platform that you can use straight out of the box and that grows and improves at an incredible rate. After you have used DNN and understand its full potential, you're more likely to ask, "How did we ever make money without it?"

A second question businesses may ask is "Do I have to tell my customers?" And the answer to this is "No, not unless you want to." Using DNN to manage your Web sites can be your own little secret if you like. The copyright is in the code, not in any visible portion of your site. The truth is that most people who run a business don't care from where or how you get the answers they need — so long as you get them!

Watch out for "resellers"! DNN is free, so you don't need to buy it. You need to buy hosting and you may need to buy designs or custom-built modules, but you don't need to buy a license to use the code.

Based on Microsoft muscle

When people talk about open-source software, they are usually thinking about platforms like Linux, Apache, MySql, PHP, or Python. When you put all these applications together, you get what is called the LAMP stack. This set of applications has been used for a long time on the Internet to host millions of Web sites around the world. These applications are popular and cover a large percentage of the hosting market because they are "free" and stable. ("Free" is not really free: One of the reasons these applications are so stable is that they are quite lightweight, which inherently makes them difficult to manage, which in turn means you need dedicated technical staff to manage these applications.) One of the great things about Microsoft products is that they build a lot of management tools into their applications, thus making them easier to manage and requiring less staff to run a hosting center. To combat the "free" argument, Microsoft has reduced the cost of their server applications and also introduced a pay-as-you-go licensing system that has allowed a lot more hosting companies to offer Microsoft platform hosting. This is a great thing for DotNetNuke because DNN needs four Microsoft Server products to function.

The base product is called Windows Server 2003. This operating system now runs some of the largest Web sites and networks in the world and has proven itself to be stable, reliable, and also easy to manage. Windows Server 2003 is now used in many large-scale Web sites that serve millions of pages an hour and has shown that it can scale out and up to massive size and still be easily managed by a small team of staff.

The next product needed to host a DNN site is called Internet Information Server (IIS). This is the Web server part of the stack and is the product that receives the requests for Web pages and then creates the HTML to send back out to the Web browsers. You can have a look at the IIS on your home computer if you are running either Windows XP Professional or Windows Vista. You can install it under Windows Update Components on the Add/Remove Programs dialog box. IIS is quite simple to use and makes it easy for a hosting company to provision new Web sites quickly and with a minimum of effort.

DotNetNuke is written in a programming language called ASP.NET, using the Visual Basic language. For IIS to be able to understand these instructions, the .NET Framework needs to be installed on the server. DNN comes in two flavors: DNN3.x.x for the .NET 1.1 Framework and DNN 4.x.x for the .NET 2.0 Framework. .NET 2.0 is a progression from .NET 1.1 as is DNN 4 from DNN 3. DNN 3 has been "sunsetted" and no further development is occurring on that code base.

Now that we have an operating system (Windows Server 2003), a Web server (Internet Information Server), and an application framework (.NET 2.0), all we need to finish off our stack to run DNN is Microsoft SQL Server 2000 or 2005. This product is a database server: It stores the data for your sites and allows users of DNN to easily add new pages, modules, and content to their Web sites. SQL Server is an enterprise-level database and is capable of storing huge amounts of data while still remaining responsive to the user. Microsoft has spent a large amount of money improving the performance of SQL Server because it forms an integral part of many applications. There is also a free version called SQL Server Express edition that you can download from the Microsoft site to try out if you like.

The pay-as-you-go licensing Microsoft has introduced is called SPLA (Service Provider License Agreement). This method of licensing is designed to encourage hosting companies to provide Microsoft hosting solutions. The license allows them to pay monthly on a per-user basis, which means there is no upfront cost and they can be profitable from the beginning.

A thriving community

By choosing DNN, you are joining a thriving and rapidly expanding ecosystem of users and suppliers. Each time a new user joins DNN, this adds to the demand for newer and improved features — which in turn spurs more innovation that attracts additional users.

The DNN community is a friendly bunch of people from around the world with a common interest in using and building DNN Web sites. DNN community members have a range of different needs and skill levels. Members range from individuals who just want to use DNN for their own personal Web site, to IT professionals who are using DNN to manage Web sites as part of their paid employment, to IT professionals who are using DNN as their Web development or Web hosting businesses. And the good news is that everyone is welcome, so don't be shy!

It is often commented on in the DNN online help forums that the DNN community is one of the most friendly and helpful online communities in the technology field. It is rare to find people being sarcastic, angry, or unkind. As such, DNN is the perfect tool for beginners because you quickly find out that no question is too small and no reasonable request is too large.

Blink and the world isn't likely to change too much, unless it's the DNN world! There are two main sections of DNN — the core framework and the add-ons that are essentially content modules and design skins. The DNN framework comes with 27 (and growing) high-quality free modules developed by the DotNetNuke Corporation itself, as well as a small number of basic skin designs.

There are also many more to be had from other providers, both free and fully commercial. This ability for development houses to build custom modules is a popular business model in the DNN community and is one of the many ways people choose to make money.

Every day someone out there in the DNN community has an idea for a new module they want to build or a skin they want to design. These may or may not be given away for free — depending on who the person is or why they were created — but every day across the wide world of DNN, something new is being developed. The good news is that these resources are always available at very affordable prices. See Chapters 12 and 13 for some examples.

Be careful when you are interacting with the DNN community: It can become very addictive when you get started! Soon you may find yourself answering questions rather than asking them and giving back just a tiny slice of your own time to the community that makes life so easy. Please do!

Finding Help Only a Hyperlink Away

There are a number of ways that you can receive help for DNN. One great way to get started with DNN is by taking the DNN Guided Tour, as shown in Figure 1-9. The Guided Tour is a very simple-to-understand 20-page Web site that will assist even the freshest DNN beginner to understand the principles of pages, modules, and the basics of using a DNN Web site (www.dotnetnuke.com/guidedtour/).

DotNetNuke provides free online help service on their Web site, shown in Figure 1-10, which is regularly updated. This is a great resource that includes how-to tutorials on nearly every function in DNN. Furthermore, the Online Help is also available in a downloadable PDF format for a small fee http://dotnetnuke.com/About/DotNetNukeOnlineHelp/tabid/787/Default.aspx.

The DotNetNuke Web site runs a wide number of forums where you can ask questions about how to install DNN, how to use DNN and its modules, and how to develop for DNN, as shown in Figure 1-11. A number of other forums enable community members to find out about the future direction of DNN, to share information about resources and cool DNN Web sites, and lots more (http://dotnetnuke.com/Community/ForumsDotNetNuke/tabid/795/Default.aspx).

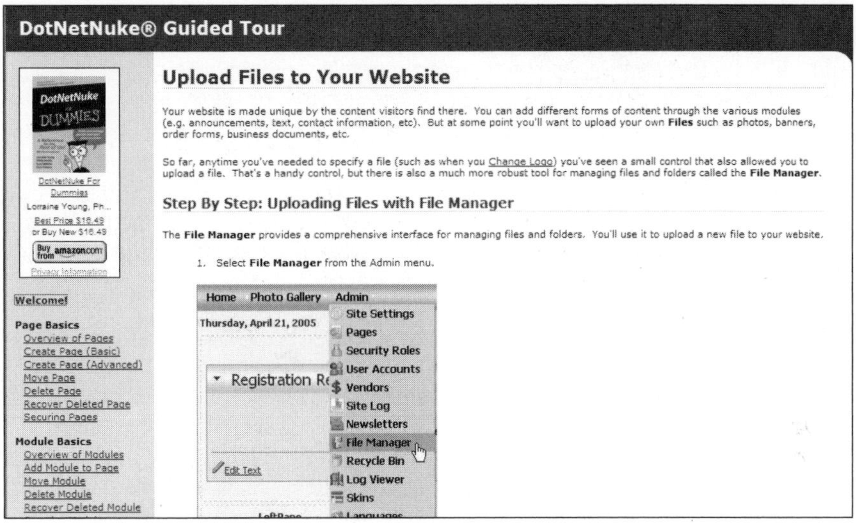

Figure 1-9: Take the free DNN Guided Tour.

Figure 1-10: Read a tutorial by using the DNN Online Help.

To make it really easy for new users to try out DNN, there is a demo site where you can sign up for your own DNN site, as shown in Figure 1-12. An online demo gives you the opportunity to experiment with the DotNetNuke Web application framework in your own virtual sandbox. Try it out at http://demo.dotnetnuke.com.

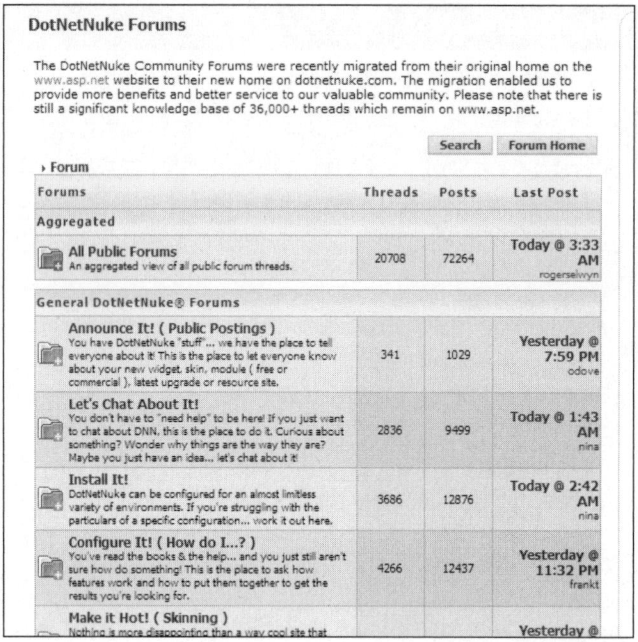

DotNetNuke Forums

The DotNetNuke Community Forums were recently migrated from their original home on the www.asp.net website to their new home on dotnetnuke.com. The migration enabled us to provide more benefits and better service to our valuable community. Please note that there is still a significant knowledge base of 36,000+ threads which remain on www.asp.net.

| | Search | Forum Home |

› Forum

Forums	Threads	Posts	Last Post
Aggregated			
All Public Forums An aggregated view of all public forum threads.	20708	72264	Today @ 3:33 AM rogerselwyn
General DotNetNuke® Forums			
Announce It! (Public Postings) You have DotNetNuke "stuff"... we have the place to tell everyone about it! This is the place to let everyone know about your new widget, skin, module (free or commercial), latest upgrade or resource site.	341	1029	Yesterday @ 7:59 PM odove
Let's Chat About It! You don't have to "need help" to be here! If you just want to chat about DNN, this is the place to do it. Curious about something? Wonder why things are the way they are? Maybe you just have an idea... let's chat about it!	2836	9499	Today @ 1:43 AM nina
Install It! DotNetNuke can be configured for an almost limitless variety of environments. If you're struggling with the particulars of a specific configuration... work it out here.	3686	12876	Today @ 2:42 AM nina
Configure It! (How do I...?) You've read the books & the help... and you just still aren't sure how do something! This is the place to ask how features work and how to put them together to get the results you're looking for.	4266	12437	Yesterday @ 11:32 PM frankt
Make it Hot! (Skinning) Nothing is more disappointing than a way cool site that			Yesterday @

Figure 1-11: Ask a question on the DNN forum.

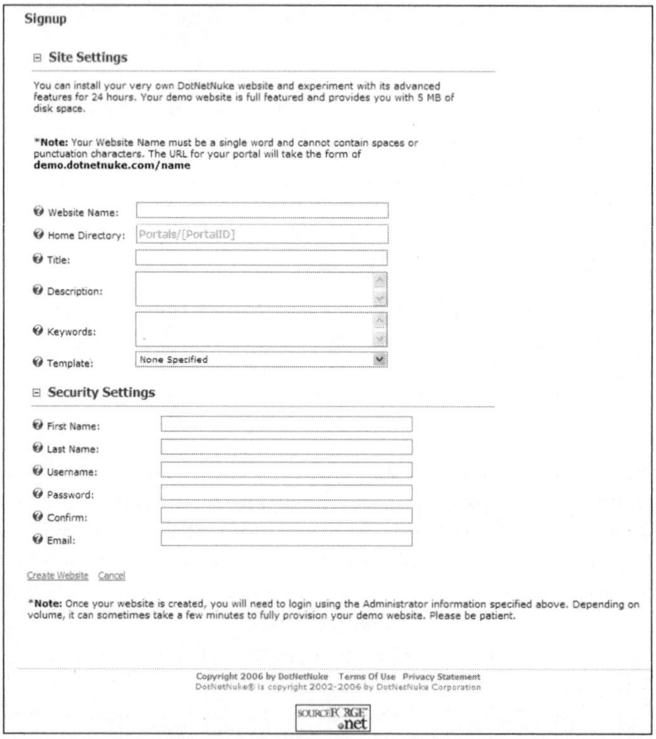

Signup

⊟ **Site Settings**

You can install your very own DotNetNuke website and experiment with its advanced features for 24 hours. Your demo website is full featured and provides you with 5 MB of disk space.

***Note:** Your Website Name must be a single word and cannot contain spaces or punctuation characters. The URL for your portal will take the form of* **demo.dotnetnuke.com/name**

❷ Website Name:		
❷ Home Directory:	Portals/[PortalID]	
❷ Title:		
❷ Description:		
❷ Keywords:		
❷ Template:	None Specified	

⊟ **Security Settings**

❷ First Name:	
❷ Last Name:	
❷ Username:	
❷ Password:	
❷ Confirm:	
❷ Email:	

Create Website   Cancel

***Note:** Once your website is created, you will need to login using the Administrator information specified above. Depending on volume, it can sometimes take a few minutes to fully provision your demo website. Please be patient.*

Copyright 2006 by DotNetNuke Terms Of Use Privacy Statement
DotNetNuke® is copyright 2002-2006 by DotNetNuke Corporation

SOURCEFORGE.net

Figure 1-12: Sign up for a demo site.

Chapter 2

Installing DotNetNuke

• •

In This Chapter

▶ Selecting the proper DotNetNuke installation package

▶ Getting DotNetNuke to your server via FTP

▶ Configuring your database connection string

▶ Troubleshooting your DotNetNuke installation

• •

*B*efore you can install DotNetNuke, you are faced with many decisions, such as determining where you want your Web site hosted, which ASP.NET framework you will be working with, and how much time you want to spend managing your Web site. This chapter helps answer some of the questions you encounter when first getting started, as well as outlines the various tasks you need to perform in order to get your DotNetNuke Web site up and running.

Making Decisions about Your DNN Installation

Faced with so many decisions prior to installation of DotNetNuke, you might find yourself in a quandary. This section of this chapter helps walk you through the decision-making process that is necessary to tailor your DotNetNuke installation to your preferences.

Which file do I download?

The first decision you need to make is which version of DotNetNuke you want to use. Because you are just starting your Web site, you should start with the newest version of DotNetNuke available at the time. This is normally your best option for new Web sites because any bugs or errors found in previous version are probably corrected in the latest version. Although the new version itself may contain a bug because of new changes, you should have some confidence in the fact that each release is tested by a private team of testers for a period of two to four weeks. Real-world people who use DotNetNuke for their business or personal Web sites conduct these tests, known as *beta tests*. This group of testers has a stake in finding and correcting these bugs prior to an official release and therefore helps identify problems before they are seen in the mainstream.

ASP.NET framework and DotNetNuke version

DotNetNuke is dependent on Microsoft's ASP.NET framework. The ASP.NET framework is a set of common functionality and methods utilized by developers to increase the speed of application development. It is freely distributed by Microsoft for the Windows operating system and is a solid foundation for any application running on a Microsoft Windows computer.

Since DotNetNuke's inception, Microsoft has released a new major version of the framework. When originally developed, DotNetNuke was dependent on version 1.0 of the ASP.NET framework. Not long after DotNetNuke's first official release on the ASP.NET 1.0 framework, an updated ASP.NET version 1.1 was released. This minor revision was a very slight change and far from a complete overhaul of the ASP.NET framework. In October of 2005, however, Microsoft released version 2.0 of their framework. With version 2.0, Microsoft made changes to the framework that forced developers to alter how certain things were accomplished via their programming.

Because of these changes and the fact that not all businesses or individuals want to adapt new technology or a new framework version so shortly after its release, DotNetNuke decided to release different major versions. This was done to allow adapters of the new framework to work with it yet still maintain the DotNetNuke versions running on the previous ASP.NET framework version. The major versions of DotNetNuke are 3 and 4. All DotNetNuke versions prior to 4 run on the ASP.NET framework version 1.1, whereas all DotNetNuke versions starting with a 4 run on the ASP.NET framework version 2.0.

Distribution packages

In addition to the versions available of DotNetNuke for download, you also need to understand what distribution packages are. *Distribution packages* are, simply put, sets of files for DotNetNuke tailored to a specific situation. The specific situations are one of three scenarios: New Installation, Upgrade of an Existing Installation, and Developer Setup.

The New Installation scenario is the one you are most likely to encounter when first getting started. These distribution packages are labeled *Install* and contain only the files necessary to run DotNetNuke on a Web server. The Upgrade scenario is very similar and contains almostall the same files as the Install distributions, with the exception of a special configuration file named Web.Config. (We discuss the Web.Config file in the "Preinstallation

Configuration" section later in this chapter.) These distribution packages have *Upgrade* in the name. The important difference to understand here is that this Web.Config file is not included in the Upgrade distribution package so that users won't replace the existing Web.Config file. Replacing this file when you don't intend to can cause all kinds of problems: The current site may break, users may not be able to log in, configuration changes to DotNetNuke and how it operates can occur, and, finally, it can cause you to lose important information that connects DotNetNuke to its database.

The third scenario, Developer Setup, is the one tailored to developers. This is actually broken out into two separate distribution packages: Source and Starter Kit. These distribution packages are distributed so developers can download and develop DotNetNuke. The reason for two separate packages is that each one is tailored for a specific developer toolset. The Starter Kit was designed to allow developers who use Microsoft's Visual Web Developer Express to program this tool, whereas the Source distribution was designed to work with Visual Studio .NET. If you are working with the ASP.NET framework version 1.1, and therefore DotNetNuke version 3, Visual Studio 2003 is required. If you are using the ASP.NET 2.0 framework, you need to use Visual Studio 2005. You should note that there is no Starter Kit distribution for the DotNetNuke 3 series because Visual Web Developer Express utilizes the ASP.NET 2.0 framework and has no ASP.NET 1.1 framework version counterpart.

Putting it all together

At this point, you should have a good idea of which distribution package and version is right for you. If you are still in doubt, start with the install distribution package for the latest DotNetNuke version released. To get the distribution package, go to www.DotNetNuke.com and register. After receiving an e-mail with your registration code, log in to the Web site and proceed to the download section of the Web site. Click on the Download links to obtain the distribution package you've chosen.

Choosing a Web host

When it comes to Web hosting, there is no shortage of companies offering this service, so choosing the right Web host is an important step in getting you closer to installing DotNetNuke. Your host should offer the following:

- ✔ Windows hosting
- ✔ ASP.NET hosting
- ✔ The ASP.NET framework version you plan on using
- ✔ Microsoft SQL Server 2000/2005 or 2005 Express database hosting

The above bullet points are requirements; however, you should also consider these other items before choosing a host. These services help you get the most out of your Web host:

- ✔ E-mail services
- ✔ Managed backups
- ✔ FTP access
- ✔ E-commerce/SSL abilities
- ✔ A sizable drive space allotment
- ✔ A large database space size allotment
- ✔ Affordable cost
- ✔ Support
- ✔ Adequate bandwidth
- ✔ DotNetNuke experience

You probably want to have e-mail available at your registered domain. If the registrar you bought the domain name from is not currently hosting your e-mail, you should get this as an added service in your hosting package. You also want to find out ahead of time the limitations on disk space size along with how much database space you are allotted. The exact requirements vary depending on how busy your site will be and how you plan to use it.

If you plan to process payments on your Web site, you may need to obtain an SSL certificate, which means you need to make sure that the host you choose supports e-commerce capabilities. Also, when selecting a host, you should educate yourself on the company's support policies as well as their experience in hosting DotNetNuke. You can always go to the DotNetNuke Web site and browse through some of the ads on the site to see a few of the hosts who are experienced in hosting DotNetNuke.

Last but not least is the cost factor. This varies greatly depending on which services you need, how busy your site is, as well as how much management you are doing on your own. You can find DotNetNuke hosting for as little as five dollars a month; on the other hand, some hosts charge over several hundred per month. The average DotNetNuke install combined with the most common services necessary to run any business online should probably run from $10 to $50 per month.

Now that you know how to choose the proper distribution package and Web host, the rest of this chapter is much more hands-on. We show you how to move files and alter their content to get your DotNetNuke Web site up and running. You should note that not all remaining sections pertain to your particular hosting situation. All commonly encountered aspects of the various hosting situations are discussed in the remainder of this chapter, so feel free to skip sections that don't pertain to your situation.

Getting DotNetNuke to Your Server

If your host does not set up the DotNetNuke Web site for you, you need to somehow get the DotNetNuke distribution package you downloaded to your Web host. This section of the chapter discusses the most common way of doing that.

When a Web hosting company sets you up as a new client, one of the first things they typically provide you is a series of usernames and passwords to access your space on the Web for administration purposes. The first combination of these usernames and passwords normally gives you the ability to access your account on the Web. At this point, some Web hosts also provide you FTP login information, whereas others require you to log in to your account management Web site to retrieve this information.

FTP, or File Transfer Protocol, is a standard method for transferring large files across the Internet. It has also become the standard in the Web hosting industry for Web hosting customers to transfer files to their Web server. All the files needed for a Web site to function properly must be transferred to the Web host so that they can be viewed by an Internet browser, such as Microsoft Internet Explorer, for viewing Web pages, images, and so on. To transfer files by using FTP, you need an FTP client program installed on your computer. If you do not have an FTP client installed, there are many free or trial versions available for you to get started with. Check out www.download.com to explore some of these clients. This chapter focuses on using a freely available open source FTP client named FileZilla, which can be found at http://filezilla.sourceforge.net.

When using FTP, you need the FTP URL to connect to, a username, a password, and, in some cases, a port to configure your FTP client to use. All the items you need to connect using an FTP client are usually provided by the Web host. If your Web host does not specify a port for use in your FTP client, it is fairly safe to assume the port is 21, which is the standard port used by FTP clients and servers for transferring data.

After you have the FTP login information, the next item on the agenda is to take the unzipped DotNetNuke install and transfer the extracted files to the Web server. An unzipped DotNetNuke install is the set of files extracted from the DotNetNuke .ZIP file you downloaded in the "Which file do I download?" section of this chapter. You can extract the files from a .ZIP file by right-clicking the .ZIP file and selecting Extract.

To transfer the files, connect to the remote Web server by using an FTP client along with the information provided by the hosting company for authentication. In most hosting scenarios, when you connect by using an FTP client, you are placed in what is called the *root level directory*.

Use the FTP authentication information given to you by your hosting company to populate the login screen within your FTP client. Figure 2-1 is an example of what a typical FTP client login screen looks like when using an FTP client application's Site Manager. You should use the Site Manager instead of the other option, Quick Connect, so you don't have to keep searching for that e-mail from the hosting company. Quick Connect allows you to connect to the remote server but doesn't save the information for later.

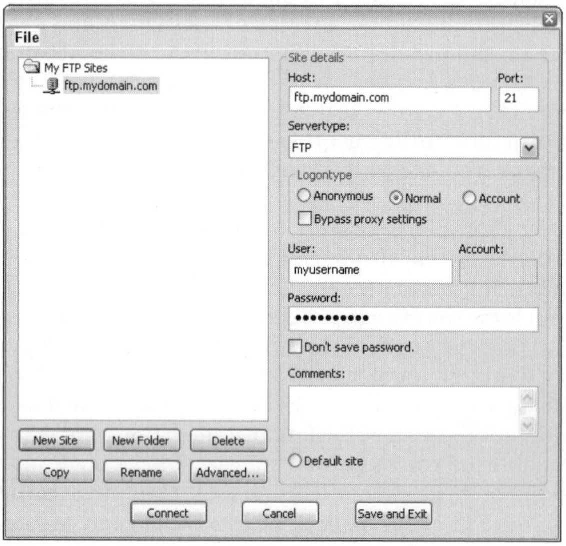

Figure 2-1:
The FileZilla
FTP client
login
screen.

The root level directory is normally the root level for the Web site; in other words, the root level for a Web site is the directory on the remote Web server where calls via a Web browser look for the Web site. What this means to you is that when you type in www.yourdomain.com in a Web browser, the Web browser is directed to this root level directory and looks for pages to display.

In some Web hosting provider setups, you may have a folder level directly below this root level directory. Typically, these directories are named similar to your domain name given to the Web hosting company at the time of your original purchase of the hosting service. Using the www.yourdomain.com example again, this directory should be named something similar to yourdomain or yourdomain_com. Just keep in mind that if this scenario of the extra level of folders applies to you, your root Web site level is actually within that folder.

After identifying your root level Web site folder, the next task is to transfer the contents of your downloaded DotNetNuke .ZIP file to the remote Web server. How this is accomplished varies depending on the FTP client you are using, but in the more popular FTP clients used today, this is as simple as dragging the local files and dropping them into the root level Web site folder on the remote server from within the FTP client.

The transferring of these files may take a long time depending on the speed of your Internet connection. Users with a broadband Internet connection can expect times of five to ten minutes or less. Most FTP clients allow you to save the login information so that you can connect to your remote Web server in a manner very similar to the way you bookmark a Web page in your Web browser. Although you mostly need FTP access to your remote Web server during the initial setup and configuration phase, you should save this information for later in case you need to make configuration changes or you want to upgrade to a newer version of DotNetNuke in the future.

When you use some form of commercial Web hosting, the host usually does a good job of setting things up on their end. They also tend to have tips and tricks to help you connect to your FTP server if you are having problems. One common problem is a conflict with a firewall setup on your home or local business network. Most networks have the common FTP port 21 open for outgoing usage, meaning you can connect from your local computer to your remote FTP server. Sometimes, however, you may need to change from what is referred to as *active mode* to *passive mode* within your FTP client. If you are using FileZilla, click the Advanced button. A dialog box appears, as shown in Figure 2-2. Click the Use Passive Mode radio button to switch to passive mode.

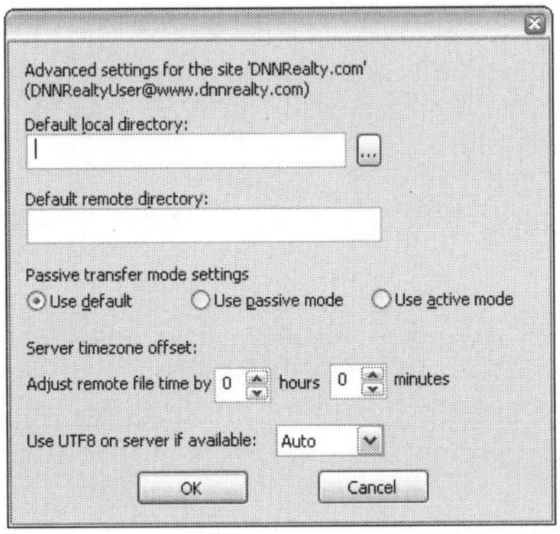

Figure 2-2:
Changing
from active
to passive
mode in
FileZilla.

Advanced settings for the site 'DNNRealty.com'
(DNNRealtyUser@www.dnnrealty.com)

Default local directory:

Default remote directory:

Passive transfer mode settings
⊙ Use default   ○ Use passive mode   ○ Use active mode

Server timezone offset:

Adjust remote file time by 0 hours 0 minutes

Use UTF8 on server if available: Auto

OK   Cancel

If it seems you are starting to connect, but you can't see any files or folders on the remote Web server after a minute, or you cannot transfer files even though it seems you are connected, try to connect again, using the opposite mode from the one you previously tried. In some situations, but not all, you receive a response in the FTP client about a directory listing error. This is normally a sign that you need to change the mode to the opposite from the one you first tried.

Setting Up IIS for DotNetNuke

If you are developing DotNetNuke, or your hosting setup is one in which you control the Web server, you will need to set up Microsoft's Internet Information server in order for your DotNetNuke Web site to be accessible via the Internet. In most situations, however, your hosting provider will handle this for you. Please note that if your hosting provider handles this for you, they will also probably handle database configuration; in that case, skip to the section entitled "Preinstallation Configuration."

Creating a Web site in IIS Manager

If you do take on the task of server administration, you are going to have to also know how to set up Microsoft's Internet Information Services, or IIS, to allow your DotNetNuke site to be displayed properly. The initial step is to open the IIS Manager. Click Start➪Administrative Tools➪Internet Information Services (IIS) Manager. With the IIS Manager open, you can begin creating a new Web site by right-clicking the Web Sites folder, as shown in Figure 2-3.

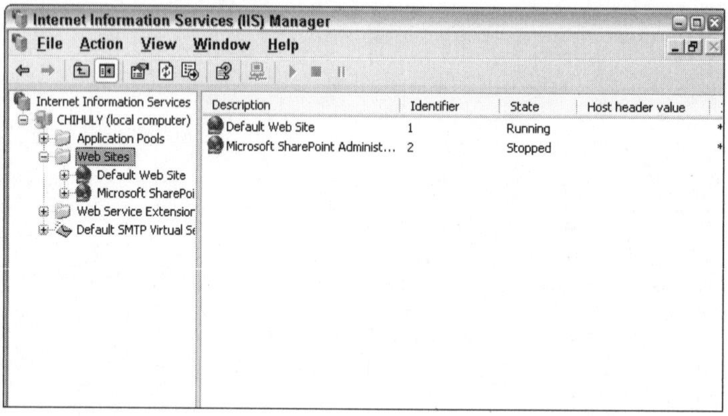

Figure 2-3:
Creating a new Web site in Microsoft's IIS Manager.

This starts the Web Site Creation Wizard, which guides you through the process of creating a new Web site. This entails first filling in a short description of what site this will represent. It is often a good idea to name the Web site something similar to your domain name, but that's not a requirement. The important thing here is that you name it something that instantly lets you as the Web Administrator know what this site is.

The next step in the wizard asks for the IP address to assign, as well as which port should be used and the host header value to assign. An *IP address* is a number that, in part, uniquely identifies the Web server so other computers and devices can communicate with it. IP, or Internet Protocol, works in combination with TCP, which we touch on shortly. An IP address consists of a series of numbers and periods that make up a set of four octets, so named because they are based on the binary system, and are in the format of xxx.xxx.xxx.xxx. If your assigned IP address looks slightly different, realize that if a 0 is at the beginning of any of these sets, the set will not be displayed. For example, the local IP address of 127.0.0.1 is actually 127.000.000.001.

When setting the IP address, leaving it as the default of "All Assigned" is often acceptable, but some situations require you to select an IP address that is accessible via the Internet. In some situations, you will have a series of local network and Internet network IP addresses available to choose from. Most local IP addresses start with 192 or 10, and you have to make sure that you are using one that is available to the Internet and not just the local network, so be careful when choosing. If you are unclear about which IP address you should be using, contact your hosting provider.

The second field available from this screen is the TCP port the Web server will be using to serve up your Web pages. TCP stands for Transmission Control Protocol, which is the method that actually allows two devices to communicate with one another.

To translate all this jargon and help make sense of it, think of the TCP/IP combination as similar to how phones work in combination with phone numbers. The IP part of TCP/IP gives us the two phone numbers that uniquely identify each telephone device. However, without the TCP part, there is no way for these two phones to communicate with each other because both phones need some type of telephone service. In this situation, the TCP part represents the active telephone service and offers the channel of communication between the two phone numbers.

By default, the TCP port you should use is port 80. Setting the TCP port to anything other than port 80 requires visitors who want to reach your site to type additional parameters after your domain name, such as `www.yourdomainname.com:8080`. It is possible to use a port other than 80 and not require users to type it in the address bar, but that varies based on network configuration, which is beyond the scope of this book.

If you are building a site that requires a Secure Socket Layer, usually referred to as simply SSL, other tasks outside the scope of this book must also be handled. If you would like further information about obtaining and installing SSL certificates, please see the VeriSign Web site at `www.verisign.com`, where you can not only find out more about SSL, but purchase certificates as well. You can identify when SSL is being used on any Web site by looking at the address bar of the Web browser. If you see https instead of the usual http, the Web site you are visiting has implemented SSL. SSL is often a requirement when processing payments online from your Web site or when security is an extremely important factor.

Please note that sites typically only use SSL on specific pages, not the entire Web site; therefore, this is normally handled by the Web server and does not require you to make any changes from the default setting. Because SSL uses TCP port 443, you may think it is necessary to set this as your TCP port, but that is not the case: Avoid doing so unless instructed to do so by your Web host. If you require SSL, you should discuss this with your hosting provider to make sure that they support it and that your server is properly configured to handle such a situation.

The final field in this screen is the host header value. This item should be set to the domain name of your site, including the extension, such as .com, in addition to the www prefix, if necessary. You may require more than one domain name, which is why we touch on the host headers again in the next section. For now, use `www.yourdomain.com` for the host headers value, unless the www part is not available to you, or you are using a subdomain, which looks similar to `my.yourdomain.com`. An example of what your wizard screen should look like just prior to completing this step is shown in Figure 2-4. Click Next to advance to the next step of the wizard.

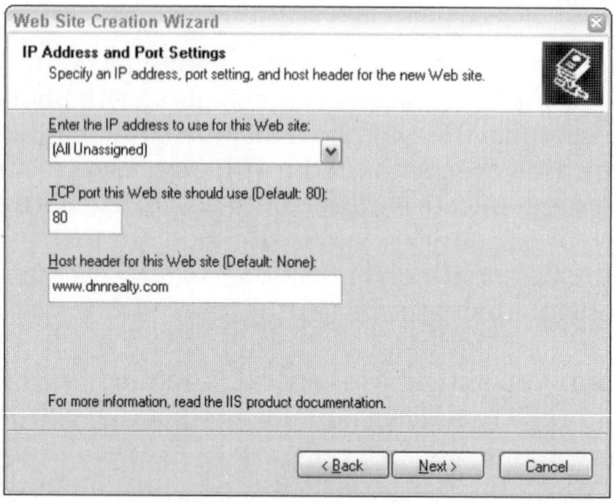

Figure 2-4:
The Web Site Creation Wizard IP Address and Port Settings window.

The next information the wizard requires is the home directory of your site. You can click the Browse button and locate the directory where your DotNetNuke install resides. Although this can be just about anywhere on the computer where there is adequate space, the normal root directory is located at C:\Inetpub\wwwroot\. Inside this directory you should create a folder to contain your DotNetNuke files. Name it something similar to your domain so you can easily identify it in the future. (Please keep in mind that it is good practice to avoid using periods in the names of your folders as well.) Click Next to advance to the next step of the wizard.

The final step requiring input from you is the Web Site Access Permissions screen. The items set here are a set of permissions used to control how your Web site behaves. Because DotNetNuke is an ASP.NET application, it needs the ability to run scripts so your Web site can be seen by others across the Internet and make use of its functionality. Check the Run Scripts (Such As ASP) check box and click the Next button, as shown in Figure 2-5.

The final screen in the wizard requires you to simply click the Finish button, and then your newly created Web site is added to the list in the IIS Manager application.

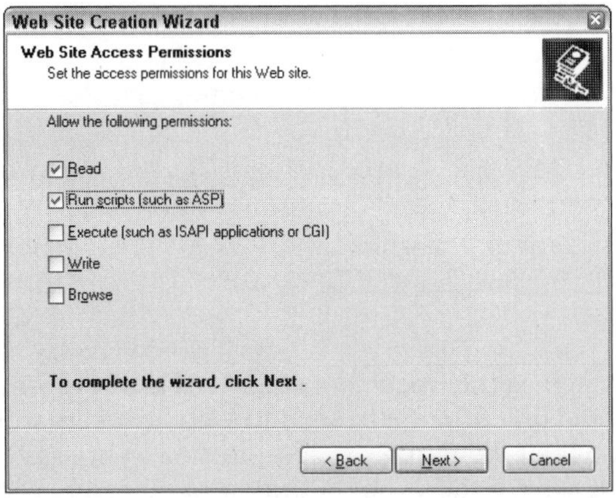

Figure 2-5:
The Web
Site
Creation
Wizard Web
Site Access
Permissions
window.

Configuring your Web site in IIS Manager

After you have created your Web site in the IIS Manager and assigned some of the configuration values, there are still several settings you may need to change to make your site viewable by the general public. What needs to be changed may differ depending on the configuration of the Web server.

To access these configuration items, right-click your Web site in the IIS Manager application and select Properties. This displays the Web Site Properties dialog box, as shown in Figure 2-6.

Most of the items in the Web Site Properties dialog box are set with default values that don't need to be changed; however, others require some changes.

When the Web Site tab is selected, you see an Advanced button. Clicking this button allows you to add additional host header values for your Web site. Host header values are simply the various domains people can type into their Web browsers to reach your Web site. When setting up your Web site by using the Web Site Creation Wizard, you assigned one host header value of www.yourdomain.com. If you want people to be able to reach your Web site by simply typing in yourdomain.com into their Web browsers, you need to add this as an additional host header value. Also, if you want people to reach your site by using completely different domain names that you have registered, you have to input those domains here as well.

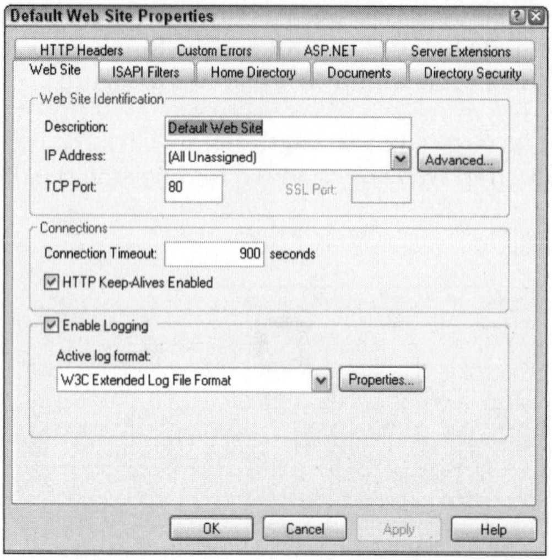

Figure 2-6:
The Web
Site
Properties
dialog box.

Another tab to check here is the Documents tab. This is where you tell IIS
what Web page it should first attempt to send to Web browsers when they
type your domain into their Web browser. The one you want listed here for
DotNetNuke is Default.aspx. If this is not in the list, you need to click the Add
button and manually type it in. After Default.aspx is in your list, select it and
click the Move Up button until it is at the top of the list, as shown in Figure 2-7.

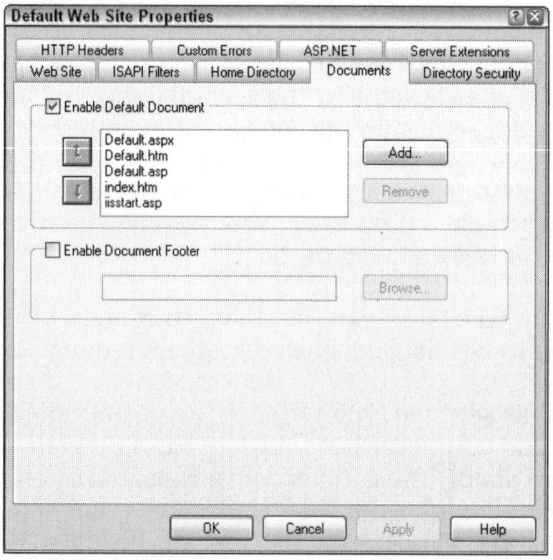

Figure 2-7:
Setting
Default.aspx
as the
default page
in the
Web Site
Properties
dialog box.

When Default.aspx is at the top of the list, click the Apply button. With that completed, the only remaining tab that requires changes is the Directory Security tab. Click the Edit button to access another property configuration screen, where you need to make sure that the Anonymous Access check box is checked, as outlined in Figure 2-8. This setting allows users to view your Web site without them entering a username and password into a popup prior to viewing your site. Leaving this unchecked requires all users to input a valid Windows username and password combination to view any page of your Web site, including the default one.

With all your changes complete, click the Apply button to apply them to your Web site. Please note that which settings need to be configured here can vary depending on how the Web server was originally configured, but this covers the most common items you have to change.

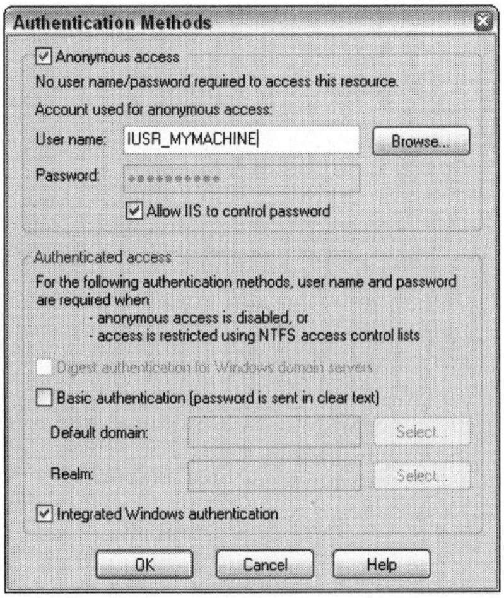

Figure 2-8: Enabling anonymous access in the Web Site Properties dialog box.

Setting Up the Database

One of the requirements to run DotNetNuke is access to a database. Although you can run DotNetNuke by using various database server systems, the recommended database server is Microsoft SQL Server. You can use either version 2000 or version 2005, but any version prior to 2000 is not supported. There are other options available such as Microsoft's Database Engine, also referred to as MSDE for short, which is part of the Microsoft Office suite, but this is normally only used in a Web development environment. In addition to the somewhat costly Microsoft SQL Server versions 2000 and 2005, the free option of Microsoft SQL Server Express 2005 is also available to you.

Creating a new database in Microsoft SQL Server 2000

The first step in creating the database is making sure that you have the database server program installed. This chapter assumes this has been installed and is properly configured for you to create new databases and database users. After the program is installed and running, you can access the administrative interface by clicking Start⇨All Programs⇨Microsoft SQL Server⇨Enterprise Manager. With Enterprise Manager open, click the plus icons until you see folder icons available for your database server name. When you can see the folders, right-click the Database folder and select New Database, as shown in Figure 2-9. (Note that if you are using SQL Server 2005, you will be using SQL Server Management Studio rather than Enterprise Manager. Aside from that, setup for both SQL Server 2000 and the 2005 version are very similar.)

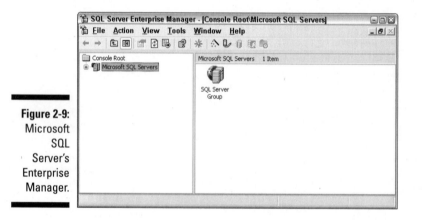

Figure 2-9:
Microsoft
SQL
Server's
Enterprise
Manager.

Clicking the new database opens a new window that allows you to give your new database a name. It is a good idea to name the database something that allows you to easily identify it, such as the name of the site. A very important note here is that you cannot use any periods in the name of the database. Doing so causes all calls to the database to look for it in the wrong place.

Microsoft SQL Server users and access permissions

There are several ways to log in to a Microsoft SQL Server database. The way you do it depends on how your Microsoft SQL Server is configured, but the most common and secure method is to create a new user in Microsoft SQL Server for each database you want to access. To create a login for your database, you need to expand the Security folder of your database server instance within Enterprise Manager. This displays the Login section. Right-click it and select New Login, as shown in Figure 2-10.

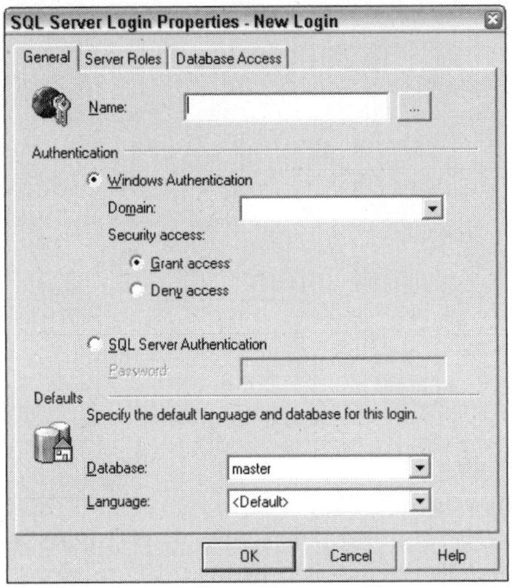

Figure 2-10:
Adding a
new
Microsoft
SQL Server
login.

In the SQL Server Login Properties screen that appears when you select New Login, you need to assign an account name. This is the username to log in to Microsoft SQL Server for DotNetNuke. Below that section is the Authentication area, where you are presented with two possibilities: Windows Authentication and SQL Server Authentication. Sticking with the more common and secure method, select SQL Server Authentication and assign a password. This password is also required later on to install DotNetNuke. After assigning the username and password, click the OK button. You see a new window that asks you to confirm the password you previously entered. Click OK in that window as well.

With the new database user created, all that is left is to give that user proper access and permissions to your DotNetNuke database. To do this, right-click your database's Users node in Enterprise Manager. Select New Database User from the menu that appears. Within the new window that appears, you can select your previously created login by using the Login Name drop-down list box. After you select the login, the username is populated and you have to assign the proper DBO (database owner) permissions by choosing the db_owner check box in Figure 2-11. Please be aware that DBO permissions are important because they allow various database calls such as insert and delete to be executed by the DotNetNuke framework and its modules.

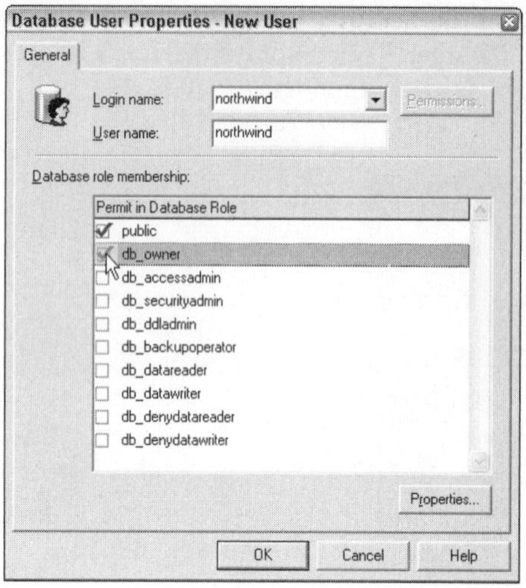

Figure 2-11:
Assigning
permissions
for a SQL
Server user.

After you click the OK button, your Microsoft SQL Server is now ready for your DotNetNuke installation. Remember that later on in the installation process, you need the database name, username, and login, along with the server name.

SQL Server 2005 Express

SQL Server 2005 Express is the free edition of SQL Server we refer to several times throughout this chapter. This version functions almost identically to its pricier counterparts, but some options are not available and it also has limitations in terms of database size. In addition to the size limitations, it does not offer administrative tools such as Enterprise Manager, found in SQL Server 2000, or its SQL Server 2005 equivalent, Management Studio. You can get a free add-on tool, however, that is not quite as detailed but still useful. It's called SQL Server Management Studio Express and can be found on the Microsoft Web site (www.microsoft.com) in the download section.

You still need the same information to connect to this database, and the way DotNetNuke operates by using SQL Server Express as its database server is identical to the SQL Server 2000 and 2005 editions. One item worth mentioning is that when you are using SQL Server Express, you are actually connecting to a database file that resides in the Database folder in your DotNetNuke install. This file is included in all DotNetNuke 4 distributions.

Preinstallation Configuration

After you have uploaded your DotNetNuke install to the remote Web host, as described in the "Getting DotNetNuke to Your Server" section, the next item on the agenda is to configure it so that the automatic installation method DotNetNuke uses functions correctly. To make sure that the installation goes as smoothly as possible, you must configure several items properly prior to calling up the Web site the first time.

The Web.Config file

DotNetNuke is often referred to as a database-driven application framework. This means that much of what you see when viewing a DotNetNuke Web site is actually pulled from the database. When it comes down to it, what is actually stored in the database is content and a series of configuration settings. Besides the content and configuration items stored in the database, there are additional configuration items that tell DotNetNuke how to function. These configuration items are settings the DotNetNuke application needs to operate — they normally need to be set only once and don't need to be changed again. The file that contains these important settings is named Web.Config and this file must reside at the root level of the Web site you want to run.

Adjusting the connection string

One of the most important items stored within the Web.Config file is the connection string. The connection string is used so your DotNetNuke Web site can communicate with your database server. A *connection string* consists of the following: database server name, database name, database username, and password. The values you need to properly configure your connection string should be provided to you by your hosting company in an e-mail or via your account management area.

After you have located this information, you are going to need to alter the Web.Config file for your installation. To do this, use your favorite text editor program or Notepad. When you open the file by using the text editing program, you see code in a structured format, referred to as XML. Locate the SiteSqlServer area, as shown in the following code:

```
<appSettings>
  <add key="SiteSqlServer" value="Server=(local);
       Database=DotNetNuke;uid=;pwd=;" />
```

You need to replace the *(local)* placeholder with the database server name supplied from the hosting company. Likewise, you need to replace *DotNetNuke* with the database name assigned to you by the hosting company. The username needs to be placed after `uid=` and ends with the semicolon. The same applies for the password except it follows the `pwd=`. The end result looks very similar to the following:

```
<appSettings>
  <add key="SiteSqlServer" value="Server=ServerName;
        Database=YourDbName;uid=DbUserName;pwd=
        DbPassword;" />
```

After you have finished adjusting the connection string, save the file. At this time, you can adjust other configuration settings stored in the Web.Config file if desired. Other settings you may want to change are discussed in Chapter 11. When you are finished making changes to the Web.Config file and have saved it, it is time for you to send those changes to the remote Web server. To do this, FTP the file as described in "Getting DotNetNuke to Your Server" section earlier in this chapter. One difference here is that if you have already transferred the Web.Config file to the remote Web server, you may be prompted by the FTP client to overwrite the original file. If you have yet to complete this site's DotNetNuke install process, simply click Yes and allow it to overwrite the existing file. If you have already installed DotNetNuke for this Web site, or you are upgrading an existing install, please make sure that you read the next section.

Getting familiar with the machine key

The machine key is another configuration setting that is stored in the Web.Config file. If you are installing DotNetNuke for the first time for a particular Web site, the existence of this configuration item is of little significance. It isn't important for a fresh install because it is changed at the time of the installation by the DotNetNuke application. The *machine key* encrypts the passwords for the user accounts that are stored in the database. If the machine key value is changed after the database is populated, it prohibits users from logging into your DotNetNuke Web site.

If you have already run your Web site, or you are upgrading an existing Web site, you need to make sure that you retain the same machine key values that were generated at the first time of installation and place them in the new Web.Config file. Normally, it is good practice to make a backup copy of your Web.Config after you have successfully installed DotNetNuke. This could prevent potential disaster in the future, so it is highly recommended. Now that you know how important the machine key is, you should probably look at an example. Machine key is actually two configuration settings located directly below the SiteSqlServer connection string, outlined in the following code. The actual value of the keys is different for every install:

```
<add key="MachineValidationKey"
     value="33EE0BD8F06F4C906AC6BB79D9B05ED099D284BA
     " />
<add key="MachineDecryptionKey"
     value="107AA92438A9A4D948CED5D75749429E55EE4EE8
     257C4BCE" />
```

DotNetNuke Automated Installation

So far in this chapter, we have covered the most important items needed to get your DotNetNuke Web site set up prior to the actual install. After you have completed all the sections outlined in this chapter, the only thing left to complete is the actual installation of the Web site. To kick off the automated installation, which DotNetNuke handles for you, all you have to do is simply navigate to the URL of your Web site in a Web browser.

Monitoring your installation

When you call up the Web site for the very first time, you should see a screen similar to Figure 2-12. This screen initially shows only the DotNetNuke logo and a few lines of text. As the installation progresses, more lines of text are displayed. Each line explains what is happening at each step of the auto-mated installation.

Figure 2-12: DotNet Nuke's automated Install screen.

If you are upgrading an existing DotNetNuke installation, you see a screen very similar to Figure 2-12 with a few minor differences pertaining to version number as well as modules being installed. In an upgrade, the previous installation's version number and the version number of the new installation is displayed at the top of the screen.

You should carefully review each line that is written to the page to view the status of that particular step of the installation process. This screen lets you know if any errors were encountered at time of installation and at which part those errors occurred. Usually, if you see the installation screen and do not immediately receive an error, the installation completes. Just because the installation completed, however, doesn't mean it was error free. If, by chance, you do encounter an error and the installation did complete, copy the errors and look for support using this book or the support forums on www.dotnetnuke.com. In the shared hosting environment, you can often ask your hosting company for support as well.

Completing your DotNetNuke installation

After installation has completed, at the bottom of the install page, you see a link that says Click Here to Access Your Portal. Clicking this link loads your newly created DotNetNuke site, which is now available to anyone who has access to the Internet. After you have clicked this link, you see the Web page shown in Figure 2-13.

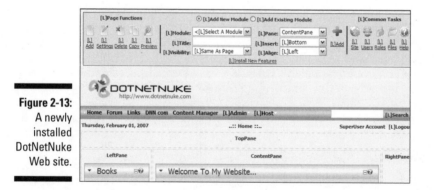

Figure 2-13:
A newly installed DotNetNuke Web site.

If you have reached this point without errors in the install screen, you have successfully set up your DotNetNuke Web site. The first thing you should do at this time is to log in by using the default host account and change the password for the host and the admin user accounts. This is very important: If you do not do this, the current username and password combinations are shown on the screen and anyone who has access to the Internet can access your site. This means they can log in to your Web site and change the passwords of these accounts, thus making the Web site no longer under your control. If this situation were to occur, you would probably have to clear out your database and install DotNetNuke again.

If you never saw the installation screen or you couldn't successfully complete your installation, read the "Troubleshooting Your Installation" section later in this chapter to see if your error is one of the common errors listed.

If you were able to install but you did see an error throughout the automated installation process, review the support Forums on `www.DotNetNuke.com` to see if others have run into the same problem you did.

Installing DotNetNuke with Control Panels

This chapter has primarily focused on shared hosting environments that involve some manual work on your end. The manual work involves things like editing your connection string, downloading a DotNetNuke installation package, and finally sending the unzipped contents of that installation package to your remote Web server. Another form of shared hosting, however, involves software called control panels.

A *control panel* is simply software that automates the DotNetNuke installation even more. Control panel software is normally developed by a third-party company and then purchased by hosting companies to offer as a service to their customers.

The control panel software makes it even easier for anyone to install DotNetNuke, but it does have limitations of its own. These limitations vary depending on the control panel software being used to control the DotNetNuke installation and the Web hosting company's policies.

Common control panel benefits

One of the huge benefits of using a host that offers a control panel setup is that it often allows you to avoid errors during the install process. Although the DotNetNuke install process is rather intuitive, some users with little or no experience setting up a Web site sometimes find the installation the most difficult part of starting with DotNetNuke. When you use a control panel, the DotNetNuke installation is normally on the server in the correct location and the control panel sets the connection string at the time of installation.

The setups are often very inexpensive, offer plenty of flexibility for very little money, and come with more than adequate support packages. They often allow you to not worry about setting up e-mail for your domain, offer Web e-mail access, and most already have DotNetNuke ready to be installed for you when you are ready to start working on your site. (That saves you the trouble of using an FTP client to transfer the files to the Web server.)

Common control panel drawbacks

One of the most common limitations when using a shared hosting environment that makes use of a control panel is that you are often limited to when you can upgrade your version of DotNetNuke. Another major limitation is not having superuser-level access. Not having superuser-level access is normally not bad unless you intend on upgrading your modules. The lack of superuser-level access means that if you want to add a new module to your Web site or you want to upgrade an existing version of a module on your Web site, you have to contact your hosting provider. Depending on the functionality you need for your Web site, you should consider this when choosing your hosting provider and verify which type of shared hosting environment they are using.

If you do not have superuser-level access but your host allows you full access via FTP, you can upgrade your DotNetNuke modules anytime you want by uploading the files via an FTP client to the proper install folder. Although this is very much possible to do, there are other settings within DotNetNuke that you may have to configure in order to enable the installation of modules from the install folder. It is worth mentioning that even if you do have superuser-level access, you may want to use this approach to install large sized modules. The FTP installation method is a great alternative for installing larger file size modules if your Internet connection speed is slow.

When choosing a hosting company, one of your decisions should be whether you want to use one that provides a control panel. If you do, you should carefully read the benefits section again and ask questions prior to committing yourself to a hosting plan. This should help you avoid making a decision now that you may want to change later.

On the other hand, if, after reading this chapter, you feel confident enough to try a hosting company that does not offer a control panel, you should still research what type of support they offer. Normally, there is plenty of free support available at the DotNetNuke forums, but you may not always get responses as quickly as you would with a paid support program.

Troubleshooting Your Installation

An installation can go wrong for many reasons: anything from configuration settings not being set up properly, files missing, permissions not properly set up by the hosting company, and the list goes on. Covering every possible problem is beyond the scope of this book, but, in this section, we cover some of the most common installation problems.

Configuration errors

If you receive a configuration error, this is most likely a problem with your Web.Config file. There are a number of reasons that this may happen. One of the more common problems is syntax in the Web.Config. While you were editing your connection string or some other part of the Web.Config file, you may have changed something into a format that the ASP.NET framework does not recognize. More than likely, if you only edited the connection string, you probably deleted something that needs to be there, like ; > / symbols, or you removed a necessary space, thus making two items that should be separate run together. Another possibility is you may have added a space inside the connection string where one shouldn't be, thus also causing the ASP.NET framework to not recognize one of the values set within the connection string item.

Figure 2-14 represents a typical ASP.NET error, although the wording may vary slightly.

Object reference error

If you are seeing an "Object reference not set to an instance of an object" error and this is the first time you are running the DotNetNuke install for this Web site, you should double-check to make sure that your Web.Config file is on the remote Web server and placed within the root level directory of your Web site. If the Web.Config file is missing, the error that you are most likely to see is shown in Figure 2-15.

There are other times you may see an object reference error; however, most of the time, when this error is seen, it's after the installation has completed.

Please note that in a future version of DotNetNuke, an installation wizard will be provided as part of the download to ease the installation process. At the time of this writing, it was not yet completed.

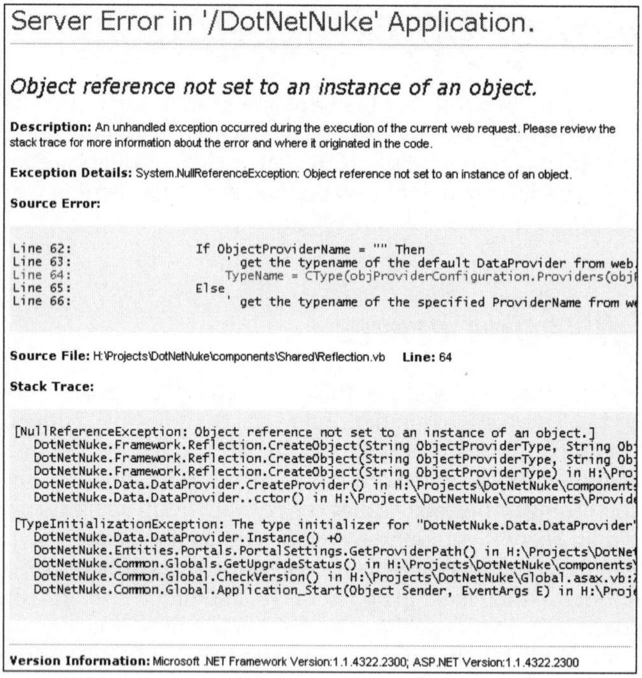

Server Error in '/DotNetNuke' Application.

Object reference not set to an instance of an object.

Description: An unhandled exception occurred during the execution of the current web request. Please review the stack trace for more information about the error and where it originated in the code.

Exception Details: System.NullReferenceException: Object reference not set to an instance of an object.

Source Error:

```
Line 62:                If ObjectProviderName = "" Then
Line 63:                    ' get the typename of the default DataProvider from web.
Line 64:                    TypeName = CType(objProviderConfiguration.Providers(obj
Line 65:                Else
Line 66:                    ' get the typename of the specified ProviderName from w
```

Source File: H:\Projects\DotNetNuke\components\Shared\Reflection.vb **Line:** 64

Stack Trace:

```
[NullReferenceException: Object reference not set to an instance of an object.]
   DotNetNuke.Framework.Reflection.CreateObject(String ObjectProviderType, String Ob
   DotNetNuke.Framework.Reflection.CreateObject(String ObjectProviderType, String Ob
   DotNetNuke.Framework.Reflection.CreateObject(String ObjectProviderType) in H:\Pro
   DotNetNuke.Data.DataProvider.CreateProvider() in H:\Projects\DotNetNuke\component
   DotNetNuke.Data.DataProvider..cctor() in H:\Projects\DotNetNuke\components\Provid

[TypeInitializationException: The type initializer for "DotNetNuke.Data.DataProvider"
   DotNetNuke.Data.DataProvider.Instance() +0
   DotNetNuke.Entities.Portals.PortalSettings.GetProviderPath() in H:\Projects\DotNe
   DotNetNuke.Common.Globals.GetUpgradeStatus() in H:\Projects\DotNetNuke\components
   DotNetNuke.Common.Global.CheckVersion() in H:\Projects\DotNetNuke\Global.asax.vb:
   DotNetNuke.Common.Global.Application_Start(Object Sender, EventArgs E) in H:\Proj
```

Version Information: Microsoft .NET Framework Version:1.1.4322.2300; ASP.NET Version:1.1.4322.2300

Figure 2-14: A typical ASP.NET error page.

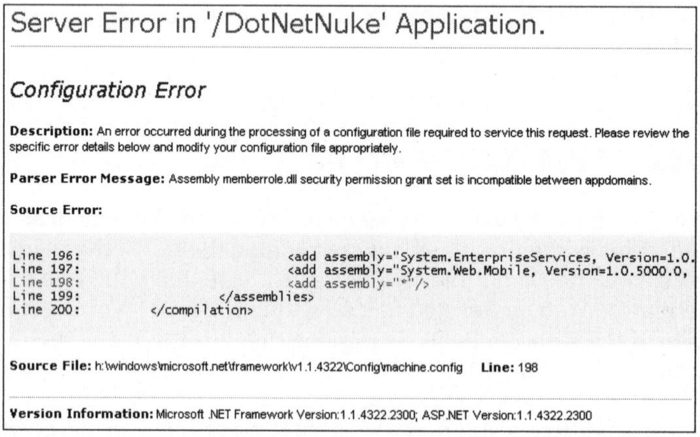

Server Error in '/DotNetNuke' Application.

Configuration Error

Description: An error occurred during the processing of a configuration file required to service this request. Please review the specific error details below and modify your configuration file appropriately.

Parser Error Message: Assembly memberrole.dll security permission grant set is incompatible between appdomains.

Source Error:

```
Line 196:                <add assembly="System.EnterpriseServices, Version=1.0.
Line 197:                <add assembly="System.Web.Mobile, Version=1.0.5000.0,
Line 198:                <add assembly="*"/>
Line 199:            </assemblies>
Line 200:        </compilation>
```

Source File: h:\windows\microsoft.net\framework\v1.1.4322\Config\machine.config **Line:** 198

Version Information: Microsoft .NET Framework Version:1.1.4322.2300; ASP.NET Version:1.1.4322.2300

Figure 2-15: A common error when the Web.Config file is missing.

Database connection errors

Database connection errors are probably the most common set of errors seen at the time of installation. The error appears as a "Cannot connect to database" message. When this happens, you need to review your connection string. Verify that you have properly filled in the database server name, database name, and database username and database password. If any one of these items is incorrect, you can't connect to your database server. An example of what this error looks like can be seen in Figure 2-16.

Figure 2-16:
A database
connection
error seen
at time of
installation.

Error Installing DotNetNuke

Current Assembly Version: 03.03.03

ERROR: Could not connect to database specified in connectionString for SqlDataProvider

This error usually appears on the install page or a very empty white Web page containing only black text.

Earlier in this chapter, we explained how to set up the connection string, which is authenticated against Microsoft's SQL Server 2000 by using the SiteSqlServer configuration variable. If you are using SQL Server version 2005, the connection string setup is exactly the same. However, if you are using the SQL Express version for your database server, you won't alter the connection string outlined in the "Adjusting the connection string" section earlier in this chapter. Instead, you'll alter this one:

```
   <appSettings>
<add name="SiteSqlServer" connectionString="Data Source=.\
        SQLExpress;Integrated Security=True;User
        Instance=True;AttachDBFilename=|DataDirectory|
        Database.mdf;" providerName="System.Data.
        SqlClient" />
```

As we mention throughout the chapter, your options for support are your hosting company and the forums located on DotNetNuke.com. If you are in need of support, you should include several things along with your request: DotNetNuke version and number, the error message displayed, and what you were trying to do. If your error seems to be specific to a particular module, you should also include the version number of that module in question.

Chapter 3

Set It and Forget It: Default Portal Settings

● ●

In This Chapter

▶ Adapting DNN to your environment

▶ Setting global preferences for new portals

▶ Installing modules and assigning them to portals

▶ Lighting up a new portal (or two, or three)

● ●

*T*his chapter shows you how to configure the default settings that apply to all new portals (Web sites) you create in your DNN installation, how to install modules to DNN, and how to control which of your Web sites have access to those modules. Finally, this chapter demonstrates how to create one, two, or more Web sites.

In the first section of this chapter, we show you how to configure the default settings that apply to all new portals (Web sites) you create with this DNN installation. To make it simple to create new Web sites, DNN lets you set a number of default settings in advance so that when you do create a new Web site, you don't need to redo each setting every time. These settings relate to things like hosting space allocation, e-mail, design, the type of files that can be uploaded, and more. These settings can later be changed on an individual Web site, if, for instance, you want to give one Web site additional hosting space. See Chapter 4 for more on this or Chapter 10 to discover more about the Site Log setting.

Also in this chapter, we show you how to install modules. DNN comes with a number of available modules that must be installed. In addition, there are many free and commercial modules out in the DNN community that you may want to install on your Web site. This chapter shows you how to do these two different types of module installation, as well as how to control which Web sites can use which modules.

Last but not least, we cover how to create new portals within this DNN installation.

Changing Settings to Adapt to Your Needs

The Site Configuration section provides information on your DNN installation and relates to every portal in this DNN application. Here you can find out the version number of your DNN application, as well as set DNN to check for version upgrades and provide you with a link to download newer versions. There is also a range of other fields that display the settings on your server. These will be of interest to you if you are running your own server. Alternatively, if you are seeking technical or development support, the support staff will need to know this information to understand your setup.

Here's how to view the Site Configuration details:

1. **Log in as the Host.**

2. **Navigate to the Host⇨Host Settings page.**

   The Host Settings page enables you to set the default details for all new Web sites in this DNN installation.

3. **Go to the Site Configuration section, as shown in Figure 3-1.**

4. **Your version number is displayed at DotNetNuke Version.**

   This is the version of DNN you are using. Typically, three new versions are released each year. This version number can be displayed in your Web browser. See "Setting the default appearance for new portals" for more information.

5. **Select Check For Upgrades? to be advised when a later version of DNN is available.**

   If you are planning to upgrade to newer versions of DotNetNuke, select this check box to find out when a new version is available.

6. **If a green button is displayed at Upgrade Available?, click to download the latest version.**

   Clicking on the button goes to the Downloads page of the DNN Web site, where you can get the latest version.

7. **Note the following information regarding your database:**

   • **Data Provider:** The name of the provider that is identified in the Web.Config file is displayed here. SqlDataProvider is the default setting for DNN; however, other database names such as OracleDataProvider may be displayed.

   • **.NET Framework:** The version of the .NET Framework that has been selected in IIS as the application pool for DNN.

- **ASP.NET Identity:** The Windows user account under which the application is running. This is the account that needs to be granted folder permissions on the server.

- **Host Name:** Displays the host name of your Web site. The host name is the name of the server that DNN is running on. If your site is running in a Web farm, this value changes depending on which server in the Web farm is serving you. A Web farm consists of multiple Web servers serving one Web site and is often used by hosting companies for large Web sites with lots of traffic.

Figure 3-1:
The Site Configuration section displays information about the DNN installation to the host.

```
⊟ Basic Settings
Enter basic settings for your Hosting Account
   ⊟ Site Configuration
   ❔ DotNetNuke Version:      04.04.01
   ❔ Check For Upgrades?      ☑
   ❔ Upgrade Available?       ◉
   ❔ Data Provider:           SqlDataProvider
   ❔ .NET Framework:          2.0.50727.42
   ❔ ASP.NET Identity:        LORRAINE\ASPNET
   ❔ Host Name:               lorraine
```

Setting the host details

In this section, we show you how to set the general contact details of the host portal. These details are used in any e-mail notifications sent to Administrators of child portals, as well as e-mail setting tests. These settings refer to the parent portal. See Chapter 9 for a list of available notification e-mails.

Here's how to set the host details:

1. **Log in as the host.**

2. **Navigate to the Host⇨Host Settings page.**

   This displays the Host Settings page, which enables you to set the default details for all Web sites in this DNN installation.

3. **Go to the Host Details section, as shown in Figure 3-2.**

   This displays details of the parent or host portal.

4. **Select the parent or host Web site for this installation from the Host Portal drop-down box.**

   The parent or host portal is typically the portal of the host. You can change the parent Web site for this installation at any time. Wherever there are references to parent and child Web sites (often called host and site), the one selected here is the host. For example, if an invalid URL to one of the portals in this DNN installation is requested, this portal is shown.

5. **Enter a title for the parent Web site into the Host Title text box.**

   This is the name of the parent Web site. This value is shown in the [HOSTNAME] skin object in the skin.

6. **Enter the URL of the parent Web site into the Host URL text box; for example,** `www.dnnangel.com`.

   This URL is the link on the [HOSTNAME] skin object you set above.

7. **Enter the contact e-mail address for the parent Web site into the Host e-mail text box; for example,** `host@dnnangel.com`.

   This is the e-mail address of the host Web site and is used in e-mails sent to and from the host. See Chapter 9 for a list of available notification e-mails.

8. **Click the <u>Update</u> link to save these settings.**

   These setting are now saved and can be edited at any time in the future if required.

Figure 3-2:
The Host
Details
section
enables the
host to set
the host
portal and
the host
contact
details for
this DNN
installation.

⊟ Host Details	
ⓘ Host Portal:	DNNAngel ⌄
ⓘ Host Title:	DNN Angel
ⓘ Host URL:	http://www.dnnangel.com
ⓘ Host Email:	support@dnnangel.com

Setting the SMTP server settings

This section enables you to set the SMTP server settings for all Web sites within this DNN installation. SMTP stands for Simple Mail Transfer Protocol, which refers to the mail settings of the server you are using. You need to set all these fields to be able to send and receive e-mails from all Web sites within this installation. Anytime an e-mail is sent, it is sent out through the SMTP server that you specify. Some hosting companies allow you to use localhost as the entry, and, if you are running DNN on your local machine, you will use localhost. Most hosting companies give you a dedicated SMTP server to send your e-mail through.

You should take care not to send large volumes of e-mail through your DNN Web site: There are harsh penalties for spam, and many hosts will ban your IP address, which means that none of your notification e-mails will work. If you need to send thousands of e-mails, you should find an e-mail sending company to do it for you as they have the right equipment and know the rules on spam.

A new security role called Subscribers was added to DNN recently. Users have the ability to unsubscribe themselves from the Subscribers role and thereby opt out of newsletters sent from the site. This was required under the new anti-spam laws. When you send mass e-mails (also known as newsletters), use this role rather than the Registered Users role. See Chapter 7 for more information on sending Newsletters.

Here's how to set the SMTP settings for all Web sites:

1. **Log in as the Host.**

2. **Navigate to the Host↪Host Settings page.**

   This displays the Host Settings page, which enables you to set the default details for all Web sites in this DNN installation.

3. **Click the Maximize button beside Advanced Settings and then click the Maximize button next to SMTP Server Settings.**

   This displays SMTP server settings, shown in Figure 3-3, which must be set to enable Web sites to send e-mails. There is also a Test button here to test these settings.

4. **Enter the address of the SMTP server into the SMTP Server text box.**

   The SMTP server name is the URL of the server that all e-mail will be sent from. This usually takes the form of mail.domain.com and is sometimes an IP address like 213.164.164.43. If you are running on your local machine, the address will be localhost.

5. **Select the type of SMTP authentication.**

   This section has three radio buttons for the three types of authentication for your SMTP server that DNN supports:

   - **Anonymous** authentication is used when the SMTP server does not need to validate which user account is trying to send an e-mail through it. A lot of hosting companies use this system because they have supplied you with a SMTP server URL that can only be discovered inside their network; therefore, to send an e-mail, you must already be on their network, so there is no need to authenticate you.

   - **Basic** authentication is simple username and password authentication. When your DNN site tries to send an e-mail, it will pass the username and password to the SMTP server, which will then attempt to authenticate the request. If the username and password are correct, the e-mail will be sent; if not, you will get an error message.

- **NTLM** authentication uses Windows Authentication to validate the account trying to send an e-mail. This is most often used when the mail server is Microsoft Exchange.

6. **Check the SMTP Enable SSL check box if your Web site requires a secure connection.**

   This option is selected when your e-mail provider requires a secure connection to the SMTP server. Some e-mail servers require a secure SSL connection when sending e-mails to try to cut down on unauthorized use of their SMTP gateway. This is not usually required for most Web sites.

7. **Enter the username of your SMTP server into the SMTP Username text box.**

   Your hosting provider supplies the username to you.

8. **Enter the password of your SMTP server into the SMTP Password text box.**

   Your hosting provider supplies the password to you.

9. **Click the <u>Update</u> link to save these settings.**

   These setting are now saved and you can test them.

10. **Click the <u>Test</u> link beside the SMTP Server field to test your settings.**

    A "Message Sent Successfully" message is displayed if the test mail was successfully sent. If it failed to send, an error message that provides information on why the message failed is displayed.

Figure 3-3:
The SMTP Server Settings section enables the Host to set the e-mail server settings for this DNN installation.

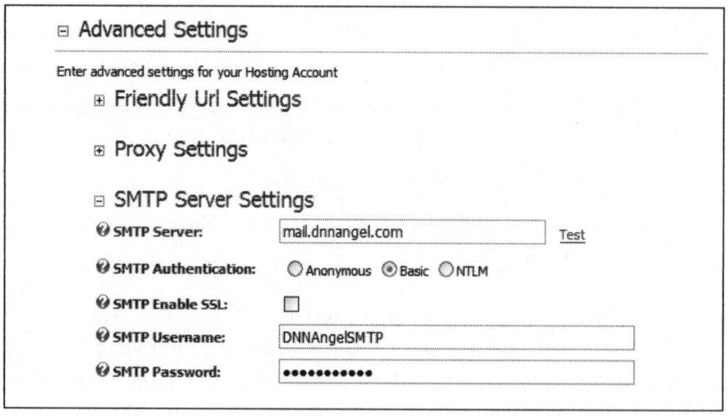

⊟ Advanced Settings

Enter advanced settings for your Hosting Account

   ⊞ Friendly Url Settings

   ⊞ Proxy Settings

   ⊟ SMTP Server Settings

   🔘 **SMTP Server:**   mail.dnnangel.com   Test

   🔘 **SMTP Authentication:**   ○ Anonymous ⦿ Basic ○ NTLM

   🔘 **SMTP Enable SSL:**   ☐

   🔘 **SMTP Username:**   DNNAngelSMTP

   🔘 **SMTP Password:**   ••••••••••

In a lot of hosting situations, the Web server your Web site runs on is also the SMTP server. This can cause your e-mail to be flagged as spam by the receiving mail servers. Mail services such as Hotmail, Google, and Yahoo! get a lot of spam, so they have strict limits on how many e-mails are sent to them.

One way to help make sure that your e-mail is not flagged as spam is to ensure that the SMTP Server address you enter at SMTP Server above is the same server name that is specified in the MX record of your domain. An MX record (Mail exchanger record) is a type of resource record in the domain name system (DNS) that sets how Internet e-mail is sent. MX records point to the servers that should receive an e-mail and their priority over each other. Ask your hosting provider about this if you have trouble sending e-mail.

In most cases, you don't need to specify the proxy server settings for DNN. However, some modules may need to use ports that may require a proxy server to function properly. Modules that use things like File Transfer Protocol (FTP), Network News Transfer Protocol (NNTP), or Really Simple Syndication (RSS) may need this setting. Talk to your hosting provider about this if you have trouble with these sorts of modules.

Enabling Friendly URLs

Enabling Friendly URLs automatically changes the format of the Web site URL address to one that is easier for users to remember and type in, as shown in Figure 3-4. See Chapter 11 for more details on why you may choose to use Friendly URLs.

Here's how to enable Friendly URLs:

1. **Log in as the Host.**

2. **Navigate to the Host⇨Host Settings page.**

   This displays the Host Settings page, which enables you to set the default details for all Web sites in this DNN installation.

3. **Click the Maximize button beside Advanced Settings and then click the Maximize button beside Friendly URL Settings.**

   This displays the Enable/Disable check box for this setting. If this box is checked, a list of editable items is displayed below.

4. **Check the check box beside Use Friendly URLs? to enable Friendly URLs.**

   A list of editable items is displayed. This list is a list of rules that are used to transform the standard DNN URLs into friendly human-readable and search engine–friendly URLs. These are called *regular expression rules* and are beyond the scope of this book. However, if you want to find out more about regular expressions, visit www.regexlib.com to see a large library of regular expressions.

Figure 3-4:
Friendly
URLs
disabled
(top image)
and enabled
(bottom
image) as
rendered in
the Web site
browser.

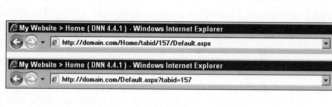

Setting auto-unlock of accounts

DNN includes a security setting aimed at preventing people from trying to log in to someone else's accounts. If someone unsuccessfully attempts to log in to a user's account five times, DNN can be set to block that user account from attempting further logins to the Web site for a set number of minutes. When a lockout occurs, the host receives a notification message telling them about this suspicious activity.

Here's how to set the auto-unlock accounts time period for all portals:

1. **Log in as the Host.**

2. **Navigate to the Host⇨Host Settings page.**

   This displays the Host Settings page, which enables you to set the default details for all Web sites in this DNN installation.

3. **Click the Maximize button beside Advanced Settings and then click the Maximize button beside Other Settings.**

   This displays a number of miscellaneous settings for all Web sites. Many have defaults set already.

4. **Enter the number of minutes until auto-unlock of an account occurs in the Auto-Unlock Accounts After (Minutes) text box; for example,** 20.

   Alternatively, you can set this field to zero (0) to disable the auto-unlock feature. If it is disabled, only the Administrator can unlock the user account.

5. **Click the __Update__ link.**

Installing Modules and Assigning Them to Portals

DNN comes with two installed modules (Links and Text/HTML) and a large number of available modules that you can choose to install. Furthermore, DNN has a large community of module developers who provide yet more additional modules. This section shows you how to install both available and new modules.

This section also shows you how to set certain modules as Premium modules. If a module is set as premium, the host can choose which portals have access to use these modules. This offers a business model for hosts or hosting companies to sell access to premium modules.

Installing the modules included with your DNN application

Here's how to install the modules that are included with your DNN application:

1. **Log in as the Host.**
2. **Navigate to Host⇨Module Definitions.**

   This goes to the Module Definitions page, which displays a list of the installed modules and the available modules.
3. **Go to the Available Modules section.**

   This displays a list of the modules included with this DNN application but are not yet installed.
4. **Select the check box beside each module to be installed.**
5. **Click the <u>Install Selected Modules</u> link.**

   The selected modules are now listed in the Installed Modules section on this page and are also listed in the Module Management section of the Control Panel.

Installing new modules

To install a new module, you need a zipped file containing all the module files. This zipped file is often referred to as the PA (private assembly) file. When you purchase a module, you purchase the PA file, which contains the compiled code for the module. Some companies also sell the source code of their modules, which contain all the code used to build and modify the module. Check the installation files provided with the module to find out which zipped file is the PA and therefore the right one to install.

Here's how to install new modules:

1. **Log in as the Host.**

2. **Navigate to Host⇨Module Definitions.**

   This displays a list of the modules included with this DNN application but are not yet installed.

3. **Select Install New Module from the module menu.**

   This goes to the File Upload module specifically for installing modules.

4. **Click the Browse button and select the PA of the module to be installed.**

5. **Click the <u>Save File</u> link.**

   This displays a report on the installation. Look out for text in red, which indicates something has failed during installation. If an error is displayed, it is a good idea to highlight and copy the whole message and send it to the module provider for help.

6. **Click the <u>Return</u> link.**

   This will return you to the Module Definitions page. The module will now be listed in the Installed Modules section.

Setting premium modules and assigning them to portals

Here's how to set premium modules and assign them to individual portals:

1. **Log in as the Host.**

2. **Navigate to Host⇨Module Definitions.**

   This displays a list of the modules included with this DNN application but are not yet installed.

3. **Go to the Installed Modules section.**

   This section lists all the modules currently installed in this DNN application.

4. **Click the Edit button beside the module to be set as premium.**

   This goes to the Edit Module Definitions page.

5. **Check the Premium? check box.**

   This displays two list boxes. The Available list displays the names of the portals in this DNN installation that this module can now be made available to, but that do not have access to this module. The Assigned list displays the names of any portals this module is assigned to.

6. **Perform one of the following to assign this module to one or more portals:**

   You must have more than one portal in this list to perform assignment and unassignment:

   • **Assign the module to a portal:** Click on the name of the portal in the Available list and then click the ≥ link. This adds the portal to the Assigned list.

   • **Unassign the module from a portal**: Click on the name of the portal in the Assigned list and then click the ≤ link. This adds the portal to the Available list.

   • **Assign the module to all portals**: Click the >> link. This adds all existing portals to the Assigned list. Portals added in the future will need to be assigned.

   • **Unassign the module from all portals**: Click the << link. This lists all existing portals in the Available list.

7. **Click the Update link.**

   This returns to the Module Definitions page.

Setting Global Preferences for New Portals

This section shows you how to configure the default settings that apply to all new portals you create within this DNN installation. To save you time, DNN lets you set a number of default settings that will be applied to each new Web site you add. These settings relate to hosting space allocation, e-mail, design, the type of files that can be uploaded, and more. These settings can later be changed on an individual Web site if, for instance, you want to give one Web site additional hosting space. See Chapter 4 for more information.

Setting the default appearance for new portals

DNN enables you to set a default skin for all new portals. This feature is particularly useful in franchising arrangements where the host needs to control how the child sites look and feel to their users. Here is how to set up the default skin and container to be used on new Web sites you create:

1. **Log in as the Host.**

2. **Navigate to Host⇨Host Settings.**

   This displays the Host Settings page, which enables you to set the default details for all Web sites in this DNN installation.

3. **Go to the Appearance section.**

   This displays the default design options set for new portals created.

4. **Check the Show Copyright Credits? check box to display the DNN copyright message in the address bar of your Web browser.**

   Check to displays the DNN version number in the Web browser title bar after the page title details, as shown in Figure 3-5; for example, (DNN4.4.1).

5. **Select the Use Custom Error Message? check box to enable DNN custom error messages.**

   When this is checked, DNN intercepts any errors that occur in the application and modules and displays friendly basic error messages to your users. If you are logged in as an Admin or host, more information is displayed to help you diagnose the problem. All error messages are recorded in the Log Viewer for your review. See Chapter 10 to find out more about the Log Viewer.

6. **Select either Host or Site in the Host Skin field to access the skins uploaded to that area.**

   Selecting Host displays all skins managed on the Host⇨Skins page; likewise, selecting Site displays all skins managed on the Admin⇨Skins. Host skins are available to all Web sites within the application, whereas Site skins are only available for use on the current Web site. The Host Skin field sets the default skin to be used on all new Web site pages apart from the Admin Skin pages, which you will set in Step 7.

7. **Select the name of skin in the Host Skin drop-down list.**

   This sets the default skin to be used on all pages of new Web sites created in this DNN installation.

8. **Click the <u>Preview</u> link to preview the skin.**

   This opens a new Web browser with an example of the skin.

9. **Repeat Steps 6-8 for the Host Container, Admin Skin, and Admin Container fields to change these settings.**

   The Host Container field sets the default container to be used on modules added. The Admin Skin and Admin Container fields set the default skin and container to be used on administration and edit pages of new Web sites.

10. **Click the <u>Update</u> link.**

    The default design for new Web sites is now set. To find how to update the design on a single Web site that has been created, see Chapter 4.

Figure 3-5:
DNN version
number not
displayed
(top) and
displayed
(bottom) in
the Web
browser.

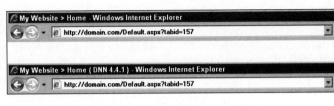

Setting the hosting space for new Web sites

When you set up your hosting arrangement with your supplier, you were allocated a certain amount of disk space, probably on the order of 100MB or more. This means you can upload files, photos, and so on until you reach that limit. If you are planning to create child portals on your DNN installation, you will need to limit the size of each one so that you don't exceed your limitation. To do this, you set the hosting space of each child portal. As part of the upload process, DNN checks to see that there is sufficient space remaining from the allocated amount for the site before it allows the upload.

If you upload files to your server by using FTP, you will bypass DNN's space allocation checking. To synchronize your Web site with the server, make sure that you run the Synchronize function on the File Manager to synchronize DNN with the File System. See Chapter 4 for more.

Here's how to specify how many megabytes (MB) of hosting space is allocated to each new Web site:

1. **Navigate to the Host⇨Host Settings page.**

2. **Click the Maximize button beside Payment Settings.**

   This displays a number of settings that control hosting capacity by hosting space, page quota, or user quota.

3. **Select one of these options to limit hosting space:**

   - **Hosting Space (MB):** Enter the hosting space allocated to all new Web sites. For example, entering **10** allocates 10 megabytes to each new Web site.

   - **Page Quota:** Enter the maximum number of pages for new portals.

   - **User Quota:** Enter the maximum number of registered users for new portals.

4. **Click the Update link.**

   The hosting space allocated to all new Web sites is now set.

Enabling the Site Log

The Site Log provides access to useful activity reports for each Web site, such as Page Popularity and Page Views. This information can be used by the Administrator to discover more about their users and page activity. See Chapter 10 for more details on how to change these settings for individuals Web sites.

Here's how to set the default Site Log for all portals:

1. **Log in as the Host.**

2. **Navigate to the Host⇨Host Settings page.**

    This displays the Host Settings page, which enables you to set the default details for all Web sites in this DNN installation.

3. **Click the Maximize button beside Advanced Settings and then click the Maximize button beside Other Settings.**

    This displays a number of miscellaneous settings for all Web sites. Many have defaults set already.

4. **Enter the number of day's history that will be stored for the site log in the Site Log History; for example,** 60.

5. **Click the Update link.**

Setting the types of files that can be uploaded

One of the most commonly used features of DNN is the ability to upload files such as photos, documents, and images to the Web site. This feature can be made available to your users by appropriate use of the security features of DNN. (See Chapter 4 for more on security roles.) The downside is that users uploading files to your server can create a security issue by uploading malicious files like viruses that could damage your server. To prevent this, DNN has a built-in list of acceptable file types that can be uploaded. When any file is uploaded, it is checked against this list: If the file extension is on the list, it can be uploaded. Otherwise, a message stating that the file type is not accepted is displayed.

Here's how to set the types of files that can be uploaded to the Host and Site File Managers:

1. **Log in as the Host.**

2. **Navigate to the Host⇨Host Settings page.**

    This displays the Host Settings page, which enables you to set the default details for all Web sites in this DNN installation.

3. **Click the Maximize button beside Advanced Settings and then click the Maximize button beside Other Settings.**

   This displays the File Upload Extensions text box, shown in Figure 3-6, where a list of the permitted file upload extensions is maintained.

4. **Review the current file types and enter any additional file types separated by a comma; for example,** MP3,DOC **allows users to upload MP3 files and Microsoft Word documents.**

   You may need to check with your hosting provider about what files they allow.

5. **Click the Update link.**

We suggest that you not let users upload executable files (EXE) as they can harbor viruses or other malicious code.

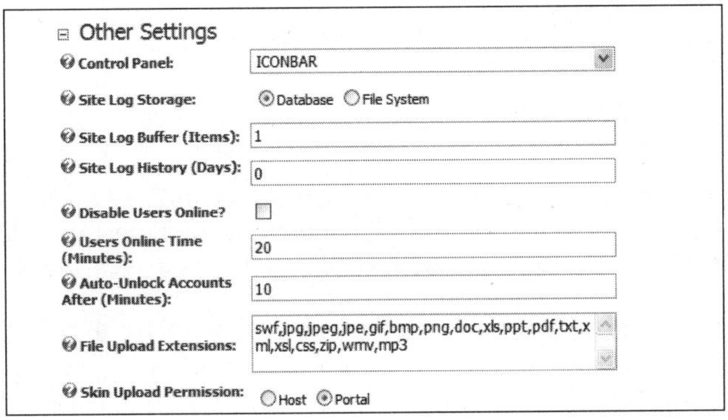

Figure 3-6:
The File
Upload
Extensions
text box
enables the
host to
control what
types of files
can be
uploaded.

⊟ Other Settings	
Control Panel:	ICONBAR
Site Log Storage:	⦿ Database ○ File System
Site Log Buffer (Items):	1
Site Log History (Days):	0
Disable Users Online?	☐
Users Online Time (Minutes):	20
Auto-Unlock Accounts After (Minutes):	10
File Upload Extensions:	swf,jpg,jpeg,jpe,gif,bmp,png,doc,xls,ppt,pdf,txt,xml,xsl,css,zip,wmv,mp3
Skin Upload Permission:	○ Host ⦿ Portal

Choosing who has permission to upload new skins

You have the ability to control who can upload skins to the DNN installation. If you are setting up the child portals to give administrators of those sites total control over the look and feel of those sites, you should allow the portal to have upload permissions for skins. However, if you want to restrict the look and feel of the child sites (for example, if the sites are part of a franchise group and you only want the child sites to have a limited list of skins), give the host upload permissions. This option means that only you can upload skins for the child sites to use.

Here's how to set DNN to enable or restrict Administrators from uploading skin packages:

1. **Log in as the host.**

2. **Navigate to the Host⇨Host Settings page.**

   This displays the Host Settings page, which enables you to set the default details for all Web sites in this DNN installation.

3. **Click the Maximize button beside Advanced Settings and then click the Maximize button beside Other Settings.**

4. **Select either Host or Portal for the Skin Upload Permission field.**

   Selecting Host restricts the ability to upload new skins to the host. Selecting Portal enables the Administrators of each Web site to also be able to upload new skins and containers to their Web sites.

5. **Click the <u>Update</u> link.**

   If you selected Portal, Administrators now have the ability to upload skins to their Web sites via the Admin⇨Skins pages of any child Web sites.

Lighting Up a New Portal (Or Two, or Three)

Each DNN installation can contain multiple portals and this section shows you how to add more portals to your DNN installation. Each new portal has its own unique security roles, user accounts, vendor banners, pages, and content.

New portals can be created with just one page that can be added to, or by selecting a template for the portal. A template consists of one or more Web pages with or without existing content. DNN comes with at least one sample template and you can create your own by copying one of your existing portals.

Creating new portals

Add new portals to your DNN installation. There are two types of portals you can add called parent and child portals. Parent portals have their own domain name, whereas child portals are a subdomain of the domain of your DNN installation. These portals inherit the defaults set in the Host Settings sections. These settings can later be modified: See Chapter 4 for more information.

 Don't get the naming of parent and child portals in this tutorial confused with the parent (Host) and child (Site) relationship discussed elsewhere. The parent and child portals referred to in this tutorial only relate to the way the URL is made.

Here's how to create a new portal:

1. **Log in as the Host.**

2. **Navigate to the Host⇨Portals page.**

   This displays a list of the portals in this DNN installation.

3. **Select Add New Portal from the Portals module menu.**

   This opens the Signup module, shown in Figure 3-7, where new portals are created.

4. **Select either the Parent or Child radio button beside the Portal Type field to select the domain type.**

   Select Parent if you have a domain name for this portal; for example, www.domain.com. Select Child if this portal will be a child of this domain; for example, www.domain.com/childportal1. Selecting Child displays the domain of your Web site in the Portal Alias field. Use this option when the portal will not have a separate domain name, or when you are waiting for one. This is also a good temporary measure so you can get a portal online straightaway while waiting for a domain to be set up. It takes about two or three days for new domains to resolve properly.

5. **Enter an alias for the Web site into the Portal Alias text box.**

   This information sets the main URL for this Web site. After the site has been created, you can add as many other aliases as you like. Many sites have multiple domains pointing to the same site. For example, you may have domains such as www.dotnetnuke.com and www.dotnetnuke. net, both pointing to the same portal.

6. **Optional. Click the <u>Customize</u> link beside Home Directory to edit this setting.**

   When you create a new portal, you also create a new folder on the Web server to store all the files associated with that site. By default, the Home Directory will be Portals/[*PortalID*], where *PortalID* is a number generated by DNN depending on how many portals there are. If you want to give the new portal a folder that is more descriptive, or if you want to store the file in a different folder structure, you can enter your own folder path in the text box. If you enter Portals/MyNewSite, all the files for the new portal go into that folder. You can also create other paths like ChildSites/MyNewSite that create a new folder under the root directory on your server.

   You cannot create folders outside of the root directory of your main site.

7. **Enter a title for the Web site into the Title text box.**

   This is the name of the Web site, such as DNNAngel. This field can be modified later if required.

8. **Enter a description of the Web site into the Description text box.**

   This is the description of the Web site, which is what is shown in search engine results. This field can be modified or completed later.

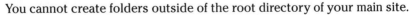

9. **Enter keywords for the Web site into the Keywords text box.**

   Keywords assist your search engine rankings and can be added or modified later.

10. **Select a template name from the Template drop-down box to set the template for this new Web site.**

    A *template* sets the initial pages and content for the new Web site. This setting displays a description of the selected template below this field. To find out which template best suits your purpose, select each one to read a description of each. For more details on templates, see "Photocopying your portal" later in this chapter.

11. **Complete the Security Settings fields to set up the Administrator account for the new portal.**

    The Administrator has full rights to build and modify the new Web site and edit all of its settings. The details entered in the Security Settings will be e-mailed to the e-mail address entered here so that the Administrator has a copy of her login details.

12. **Click the <u>Create Portal</u> link to create the new portal.**

    The new portal has now been created and you are now taken to the home page of the new portal. You are still logged in as the host for all Web sites. If you return to the Host⇨Portals page, you will see that the new Web site is listed in the Portals module.

There is no host password for this new portal, only the host portal.

Photocopying your portal

Imagine you have built a portal for your local church. The church community is growing and now has three regional branches. The portal you built is central to the growth of the church and so you want to provide each branch with a template of your portal to get them started. Typically, this would be quite a challenge, but not with DNN! Using DNN, you can create a copy of a portal called a *template,* which can then be used again and again. The template includes each of the pages and modules within your portal. The pages and modules are named the same as the original portal. Module content can be optionally included. Templates use the same skin and containers as the original portal. By changing a few contact details, each branch will have a ready-to-go Web site in just a few clicks.

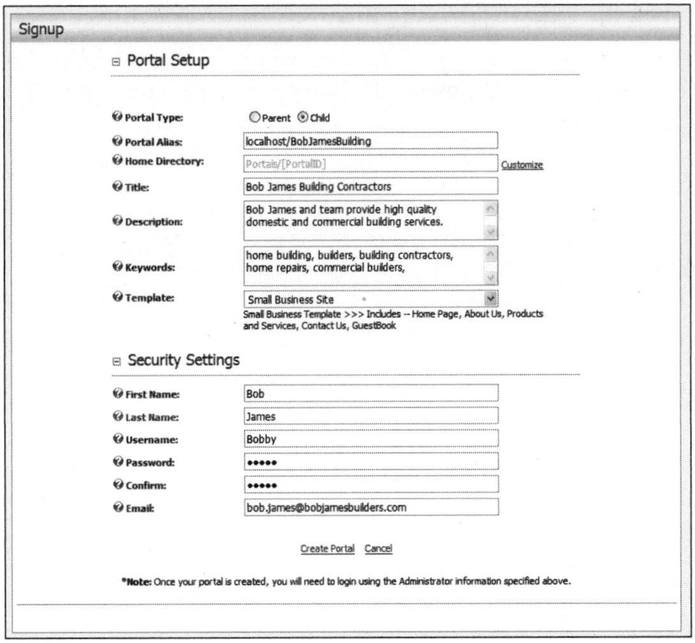

Figure 3-7:
Creating a
second Web
site within
this DNN
installation.

Here's how to export a template of a Web site, with or without module content:

1. **Log in as the Host.**

2. **Navigate to the Host⇨Portals page.**

   This displays a list of the existing portals in this DNN installation.

3. **Select Export Portal Template from the module menu.**

4. **Select the portal you want to template from the Portal drop-down box, as shown in Figure 3-8.**

5. **Enter a name for the new template into the Template File Name text box; for example,** Real Estate Franchise.

6. **Enter a description of the new template into the Template Description text box; for example,** Franchisees Web site: Home, For Sellers, For Buyers, Client Center, and Contact Us pages.

   This information helps you identify the template in the future.

7. **Choose whether to include module content by checking or not checking the Include Content check box.**

   Checking this option exports all the modules, including content. If this option is not checked, the template exports all the modules without content. The titles and other modules settings are still exported.

8. Click the Export Template link.

The selected portal has now been saved as a template and is listed in the Template drop-down list when you create a new portal.

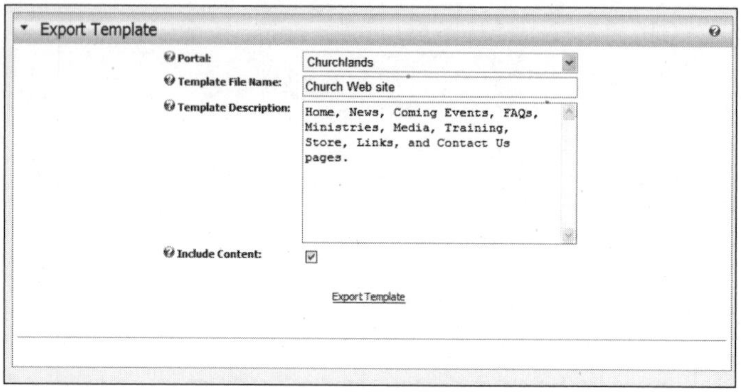

Figure 3-8:
Create a
template
of your
Web site
including all
pages and
optional
content —
perfect for
franchising
businesses
or Web
design
companies.

Part II
Putting the Power of DotNetNuke to Work

The 5th Wave   By Rich Tennant

"I have to say I'm really impressed with the interactivity on this car wash Web site."

In This Part . . .

This Part covers the building of your DNN Web site. It covers the main activities of the portal Administrator, including how to create pages and add content to the Web site. We also discuss how to create registered Web site users and how to control which users can see what information. The section is written sequentially, with each chapter covering a slightly more complex task or tool. Mastering this Part means you are a skilled DNN Administrator.

Chapter 4

Getting Your Site Started on the Right Foot

. . . .

In This Chapter

▶ Setting defaults for a particular Web site

▶ Getting your users into roles

▶ Adding and managing pages

▶ Dropping content on a page

▶ Managing Web site files

▶ Making your site look good with skins and containers

. . . .

*T*his chapter explains how to configure basic Web site settings such as the name of your Web site, a description of its purpose, and key words for search engines. If you have host access, this chapter also explains how to set the disk space and billing period for an individual Web site.

Also in this chapter, we explain how to register and manage users, how to add and manage Web pages, how to begin adding content to your Web site, and how to add and manage Web site files such as documents, images, and movies. Finally, we wrap up this chapter by demonstrating how to change the design used on your Web site.

Setting Defaults for a Web Site

In Chapter 3, we cover various host settings that set the defaults for all new Web sites created by using this DNN installation. In this chapter, we cover many of the same settings; however, these are site settings rather than host settings. *Site settings* affect only a particular Web site and do not affect the default settings of any new Web sites you create.

Setting Site Details

The Site Details section enables you to enter a title and description of the Web site and key words that describe its purpose. Search engines use this information to index your Web site on the World Wide Web.

Here's how to set the basic site details:

1. **Click the Site button located in the Common Tasks section of the Control Panel.**

   This displays the Admin⇨Site Settings page, where you can set details specific to this Web site.

2. **Go to the Basic Settings, Site Details section, as shown in Figure 4-1.**

3. **Enter a title for the Web site into the Title text box.**

   This is the main title for your Web site, such as your business name. This title appears in the title bar of your Web site browser, which is located in the top-left corner.

4. **Enter a description of the Web site into the Description text box.**

   Write a brief description of the purpose of your Web site.

5. **Enter keywords for the Web site into the Key Words text box.**

   Enter keywords and phrases that describe the purpose of your Web site.

6. **Click the <u>Update</u> link.**

   This saves these settings.

TIP

Increase the effectiveness of your keywords by using them frequently within the content of your Web site. This confirms for search engines that these really are the keywords for your Web site and not just some words you typed in to get more traffic.

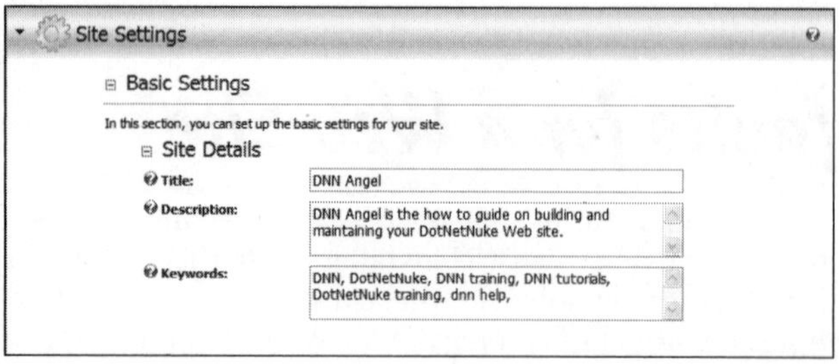

Figure 4-1:
Search engines use site details to help index your site.

Site Settings

☐ **Basic Settings**

In this section, you can set up the basic settings for your site.

☐ Site Details

Title: | DNN Angel

Description: | DNN Angel is the how to guide on building and maintaining your DotNetNuke Web site.

Keywords: | DNN, DotNetNuke, DNN training, DNN tutorials, DotNetNuke training, dnn help,

Setting Payment Details

In a later section of this chapter, "Getting Your Users into Roles," we cover how to create subscription roles. *Subscription roles* enable you to designate areas of your Web site that users must pay a fee to access. Setting a fee for Subscription roles is optional. If you do choose to charge a fee, use the Payment Details to set the payment gateway or payment provider you will use to collect the funds for you. DNN is integrated with a handful of different companies, so you should investigate them to see which suits you best. A full list of these companies is displayed in the drop-down list box of the Payment Processor field. After you have chosen your payment provider and signed up for an account with them, you can complete this section.

1. **Click the Site button located in the Common Tasks section of the Control Panel.**

   This displays the Admin⇨Site Settings page, where you can set details specific to this Web site.

2. **Click the Maximize button beside Advanced Settings.**

   This displays the advanced settings that are specific to this Web site.

3. **Click the Maximize button beside Payment Settings.**

   This displays the Payment Settings section, as shown in Figure 4-2.

4. **Select the currency you will be receiving payment in from the Currency drop-down box.**

   Be sure that your payment provider offers the currency you choose. Some companies only process U.S. dollars.

5. **Select the payment processing company you have an account with from the Payment Processor drop-down box.**

   If you haven't signed up for an account yet, you can select a company and then click the <u>Go To Payment Processor Web Site</u> link to find out more about each company.

6. **Enter your user ID into the Processor UserID text box.**

   This is the user ID you chose when signing up for an account with the payment processing company.

7. **Enter your password into the Processor Password text box.**

   This is the password you chose when signing up for an account with the payment processing company.

8. **Click the <u>Update</u> link.**

   The payment details are now set for this Web site.

Figure 4-2:
These
payment
settings
enable you
to receive
payment
from users
who
subscribe to
certain
roles.

⊟ Payment Settings

@ **Currency:**   U.S. Dollars (USD)

@ **Payment Processor:**   Authorize.net
         Go To Payment Processor WebSite

@ **Processor UserId:**   cnpdev9012

@ **Processor Password:**   ●●●●●●●●●●

Setting other miscellaneous settings

A variety of miscellaneous settings can be found under the Other Settings section of the Site Settings page. These advanced site settings enable you to display a copyright message on your Web site, to display vendor banner advertising, and to set the language and time zone for the Web site.

1. **Click the Site button located in the Common Tasks section of the Control Panel.**

   This displays the Admin⇨Site Settings page, where you can set details specific to this Web site.

2. **Click the Maximize button beside Advanced Settings.**

3. **Click the Maximize button beside Other Settings.**

   This displays the Other Settings section.

4. **Enter a copyright notice into the Copyright text box; for example,** Copyright(c)2007.

   The copyright notice is displayed at the bottom of all Web site pages. Leave this field blank to hide the copyright message or enter any other text you want to display in this location.

5. **Select either the None, Site or Host radio button displayed at the User Registration field to select the banner advertising source.**

   This sets the universal banner advertising displayed on your Web Site. Select None to hide banner advertising. Select Site to display banners that you can set up on the Admin⇨Vendors page. These site banners are only available to this Web site. Select Host to display banners that the host can set up on the Host⇨Vendors page. These Host banners are available to all Web sites within this DNN installation. See Chapter 6 for details on adding banners.

6. **Select the name of the primary Administrator for the Web site from the Administrator drop-down box.**

   This field sets the primary administrator for the Web site. This Administrator receives notification e-mails when new users register, change their account details, or perform some other action. See Chapter 9 for a full list of notification e-mails.

7. **Select a new default language from the Default Language drop-down box if required.**

   This is the primary language on the Web site. Changing this setting changes the language used on common fields like the Date and the Terms of Use. See Chapter 9 to find out how to add new languages to this list.

8. **Select your time zone from the Portal TimeZone drop-down box.**

   This sets the time zone of your Web site.

9. **Click the Update link.**

   This saves these site settings.

Maintaining host-only settings

The Site Setting page is located under the Admin page, which makes it accessible to the Administrator; however, there are a few host-only settings on this page. When you are logged in as the host, these fields can be viewed and changed; they are hidden from you when you are logged in as the Administrator.

Here's how you, if you have host-level access, can update the default host settings just for this portal:

1. **Log in as the host.**

2. **Click the Site button located in the Common Tasks section of the Control Panel.**

   This displays the Admin⇨Site Settings page, where you can set details specific to this Web site.

3. **Click the Maximize button beside Advanced Settings.**

4. **Click the Maximize button beside Host Settings.**

   This displays the host-only settings, as shown in Figure 4-3.

5. **Click the Calendar link beside the Expiry Date field and select a date when the hosting for this Web site expires.**

   When this date is reached, the Web site is longer available. Visitors see a message stating that the hosting contract for this Web site has expired. Leave this field blank if there is no expiry date.

6. **Enter the monthly fee charged to host this Web site into the Hosting Fee text box.**

7. **Enter the maximum number of megabytes allowed for this Web site into the Disk Space text box.**

   When the maximum space has been filled, Administrators can't upload any more files. Instead, they see a message asking them to contact their host. Leave this field blank for unlimited space.

8. **Enter the maximum number of pages allowed for this Web site into the Page Quota text box.**

   When the maximum number of pages is reached, Administrators can't add any more pages. Instead, they see a message explaining that adding a page will exceed their page quota and asking them to contact their host. Leave this field blank for unlimited space.

9. **Enter the maximum number of users allowed for this Web site into the User Quota text box.**

   When the maximum number of users is reached, Administrators can't add any more users. Instead, they see a message explaining that adding a page will exceed their page quota and asking them to contact their host. Leave this field blank for unlimited space.

10. **Enter the number of days of history that should be kept for site log reporting into the Site Log History (Days) text box.**

    The Site Log is located under the Admin⇨Site Settings page and gives the Administrator access to reports on the activities of the Web site relating to users and Web site traffic. Leave this field blank to disable the Site Log of this Web site.

11. **In the Available box beside the Premium Modules field, click on the name of a module and then click the right angle bracket (≥) link to assign it to this Web site.**

    This adds the selected module to the Assigned box which lists the special modules assigned to this Web site. This setting lets the host make more or fewer modules available to this Web site. See Chapter 3 to find out how to set a module as Premium.

12. **Click the Update link.**

    This saves these host settings for this Web site only.

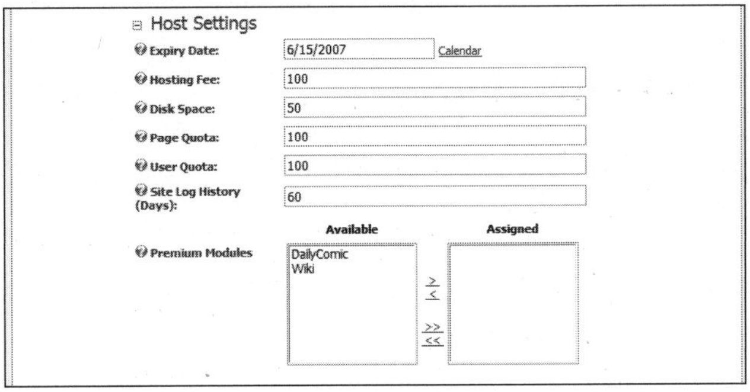

Figure 4-3:
These host
settings
manage
hosting for
this Web
site and
are only
displayed to
the host.

```
⊟ Host Settings
  ⊘ Expiry Date:        6/15/2007          Calendar
  ⊘ Hosting Fee:        100
  ⊘ Disk Space:         50
  ⊘ Page Quota:         100
  ⊘ User Quota:         100
  ⊘ Site Log History    60
    (Days):
                               Available              Assigned
  ⊘ Premium Modules    DailyComic
                       Wiki
                                          >
                                          <
                                          >>
                                          <<
```

Getting Your Users into Roles

In Chapter 1, we discuss the basic concepts of membership and security
roles. In this chapter, we delve further into how to set up the roles for your
Web site and how to add users (members) to these roles.

Every DNN Web site comes with a couple of built-in roles. These are
Administrator, Registered Users, and Subscribers. Every user you add to your
Web site is automatically added to the Registered Users role. You can create
as many other roles as you need to control who can access the different
areas of your Web site.

Adding a new role

Here's how to add a new role to this Web site that you control access to:

1. **Click the Roles button located in the Common Tasks section of the
   Control Panel.**

   This displays the Admin⇨Security Roles page and lists the existing roles
   on this Web site, as shown in Figure 4-4.

2. **Select Add New Role from the module menu.**

   This goes to the Edit Security Roles page, where you can create a new
   role for this Web site.

3. **Enter a name for the role into the Role Name text box.**

   For example, **Client File Access**.

4. Enter a description of the role into the Description text box.

For example, **Members of this role are clients who are able to download files from this Web site**.

5. If the role belongs to a role group, select the group name from the Role Group drop-down box. If the role isn't part of a role group, leave this setting on <Global Roles>.

Find out more about how and why to create role groups in the next section, "Adding a new role group."

6. Click the <u>Update</u> link.

This returns you to the Security Roles page where the new role is now listed. If you added a role that belongs to a role group, you need to select the group name from the drop-down box above or select <All Roles>.

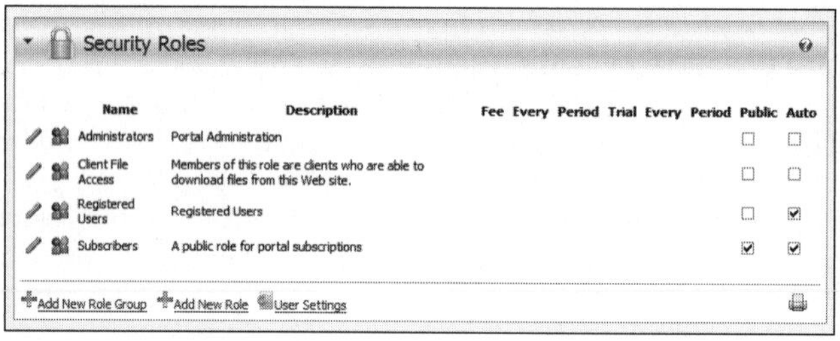

Figure 4-4:
The
Admin⇨
Security
Roles page
lists the
security
roles.

	Name	Description	Fee	Every	Period	Trial	Every	Period	Public	Auto
🔒 Security Roles										?
✏ 🏬	Administrators	Portal Administration							☐	☐
✏ 🏬	Client File Access	Members of this role are clients who are able to download files from this Web site.							☐	☐
✏ 🏬	Registered Users	Registered Users							☐	☑
✏ 🏬	Subscribers	A public role for portal subscriptions							☑	☑

➕ Add New Role Group ➕ Add New Role 👤 User Settings 🖨

Adding a new role group

Because your Web site can include as many roles as you like, you can end up with 20, 30, or even 100 different roles. To make it easier to manage your roles, group similar roles together by creating a *role group*. For example, you might have a role group called Staff and create a number of roles within this group such as Marketing, Telemarketing, Sales, and so on. Roles that don't belong to a role group are called *global roles*.

Here's how to create a role group:

1. Click the Roles button located in the Common Tasks section of the Control Panel.

This displays the Admin⇨Security Roles page, which lists existing roles on this Web site.

2. **Select Add New Role Group from the module menu.**

   This goes to the Edit Role Group page, where you can create a new role for this Web site.

3. **Enter a name for the role group into the Group Name text box.**

   For example, **Staff**.

4. **Enter a description of the role group into the Description text box.**

   For example, **Staff members only**.

5. **Click the <u>Update</u> link.**

   You can now add one or more roles to this group.

Creating an opt-in/opt-out role

Creating opt-in/opt-out roles enables users to control the information they can access on your Web site. For example, you may create an opt-in role called "Jokes and Riddles" that enables members to view a page that has funny stuff on it. Users can choose whether to see this page or not by opting in and out of this role.

Another way to use this type of role is to enable users to subscribe and unsubscribe from newsletters. (See Chapter 9 to find out how to send newsletters.)

Here's how to create a role that users can opt in and opt out of at any time:

1. **Click the Roles button located in the Common Tasks section of the Control Panel.**

   This displays the Admin⇨Security Roles page, which lists existing roles on this Web site.

2. **Select Add New Role from the module menu.**

   This goes to the Edit Security Role page, shown in Figure 4-5, where you can create a new role for this Web site.

3. **Enter a name for the role into the Role Name text box.**

   For example, **News and Gossip**.

4. **Enter a description of the role into the Description text box.**

   For example: **Find out the latest celebrity gossip by subscribing to our monthly newsletter**.

5. **If the role belongs to a role group, select the group name from the Role Group drop-down box. If the role isn't part of a role group, leave this setting on <Global Roles>.**

6. **Check the Public Role? check box.**

   This makes access to opt in and opt out of this role public to all users on their own profile page.

7. **Check the Auto Assignment check box if you want new users to be automatically added to this role.**

   This sets the role to automatically add all new users to it. If this option is not checked, users must subscribe to the role on their profile page.

8. **Click the <u>Update</u> link.**

   This returns you to the Security Roles page where the new role is now listed. If you added a role that belongs to a Role Group, you need to select the group name from the drop-down box above or select <All Roles>.

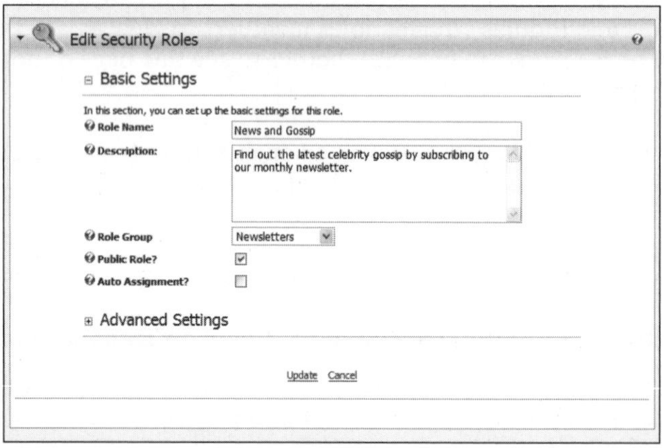

Figure 4-5:
Adding an
opt-in/opt-
out role to
your Web
site.

> **Edit Security Roles**
>
> ⊟ **Basic Settings**
>
> In this section, you can set up the basic settings for this role.
>
> **Role Name:** News and Gossip
>
> **Description:** Find out the latest celebrity gossip by subscribing to our monthly newsletter.
>
> **Role Group** Newsletters
>
> **Public Role?** ☑
>
> **Auto Assignment?** ☐
>
> ⊞ **Advanced Settings**
>
> Update Cancel

Setting user registration

Registration on your Web site can be made available to anyone who visits the Web site, or it can be managed exclusively by the Administrator. When a user registers, they receive an e-mail containing all of their account and login details.

Here's how to set up user registration for the Web site:

1. **Click the Site button located in the Common Tasks section of the Control Panel.**

2. **Click the Maximize button beside Advanced Settings.**

3. **Go to the Security Settings section.**

   This displays the User Registration options.

4. **Select the required user registration from the options listed at the User Registration field.**

   - **None:** Only the Administrator is able to register new users.

   - **Private:** Visitors can complete a registration form to express their interest in becoming a member of the Web site; however, they can't log in to the Web site until the Administrator gives them access by authorizing their account. The Administrator receives an e-mail notification when this type of registration occurs.

   - **Public:** All visitors can register and are given immediate access to areas of the Web site, including areas restricted to registered user access only.

   - **Verified:** All visitors can register, but can't log in to the Web site until they enter a verification code that is e-mailed to them. This verifies that they have provided a valid e-mail address.

5. **Click the <u>Update</u> link.**

   The registration type is now set. If None has been selected, the Register link is no longer displayed in the top-right corner of the Web site. This link is displayed for all other registration options.

Adding a new user

The Administrator can add new users to the Web site at any time. Here's how:

1. **Click the Users button located in the Common Tasks section of the Control Panel.**

   This displays the Admin⇨User Accounts page.

2. **Select Add New User from the module menu.**

   This displays the Edit User Accounts page, shown in Figure 4-6, where you can add the new user to this Web site.

3. **Enter a username for this user into the User Name text box.**

   Users need to enter a username and a password when they log in to the Web site. Usernames are unique and they cannot be changed.

4. **Enter the person's first name into the First Name text box.**

5. **Enter the person's last name into the Last Name text box.**

6. **Enter the name that will be displayed to others into the Display Name text box.**

   This might be a nickname or perhaps just their first name. This lets people keep their real name private if they like.

7. **Enter the person's e-mail address into the E-mail Address text box.**

8. **In the Password section, select Random Password to automatically generate a password for this person.**

   This lets you generate a random password for this person, relieving you from thinking up a new password each time. The person can change the password later. If you prefer to create a password, you can do so by entering it into both of the password text fields in Figure 4-6. Note: The password must be at least seven characters in length.

9. **Click the <u>Register</u> link.**

   The user account has now been created and you are returned to the User Accounts page. To view the new user account, click on the <u>All</u> link, which will display all the user accounts, or click on the letter that is the first letter of their first name.

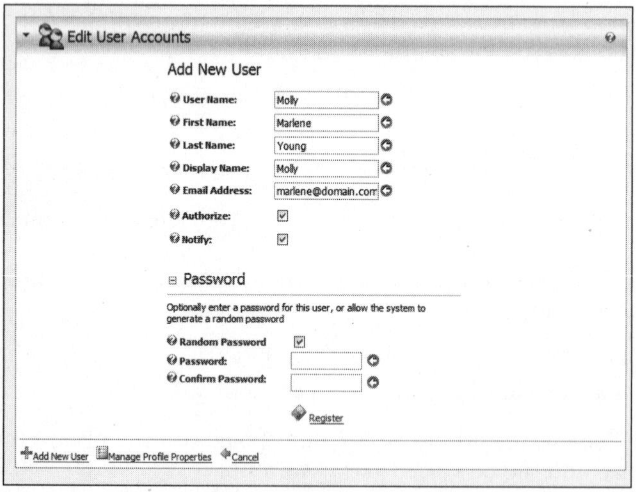

Figure 4-6:
Adding a
new user to
the Web
site.

Adding and Managing Pages on Your Web Site

This section explains how to add and set pages on your Web site. If you need a refresher on the basic concepts of pages and how they apply to DNN, flip back to Chapter 1.

Adding a page

Here's how to add a new page to the Web site:

1. **Click the Add button located in the Page Functions section of the Control Panel.**

   This displays the Page Management page, shown in Figure 4-7, where you set the information of the new page.

2. **Enter the name of the page as it will be displayed in the Web site menu into the Page Name box.**

   If you want to add your page quickly, you can skip Steps 3-6, which assist search engines in ranking your Web site.

3. **Enter a descriptive title for the page in the Page Title text box.**

   This title will be displayed in the very top-left corner of the Web site browser and is used by search engines to list your Web site. If you don't enter a title, the page name will be displayed. Your title should describe the information people can find on the page. The title should be between 60–90 characters.

4. **Enter a description for the page in the Description text box.**

   Search engines will use this description to index and describe the page. The description should be between 170–200 characters.

5. **Enter keywords and phrases for the page in the Key Words text box.**

   These are words and phrases that describe the page content. Separate each word or phrase with a comma. Try to anticipate the words or phrases someone would enter into a search engine to find your content. Your search engine ranking should use words and phrases that are included in the content of this page.

6. **At the Parent Page drop-down box, select a page to position this page beneath or leave this field as <None Selected> if the page doesn't belong under another one.**

   DNN uses the terms *parent* and *child* to explain the relationship between pages on the Web site. A parent page is displayed in the menu and can have one or more child pages belonging to it. Positioning your mouse over a parent page displays its child pages. This grouping of pages makes it easy for people to find their way around the Web site.

7. **Select <All Roles> at the Filter by Group box beside Permissions to view a full list of all roles.**

   This option is visible only if one or more role groups have been added to the Web site as shown in "Adding a new role group" earlier in this chapter. If this option isn't displayed, skip to Step 8.

Alternatively, you can filter groups by selecting a role group name, or selecting global roles, which are roles that don't belong to a group.

8. **Select the check box beside any role in the View Page column of the Permissions field to enable that role to view the page.**

   To make the page viewable by everyone, select All Users. If the page is not viewable by All Users, only logged-in members of roles selected here can view the page. Role members can also view any modules added to this page unless the modules have different permissions set. Only Administrators are selected to view the page by default at this setting. This can be useful when building your Web site live on the Internet, as you can add content to the page before you set it as viewable by All Users.

9. **Select the check box beside any role in the Edit Page column of the Permissions field to enable that role to edit the page.**

   If only Administrators can edit the page, you can leave these settings as they are. Providing role members permission to edit a page gives them the ability to change the whole page. These users are sometimes called Page Editors because they have permission to edit an entire page, although this isn't an actual security role. Members of selected roles will have the Control Panel displayed on this page, providing them with the ability to add and edit pages below this page and add and edit modules on this page. (In this scenario, the Common Tasks section of the Control Panel, which provides access to site settings, user accounts, security roles, and the file manager, will be disabled. The Help button in the Common Tasks section will still be enabled.) Page Editors can delete the page and edit most of the page settings; however, they cannot move the page. They can add and copy new child pages below this page and add content to those pages. They can add new modules to the original page and, by default, they can edit all module content on that page.

10. **Click the <u>Update</u> link.**

    The page name is now displayed in the menu unless it was set with a parent page; in that case, you will need to mouse over the parent page and click on the page name to view it.

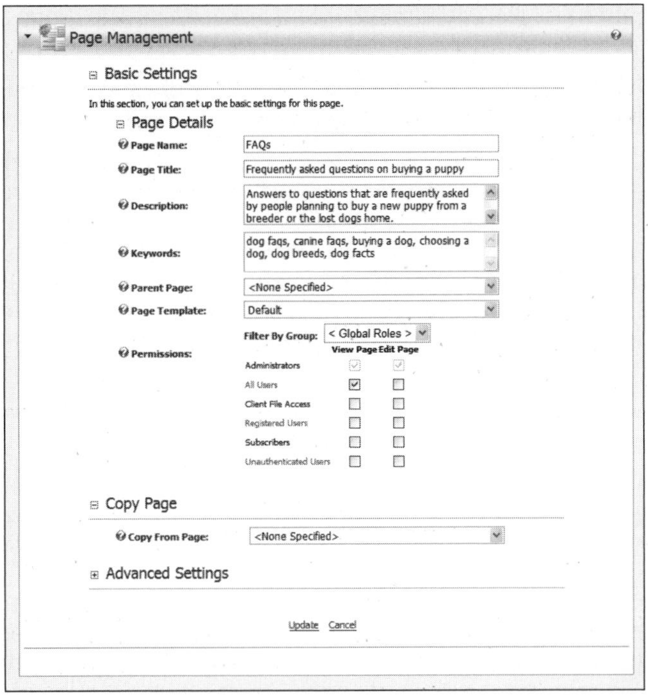

Figure 4-7:
Adding a
new page to
the Web
site. The
permission
settings
here enable
everyone
(All Users)
to view the
page, but
only
Adminis-
trators can
edit it.

Setting view and edit permissions for a page

Here's how to set the view and edit permissions on a page:

1. **Click the Settings button located in the Page Functions section of the Control Panel.**

   This displays the Page Management page, where you can set and edit the page.

2. **Select <All Roles> at the Filter by Group box beside Permissions to view a full list of all roles.**

   This option will only be visible if one or more role groups have been added to the Web site, as shown in "Adding a new role group" earlier in this chapter. If this option isn't displayed, skip to Step 3.

Alternatively, you can filter groups by selecting a role group name, or selecting global roles.

3. **Select and deselect the check boxes beside each role in the View Page column of the Permissions field to set which roles can view the page.**

   To make the page viewable by everyone, select All Users. If the page is not viewable by All Users, only logged-in members of roles selected here can view the page. Role members can also view any modules added to this page unless the modules have different permissions set. Only Administrators are selected to view the page by default at this setting. This can be useful when building your Web site live on the Internet, as you can add content to the page before you set it as viewable by All Users.

4. **Select and deselect the check boxes beside each role in the Edit Page column to set which roles can edit the page.**

   If only Administrators can edit the page, you can leave these settings as they are. Providing role members with permission to edit a page gives them the ability to change the whole page. These users are sometimes called Page Editors because they have permission to edit an entire page, although this isn't an actual security role. Members of selected roles will have the Control Panel displayed on this page, providing them with the ability to add and edit pages below this page and add and edit modules on this page. (In this scenario, the Common Tasks section of the Control Panel, which provides access to site settings, user accounts, security roles, and the file manager, will be disabled. The Help button in the Common Tasks section will still be enabled.) Page Editors can delete the page and edit most of the page settings; however, they cannot move the page. They can add and copy new child pages below this page and add content to those pages. They can add new modules to the original page and by default they can edit all module content on that page.

5. **Click the <u>Update</u> link.**

   The page name is now displayed in the menu, unless it was set with a parent page; in that case, you will need to mouse over the parent page and click on the page name to view it.

Copying view and edit permissions to child pages

DNN enables you to bulk update the view and edit permissions of the child pages of a single parent page to match their parent page. Keep this feature in mind when deciding how to organize your Web site. Keeping the permissions to view and edit pages organized by parent page makes the Web site both easy for you to manage and easy for your users to know what to expect.

Here's how to set the view and edit permissions on a page:

1. **Click the Settings button located in the Page Functions section of the Control Panel.**

   This displays the Page Management page, where you can set and edit the page.

2. **Select <All Roles> at the Filter by Group box beside Permissions to view a full list of all role.**

   This option will only be visible if one or more role groups have been added to the Web site as shown in "Adding a new role group" earlier in this chapter. If this option isn't displayed, skip to Step 3.

   Alternatively, you can filter groups by selecting a role group name, or selecting global roles.

3. **Select and deselect the check boxes beside each role in the View Page column of the Permissions field to set which roles can view the page.**

   To make the page viewable by everyone, select All Users. If the page is not viewable by All Users, only logged-in members of roles selected here can view the page. Role members can also view any modules added to this page unless the modules have different permissions set. Only Administrators are selected to view the page by default at this setting. This can be useful when building your Web site live on the Internet, as you can add content to the page before you set it as viewable by All Users.

4. **Select and deselect the check boxes beside each role in the Edit Page column to set which roles can edit the page.**

   If only Administrators can edit the page, you can leave these settings as they are. Providing role members with permission to edit a page gives them the ability to change the whole page. These users are sometimes called Page Editors because they have permission to edit an entire page, although this isn't an actual security role. Members of selected roles will have the Control Panel displayed on this page, providing them with the ability to add and edit pages below this page and add and edit modules on this page. (In this scenario, the Common Tasks section of the Control Panel, which provides access to site settings, user accounts, security roles, and the file manager, will be disabled. The Help button in the Common Tasks section will still be enabled.) Page Editors can delete the page and edit most of the page settings; however, they cannot move the page. They can add and copy new child pages below this page and add content to those pages. They can add new modules to the original page and by default they can edit all module content on that page.

5. **Click the <u>Update</u> link.**

   The page name is now displayed in the menu, unless it was set with a parent page; in that case, you will need to mouse over the parent page and click on the page name to view it.

Copying a page

Here's how to copy an existing page:

1. **Click the Copy button located in the Page Functions section of the Control Panel.**

   This displays the Page Management page where you set the information of the new page.

2. **Complete all the Page Details settings.**

   See Steps 2-9 in "Adding a page" earlier in this section for more details.

3. **Select the name of the page you want to copy from the Copy Modules From field in the Copy Page section.**

   The page you were last on will be selected by default. The title and location of each module on the selected page is now displayed at the Copy Content field. Note: If the page doesn't have any modules, there is no benefit to copying it!

4. **Clear the check box beside any module that you don't want to copy.**

5. **Enter a new title for each module to be copied.**

   Alternatively, you may prefer to keep the original title.

6. **Select the New, Copy, or Reference radio button to define the content you want to copy from each module.**

   Select New to copy the module without any content. Select Copy to copy the module and its content. This creates a new version of this content, which can be edited independently of the original content. Select Reference to copy the module and create a new version of the content inside the module. Editing content in a referenced module also updates the content in the original module.

7. **Click the <u>Update</u> link.**

   The page name is now displayed in the menu, unless it was set with a parent page; in that case, you will need to mouse over the parent page and click on the page name to view it. Any copied modules will be displayed on the page.

Adding a page set as a link to a URL, page, or file

DNN provides you with the ability to create a page that links to another Web page or file. This feature is a great shortcut when you want to display one page in two different locations on the Web site menu, or if you want to use the menu to provide people with access to commonly request files.

Here's how to add a page that links to a URL, page, or file:

1. **Click the Add button located in the Page Functions section of the Control Panel.**

   This displays the Page Management page where you set the information of the new page.

2. **Complete all the Page Details settings.**

   See Steps 2-9 in the section called "Adding a page" earlier in this chapter for more details.

3. **Click the Maximize button at Advanced Settings.**

   This displays all the advanced page settings. The link settings are located in the Other Settings section.

4. **Select URL (A Link to an External Resource), Page (A Page on Your Site), or File (A File on Your Site) from the Link Type options listed for the Link URL field.**

   Selecting URL displays a text box where you can enter a Web site address. This option takes the person to that Web site when they click on this page in the menu. Selecting Page displays a list of pages on the Web site that you can select from. This option takes the person to that page on this Web site when they click on this page in the menu. Selecting File displays a list of files uploaded to the File Manager. This option displays the selected file to the person when they click on the page in the menu.

5. **Enter the URL, or select the page or file per your selection at Step 4.**

6. **Click the Update link.**

Changing the order of your pages

The Control Panel across the top of each page enables Administrators to perform most of the tasks required to manage pages; however, one task that can't be managed here is changing the order of pages in the menu.

Here's how to move a page to a new location in the menu:

1. **Select Admin⇨Pages from the module menu.**

   This displays the Pages page, where you can change the order of pages in the menu. All pages are listed here. Parent pages are listed to the left. Child pages are indicated by . . . *PageName,* where *PageName* is replaced by the actual name of the page.

2. **Locate and click on the name of the page you want to move in the list of pages.**

3. Select one of the following options.

- Click the left arrow to move a child page up one position within the parent/child hierarchy. Any child pages of this page retain their relationship with this page.

- Click the right arrow to move a child page down one position within the parent/child hierarchy. Any child pages of this page retain their relationship with this page. For example, in Figure 4-8, clicking the right arrow makes the FAQs page a child of the Services page. The two child pages of the FAQs page (For Builders and For Individuals) remain children of the FAQs page.

- Click the up arrow to move the page up one position within the current level. Any child pages of this page retain their relationship with this page. For example, in Figure 4-8, clicking the up arrow moves the FAQs page above Services page, displaying itfarther left in the menu. The two child pages of the FAQs page (For Builders and For Individuals) remain children of the FAQs page.

- Click the down-arrow button to move the page down one position within the current level. Any child pages of this page retain their relationship with this page. For example, in Figure 4-8, clicking the down arrow moves the FAQs page below the Contact Us page, displaying it one position farther right in the menu. The two child pages of the FAQs page (For Builders and For Individuals) remain children of the FAQs page.

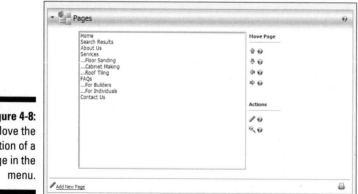

Figure 4-8:
Move the position of a page in the menu.

Adding Content to a Page

After you have added one or more pages to your Web site, you can begin adding content modules to those pages. A module manages content of a particular flavor. The name of a module usually gives a good clue as to the type of content it manages. For example, the Links module allows you to display a list of links, the Feedback module displays a feedback form, and the Text/HTML module allows you to add text or HTML. Chapters 5, 6, and 7 provide detailed explanations of the purpose of each module and info on how to manage records for each module. In this section, we provide an overview of how to add and delete modules from a page and discuss some of the many settings available on each module.

Adding a new module to a page

You must be logged in as the Administrator or as a user with permission to edit a page to add modules to the Web site. See "Setting view and edit permissions for a page" to find out how to enable users to also add modules to a page. After you're logged in, the Control Panel will be displayed above the menu. The middle section of the Control Panel manages adding modules.

Here's how to add a new module to a page:

1. **Navigate to the page you want to add the module to.**

2. **Leave the Add New Module radio button selected.**

3. **Select Text/HTML from the drop-down box beside the Module field, as shown in Figure 4-9.**

4. **(Optional.) Enter a title for the module into the Title text box.**

   The title is displayed as a heading in the module container above any content you later add to the module. If you don't enter a title, the name of the module will be added automatically.

5. **Leave the Visibility field set to Same As Page.**

   This means that all roles that have been given View Page permissions are able to view the module. The other option is Page Editors Only. This option means that only members of roles with Edit Page permissions are able to view the module. This option is useful if you are adding the module to a page that is visible to all users and you want to set it up and add content to it before your visitors see it.

6. **(Optional.) Select the name of the pane you want to add the module to.**

   The main pane in the center of the page is called the ContentPane. This is the default pane the module will be added to. Selecting a different pane here adds the module into that pane instead. You can easily move the module to another pane later if you need to.

7. **Leave the Insert field set on Bottom.**

   This adds the module below any other modules that are located inside the pane selected at Pane. Alternatively, you can choose to insert the module on top of any existing modules. It is easy to move modules around if you later choose to do so.

8. **Leave the Align field set on Left.**

   This sets the alignment of content within the module.

9. **Click the Add button.**

   The module is now displayed on the page, awaiting your witty prose. Figure 4-9 displays an example of the Add New Module section of the Control Panel, as well as a Text/HTML module that has previously been added to the ContentPane of this page.

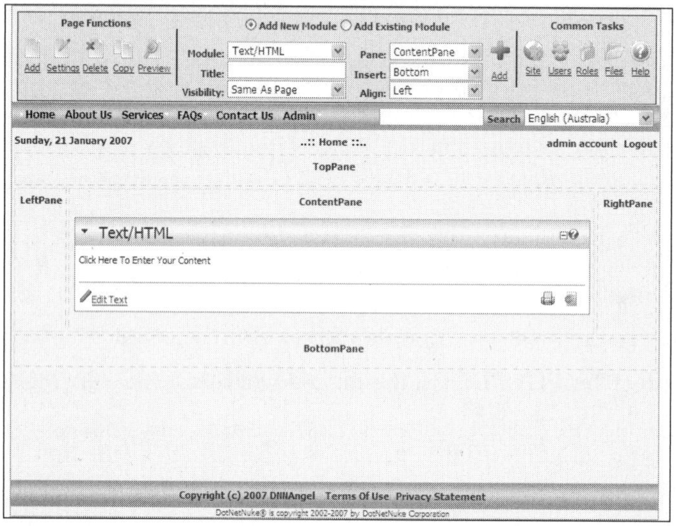

Figure 4-9:
Adding a new module to a page.

Adding an existing module to a page

To save you time when building your Web site, DNN provides you with the ability to display an existing module and its content on more than one page. This is a great timesaver if, for example, you want to display a list of important links on two pages of the Web site. By copying an existing module, you don't have to reenter all the links on the second page. You can also update a link on one instance of the module and the change will appear in both lists.

Here's how to add an existing module to a page:

1. **Navigate to the page you want to add the module to.**

   You can't add a second copy of the module to the same page.

2. **Select the Add Existing Module radio button from the Control Panel.**

3. **Select the page name from the drop-down box beside the Page field.**

4. **Select the module title from the drop-down box beside the Module field.**

5. **Select the name of the pane you want to add the module to.**

   The main pane in the center of the page is called the ContentPane. Selecting a different pane name here adds the module into that pane instead. You can easily move the module to another pane later if you need to.

6. **Leave the Insert field set on Bottom.**

   This adds the module below any other modules that are located inside the pane selected at Pane. Alternatively, you can choose to insert the module on top of any existing modules. It is easy to move modules around if you later choose to do so.

7. **Leave the Align field set on Left.**

   This sets the alignment of content within the module.

8. **Click the Add button.**

   The module is now copied to the page and any future content changes will be displayed on both instances of the module.

Deleting, moving, and performing other module tasks by using the module menu

When you are logged in as the Administrator, a small arrow is displayed to the left of the module title. Mouse over that arrow and you will see a drop-down menu, shown in Figure 4-10, that enables you to do all the things you want to do with a module, such as deleting and moving modules. It also provides access to the Module Settings page where module details, permissions, design, and more can be changed.

Here's an overview of the functions on the module menu in the order they appear on the menu:

✔ **Edit** or **Add New:** Click this option to add or edit module content. This option is displayed to Administrators and role members with edit rights to the module. See "Setting module permissions" later in this chapter to find out how to set edit and view rights to modules.

✔ **Import Content:** Click this option to import content to this module. Content must first be exported before it can be imported. For example, you could import a list of links from one links module to another links module. This creates a brand-new version of the content that can be edited independently of the module that the content was exported from. This option is only available to Administrators and Page Editors (that is, role members who have been given edit page permissions), and is only available on some modules.

✔ **Export Content:** Click this option to export the content of this module for future importing to another module of the same type. This option is available to Administrators and Page Editors. See the earlier section "Setting view and edit permissions for a page" for more details.

✔ **Help:** Click this option to view basic information on using this module. This option is displayed to Administrators, Page Editors, and Module Editors (that is, members of roles with edit rights to the module). See "Setting module permissions" later in this chapter for more information.

✔ **Online Help:** Click this option to view detailed online help on using DNN. This help is written and maintained by Lorraine Young, one of the authors of this book, for the DNN Core Team. This option is displayed to Administrators, Page Editors, and Module Editors.

✔ **Print:** Click this option to view a print version of the content within this module. This option is displayed to Administrators, Page Editors, and Module Editors.

✔ **Settings:** Click this option to view and manage the settings of this module. Module settings are discussed in detail later in this chapter: See "Tweaking module settings." This option is only available to Administrators and Page Editors.

✔ **Delete:** Click this option to delete the module from the page. This option is only available to Administrators and Page Editors.

✔ **Clear Cache:** Click this option to refresh the stored information of this module. This ensures that other people browsing your Web site only see the latest updated information inside this module. This option is only available to Administrators and Page Editors.

✔ **Move:** Mouse over this option to see a list of panes on this page and then select the name of the pane you want to move it to. This option is only available to Administrators and Page Editors.

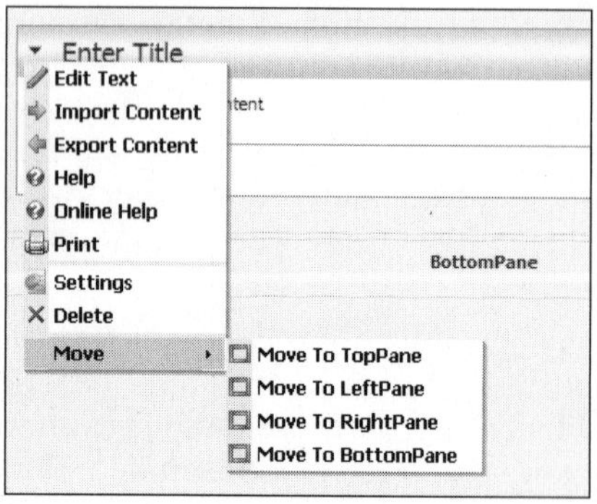

Figure 4-10:
The module
menu
enables
Adminis-
trators to
perform a
wide range
of module
tasks.

Setting module permissions

Module permission settings enable the Administrator to control which roles can view the module (View Module permissions) and which roles can add, edit, and delete content within the module (Edit Module permission). Some advanced modules have additional role settings, which provide more refined permissions; however, View Module and Edit Module permissions are the most common.

Here's how to set the permissions on a module to control which roles can view a module and manage its content:

1. **Select Settings from any module menu.**

   This goes to the settings page for this module.

2. **In the Basic Settings section, select <All Roles>from the Filter by Group drop-down box beside Permissions to view a full list of all roles.**

   This option is only visible if one or more role groups have been added to the Web site as shown in "Adding a new role group" earlier in this chapter. If this option isn't displayed, skip to Step 3.

   A checked box in the Edit Module column indicates that members of the role can edit the content of the module.

3. **Deselect the Inherit View Permissions from Page check box if you want to change the roles that can view the module.**

   This makes all the check boxes in the View Module column available for selection. Changing this setting allows you to hide this module from one or more roles that have access to view this page. The Inherit View Permissions from Page check box is selected by default, which means all roles that can view the page can also view the module. If you don't want to change view permissions, skip to Step 5.

4. **Select the check box for each role in the View Module column of the Permissions field that you want to be able to view the module.**

   The Administrators role is automatically checked and can't be unchecked. Members of roles selected here can view the module and its content but do not have any editing rights.

5. **Select the check box beside each role in the Edit Module column of the Permissions field that you want to be able to edit the module.**

   The Administrators role is automatically checked and can't be unchecked. Members of roles selected here can add, edit, and delete module content; however, they can't modify the module settings, move, or delete the module itself.

6. **Click the <u>Update</u> link.**

   You are now returned to the page.

Tweaking module settings

If you need to change something apart from the content of the module, the Module Settings page is the place to come. Module settings enable you to control all aspects of a module apart from its content. Module settings include module permissions (as discussed above), module publishing dates, module title, module layout, the location of the module on the Web site, container design, and more.

Here's how to change module settings:

1. **Select Settings from the module menu.**

   This opens the Module Settings page of this module, as shown in Figure 4-11.

2. **Edit any of the Basic Settings. These settings apply to every instance of this module on the Web site:**

   - **Modify the Module Title:** The module title is displayed above the module content. Alternatively, you can edit this on the page by clicking on it.

   - **Modify module Permissions:** This controls which roles can view and edit the module. See "Setting module permissions" earlier in this chapter for more details.

3. **Click the Maximize button beside Advanced Settings to edit more options:**

   - **Display Module on All Pages?:** Select this check box to display this module on every page of the Web site. The module will be displayed in the same pane as this module; however, you can move the module to a different pane on any page without affecting other pages.

   - **Header:** Enter any text to be displayed between the module title and module content. For example, if the module contains a list of documents, the header may offer assistance or more information, such as **Our product price lists are listed below. Click on the link beside a price list to download it.**

   - **Footer:** Enter any text to be displayed below the module content.

   - **Start Date:** Click the <u>Calendar</u> link and select the first day you want the module to appear on the Web site. Prior to this date, the module will only be displayed to Administrator and Page Editors.

   - **End Date:** Click the <u>Calendar</u> link and select the last day you want the module to appear on the Web site. The module will only be displayed to Administrator and Page Editors after this date.

4. **Click the <u>Update</u> link.**

   The changes will be applied to the module.

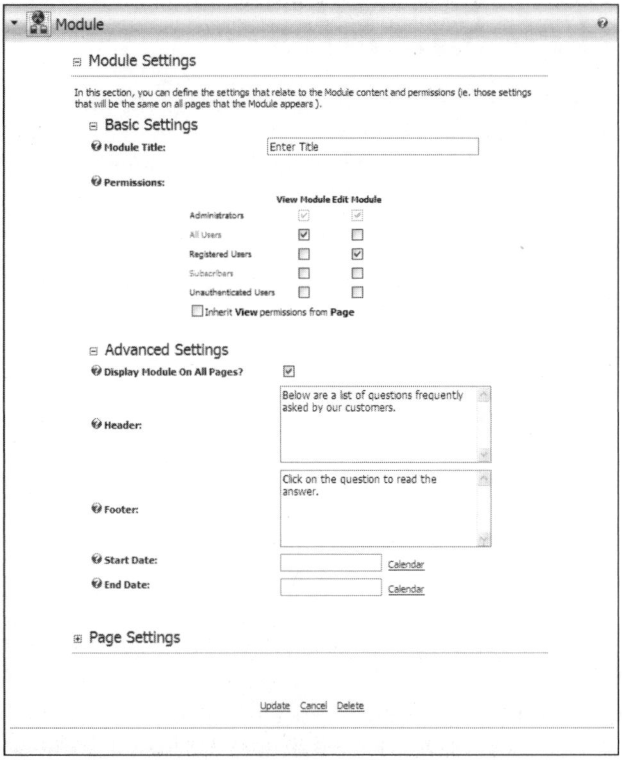

Figure 4-11:
Manage all modules settings here.

Moving a module to another page

Here's how to move a module to another page:

1. **Select Settings from the module menu.**

   This opens the Module Settings page of this module.

2. **Click the Maximize button beside Page Settings.**

3. **Click the Maximize button beside Advanced Settings.**

4. **Select the page to move the module to from the Move To Page field.**

5. **Click the Update link.**

   This module is now located on the selected page. It will be positioned at the bottom of the same pane as the previous page. If the same pane doesn't exist on the new page, it will instead be added to the bottom of the content pane.

Managing Web Site Files

DNN provides a central place to upload and manage the images, movies and other types of files that can be viewed and downloaded from your Web site. That place is called the File Manager and it is located under the Admin page on the Web site menu.

Only Administrators can access the File Manager; however, they can enable roles to view the files within one or more folders and upload files to one or more folders.

Getting familiar with the File Manager

The File Manager is divided into the following six sections, as shown in Figure 4-12:

- ✔ **Folders toolbar:** This toolbar enables the Administrator to perform administrative tasks on a folder that is selected in the Folders window.

- ✔ **Files toolbar:** This toolbar enables the Administrator to manage the files selected in the Files window.

- ✔ **Folders window:** This area displays a list of folders in a hierarchical tree structure. When a folder is selected, any files inside that folder are displayed in the Files window to the right.

- ✔ **Files window:** This area displays the files associated with the selected folder. Ten (10) files are displayed by default. The filename, date, and size of the files are displayed. The default order of these files is alphanumeric by filename; however, they can be reverse ordered or ordered by another field by clicking on a linked heading above the files.

An Edit and Delete button is displayed beside each file enabling Administrators to edit or delete a single file. A check box beside each file enables one or more files to be modified simultaneously, and the Select All button enables all displayed files to be modified. The check boxes are used in conjunction with the Files toolbar.

Below the listed files are details of how many pages of files are contained within the currently selected folder and navigation buttons to move between these pages.

✔ **File Manager Details bar:** The information bar displayed across the bottom of the File Manager window displays the location of selected folders on the left side. The middle of the bar tells you how full the File Manager is and the maximum space allocated to this Web site by the host. The right side of this bar enables you to set the number of files displayed in the Files window. This setting defaults back to ten when you leave the File Manager or upload a file.

✔ **Folder Security Settings:** This section displays all the security roles for this Web site and displays the View and Write (upload) permissions allocated for the selected folder. These permissions can be updated at any time.

Files toolbar

Folders toolbar

Folders window

Figure 4-12:
The
Admin➪File
Manager
provides a
central
location to
store and
manage
files,
such as
documents
and images
that are
used on the
Web site.

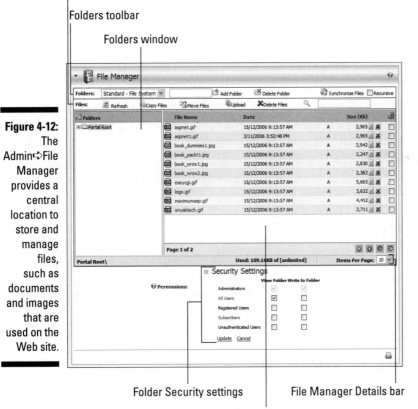

Folder Security settings   File Manager Details bar

Files window

Uploading a file to the File Manager

Here's how the Administrator can upload one or more files to the File Manager:

1. **Click the Files button located in the Common Tasks section of the Control Panel.**

   This goes to the Admin⇨File Manager page where the File Manager is located. Folders are listed down the left and the files inside each folder are displayed to the right.

2. **Click the Upload button located above the list of files.**

   This takes you to the File Upload page.

3. **Click the Browse button and select the file from your computer.**

   You can either upload a single file or save time by uploading a .ZIP file containing several files.

4. **Select the folder that you want to upload the file to from the drop-down box below.**

   You can only upload one file or one .ZIP file to one folder at a time.

5. **Select the Decompress .ZIP Files? check box if you are uploading a .ZIP file that you want to decompress.**

   When uploading a .ZIP file, you have two options. Selecting this option enables you to decompress the file so that each of the files appears separately in the folder as well as the .ZIP file. Alternatively, if you do not check this option, the .ZIP file uploads as a single file.

6. **Click the <u>Save File</u> link.**

   You are now returned to the File Manager.

If you receive a warning message that the file is a restricted file type, your Web site doesn't allow you to upload this type of file. See Chapter 3 to find out how to change this: You need host access to do so.

Delete a single file

Here's how to delete a single file:

1. **Click the Files button located in the Common Tasks section of the Control Panel.**

2. **Click the Maximize button beside Portal Root folder in the Folders Window.**

This displays any folders inside the Portal Root folder. Repeat this step to open additional folders.

3. **Click on a folder name in the Folders window to select it.**

   This displays the first ten files inside this folder in the Files window. If the required file isn't displayed, use the navigation buttons to move to it. Alternatively, you can search for the file.

4. **Click the Delete button beside the file to be deleted.**

Working with multiple files inside the File Manager

The File Manager uses a folder and file organization structure that is familiar to most computer users. A list of folders appears down the left side. When a folder name is selected, the files inside that folder are displayed.

Here are a number of tasks you can perform on files within the File Manager:

1. **Click the Files button located in the Common Tasks section of the Control Panel.**

2. **Click on the Maximize button beside Portal Root folder in the Folders Window.**

   Repeat this step to access additional folders.

3. **Click on a folder name in the Folders window to select it.**

   This displays the first ten files inside this folder in the Files window. If the desired files are not displayed, use the navigation buttons below to navigate to them.

4. **Select the check box beside one or more files, or click the Select All button above the check boxes.**

   The checked files are now selected. Note: The Select All button only selects all the files on the displayed page. To manage a larger number of files at one time, change the Items Per Page field to 15, 20, 30, 40, or 50.

5. **Here are some of the tasks you can now perform on these files:**

   • **Copy Files**: Click the Copy Files button to copy the files to another folder. Click OK and repeat Steps 2 and 3 to select the folder and then click OK again.

   • **Move Files**: Click the Move Files button to move the files to another folder. Click OK and repeat Steps 2 and 3 to select the new folder and then click OK again.

When a file is moved, the new location of the file is updated across the site wherever the file is in use. The exception is when a file such as a file link or an image that is displayed in the Rich Text Editor (RTE) is moved. In this case, the file link will not work or the image will no longer be displayed. This happens because the location of the path is saved into the RTE. If this occurs, you will need to reselect the image in the related RTEs.

• **Delete Files**: Click the Delete Files button to delete the files and then click OK.

Creating a new folder

Only Administrators can add folders to the File Manager. Folders let you organize the files used on your Web site, similar to the way you do it on your personal computer. Each folder can be set to enable one or more roles to have access to view the files in the folder and to upload files to the folder. See the next section, "Setting the role permissions for a folder," for details.

Here's how to add a new folder to the File Manager:

1. **Click the Files button located in the Common Tasks section of the Control Panel.**

2. **Navigate to and click on the name of the folder you want to add the new folder underneath in the Folders list.**

3. **Enter a name for the new folder into the text box on the Folders toolbar.**

4. **Click the Add Folder button.**

   The folder is now displayed in the Folders list. By default, new folders are set to enable All Users to view any files added to the folder and only Administrators can upload files to the folder. You may now want to set role permissions to this file.

Setting the role permissions for a folder

Administrators can set folders to enable one or more roles to have access to view the files in the folder and to upload files to the folder via the add/edit page of certain modules.

Here's how to set the role permissions on a folder in the File Manager:

1. **Click the Files button located in the Common Tasks section of the Control Panel.**

2. **Navigate to and click on the name of the folder you want to set permission for.**

3. **Go to the Folder Security Settings section and select <All Roles> if the Filter by Group field is displayed.**

   This option is only visible if one or more role groups have been added to the Web site as mentioned in "Adding a new role group" earlier in this chapter. If this option isn't displayed, skip to Step 4.

4. **Select the check box beside each role in the View Folder column to enable members of that role to view files in this folder.**

   This enables these role members to view the files within this folder when they are displayed on the Web site. All Users is checked by default. If All Users is not checked, people who aren't logged in to Web site won't be able to view these folder files on their page and only members of the selected roles will be able to see the files when logged in.

5. **Select the check box beside each role in the Write to Folder column to enable members of that role to upload files to this folder.**

   This enables these role members to upload new files to this folder. Because these users cannot access the File Manager itself to upload new files, access to upload files is achieved through adding or editing module content. See "Uploading files without Administrator rights" later in this chapter for more details.

6. **Click the <u>Update</u> link.**

Deleting an existing folder

Here's how to delete a folder from the File Manager:

1. **Click the Files button located in the Common Tasks section of the Control Panel.**

2. **Navigate to and click on the name of the folder you want to delete.**

   Any files within the selected folder are displayed in the Files window to the right. These files must be deleted or moved to another folder before this folder can be deleted. Likewise, if this folder has any subfolders, these must be deleted first.

3. **Click the Delete Folder button on the Folder.**

   This displays a message box confirming the name of the folder to be deleted.

4. **Click OK.**

   The folder will now be deleted.

Synchronizing one or more folders with your database

If you have access to upload files directly to your Web site server with a protocol such as FTP, or someone else has uploaded files for you in this way, you need to synchronize your File Manager to ensure that the files changed via the server are accurately reflected in the File Manager.

Here's how to synchronize File Manager folders:

1. **Click the Files button located in the Common Tasks section of the Control Panel.**

2. **Navigate to and click on the name of the folder you want to synchronize in the Folders window.**

   To synchronize one or more child folders at a time, select their parent folder.

3. **Check the Recursive check box on the Folders toolbar if you want to synchronize all the child folders of the selected folder.**

   Selecting the Recursive check box synchronizes all files inside both the selected folder and any child folders. If this option isn't selected, only the selected folder is synchronized.

4. **Click the Synchronize Files button on the Folder toolbar.**

   The folder will begin synchronizing. If the Recursive check box is selected, all child folders will also be synchronized.

Uploading files without Administrator rights

Only Administrators can upload files with the File Manager interface; however, users can upload files via the Add/Edit page of some modules. To do so, the user must be a member of a role with access to upload files to one or more File Manager folders. See "Setting the role permissions for a folder" for more details.

The user must also be a member of a role with edit permissions of a module that enables file upload. Modules that enable file upload are those that display the Link Type field on the Add/Edit page. For example, the Announcements, Blog, Documents, Links, News Feeds (RSS), and Media modules.

Here's how role members with edit module permissions can view or upload a file to the File Manager:

1. **Select Add from the module menu.**

   This is the first item listed in the module menu. Depending on the module you are using, the actual words displayed here will vary. For example, the Links module displays Add Link, whereas the Announcements module displays Add New Announcement.

2. **Ensure that the page displays the Link Type field.**

   If the Link Type control is not displayed, this module does not allow files to be uploaded.

3. **Select the File (A File on Your Site) radio button below the Link Type field.**

   This displays the File Location and File Name drop-down boxes. Any File Manager folders that the user has view access to will be listed in the File Location drop-down box.

4. **Select the folder to view or upload the file to from the File Location drop-down box.**

   This will list the files within the folder in the File Name drop-down box.

5. **Click the Upload New File link.**

   If the Update New File link is not displayed, the user doesn't have access to upload files to this folder.

6. **Click the Browse button and locate and select the file from your computer.**

   This displays the filename in the text box to the left of the Browse button.

7. **Click the Upload New File link.**

   This uploads the file to the File Manager and displays the filename in a drop-down box. To upload more files, repeat Steps 4 through 7.

Making Your Site Look Good

One of the early accomplishments of DNN was to achieve separation between the content within the Web site and the design used on the Web site. Unlike common HTML editing programs, where you design a Web page and then add the content directly inside the designed page, DNN manages these two elements separately, enabling one to be changed independently of the other.

The design of a DNN Web site is broken down into two main elements called skins and containers. A *skin* refers to the design of the page and a *container* refers to the design of a module. Typically, a designer creates a Skin Package for a DNN Web site that consists of a number of different skins and containers with the same look and feel. Because the design and content of a DNN Web site are completely separate from each other, the skin and container can be changed as often as you like. You can set a default skin and container for all pages and modules on your Web site, as well as select different skins or containers for any page or module.

As well as containing skins and containers that provide designs for pages and modules respectively, a Skin Package also contains a style sheet. A *style sheet* is a document that sets the styles used in the skin. (Styles control elements like the text color, size and font, the colors used in the menu, and so on.) A Skin Package can include one style sheet to be used for all skins and containers in that package, or it may include a different style sheet for each skin and container. DNN style sheets are Cascading Style Sheets (CSS). Detailed coverage of CSS is outside the scope of this book, but you can find lots of information on the WWW on writing CSS if you're interested. If you do have a design bent or are interested in understanding more about skinning, DNN core has produced a document on building skins and containers called *Skinning Guide*. You can download it from `www.dotnetnuke.com/About/Documentation/ProjectDocuments/tabid/478/Default.aspx`.

Skins are stored in two areas of DNN: One is at Host⇨Skins and the other is at Admin⇨Skins. Host skins are uploaded and managed by the host and Admin skins are uploaded and managed by the Administrator. Skins maintained under host are available to all portals, whereas skins maintained under Admin are unique to that Web site.

Changing the site logo

Web sites typically display a logo image in the top-right corner of each page. Most DNN skins also use this format.

Here's how to set the site logo:

1. **Upload the logo to the Admin⇨File Manager.**

   See "Uploading a file to the File Manager" earlier in this chapter for more details.

2. **Click the Site button located in the Common Tasks section of the Control Panel.**

3. **Go to the Appearance section.**

4. **Select the folder where the logo is located from the File Location drop-down list beside the Logo field.**

   This displays a list of images within this folder in the File Name drop-down list below.

5. **Select the logo from the File Name drop-down list.**

6. **Click the <u>Update</u> link.**

   This saves these settings.

Changing the default skin and containers

The Administrator can set a default skin and container to be used on all new pages added to the Web site. Skins and containers can be stored in two places — under Host⇨Skins and under Admin⇨Skins. Skins under Host are maintained by the host account, whereas the Administrator maintains those under Admin.

Here's how to set the default skin and container:

1. **Navigate to the Admin⇨Site Settings page.**

   This displays the Site Settings page, where you can set details specific to this Web site.

2. **Go to the Appearance section.**

3. **Select either the Host or Site radio button at the Portal Skin field to view the skins uploaded to that area.**

   Selecting Host displays the skins managed on the Host⇨Skin page; selecting Site displays the skins managed on the Admin⇨Skin page. Host skins are available to all Web sites within the portal, whereas Site skins are only available for use on this Web site. The Portal Skin field sets the default skin to be used on all new Web site pages apart from the Admin Skin pages, which you will set at Step 6.

4. **Select the skin from the drop-down list.**

5. **Click the <u>Preview</u> link to see what the skin looks like.**

   This opens a new Web browser with an example of the skin.

6. **Repeat Steps 3 through 5 to set the Portal Container, Admin Skin, and Admin Container fields.**

   The Portal Container field sets the default container to be used on all modules. The Admin Skin and Admin Container fields set the default skin and container to be used on Administration (Admin) and add/edit pages. Typically, the Admin Skin only has one large pane. The Admin Skin and Admin Container are also used on the default Login and User pages.

7. **Click the Update link.**

   This saves and immediately applies these settings.

 Every page and module has its own settings page where the skin and container to be used on it can be set. Setting the default designs for the Web site doesn't override these individual settings. See "Setting the skin and container designs for an individual page" to find out how to change the designs set on an individual page, or see "Setting the container for an individual module" to find out how to set the container design on an individual module.

Viewing and applying skins

DNN provides administrators with a skins Gallery where they can view and select skins and containers to be used on the Web site, and where they can upload new skins, containers, and skin packages.

Here's how to view and apply skins to the Web site:

1. **Select Admin⇨Skins from the main menu.**

   This opens the Skins page for this Web site, which displays thumbnail images of the skins and containers on your Web site, as shown in Figure 4-13. The name of the displayed skins package is shown at the Skins field.

2. **Select the skins you want to preview by checking one or both of the Host and Site check boxes at the Skin Type field.**

3. **Select the name of a skin or skin package from the Skins drop-down box to view a thumbnail image of all the skins and containers within that Skin Package.**

   Thumbnail images of the related skins and containers are displayed.

4. **Click the Preview link below any skin to preview it.**

   This opens a new Web browser with an example of that skin.

5. **Select either or both of the Portal or Admin check boxes beside the Apply To field below the thumbnail images to choose where you would like to apply the new skin or container.**

Selecting Portal will apply your selection to all Web site pages or containers except on the Administration pages, and the Login and Registration pages. Selecting Admin will apply your selection to the Administration pages, and the Login and Registration pages.

6. Click the <u>Apply</u> link below any skin or container to apply it.

This applies the selected skin or container to either the portal or admin pages or containers as selected at Step 5.

This setting overrides but doesn't change the Default skin we show you how to set in the previous section. You can restore the Default skin at any time by clicking the <u>Restore Default Skin</u> link on the Admin⇨Skins page.

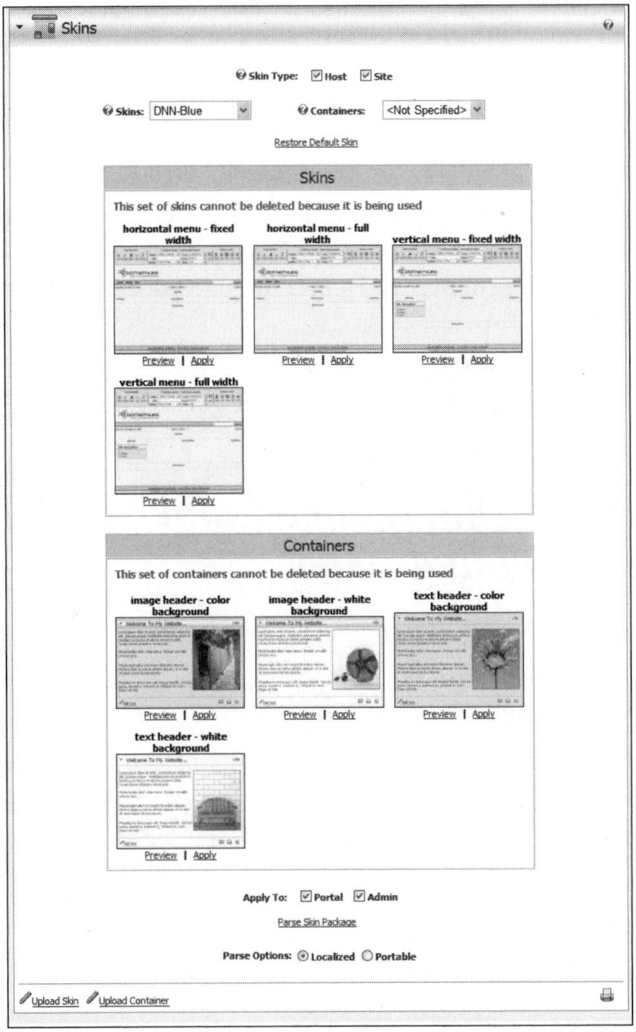

Figure 4-13:
Previewing
and
applying
skins and
containers
to the Web
site by
using the
Admin⇨
Skins page.

Uploading a skin to your Web site

DNN comes with a selection of skin packages; however, if you want something more special, you can buy or design a skin just for you. After you have your new skin, you will need to upload it to your Web site.

You can download information on how to build a skin from www.dotnetnuke. com/About/Documentation/ProjectDocuments/tabid/478/Default. aspx.

Here's how to upload a skin to your Web site:

1. **Select Admin⇨Skins from the main menu.**

   This opens the Skins page for this Web site. Depending on the settings given to you by your host, or set by you under host, Administrators may or may not be able to upload a skin. For this example, we assume you have been given the ability to upload skins. See Chapter 3 to find out how to enable Administrators to upload skins.

2. **Select Upload Skin from the Skins module menu.**

   This opens the File Upload page specifically for uploading skins and skin packages.

3. **Click the Browse button and select the skin package from your computer.**

4. **Click the <u>Save File</u> link.**

   This adds the skin to the Admin ⇨Skin page.

Setting the skin and container designs for an individual page

Here's how to set the skin and containers used on an individual page:

1. **Go to the page and click the Settings button located in the Page Function section of the Control Panel.**

   This displays the Page Management page, where you can configure the setting of this page.

2. **Click the Maximize button at Advanced Settings.**

   This displays all the advanced page settings for this page.

3. **Select either the Host or Site radio button at the Page Skin field to view the related skins.**

   Selecting Host displays a list of the skins managed on the Host⇨Skins page; selecting Site displays a list of the skins managed on the Admin⇨Skins pages.

4. **Select a skin from the drop-down list.**

5. **Click the Preview link to see what the skin looks like.**

   This optional setting opens a new Web browser with an example of the skin. Repeat Steps 4 and 5 to choose another skin.

6. **Repeat Steps 3 through 5 at the Page Container field to set the containers for this page.**

   This sets the container applied to all modules on this page. This setting overrides the default container setting but does not override the container where it is set on the settings page of an individual module.

7. **Click the Update link.**

Setting the container for an individual module

A *container* is the design applied to a module, and changing it can transform the appearance of a module and its content. Containers set all the design elements of a module, as well as the styles applied to the content within the module such as the default font type, size, and color. Each module can be set to display a different container, including instances of the same module located on different pages.

Here's how to set the container on a module:

1. **Select Settings from the module menu.**

   This opens the Module Settings page for this module.

2. **Click the Maximize button beside the Page Settings section.**

   This section enables you to define settings specific to this particular occurrence of this module.

3. **Select the check box beside the Display Container? field.**

   This setting must be selected for the container to be displayed.

4. **Select either the Host or Site radio button beside the Module Container field to view the containers within that area.**

5. **Select a container from the drop-down list.**

6. **Click the Preview link to see what the container looks like.**

   This opens a new Web browser showing how the container looks when it's applied to this module.

7. **Click the Update link.**

   The selected container is now displayed on the module.

Setting advanced design options for an individual module

Here's how to set more advanced design options for an individual module:

1. **Select Settings from the module menu.**

   This opens the Module Settings page for this module.

2. **Click the Maximize button beside the Page Settings section.**

   This section enables you to define settings specific to this particular occurrence of this module.

3. **Edit any of these Basic Settings, as shown in Figure 4-14:**

   • **Icon:** Select an image to be displayed beside the module title. See "Uploading files without Administrator rights" earlier in this chapter for more details.

   • **Alignment:** Select Left, Center, or Right to set the alignment of content within the module. Note: this does not affect the content with Text/HTML module.

   • **Color:** Enter the name of a color or hexadecimal color value to set the background color of the module. Note: The color may not be visible depending on the design of the container applied to the module.

   • **Border:** Enter a number to set the border width for the module. Note: At the time of writing, this option was only working when the container displayed.

- **Visibility:** This setting controls the display of the Minimize/Maximize button that is typically located in the top-right corner of module containers. This button is the same as the Maximize button displayed beside the headings on this page. It enables you control the way module content is displayed to users and also provides users with the ability to change how module content is displayed to them personally.

  Select Maximized to display the module content and to display the minimize button. Users can click the Minimize button to hide the content.

  Select Minimized to minimize the module to hide the content and to display the maximize button. Users can click the Maximize button to view the content.

  Select None to remove this feature.

- **Display Container?:** Check to display a container for this module. If the container is not displayed, the module title is also hidden.

- **Allow Print?:** Check to display a Print button in the bottom right corner of the module. This button enables users to print the content of the module. Display Container? must be selected for this option.

- **Allow Syndicate?:** Check to display a Syndicate button in the bottom right corner of the module. This button enables users to syndicate the content of the module. Display Container? must be selected for this option.

- **Module Container:** Select the container for this module. See "Setting the container for an individual module" earlier in this chapter for more details.

- **Cache Time (secs):** Enter how often, in seconds, you want this module to refresh.

4. **Edit any of the Advanced Settings:**

   - **Set As Default Settings?:** Set the Basic Page Settings applied to this module as the default settings to be used on new modules added to the Web site.

   - **Apply to All Modules?:** Set the Basic Page Settings applied to this module as the default settings to be used on all existing modules on the Web site.

5. Click the <u>Update</u> link.

The module settings are saved and immediately applied to the module. To view the changes, click the Preview button in the Control Panel or log out of the Web site.

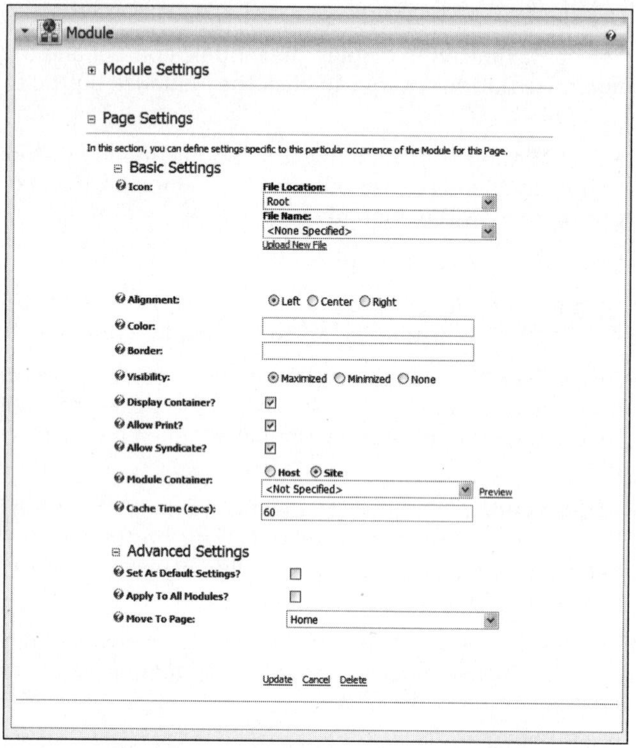

Figure 4-14: These settings manage module design and moving the module to another page.

Chapter 5

Delivering Content Right Out of the Box

*W*hen buying a new home, the catch phrase you hear is, "Location, location, location." When building a new Web site, the catch phrase is "Content, content, content!" No one is interested in visiting a Web site with little or no content, out-of-date content, or really boring content. Content is king! And if you haven't written, obtained, or stolen some yet, now's the time.

In this chapter, we show you how to use eight different modules that come with DNN. These are the modules that display static information such as a list of frequently asked questions, a list of announcements, or a list of downloadable documents.

This chapter shows you how to use two of the fundamental tools of most modules you encounter. The first is the Rich Text Editor (RTE), which enables you to manage and format rich text. The second is the Link tool used in the Links module. This tool is used wherever you need to set a link to a page, a URL, or a file on your Web site. Master these and you are well on your way with DNN.

Doing Almost Anything with Text/HTML

The DNN Text/HTML module enables you to add text, images, links, and tables to the pages of your Web site. Essentially, this module is the Swiss Army knife of modules as it offers all the functionality of a word processor. In fact, you could build your whole Web site by using only this module.

The Text/HTML module provides you with a variety of ways to create and edit text including editing directly on the Web page, by using a Rich Text Editor, and by using an HTML editor.

Plain text editing

Here's how to create and edit text directly on your Web site page:

1. **Click on some text in a Text/HTML module.**

   If this is the first time you have edited this module, the text will read "Click Here To Enter Your Content." Clicking on the text displays a red box around it, which indicates that you can now edit the text.

2. **Edit the text as required.**

   Common word processing shortcuts work in this editing window, so experiment for a while. Don't worry: You can't break it! Some of the shortcuts that work include pressing Ctrl+B to bold a word, Ctrl+U to underline a word, or Ctrl+I to italicize a word.

3. **Click outside the red box to exit editing.**

   The red box disappears and you are taken out of editing mode.

Working with the Basic Text Box

Another way to enter text into the Text/HTML module is by using the Basic Text Box feature. In this section, we show you how to copy only the text from another source, such as an e-mail or an existing Web site, leaving behind any text formatting so the text uses the same layout and fonts as the rest of your Web site.

Here's how to add plain text into a Text/HTML module:

1. **Select Edit Text from the module menu.**

   This takes you to the Edit Text/HTML page.

2. **Click the Basic Text Box radio button above the Editor.**

   The Basic Text Box is now displayed.

3. **Enter text into the Basic Text Box.**

   You can also cut and paste text from an e-mail, word document, and so on. Because you are not using a Rich Text Editor, any Word formatting is discarded.

4. **Click the <u>Update</u> link.**

   The text is now displayed, as shown in Figure 5-1.

Because you updated the Text/HTML module when it was switched to Basic Text Box, the next time you use a Text/HTML module, the Editor will display in the Basic Text Box.

Figure 5-1:
The
Text/HTML
module is
similar to
a word
processor.
You can add
and format
text, images,
links, and
tables.

From rags to riches with Rich Text Editor

The Text/HTML module includes a text editor called the Rich Text Editor (RTE). The RTE is used in many other DNN modules, so it is worthwhile for you to get familiar with this module first. After you have mastered it, you're well on your way to understanding how to use a whole bunch of other modules.

The Rich Text Editor includes nearly all the features you expect from a word processor. The RTE contains more than 40 different buttons, so it would be a waste of space to talk you through each of them, but here's how you can see what the RTE buttons do:

1. **Select Edit Text from the module menu.**

   This takes you to the Edit Text/HTML page.

2. **Ensure that the Rich Text Editor radio button is selected.**

   This displays the RTE.

3. **Click inside the RTE window and type some text.**

4. **Select some of your text.**

5. **Place your mouse over any button.**

   This displays a tooltip explaining what the button does; for example, the Underline button underlines any selected text.

6. **Click a button to try it out.**

   You can experiment all you like and the text won't be displayed on the page until you click the Update link. Go wild!

Discarding unwanted text formatting

When you are building a new Web site, you often need to transfer existing information into the Web site. Maybe you need to transfer information from your old Web site, or existing documents such as Microsoft Word files. One of the problems with doing this is that the text may include formatting that will override the styles set in the style sheet you have applied to your Web site. This means the text won't be standardized, especially if you are cutting and pasting text from a number of different sources. The effect can be unprofessional and tacky. This can all be avoided by cleaning the text. *Cleaning* removes all the unnecessary formatting from the text so it looks good on the page and matches the rest of your Web site.

Here's how to copy text from another source and discard unwanted formatting:

1. **Select Edit Text from the module menu.**

   This displays the Edit Text/HTML page.

2. **Ensure that the Rich Text Editor radio button is selected.**

   This displays the RTE.

3. **Open your document and copy the information you want to add to this Text/HTML module.**

   You can copy text from another Web site, a Word document, a PDF, and so on. You can't copy images into the Web site this way. See "Inserting images into the RTE" later in this chapter for more details.

4. **Click inside the RTE window in the place where you want to insert the information and then click the Paste button.**

   The text is now displayed inside the RTE.

5. **Click the Clean MS Word HTML button.**

   The layout and style of the text will change and only basic formatting like headings remains. Depending on the amount of formatting that has been removed, you will probably need to modify the layout of the text now. Don't be dismayed: It's worth the effort in the long run!

6. **Click the <u>Preview</u> link below the RTE to see how the text will look on the page.**

   Clicking Preview displays the text at the bottom of the page. The text in the RTE window doesn't display the styles from your style sheet, only those set by using the RTE. Previewing your text lets you see how it will look after the styles have been applied.

7. **Click the <u>Update</u> link to save.**

   This returns you to your Web page.

The Clean MS Word HTML button also removes any formatting added by using the Styles, Paragraph, Font, and Size drop-down selection boxes. If you have gone too wild with adding headings and styles and fonts and colors, clicking the Clean MS Word HTML button is the best way of starting afresh!

Adding styles to text

One toolbar worth a bit of explanation is the Styles toolbar at the very top of the RTE. This toolbar lets you change the size and font of your text by selecting options from the Size and Font drop-down boxes respectively.

This tool bar also includes two additional drop-down list boxes called Styles and Paragraph. The Paragraph option lets you select text and change it to a Heading style such as Heading 1, Heading 2, and so on. The styles of these headings are set up in the style sheet applied to this page. See Chapter 4 for more details.

The final option is the Styles drop-down selection box. Like the Paragraph drop-down list box, it applies formatting to your text according to the style sheet applied to this page. The Styles drop-down list box displays all the styles from your style sheet.

Adding a Web site link to the RTE

Here's how to add a link to another Web site by using the Text/HTML module:

1. **Select Edit Text from the module menu.**

   This displays the Edit Text/HTML page.

2. **Ensure that the Rich Text Editor radio button is selected.**

   This displays the RTE.

3. **Highlight the text or image you want to add the link to and click the Create Link button.**

   This displays the Insert Link window, as shown in Figure 5-2.

4. **Enter the Web site URL into the text box below Location:**

   Ensure that http:// is only entered once in this box.

5. **(Optional.) Select the Open Link in New Browser Window? check box**

   This setting is optional; however, opening a new browser is the typical way Web sites work when linking to a different Web site.

6. **Click the OK button.**

   The link will now be added; however, it is not clickable within the editor.

7. **Click the <u>Update</u> link.**

   This returns you to your Web page, where you will be able to click on the link.

See the "Getting Around with Links" section later in this chapter to find out how to set links to pages and files within your Web site. Along with getting comfortable with the RTE, discovering how to work with links is the other major "must-know" of building DNN Web pages.

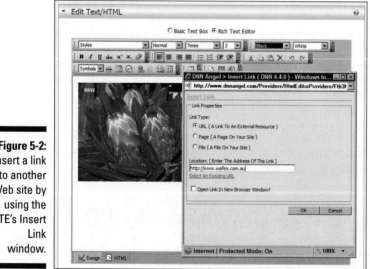

Figure 5-2:
Insert a link to another Web site by using the RTE's Insert Link window.

Inserting images into the RTE

Here's how to insert an image by using the RTE:

1. **Select Edit Text from the module menu.**

    This displays the Edit Text/HTML page.

2. **Ensure that the Rich Text Editor radio button is selected.**

    This displays the RTE.

3. **Position the cursor where you want to add the image.**

4. **Click the Insert Image from Gallery button.**

    This displays the Image Gallery window, as shown in Figure 5-3. An icon for each folder in the Administrator's File Manager is displayed, as well as a thumbnail picture of any image inside the root folder.

5. **Double-click on a folder to view the images inside it and then single-click on the image to preview it.**

    The image you select for previewing is displayed in the Preview window to the right. The Dimensions section displays size information and enables modifying of these values. The Properties section lets you add borders and align the image. You don't have to modify any of these sections to insert the image. Skip to Step 8 if you just want to add the image without changing its size or alignment.

6. **To scale the image, click the Percentage radio button beside Percentage and enter a percentage.**

    For example, entering **50** scales the image down to 50% of its original height. The size of the scaled image is displayed in the Preview window above.

7. **To set the alignment of the image in the RTE, select an option from the Align drop-down box in the Properties section.**

    The default setting of NotSet aligns the bottom of the image with the bottom of any text on the same line. The other options are

    - **Top:** Aligns the top of the image with the top of the text
    - **Bottom:** Aligns the bottom of the image with the bottom of the text
    - **Left:** Aligns the image to the left of the module
    - **Right:** Aligns the image to the right of the module
    - **AbsMiddle:** Aligns middle of the image with the middle of the text
    - **Center:** Aligns middle of the image with the middle of the text

Do not use the Center option to center align an image. Instead, you are better off inserting the image and then using the Center button on the main RTE toolbar. The Center option in the Insert image dialog box appears to have the same effect as the Absolute Middle. Using the Center align button on the toolbar after you have inserted the image gives a more logical result.

8. Click the Insert button.

The image is now added into the RTE.

9. Click the <u>Update</u> link.

This returns you to your Web page where you will be able to view the image.

You can move the position of the image by clicking on the image and then dragging and dropping it in a new position.

If a file link or an image inserted into the RTE moved to a new File Manager folder, the file link will no longer work and the image will no longer be displayed. This happens because the location of the path is saved into the RTE. If this occurs, you will need to reselect the image in the related RTEs.

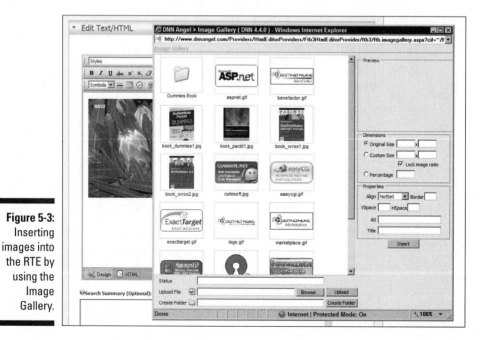

Figure 5-3:
Inserting images into the RTE by using the Image Gallery.

Uploading images to the RTE Image Gallery

Here's how to upload an image into the File Manager via the RTE interface:

1. **Select Edit Text from the module menu.**

   This displays the Edit Text/HTML page.

2. **Ensure that the Rich Text Editor is selected.**

   This displays the RTE.

3. **Click the Insert Image from Gallery button.**

   This displays the Image Gallery window. You can see folders within the Administrator's File Manager as well as thumbnail pictures of any images inside the root folder.

4. **Double-click on the Folder you want to upload the image to.**

   This opens the folder and displays any existing images inside this folder.

5. **Click the Browse button beside Upload File.**

   This opens a dialog box enabling you to locate the image on your computer.

6. **Select the image from your computer and click the Upload button.**

   A thumbnail picture of the image is now displayed in the folder. You can now close the Image Gallery window, or if you want to use the image in your Web site now, select the image and insert it.

Adding a table

The RTE provides you with the ability to create tables. I personally prefer to use the User Defined Table module to manage tables of information and suggest you take a look at this module as a better alternative. (Flip to Chapter 6 for more on User Defined Tables.) However, for creating simple tables, you might like to give the RTE a try.

Here's how to create a table by using the RTE:

1. **Select Edit Text from the module menu.**

   This displays the Edit Text/HTML page.

2. **Ensure that the Rich Text Editor radio button is selected.**

   This displays the RTE.

3. **Position your cursor where you want to add the table and click the Insert Table button.**

   This displays the Table Editor window, as shown in Figure 5-4.

4. Enter a number into the Rows text box to set the number of rows in the table.

Rows go down the page. The default setting is two rows.

5. Enter a number into the Cols text box to set the number of columns in the table.

Columns go across the page. The default setting is four columns.

6. Click the OK button to insert your table.

The empty table is now displayed in the RTE and you can add text or images to each table cell.

7. Click the Update link.

This returns you to your Web page, where you can view the table.

To edit a table click inside the table and click the Edit Table button.

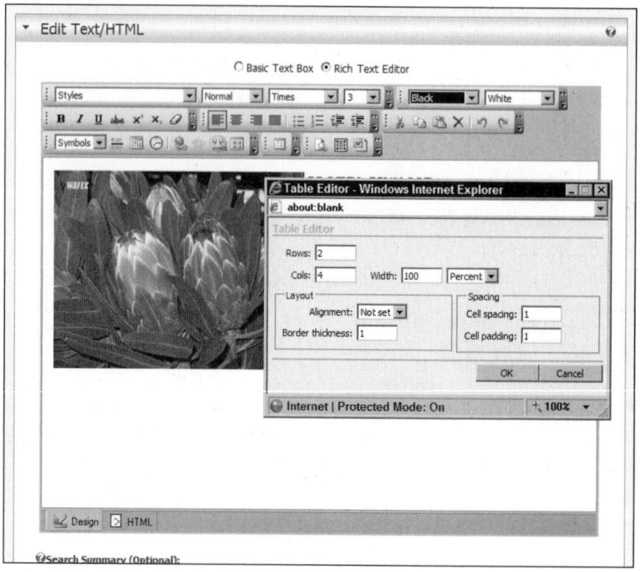

Figure 5-4:
Create tables in the RTE by using the Table Editor.

Accessing the HTML code

This book won't attempt to show you how to write HTML code. If you are interested in mastering HTML, you can find lots of books and online resources to help you do this. (Check out *HTML 4 For Dummies*, by Ed Tittel and Mary Burmeister, published by Wiley, for starters.) However, if you do know how to write HTML, you can either create it in your favorite HTML editor and copy and paste it into the RTE, or you can code straight into the RTE. The choice is yours.

As we mention previously, we recommend the User Defined Tables module over the RTE Table Editor. This isn't because the RTE Table Editor is faulty, but you need some HTML knowledge to get the most out of it. If you do know some HTML, you will be confident enough to switch to the HTML tab below the window and edit the table HTML. If you aren't confident, give it a try anyway.

Here's how to access the HTML editor of the Rich Text Box:

1. **Select Edit Text from the module menu.**

   This takes you to the Edit Text/HTML page.

2. **Ensure that the Rich Text Editor radio button is selected.**

   This displays the RTE.

3. **Select the HTML tab below the RTE window.**

   This displays the HTML code for the page.

4. **Create or paste your HTML code.**

5. **Click the Update link.**

This saves your HTML and returns you to the page.

If you do feel comfortable tinkering, at least a little, with the HTML, you can fix a few common problems that you may experience with your RTE tables. For example, you may notice that the text inside the table is larger than the text on the rest of the page. Here's how to make the table text the same size as the normal text size:

1. **Click the HTML tab at the base of the RTE window.**

   This displays the entire HTML code for this page, but don't panic just yet!

2. **Find the `<TABLE` tag inside the HTML code.**

   You can do this quickly by pressing Ctrl+F and entering `<TABLE` into the Find box that appears.

3. **Replace `<TABLE` with `<TABLE class="normal"`.**

   This step changes all the text in the table to the normal style used on your Web site.

4. **Click the Design tab.**

   This displays the table and other content in Normal view.

5. **Click the Update link.**

   This returns you to your Web page, where you will be able to view the table.

You do not need to enter text in each table cell; however, if a cell is empty, its border won't display correctly. To fix this, simply add a space into the cell.

The width of table cells changes as you add text and images to them. This can result in scrappy-looking tables. The Table Editor gives you an option to create tables with a pixel width setting rather than a percentage setting, but if you enter too much text into a cell, it will simply push out the size of the table anyway.

Here's how to make all table cells the same width:

1. **Count the number of columns in your table and formulate a percentage for each one totaling 100%.**

   For example, if you have four columns and want to set them all to the same width, they should be 25% each.

2. **Select the HTML tab below the RTE window.**

   This displays the HTML code for the page.

3. **Locate the HTML code that reads <TR><TD>.**

   If the <TD> doesn't have <TR> before it, it isn't the right code. The HTML is displayed on separate lines, like this:

   ```
   <TR>
         <TD>
   ```

4. **Edit all four of the <TD> code sections so that they read <TD width="25%">.**

   This sets the width for each section to 25%.

   The HTML now looks like this:

   ```
   <TR>
               <TD width="25%">
   ```

5. **Click the Update link.**

   This saves your changes and returns you to the page.

If you are already familiar with a HTML editor such as Microsoft FrontPage, you can create your tables in FrontPage and cut and paste them into the RTE.

Keeping Users Informed with FAQs

The World Wide Web, better known as the WWW, is full of acronyms. Here's another one for you: FAQ is the acronym for frequently asked question. The FAQs module is designed to manage and display a list of frequently asked questions and their answers. The benefit of this module is that it provides visitors to your Web site with a place to go and find answers to their questions. It also gives you a place to continuously add new questions and answers, or modify questions and answers as the need arises.

The FAQs module displays each question as a link. Site users must click on a question to view the related answer, as shown in Figure 5-5. This layout ensures that the module doesn't take up too much space on the page and makes it easy for users to quickly scan for their question.

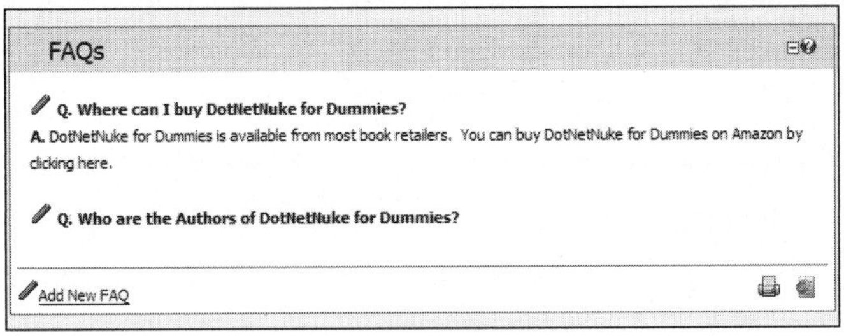

Figure 5-5:
The FAQs
module
displays
each
question as
a link. When
a user
clicks on
a question,
the answer
is displayed.

Adding an FAQ

Here's how to add a frequently asked question and answer to the FAQs module:

1. **Select Add New FAQ from the module menu.**

   This displays the Edit FAQs page.

2. **Enter the question into the RTE displayed below the Question field.**

   You can use any of the RTE features to best describe the question, such as inserting an image. See the section called "Doing Almost Anything with Text/HTML" earlier in this chapter for more details. The module automatically displays Q. before the question so you don't need to type anything to indicate that it is the question.

3. **Enter the answer into the RTE displayed below the Answer field.**

   As with the question field, you can insert any images, links, and so on, to best illustrate the answer.

4. **Click the <u>Update</u> link.**

   The question is now displayed on the page. Click on the question to view the answer.

FAQs are displayed in the order that they are entered: The first FAQ you enter is displayed at the top of the module, and the most recently entered is displayed last. Because there is no way of reordering FAQs, be sure to plan the order in which you would like them to appear before adding them.

Editing an FAQ

The FAQ module uses one of the most common methods for editing modules with multiple records. Here's how to edit an FAQ:

1. **Click the Edit button displayed to the left of the question to be edited.**

   This takes you to the Edit FAQs page.

2. **Edit the question into the RTE displayed below the Question field.**

3. **Enter the answer into the RTE displayed below the Answer field.**

4. **Click the <u>Update</u> link.**

   The question is now displayed on the page. Click on the question to view the answer.

To delete an FAQ, simply click the <u>Delete</u> link after Step 1.

Getting Around with Links

Links (short for *hyperlinks*) are the key to any Web site and one of the best ways of accessing and reading documents. The use of links means that users are no longer forced to skim through a full page of text to seek out relevant information. Links can be added throughout the main text of a Web page (see "Doing Almost Anything with Text/HTML" earlier in this chapter) or grouped together in a list by using the Links module, as shown in Figure 5-6. Using the Links module on a page to list one or more links allows you provide users with one place to quickly find relevant topics to the current page, or draw their attention to pages you want to promote.

The Links module uses a tool called Link Type. This tool is used throughout DNN whenever you have the option to set a link. Any modules or Administration pages that enable you to set a link use the Link Type tool. Examples of these modules include the Announcements and Documents modules.

Figure 5-6:
The Links
module
displays a
list of links.

Adding a link to another Web site

Here's how to add a link to another Web site by using the Links module:

1. **Select Add Link from the module menu.**

   This displays the Edit Links page.

2. **Enter a title for the link into the Title text box.**

   The title of the link is displayed on the page. For example, if you enter Local Schools as the title, this is the text displayed on the page.

3. **Ensure that URL (A Link to an External Resource) is selected as the Link Type.**

4. **Enter the URL to the Web site you want to link to in the Location: (Enter the Address of the Link) field.**

   For example, enter `www.localschools.com` to link to that Web site.

5. **Enter a description of the link into the Description text box.**

   The description displays as a tooltip when the user hovers their mouse pointer over the link title or when they click the ellipsis (. . .) after a link.

6. **Check the Open Link In New Browser Window? check box if required.**

   This option allows you to set how the link will work. It is common practice when linking to another Web site to set the link to open a new browser window to display the new site. This means the user will then have two browser windows open: The original browser displays the page where they clicked from, and the new one displays the Web site they click to get to. This makes it easy for users to get back to your Web site after they have browsed around the new Web site.

7. **Click the <u>Update</u> link.**

   The link is now displayed in the Links module. Mouse over the link to view the tooltip and click on the link to go the Web site.

   The URL you enter at Step 4 can be to a Web site, a page on a Web site, or a file on a Web site.

Linking to pages, files, or users within your site

As well as linking to another Web site, you can also link to a page, file, or user on your Web site. (Depending on which module the Link Type control is being used in, however, some of these options may not be available.) These options show as radio buttons directly under the Title.

Here's how to link to a page, file, or user on your Web site:

✔ **Page (A Page on Your Site):** This option displays a drop-down box labeled Select a Web Page from Your Site, where you can view a list of all the pages on your site and select the one you want to link to.

✔ **File (A File on Your Site):** This option displays two drop-down boxes that let you set the link to a file that has been uploaded to the File Manager located on the Admin page. Select the File Location, which is the folder where the file was placed, and then the File Name. This option also allows you to upload a new file if you haven't uploaded it already. See "Selecting and uploading a file on the fly" later in this chapter for full details.

✔ **User (A Member of Your Site):** This option displays a text box labeled Enter The Username of a Member of Your Site. This option displays the profile of the user. Details displayed can include their name, address, contact information, and preferences. See Manage Profile Properties under Admin⇨User Accounts to find out how to set the details that will be displayed.

Selecting and uploading a file on the fly

Just to make your life easier, the Link Type control allows you to upload a file to the File Manager while you are setting the link. This is great because it means your workflow isn't interrupted. Here's how to upload a file to the Admin⇨File Manager while you are adding a link to a file:

1. **Ensure that File (A File on Your Site) is selected as the Link Type.**

   This displays the File Location and File Name drop-down boxes.

2. **Select the folder to upload the file to from the File Location drop-down box.**

   This lists all the folders within the Administrators File Manager that you have been given Read Access to. You cannot add a new folder from here. If you have also been given Write Access, you will see the Upload New File link. If you are logged in as an Administrator, you will see all the folders and be able to write to them as well.

3. **Click the Upload New File link.**

   This displays a Browse button and two new links.

4. **Click the Browse button and locate and select the file from your computer.**

   This displays the filename in the text box to the left of the Browse button.

5. **Click the Upload Selected File link.**

   This uploads the file to the File Manager and displays thefilename in a drop-down box. If you want to upload more files, repeat Steps 3 through 5.

Tracking clicks on your links

The Link Type tool provides some simple tools to help you track the popularity of your links. You can use this information to find out what people are most interested in. These are the click tracking tools available when setting a link by using the Link Type tool:

- ✔ **Track Number Of Times This Link Is Clicked?** Leave this option selected (it is selected by default) to display information about this link on the Edit screen of the module below any editable fields. It displays the Tracking URL info for this link (that is, the URL for the link, the number of times the link has been clicked on your Web site, and the last time the link was clicked).

  Note: The page must be updated before the information is displayed.

- ✔ **Log the User, Date, and Time for Every Link Click?** Select this option to display two fields with Calendar links, and a Display link. Clicking Display gives you a report of all the times the link has been clicked on between the two selected dates.

Changing the layout of links

Each Links module has four different settings that Administrators can use to change the way links are displayed for that module. By changing one or more of these settings, you can achieve a variety of layouts and customize the layout of each Links module to best suit the page you are designing. Here's how to change the layout of a Links module:

1. **Select Settings from the Links module menu.**

   This takes you to the Module Settings page for this module.

2. **Click the Maximize button beside Links Settings.**

   This displays the different settings available for this module.

3. **Select either List or Dropdown as the Control Type setting.**

   Select List if you want to display all the links in a list. This is the default setting. Select Dropdown if you want to the links to be displayed in a drop-down box. Using Dropdown is a good way to save space on a page.

4. **Select either Vertical or Horizontal as the List Display Format setting.**

   This setting only applies when List is selected as the Control Type. As the options suggest, you can set the links to display Vertically down the page, which is the default option, or Horizontally across the page. If you choose to display links horizontally, make sure that the titles aren't too long to fit in the selected pane.

5. **Select either Yes or No for the Display Info Link setting.**

   This setting changes the way the description of a link is handled. The default option for this setting is No, which means the description of the link is displayed when a user mouses over the link title. By setting this option to Yes, an ellipsis (. . .) link is displayed beside each link title. Clicking on the ellipsis displays the description below the link title.

6. **Select an image as the Display Icon.**

   This setting lets you choose an image to be displayed beside each link. The prettiest option is to choose a small image or icon.

7. **Click Update to save the new settings.**

   The links now display differently in the module, depending on the setting you selected. Go back and try it again with another combination. You can't break anything, so don't worry!

Letting Everyone Know with Announcements

The Announcements module displays a list of items, each consisting of a text title, the date the item was published, a rich text description, and an optional link to read more about it, as shown in Figure 5-7. Typically this module is used to briefly announce topical items. Write a catchy title and a brief description to enable your Web site users to quickly scan through the items and decide if they want to read more about any of these topics.

Figure 5-7:
The
Announce-
ment module
displays a
list of
announce-
ments with
an optional
link to
read more.

Adding an announcement

Here's how to add an announcement to the Announcements module:

1. **Select Add New Announcement from the module menu.**

   This takes you to the Edit Announcements page.

2. **Enter a title for the announcement into the Title text box.**

   The title of the announcement is displayed on the page. For example, if you enter **First Home Buyer Grant** as the title, this is the text displayed on the page.

3. **Enter a description of the announcement into the Description text box.**

   The description is displayed in the module below the title. The description can include links, images, and all the usual RTE formatting options.

4. **(Optional.) Select the Link Type.**

   Selecting a link for an announcement is optional. If you leave the Link Type set to None, no link is added. See "Getting Around with Links" earlier in this chapter for details on the other types of links you can set.

5. **Click the Calendar link and select the Publish Date.**

   The date you select here will be displayed beside the announcement title for this item and the announcement will not be displayed on the Web site until that date. This means you can create announcements in advance to ensure that your Web site information is always up-to-date.

6. **(Optional.) Enter the position of the announcement into the View Order text box.**

   This step is optional. Entering a number here sets the order of each announcement. For example, enter **1** to make it the top announcement. If you don't enter a number here, the announcements are all given a zero (0) and order themselves according to their publish date, with the most recent publish date at the top of the module.

7. **Click the <u>Update</u> link.**

   The announcement is now displayed in the Announcements module. The current date is displayed beside the module title and a <u>Read More . . .</u> link provides access to the link.

Setting the displayed announcements

Each Announcements module includes two settings that enable you to control which announcements are displayed based on their publish date.

Here's how to set the displayed announcements:

1. **Select Settings from the module menu of an Announcements module.**

   This takes you to the Module Settings page for this module.

2. **Click the Maximize button beside Announcements Settings.**

   This displays the different settings available for this module.

3. **Enter a number into the History (Days) text box.**

   The number controls how many days' old displayed announcements can be. For example, entering **3** displays announcements from today, yesterday, and the day before. Any older announcements will not be displayed.

4. **Check the Display Future Items check box if required.**

   Check this box to set this module to display announcements that have not reached their publish date yet. This lets you use the module to announce upcoming events in advance. Leaving this box unchecked keeps future announcements hidden. This setting doesn't affect the History setting above.

5. **Click the <u>Update</u> link.**

   The announcements module will now be displayed and any existing announcements affected by your changes will be hidden or displayed accordingly.

Listing Your Contacts

For many people, your Web site is the first place they come to find out about your business. If they like what they see, you want to make it easy for them to contact you. We find it really annoying when a Web site doesn't provide you with a way to contact anyone who actually works there. This is fine for multi-nationals, but for most businesses, you want to encourage customers to come to you. The Contacts module, shown in Figure 5-8, is a great way to give visitors quick access to contact information. Alternatively, you can use the module on pages that are only visible to your customers or your staff, thereby limiting who can access the information.

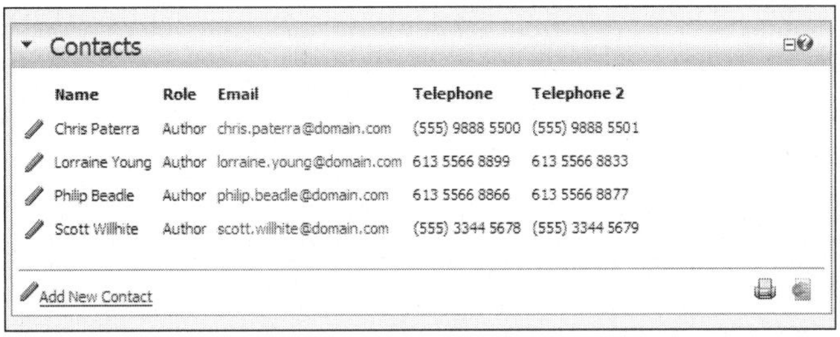

Figure 5-8:
The
Contacts
module
displays a
list of
Contacts
within your
business
and their
contact
details.

Here's how to add a contact to the Contacts module:

1. **Select Add New Contact from the module menu.**

   This takes you to the Edit Contacts page.

2. **Enter the person's full name in the Name text box.**

   You can enter the person's name however you like; for example title, first name, last name; or last name, first name, and no title. For instance, you could enter the name as either Mr. Luke Marshall, or as Marshall, Luke. Keep in mind that the contacts will be listed in alphabetical order based on the name you enter. The Name field is the only mandatory field on this module, so you can choose what other information you want to fill in for each contact.

3. **Enter the person's role within your business into the Role text box.**

   For example, Senior Accountant.

4. **Enter the person's e-mail address into the E-mail text box.**

   For example, `Luke.Marshall@marshallsaccounting.com`.

5. **Enter the person's telephone numbers into the Telephone 1 and Telephone 2 text boxes.**

6. **Click the <u>Update</u> link.**

The contact will now be displayed in the Contacts module. Users can click on the E-mail address to send an e-mail to the person.

The E-mail address field has been created in a tricky way to prevent spamming software from reading it and sending you buckets of spam.

Downloading with Documents

The Documents module displays a list of documents, shown in Figure 5-9, that are located either within your Web site or on another Web site. Each document listing includes a link to view the document and one to download it.

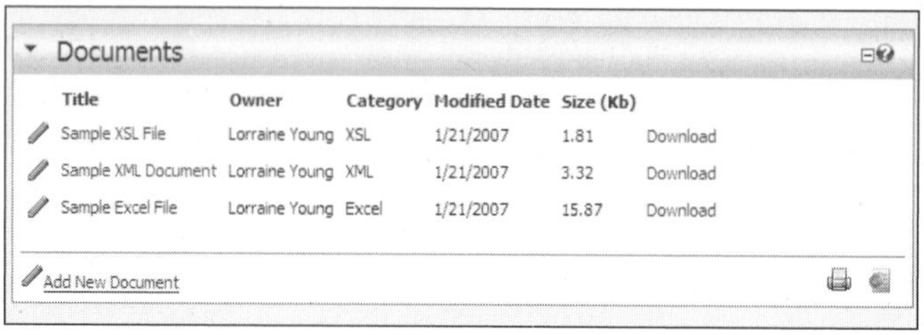

Figure 5-9:
The Documents module displays a list of documents with links to browse or download the document.

▾ Documents						▤❷
Title	**Owner**	**Category**	**Modified Date**	**Size (Kb)**		
✎ Sample XSL File	Lorraine Young	XSL	1/21/2007	1.81	Download	
✎ Sample XML Document	Lorraine Young	XML	1/21/2007	3.32	Download	
✎ Sample Excel File	Lorraine Young	Excel	1/21/2007	15.87	Download	
✎ Add New Document						🖶 ▨

Here's how to add a document to the Documents module:

1. **Select Add New Document from the module menu.**

This takes you to the Edit Documents page.

2. **Enter a title for the document into the Title text box.**

The title of the document is displayed on the page. For example, if you enter Newsletter as the title, this will be the text displayed on the page. This field and the Link field are both mandatory. All other fields are optional.

3. **(Optional.) Enter a description of the document into the Description text box.**

   The description is not displayed in the module by default.

   You can change which fields are visible by using Module Settings.

4. **(Optional.) Enter a category for the document into the Category text box.**

   For example, PDF format. The category will be displayed in the module by default.

5. **(Optional.) Click the <u>Change Owner</u> link and select a new owner if required.**

   Your first and last name is displayed in the Owner column for each document you add. This setting lets you change the owner to any other user. You may want to do this if you are loading a bunch of documents that belong to other people. For example, if you are a Web site Administrator and need to manage a list of documents for someone else, you would change the Owner field to that person so that users of the module know who to talk to about the document.

6. **Set the Link by using the Link Type control.**

   See "Getting Around with Links" for details on the types of links you can set.

7. **Click the <u>Update</u> link.**

   The document is now displayed in the Documents module. Other information such as the Owner (your name), the date the document record was last updated, and the size of the document will also be displayed. Click on the document title to view the document in a Web browser, or click the Download link to download it to your computer.

If the document is located on an external resource, the size of the document will be displayed as Unknown.

Sneaking a Peek with IFrame

The IFrame module can *frame* either a page from another Web site or a file within your Web site inside a page on your site, as shown in Figure 5-10. In other words, the IFrame module displays a page from another Web site on a page of your Web site. If the IFrame frames a Web site page, that page still has all of its functionality intact, so you can navigate around the Web site all from the armchair comfort of your own Web page.

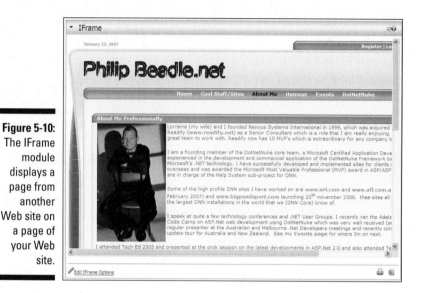

Figure 5-10:
The IFrame
module
displays a
page from
another
Web site on
a page of
your Web
site.

Here's how to display another Web site within a page on your Web site:

1. **Select Edit IFrame Options from the module menu.**

   This displays the Edit IFrame page.

2. **Select URL (A Link to an External Resource) as the Link Type for the Source field.**

   This displays a text box.

3. **Enter the URL for the Web site into the text box below Location: (Enter the Address of the Link).**

   Ensure that you have entered http:// only once for the URL.

4. **Enter a number to set the width in pixels for the IFrame into the Width text box.**

   For example, enter **500** to set the width to 500 pixels. You can also set the width as the full width of the pane by entering **100%**.

5. **Enter a pixel amount to set the height of the IFrame into the Height text box.**

   For example, enter **800** to set the width to 800 pixels. You cannot enter a percentage in this field.

6. **Choose to hide or display vertical and horizontal scroll bars on the IFrame by selecting an option from the Scrolling drop-down box.**

   This field is set to Auto by default, which displays scroll bars only when required to view the whole Web page. The other options are No, which doesn't display any scroll bars, and Yes, which always displays scroll bars.

7. **Choose to hide or display a thin border around the Web page by setting the Border drop-down box.**

   Select No to hide the border or Yes to display the border.

8. **Click the Update link.**

   This displays the Web page within the IFrame. You might need to change the settings a few times to get it to look right.

Showing Pictures, Movies, and More with the Media Module

The Media module allows you to display image, video, and audio files, shown in Figure 5-11, on your Web page. The media can either be located on another Web site, or uploaded to your Web site. The Media module also lets you add a link from an image.

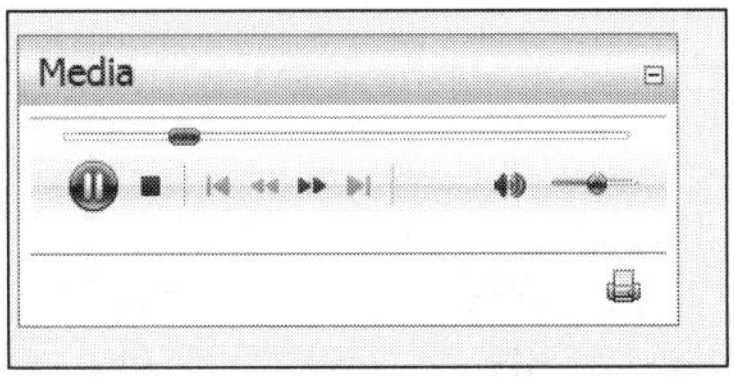

Figure 5-11:
The Media module displaying an audio file.

Displaying an image with a link to another Web site

Here's how to display an image with a link to another Web site:

1. **Select Edit Media Options from the module menu.**

   This displays the Edit Media page.

2. **Select a Link Type at the Media field and enter or select the image.**

   The image can either be located in the Administrator's File Manager (File) or on another Web site (URL). See "Getting Around with Links" for more information on how to select the image.

   Make sure your media files have their file extensions such as jpg in lowercase.

3. **Enter a description of the link into the Alternate Text text box.**

   This is the text that displays when the user mouses over the image; for example, Click Here to Search for Property.

4. **(Optional.) Enter a width in pixels for the image into the Width text box.**

   This field lets you modify the width of the displayed image. Leave this field blank to display the true width of the image.

5. **(Optional.) Enter a height in pixels for the image into the Height text box.**

   This field lets you modify the height of the displayed image. Leave this field blank to display the true height of the image.

6. **(Optional.) Select the Link Type for the link at the Link field.**

   The link can go to another Web site, another page on this Web site, or to a file on this Web site. See "Getting Around with Links" for more information on how to set the Link Type.

7. **Click the <u>Update</u> link.**

   The image is now displayed, as shown in Figure 5-12. Clicking on it takes the user to the selected link.

The Media module provides a simple way to create buttons. Just hide the module container, and voilà! See Chapter 4 for more details.

Displaying a movie

Your Web site hosting company controls the formats you can upload to and display on your Web site. If you want to include MP3 or WMV movie files, you need to ask your host set this up for you. See Chapter 3 for more details.

Here's how to display a movie that has been uploaded to your File Manager by using the Media module:

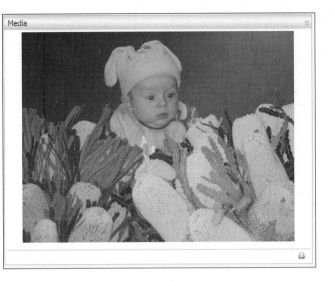

Figure 5-12:
The Media module displaying an image with a link. This is a simple way of creating buttons.

1. **Select Edit Media Options from the module menu.**

   This displays the Edit Media page.

2. **Select File (A File on Your Site) as the Link Type and select the movie.**

   See "Getting Around with Links" for more information on how to set the link to the movie.

3. **Enter a description of the movie into the Alternate Text text box.**

   This is the text that displays when the user mouses over the movie. Note: At the time of writing, the Alternate Text wasn't actually displaying, but was still a required field.

4. **Enter a width in pixels for the movie into the Width text box.**

   This field lets you set the width of the movie. Leave this field blank to display the standard size for this movie.

5. **Enter a height in pixels for the image into the Height text box.**

   This field lets you set the height of the movie. Leave this field blank to display the standard size for this movie.

6. **Click the <u>Update</u> link.**

   The movie is now displayed on the page inside your usual media player, as shown in Figure 5-13. You have buttons to control the playback of the movie.

Figure 5-13:
The Media module displaying a movie from another Web site on a page of your Web site.

Chapter 6

Adding Bells and Whistles to Your Site

*T*here are a lot of sites out there on the World Wide Web today. We haven't quite managed to count them all, but there are millions! Standing out among the crowd can sometimes be difficult. Luckily the modules included with DNN let you add some special touches to your Web site.

The modules covered in this chapter offer interesting, attractive, and useful ways to do it. This chapter shows you how to use seven modules that are included with DNN. These modules require a small amount of configuration but aren't at all complicated.

The Events and User Defined Tables modules present content in an interest and interactive layout. The News Feeds module and XML/XML modules display data created outside of DNN. The Survey module lets you create online surveys, and the UsersOnline module displays information and statistics on your user membership. Read on to find out how to make your Web site stand out with these great modules.

This chapter also explains how to add vendor accounts to your Web site. Vendors are companies that have advertising banners or messages on your Web site. The Administrator manages the vendor account, the uploading of banners, and has access to banner reports.

Keeping Track of Dates with the Events Module

The Events module displays a list of events in a monthly calendar, as shown in Figure 6-1. Users can click through different months, go to events for any day, or view a list of all events for any given day.

This module has a large number of settings on the Module Settings page that provide you with ways to make your Events module more interactive, or you can let your users choose to be notified of events or to enroll for events. These settings are out of the scope of this book.

Figure 6-1:
The Events module displays a monthly calendar of events.

Setting up the events calendar

You have to update the module settings page of the Events module before you can see the event calendar inside the module. You can do this simply by going to the page and clicking Update; however, it is a good idea to set the General Settings at this point.

Here's how to set the general settings of the Events module:

1. **Add an Events module to a page.**

   The module displays the message Please Select Settings to configure Events Module... .

2. **Select Settings from the Events module menu.**

   This takes you to the Module Settings page.

3. **Click the Maximize button beside the Event Module Settings section.**

   This takes you to the Module Settings page. If you want to perform a super-speedy setup, you can accept all the default general settings and skip to Step 9.

4. **Enter a time interval in minutes into the Edit Time Interval.**

   This setting controls the time periods displayed when you are adding events to the calendar. For example, entering 60 enables you to schedule events only on the hour. The default setting is 30 minutes.

5. **Select one or more of the following options, which can be updated later:**

   - **Display Tooltip**: Select to display additional event information as a mouseover tooltip.

   - **Disable Month View Cell Display**: Select this option to display the calendar with event details below. Don't select this option if you want to display the events inside the calendar.

   - **Set Event Cell Background Color**: Select a background color for calendar dates with an event. This is useful if you want the events to stand out in the calendar.

   - **Disable Event Month View Inline Styles**: Select to prevent styles being changed in the calendar design and includes the above field.

   - **Disable Event Month View Navigation Controls**: Select to hide the View Week, Today, and View Date links displayed above the calendar.

   - **Disable Event Month View Table for non-edit users**: Select to hide a list of events below the calendar. The list will still be displayed to users with edit rights to this module.

   - **Permit Recurring Events**: Select to enable recurring events to be added.

   - **Prevent Schedule Conflict**: Select to stop overlapping events being added to the calendar.

   - **Show Events on Next Month (or Prev Month)**: Select to display all events in the displayed calendar month including events that occur in the previous or subsequent month.

   - **Enable DNN Search**: Select to make these events searchable by using the Search module and DNN Searching.

   - **Weekend Starts Friday**: Select to set the weekend as Friday and Saturday. The default setting is Saturday and Sunday.

6. **Click the Update link.**

   This displays a monthly calendar.

Adding event categories

When you add an event, you can select a category for the event. You need to add the categories yourself. The selected category is displayed on the Event Detail page.

Here's how to add event categories:

1. **Select Edit Categories from the module menu.**

   This displays the Edit Categories page.

2. **Enter a title for the category into the Category text box.**

   The title is displayed in the Categories drop-down box on the Edit Events page where you add and edit the event.

3. **(Optional.) Select a color for the event from the drop-down box.**

   This sets the background color of the event details displayed in the calendar but not the whole day cell. Leave the field as None for no background color.

4. **Click the Update link.**

   This displays category below.

5. **Repeat Steps 2 through 4 for each new category.**

You can delete categories but you can't edit them. To change the name or color of a category, you must delete it and then add it again with the new details. Unfortunately, this removes it from any associated events. Reduce or avoid this by planning and adding them before adding events.

Adding event locations

When you add an event, you have the option of selecting a location for the event. You need to add the locations yourself. Location can be created with an option link that displays a map of the location.

Here's how to add event locations:

1. **Select Edit Locations from the module menu.**

   This displays the Edit Locations page.

2. **Enter a title for the location into the Location text box.**

The title is displayed in the Location drop-down box on the Edit Events page where you add and edit the event. Locations can be general or specific. They can be a list of different rooms in your building, such as Board Room or Conference Room 1; or they can be full addresses such as Lvl 1, 11 St Kilda Rd, Melbourne, Australia.

3. **(Optional.) Enter a URL to a map or directions to the location into the Map URL text box.**

   You can add any URL here. It may be to a page on your Web site where you have directions and more information on the location. Alternatively, it may link to a Web site such as Google Maps (`www.google.com/maps`), which enables you to locate a map and link to that page.

4. **Click the <u>Update</u> link.**

   This displays the location on this page and adds it to the location drop-down box.

5. **Repeat Steps 2 through 4 for each new location.**

You can delete locations but you can't edit them. To change the title or map URL of a location, you must delete it and then add it again with the new details. Unfortunately, this removes it from any associated events. Reduce or avoid this by planning ahead and adding locations before adding events.

Adding events

Here's how to add an event to the calendar:

1. **Select Add Events from the module menu.**

   This displays the Edit Events page, as shown in Figure 6-2.

2. **Enter a title for the event into the Title text box.**

   The title of the event is displayed on the page. For example, if you enter **Learn How to Fly a Kite** as the title, this is the text displayed in the calendar.

3. **Select the start date and time of the event from the Start Date/Time field.**

   This is the first date when the event is listed in the calendar. The time is also displayed.

4. **Select the end date and time of the event from the End Date/Time field.**

   This is the last date when the event is listed in the calendar. The time is also displayed.

5. Set the Time Zone field to the correct time zone for the event.

If you don't set the time zone field, it defaults to the user's own time zone, which he can set on his Profile page.

6. Select an option from the Importance drop-down box.

Select Low, Normal, or High as the importance of this event. The selected option is displayed on the Event Detail page. If the user chooses to export details of the event to the desktop of his computer, the importance is also saved.

7. Select a category from the Category drop-down box.

The Category name is displayed on the Event Detail page, as shown in Figure 6-3. See "Adding event categories" earlier in this chapter to find out how to add categories to this list. If the user chooses to export details of the event to the desktop of her computer, the category information is not saved.

8. Select a location from the Location drop-down box.

The location name is displayed on the Event Detail page. See "Adding event locations" earlier in this chapter to find out how to add locations to this list. If the user chooses to export details of the event to the desktop of her computer, the location information is not saved.

9. (Optional.) Enter any additional information into the Notes RTE.

Notes entered here will be displayed in the calendar.

10. (Optional.) Display an image for the event by setting these Images settings or skip to Step 11 if you don't want to add an image.

    a. Click the Maximize button beside the Image Settings section.

    b. Select the Display Image? check box.

    c. Choose a Link type and select the Image URL.

    d. (Optional.) Enter the pixel width into the Width field.

    This setting overrides the original image width.

    e. (Optional.) Enter the pixel height into the Height field.

    This setting overrides the original image height.

11. Click the <u>Update</u> link.

This displays the event in the calendar. Click on the linked event title to view full details of the event.

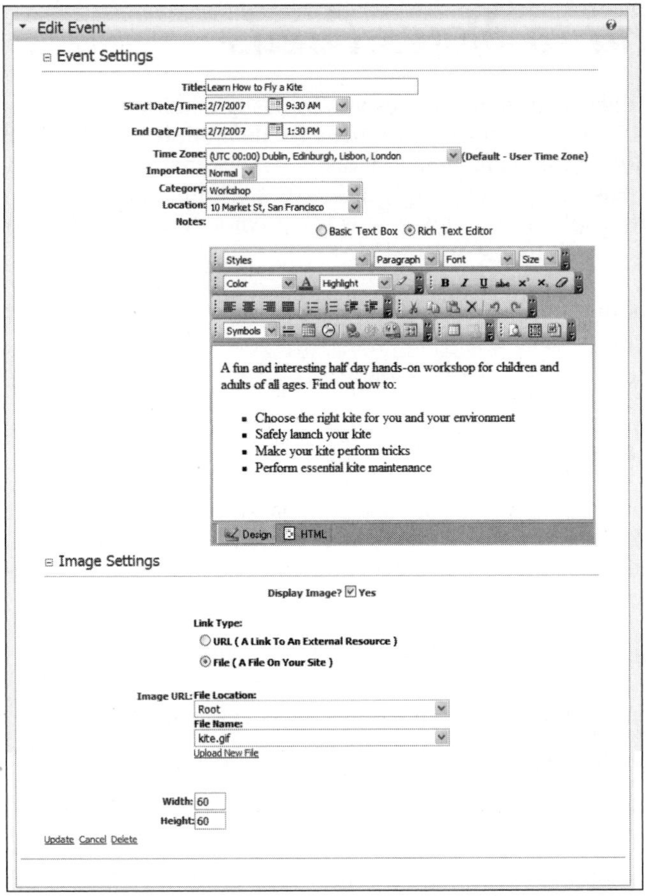

Figure 6-2:
The Edit
Event page,
where you
add new
events and
edit existing
ones.

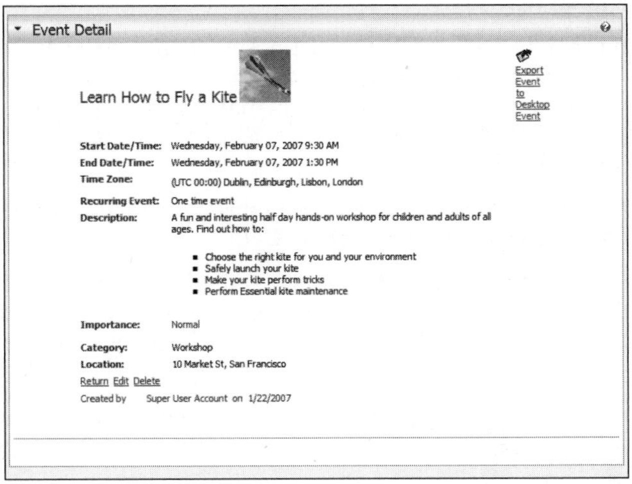

Figure 6-3:
Clicking the
event in the
calendar
displays this
detailed
event page.

Subscribing to News Feeds

The News Feeds module enables you to easily display content from other Web sites on your Web site. The News Feeds module uses Really Simple Syndication (RSS), which lets you display news that is syndicated by another Web site. Such Web sites supply a URL that is entered into the News Feeds module to displays their news. This is a great way of displaying instant content without writing a word!

If this module is not installed, see Chapter 3 for more on how to install included modules.

Displaying a news feed

A news feed typically consists of a summary of news items, as shown in Figure 6-4. Each item has a link to read more about that news item. Clicking on the link takes the visitor away from your Web site and to the Web site providing the news service.

Here's how to display a news feed in the News Feeds module:

1. **Select Edit News Feed from the News Feeds module menu.**

   This takes you to the Edit News Feeds screen.

2. **Select URL (A Link to an External Resource) as the Link Type for the News Feed Source field.**

   This displays the Location: (Enter The Address Of The Link) field.

3. **Enter the URL of the news feed into the Location: (Enter the Address of the Link) text box.**

   In this example, we use the free Latin American and Canadian News from World Press Review. The URL is `www.worldpress.org/feeds/americas.xml`. Look for news feeds that display the commonly used little orange XML button beside them as this indicates that the feed will work in this module.

4. **If a style sheet is required, set the Link Type to the required style sheet at the News Feed Style Sheet field.**

   Some news feeds require you to set a style sheet here so that the news feed displays correctly on the Web page. If this is the case, you can get the link to the style sheet file or download the style sheet file from the news feed service.

   If you are using our sample URL, you won't need to do this step.

5. Click the <u>Update</u> link.

The news feed is now displayed on your Web page. Click on a link to see how the news feed works. Note: The link will open inside the same Web browser.

Subscribing to a news feed

News feeds are available on every topic you can imagine. When we did a Google search on "free news feeds" at the time of writing, we got more than 50,000 results! If, on the other hand, you choose to subscribe to a paid news feed service, the News Feeds module includes security options that allow you to enter your account information for the paid service.

Here's how to set the security options on a news feed:

1. Select Edit News Feed from the News Feeds module menu.

This takes you to the Edit News Feeds screen.

2. Add the news feed.

Set the details of the news feed as described in Steps 2 through 4 in the preceding section.

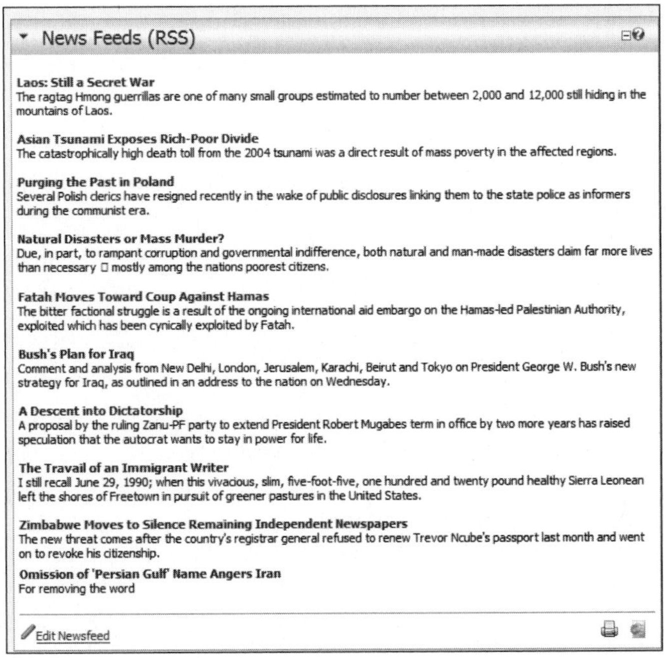

Figure 6-4: The News Feeds module.

News Feeds (RSS)

Laos: Still a Secret War
The ragtag Hmong guerrillas are one of many small groups estimated to number between 2,000 and 12,000 still hiding in the mountains of Laos.

Asian Tsunami Exposes Rich-Poor Divide
The catastrophically high death toll from the 2004 tsunami was a direct result of mass poverty in the affected regions.

Purging the Past in Poland
Several Polish clerics have resigned recently in the wake of public disclosures linking them to the state police as informers during the communist era.

Natural Disasters or Mass Murder?
Due, in part, to rampant corruption and governmental indifference, both natural and man-made disasters claim far more lives than necessary □ mostly among the nations poorest citizens.

Fatah Moves Toward Coup Against Hamas
The bitter factional struggle is a result of the ongoing international aid embargo on the Hamas-led Palestinian Authority, exploited which has been cynically exploited by Fatah.

Bush's Plan for Iraq
Comment and analysis from New Delhi, London, Jerusalem, Karachi, Beirut and Tokyo on President George W. Bush's new strategy for Iraq, as outlined in an address to the nation on Wednesday.

A Descent into Dictatorship
A proposal by the ruling Zanu-PF party to extend President Robert Mugabes term in office by two more years has raised speculation that the autocrat wants to stay in power for life.

The Travail of an Immigrant Writer
I still recall June 29, 1990; when this vivacious, slim, five-foot-five, one hundred and twenty pound healthy Sierra Leonean left the shores of Freetown in pursuit of greener pastures in the United States.

Zimbabwe Moves to Silence Remaining Independent Newspapers
The new threat comes after the country's registrar general refused to renew Trevor Ncube's passport last month and went on to revoke his citizenship.

Omission of 'Persian Gulf' Name Angers Iran
For removing the word

Edit Newsfeed

3. Set the account information in the Security Options (optional) section.

Enter the username and password details provided by the news service.

4. Click the <u>Update</u> link.

The news feed is now displayed on your Web page. Click on a link to see how the news feed works. Note: The link will open inside the same Web browser.

Going Ad Hoc with the User Defined Table Module

The User Defined Table (UDT) module provides Administrators with the ability to design and populate a table of information, as shown in Figure 6-5. Using this module is a great alternative to the Table tool provided in the RTE because you can design and manage the table separately from its content. Columns are set to enable one of these types of information to be entered or selected: Text, Rich Text (HTML), Integer, Decimal, Date and Time, Date, Time, True/False, Email, Currency, URL, Image, file Download, or a Calculated Column.

After the table is designed, you can add one or more rows of information into the table, similar to the way you add a row of information to the Contacts module or the Documents module.

If this module is not installed, see Chapter 3 for more on installing the included modules.

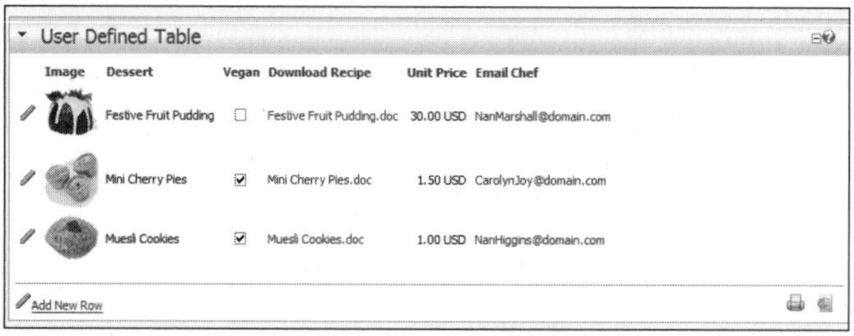

Figure 6-5:
A table designed by using the User Defined Table module.

	User Defined Table					
Image	Dessert	Vegan	Download Recipe	Unit Price	Email Chef	
	Festive Fruit Pudding	☐	Festive Fruit Pudding.doc	30.00 USD	NanMarshall@domain.com	
	Mini Cherry Pies	☑	Mini Cherry Pies.doc	1.50 USD	CarolynJoy@domain.com	
	Muesli Cookies	☑	Muesli Cookies.doc	1.00 USD	NanHiggins@domain.com	
Add New Row						

Building a UDT table

Here's how to build a table in the UDT module:

1. Select Manage User Defined Table from the module menu.

This takes you to the Manage User Defined Table page, shown in Figure 6-6, where you can build and edit the table design. The page displays an area where you can add columns to the table, as well as Global Settings and Display Settings, which set the way information is displayed in the table. Four existing table columns are displayed at the top of this page. These columns cannot be deleted but they are not displayed in the UDT unless you set them as Visible.

2. **Click the <u>Add New Column</u> link.**

   This creates a row of text boxes where you can enter values for this column.

3. **Check the Required box if this row is mandatory.**

   Mandatory fields *must* be filled in when entering data into the table. If you don't check this option, the field will be optional.

4. **Enter a unique column title in the Title text box.**

   The title is displayed at the top of this column when the table is saved.

5. **Select the type of information that will be entered into this column into the Type text box.**

   There are 14 different options to select from, including Text, Decimal, Date, Time, and so on. Choose the type that reflects the information you plan to add to this column.

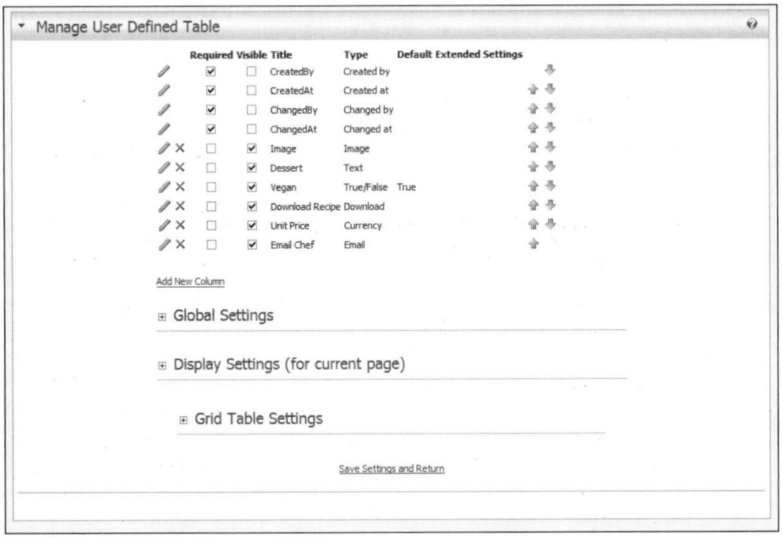

Figure 6-6:
Design and manage the UDT on the Manage User Defined Table screen.

	Required	Visible	Title	Type	Default	Extended Settings
✎	✔	☐	CreatedBy	Created by		
✎	✔	☐	CreatedAt	Created at		
✎	✔	☐	ChangedBy	Changed by		
✎	✔	☐	ChangedAt	Changed at		
✎ ✕	☐	✔	Image	Image		
✎ ✕	☐	✔	Dessert	Text		
✎ ✕	☐	✔	Vegan	True/False	True	
✎ ✕	☐	✔	Download Recipe	Download		
✎ ✕	☐	✔	Unit Price	Currency		
✎ ✕	☐	✔	Email Chef	Email		

<u>Add New Column</u>

⊞ Global Settings

⊞ Display Settings (for current page)

⊞ Grid Table Settings

<u>Save Settings and Return</u>

Avoid the Calculated Column field if you can. It requires some pro-gramming to make it work. If you want to find out more about this option, visit the Project page of the User Defined Table Module on the DNN Web site (www.dotnetnuke.com/DotNetNukeProjects/ ModuleUserDefinedTable/tabid/877/Default.aspx). Click the Project Downloads link and download the User Manual, which has more information on this field.

6. **(Optional.) Enter the default information for this column in the Default text box.**

   The information entered here is displayed in this column when you are entering data into the table later. You can delete or change the default value at any time.

Do not enter a default value for a Download type field as it will cause an error. If you do choose to enter a default value for other types, make sure that it is the right value for the field type. For example, if the field type is set to Date, you can only enter a date in the Default field. Entering text, such as "Enter a date here," will cause an error.

Here are examples of default values for each column type:

- **Text**: Enter any text. For example, Enter your text here.

- **Rich Text (HTML)**: Enter any text or HTML. For example, Enter a short description here.

- **Integer**: Enter any whole number. For example, 1129.

- **Decimal**: Enter any decimal number. For example, 1129.11.

- **E-mail**: Enter an e-mail address here. For example, Jessie. Saide@domain.com.

- **Date and Time**: Enter a date and/or time. For example, 01/01/2007 09:00 AM.

- **Date**: Enter a date. For example, 01/01/2007 09:00 AM.

- **Time**: Enter a time. For example, 09:00 AM.

- **True/False**: Enter either true or false to display either a selected or unselected check box, respectively. For example, True.

- **Currency**: Enter a currency amount. For example, 80.00.Currency type will automatically be displayed in each row. See Chapter 4 to find out how to update this setting.

- **URL**: Enter a URL. For example, www.dotnetnuke.com.

- **Image**: Enter a URL to an image. For example, www.dotnetnuke.com/Portals/_default/Skins/ DNN-Minimal/images/dotnetnukelogo.gif.

- **Download**: *Do not* enter a default value as it will cause an error. This field enables an uploaded file to be downloaded.

7. **Click the Save button to the left of this row of text boxes to save the column.**

The column is now saved and displayed on the page.

8. **Repeat Steps 2 through 7 to add additional columns.**

9. **Click the <u>Save Settings and Return</u> link to return to the Web page.**

Do not change the Type setting on a column as this will display a Warning message and may require you to rebuild your table. Be sure to design and build your table before you start adding information (rows) to it.

Adding data to a UDT table

The first couple of times you enter data into the table, you may want to have a piece of paper with the structure of the table written down to remind you what type of information needs to entered into each column. This depends on how big your table is, how many different information types you are using, and how self-explanatory the titles of the columns are.

Here's how to add data to a UDT table:

1. **Select Add New Row from the module menu.**

   This opens the Edit User Defined Table page shown in Figure 6-7. The first four lines of information (CreatedBy, CreatedAt, ChangedBy, ChangedAt) are automatically recorded when you save the data for this row. You can see this information each time you edit this row.

2. **Enter data into each field.**

   Required fields are denoted by an asterisk (*) and must be completed. Usually you can guess the types of data permitted by the type of text field displayed beside the column title. For example, if the Link Type tool is displayed for the field and only displays images, you can guess that it is an image data field.

   Number and decimal fields display entered values in the right side of the field, whereas text fields display data to the left of the field.

3. **Click the <u>Update</u> link to save the data.**

   This returns you to your Web page. If the wrong type of information has been entered into a field, you will remain on the Edit User Defined Table page. In this case, an error message is displayed at the top of the page detailing which data needs to be modified.

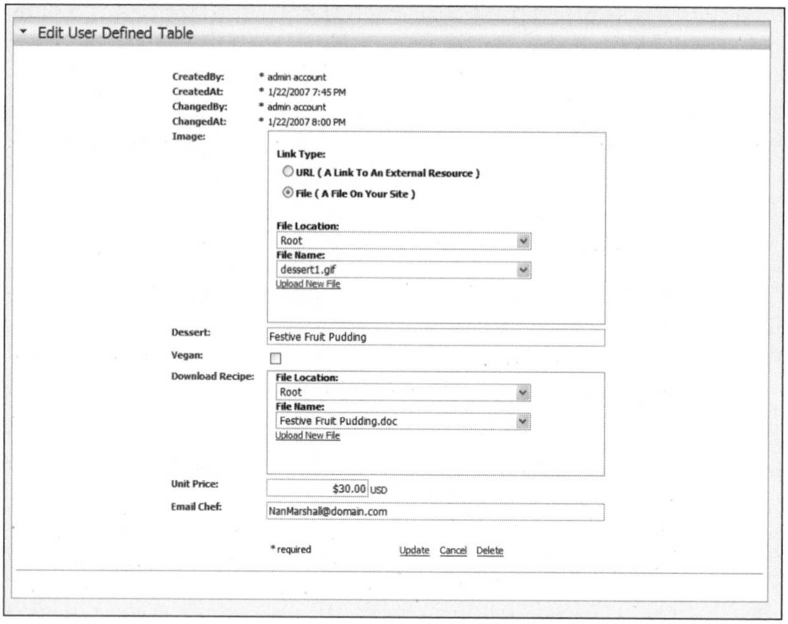

Figure 6-7:
Add data to
your table
on the Edit
User
Defined
Table
screen.

Sharing Spreadsheets and Data with XML/XSL

The XML/XSL module, shown in Figure 6-8, enables the data within an XML file to display on a Web page by applying an XSL style sheet to it. Although we've been building Web sites by using DNN for several years, we still find the title of this module a bit intimidating. Never fear! You can use this module even if, like us, you don't really understand XML or XSL.

So what are XML and XSL, you ask? XML stands for eXtensible Markup Language, which may sound a bit confusing. Any search on the Web will give you a detailed explanation of XML, but, in a nutshell, XML is like HTML in that it is a computer language that marks up text with special tags. The difference between the two technologies is that HTML uses the same tags to mark up the text, whereas XML creates unique tags to mark up the text, depending on the type of data you are saving.

XSL is an acronym for eXtensible Stylesheet Language. For this module, XSL or XSLT (eXtensible Stylesheet Language Transformation) refers to a style sheet designed to transform an XML file into HTML so it can be displayed on a Web page. Without the XSL file, the data doesn't display correctly on the Web page.

To summarize, you need an XML file with a matching XSL file to display data by using this module. If you don't know how to create an XSL file, you either need to find out how to write one or get someone else to write one for you.

Creating an XML file from an Excel spreadsheet

Many different programs can be used to create XML files. In this example, we use Excel to create an XML file. Here's how to transform an Excel spreadsheet into an XML file:

1. **Create an Excel spreadsheet, enter your data, and save the file.**

   You may want to download our sample Excel spreadsheet from `http://dnnrealty.com/ForSellers/tabid/214/Default.aspx` to use for this example.

2. **Select File⇨Save As from the Main menu.**

   This opens the Save As dialog box.

3. **Navigate to the location where you want to save the XML file.**

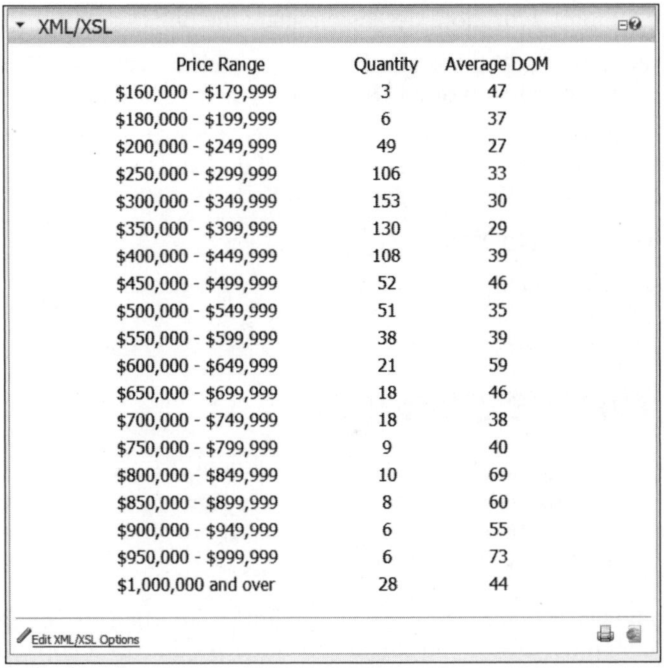

Figure 6-8:
The
XML/XSL
module.

▾ XML/XSL			▭❷
Price Range	Quantity	Average DOM	
$160,000 - $179,999	3	47	
$180,000 - $199,999	6	37	
$200,000 - $249,999	49	27	
$250,000 - $299,999	106	33	
$300,000 - $349,999	153	30	
$350,000 - $399,999	130	29	
$400,000 - $449,999	108	39	
$450,000 - $499,999	52	46	
$500,000 - $549,999	51	35	
$550,000 - $599,999	38	39	
$600,000 - $649,999	21	59	
$650,000 - $699,999	18	46	
$700,000 - $749,999	18	38	
$750,000 - $799,999	9	40	
$800,000 - $849,999	10	69	
$850,000 - $899,999	8	60	
$900,000 - $949,999	6	55	
$950,000 - $999,999	6	73	
$1,000,000 and over	28	44	

✎ Edit XML/XSL Options

4. **Select XML Spreadsheet (*.xml) from the Save As Type drop-down box and then click the Save button.**

   This saves the Excel spreadsheet as an XML file.

Displaying a custom spreadsheet from Excel

To display an Excel spreadsheet on your Web site, you must first save it as an XML file as we discussed in the preceding section. You must also have an XSL file (style sheet) that has been created to match the data in the XML file. If you don't have an XSL file, the XML data may not display correctly. You can download our sample XML and XSL files from `http://dnnrealty.com/ForSellers/tabid/214/Default.aspx` to use in this example, if you like.

Here's how to display an Excel spreadsheet on your Web page:

1. **Select Edit XML/XSL Options from the module menu.**

   This takes you to the Edit XML/XSL page.

2. **Select or enter the XML file by using the Link Type tool displayed for the XML Data File field.**

   See Chapter 4 for more details on using the link type tool.

3. **Select or enter the XSL file by using the Link Type tool displayed for the XSL Transformations File field.**

   It is called a transformation file because it transforms the XML data into something readable on the Web site. If you don't select an XSL file here, the XML data will not display correctly.

4. **Click the Update link.**

   Your XML data is now displayed on the Web page.

Creating online surveys

The Survey module enables you to create an online survey consisting of one or more questions with answers, as shown in Figure 6-9. The Survey module enables users to submit their answers once and to view survey results displayed in an attractive bar graph.

This module is popular with users who want to add their two cents or see what others have to say. You can also use this module as a pop quiz, meaning that the questions can have correct and incorrect answers, instead of just using it to gather opinions. The results can also be kept private.

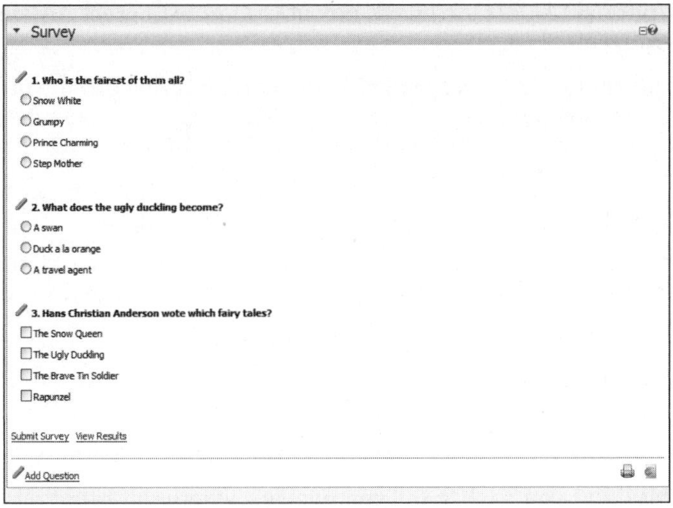

Figure 6-9:
The Survey
module
displaying
survey
questions.

Creating a survey

Here's how to create a survey by adding questions to the Survey module:

1. **Select Add Question from the module menu.**

   This takes you to the Create Survey page.

2. **Enter a question into the Question text box.**

   For example, **Who is the fairest of them all?**

3. **Select the type of answer that can be given to the question from the Type drop-down selection box.**

   There are two types of questions you can add. The Single Selection option permits survey respondents to select only one answer by using radio buttons. The Multiple Selection option permits survey respondents to select multiple answers by using check boxes.

4. **If this survey contains more than one question, enter the question number here.**

   This sets the order of questions. For example, enter **5** to make this the fifth question in the survey.

5. **Enter an answer option for the question into the New Option text box.**

   For example, **Snow White**.

6. **(Optional.) Select the check box at Option Is Correct Answer? If required.**

    If the option entered at Step 5 is the correct answer to the question, you can denote this here. Don't select this option if there is no correct answer, or you don't want to share the correct answer. Questions can have more than one correct answer.

7. **Click the <u>Add Option</u> link to save the answer option.**

    The option is displayed in the Options list on this page. Options that are set as correct are displayed like this: >Correct Answer<.

8. **Repeat Steps 6 and 7 to add additional options.**

    This adds other answer options to this question. Each additional answer option added is displayed in the Options list below.

9. **Click the <u>Update</u> link to save this question and answer options.**

    This takes you back to the survey page, where this question is now displayed.

10. **Repeat Steps 1 through 9 to add additional questions and answers to the survey.**

    After you have finished adding questions, your survey is ready for people to start submitting answers. You might like to keep your survey visible only to Administrators while you are in the process of building it to prevent people from submitting answers when it is half-built.

The Create Survey screen displays a check box titled Option Is Correct Answer?. By checking this when creating one or more options for a question, you can use the survey as a multiple-choice questionnaire or as a pop quiz.

Settings to enhance your survey

Here are three optional settings to customize a survey:

1. **Select Settings from the module menu.**

    This takes you to the Module Settings page.

2. **Click the Maximize button beside Survey Settings.**

    This displays the four settings you can modify for this survey module.

3. **Click the <u>Calendar</u> link and select the last date for survey responses into the Survey Closing Date field.**

    By selecting a date here, you close the survey from further responses at the end of that day. The next day, the <u>Submit Survey</u> link that enables responses to be recorded will be removed from the page, thus preventing any more answers from being submitted. The results to date are displayed to those authorized to view them.

4. **Enter a pixel value to set the maximum width for the bar graph into the Maximum Bar Graph Width text box (for example, 200).**

    The bar graph set to 200 pixels is shown in Figure 6-10. When this setting is left blank, the width of the bar graph is 100% of the pane. This doesn't always look right, especially for a small survey with only a couple of short questions. Setting the width is a good way to establish the importance of the survey to your visitors.

5. **Select an option to set how the survey results are controlled in the Vote Tracking field.**

    Selecting Vote Tracking Via Cookie saves a cookie to a person's computer, preventing them from submitting the survey more than once. Selecting 1 Vote/Registered User allows registered users to submit results only once.

6. **Select either Public or Private at the Survey Results field to set access to survey results.**

    Selecting Public permits everyone with View Module permissions to view the survey results. If Private is selected, only Administrators can view the results.

7. **Click the __Update__ link.**

    This takes you back to the survey page and the question is displayed.

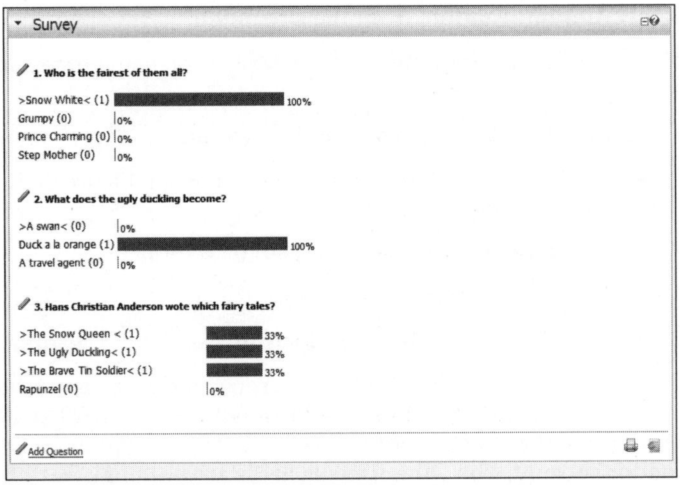

Figure 6-10: After a user submits a response, the survey results are shown, unless the survey results are set as private.

Leveraging Partnerships with Banners

The Banners module displays advertising for other companies, which DNN calls vendors. You are in control of the management of both vendor accounts and their advertising banners. For example, if another company sells complementary products to that of your company, you may choose to give free advertising to each other on your respective Web sites. Alternatively, if your Web site has lots of traffic, you may want to sell advertising space to other companies as a revenue raiser.

To use the Banners module, you must have vendors with banners. To do this, you must first create accounts for your vendors. After you have created vendor accounts, which are completely separate from your user accounts, you can create advertising banners for them. When that is done, you can set the Banners module to display these banners.

Creating a vendor account

DNN manages two separate vendor directories. One is located under Admin⇨ Vendors, which is maintained by Administrators, and the other is under Host⇨ Vendors, which is maintained by the host. Site banners are only available for display on this particular Web site, whereas host banners are available for display on all Web sites in this DNN installation.

Here's how to add a vendor to the Admin⇨Vendors page:

1. **Select Admin⇨Vendors from the site menu.**

   This takes you to the Vendors page, where you can view existing vendor accounts.

2. **Select Add New Vendor from module menu.**

   This takes you to the Edit Vendor page, shown in Figure 6-11, where you can add new vendor accounts.

3. **Complete all fields in the Vendor Details section.**

   All fields are mandatory.

4. **Complete all required fields in the Address Details section.**

   An asterisk indicates required fields. You can change any address field from required to optional by deselecting the check box beside it. These settings are then saved for the next time you are adding or editing a vendor account. The Other Details fields are optional.

5. **(Optional.) Enter the vendor's Web site URL into the Web Site text box in the Other Details section.**

6. **Click the Update link to save the new vendor.**

   You are now back on the Vendors page and the vendor you added is displayed. You can now add banners to this vendor.

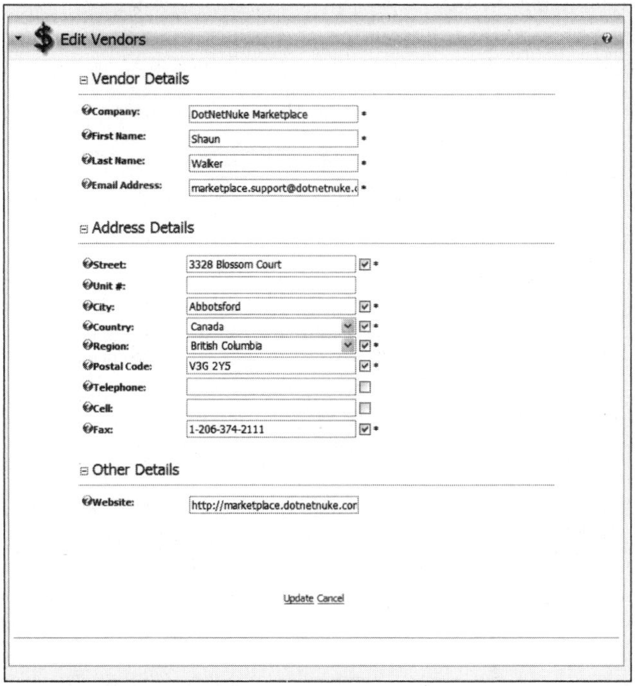

Figure 6-11:
Add a new
vendor on
the Edit
Vendors
page.

Adding an image banner to a vendor

Here's how to add an image banner with a link to the vendor's Web site:

1. **Select Admin➪Vendors from the site menu.**

   This takes you to the Vendors page, where you can view existing vendor accounts.

2. **Click the All link.**

   This displays all existing vendor accounts. Use the Next link to view more vendors if the one you want isn't displayed.

3. **Click the Edit button beside the vendor you want to add the banner to.**

   This displays the Edit Vendors page, where you can view this vendor's details.

4. **Click the Maximize button beside the Banner Advertising section.**

   This displays any existing banners for this vendor.

5. **Click the <u>Add New Banner</u> link.**

   This displays the Edit Banner page, shown in Figure 6-12, where you can add and edit banners.

6. **Enter a name for the banner into the Banner Name field.**

   The name is displayed as alternative text (tooltip) for the banner.

7. **Select the type of banner from the Banner Type drop-down box, for example, Banner.**

   The first five options (Banner, MicroButton, Button, Block, and Skyscraper) denote different sizes of image banners. Categorizing banners by sizes helps you design and control the layout of your pages. For example, you should place banners that are the Banner sizes in the Content Pane as they are wide. The other types of images look best in the side pane because they are long and skinny.

8. **(Optional.) Enter a word or phrase into the text box at Banner Group.**

   This text helps you define banners that you want to group together. The group can be just for one vendor, or for more than one vendor. When you want to identify banners as belonging to the same group, enter that name into this field. When you set up the Banners module, you can then enter this text and set the module to only display banners belonging to this Banner Group name.

9. **Select the image by using the Link Type tool displayed for the Image/Link field.**

10. **(Optional.) Enter the pixel width for the banner into the text box of the Width field.**

    This sets the width of the image. Leave this field blank to display the original image width.

11. **(Optional.) Enter the pixel height for the banner into the text box of the Width field.**

    This sets the height of the image. Leave this field blank to display the original image height.

12. **(Optional.) Enter a tooltip for the image into the text box of the Text/Script field.**

    Leave this field blank to display the Banner Name as the tooltip.

13. **Select the image by using the Link Type tool displayed for the Image/Link field.**

14. **Select the URL the user will be taken to when they click on the banner; for example, `www.dnnangel.com`.**

15. **Click the <u>Update</u> link to save the banner.**

    This takes you back to the Edit Vendors page. The banner is listed in the Banner Advertising section of the Edit Vendor page.

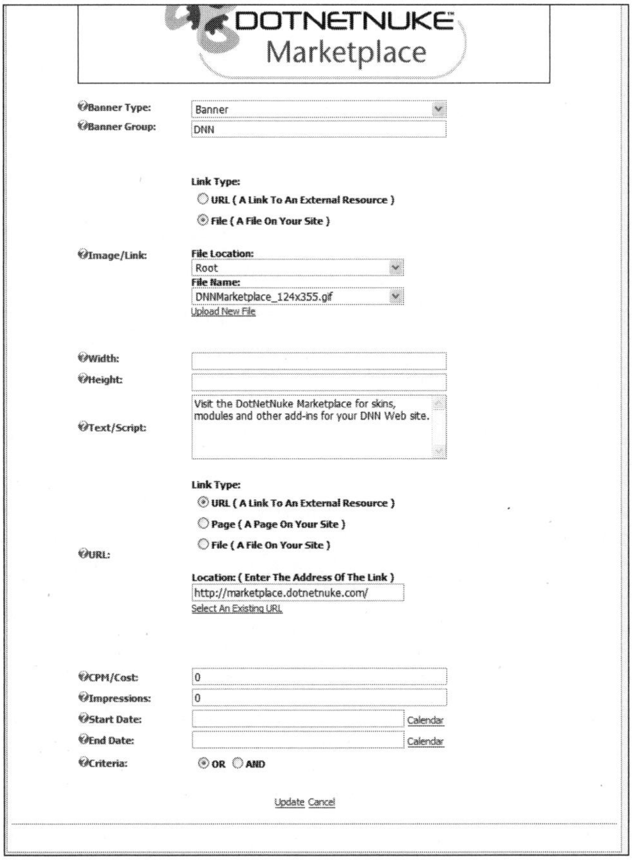

Figure 6-12:
Add and edit banners on the Edit Banner page. When editing a banner, the banner image is displayed at the top of the page.

Adding a text banner to a vendor

Here's how to add a text banner with a link to the vendor's Web site:

1. **Select Admin⇨Vendors from the site menu.**

   This takes you to the Vendors page, where you can view existing Vendor accounts.

2. **Click the <u>All</u> link.**

   This displays all existing vendor accounts. Use the <u>Next</u> link to view more Vendors if the one you want isn't displayed.

3. **Click the Edit button beside the Vendor you want to add the banner for.**

   This displays the Edit Vendors page, where you can view Vendors details.

4. **Click the Maximize button beside the Banner Advertising section.**

   This displays any existing banners for this vendor.

5. **Click the <u>Add New Banner</u> link.**

   This displays the Edit Banner page, where you can add and edit banners.

6. **Enter a name for the banner into the Banner Name field.**

   The name is displayed as alternative text (a tooltip) for the banner.

7. **Select Text from the Banner Type drop-down box.**

   Text denotes banners that aren't images but rather blocks of plain or HTML text.

8. **(Optional.) You can enter a word or phrase into the Banner Group field.**

   This text helps you define banners that are grouped together. The group can be just for one vendor or for more than one vendor. When you want to identify banners as belonging to the same group, enter that name into this field. When you set up the Banners module, you can then enter this text and set the module to display only banners belonging to this banner group.

9. **Enter the text to be displayed as this banner into the Text/Script field.**

10. **Select the URL the user will be taken to when they click on the banner; for example, `www.dnnangel.com`.**

11. **Click the <u>Update</u> link to save the banner.**

    This takes you back to the Edit Vendors page. The banner is listed in the Banner Advertising section of the Edit Vendors page.

Displaying a banner on your site

Here's how to display a banner on your site:

1. **Add a Banners module to a page.**

   The module is now displayed on the page.

2. **Select Banner Options from the module menu.**

   This displays the Edit Banner page, where you can set the banners to be displayed in this module.

3. **Be sure that the Site radio button is selected.**

   This ensures that the banners that are displayed are those that you create and maintain. Host banners are ones maintained by the host. You can choose host to display those banners instead if you want.

4. **Select a banner type from the Banner Type drop-down box.**

   To display banners of all sizes, leave this option as <All Types>.

5. **(Optional.) Enter the banner group name into the Banner Group text box.**

   This optional setting corresponds with the text entered into the field of the same name when you created the banner.

6. **Enter the number of banners you want displayed in this module in the Banner Count text box.**

   This sets the number of banners displayed at any time inside this module. The banners are randomly selected from all banners within the selected Banner Type and Banner Group. Each time this Web page is refreshed or revisited, new banners from the selected Banner Type and Banner Group are displayed.

7. **(Optional.) Set one or more of the layout options available to customize the look of banner in the module:**

   • **Orientation:** Choose whether to display banners vertically down the module or horizontally across the module.

   • **Border Width:** Specify the pixel width of a border displayed on each banner. Figure 6-13 displays a 4-pixel-wide border.

   • **Border Color:** Enter a hexadecimal or color name to set the border color. For example, red.

   • **Cell Padding:** Enter the space in pixels between the banners and the border. Figure 6-13 displays cell padding of 3 pixels.

   • **Row Height:** Enter the pixel height of each banner cell. This lets you set the spacing between banners to improve the layout.

   • **Column Width:** Enter the pixel width of each banner cell. This lets you set the spacing between banners to improve the layout.

8. Click the <u>Update</u> link to save your settings.

You can now see your banners displayed.

Figure 6-13:
The Banners
module
displays
advertising
banners for
vendor
accounts
that you
manage on
your Web
Site.

Sending a banner status e-mail to a vendor

Here's how to send a banner status e-mail to a vendor:

1. Select Admin⇨Vendors from the site menu.

This takes you to the Vendor page, where you can view existing vendor records.

2. Click the <u>All</u> link.

This displays all existing vendor accounts. Use the <u>Next</u> link to view more vendors if the one you want isn't displayed.

3. Click the Edit button beside the Vendor you want to send a status e-mail to.

This goes to the Edit Vendors page, where vendor account details are managed.

4. Click the Maximize button beside the Banner Advertising section.

This displays a list of this vendor's banners along with details of the number of times the banner has been viewed or clicked and more.

5. Click the Edit button beside the banner you want to send a status e-mail for.

This displays the Edit Banners page with details of the selected banner.

6. Click the <u>Email Status to Vendor</u> link.

A message confirming that the e-mail was sent successfully is displayed.

Seeing Who Is at Home with UsersOnline

The UsersOnline module, shown in Figure 6-14, enables the Administrator to view and share information about registered users of the Web site. This module can be set to display one or all of the three following types of user details:

- ✔ **Membership:** The Membership section of this module displays the username of the most recent registered user, how many users registered today, how many registered yesterday, and the total number of users for this Web site.

- ✔ **People Online:** The People Online section displays statistics about the number of people currently visiting this Web site. This section displays the number of visitors (unauthenticated users) currently online, the number of members (authenticated users), and the total number of all users currently online.

- ✔ **Online Now:** The Online Now section displays the usernames of all people who are currently online.

Figure 6-14:
The UsersOnline module can be set to display Membership, People Online, and Online Now information.

```
▼  UsersOnline▣❼

👥 Membership:
  Latest:
  philip.beadle
  New Today: 0
  New Yesterday: 0
  Overall: 9

👥 People Online:
  Visitors: 5
  Members: 1
  Total: 6

👥 Online Now:
01: philip.beadle
```

Enabling the UsersOnline module

This task must be performed to enable the UsersOnline module to display People Online and Online Now information. Host access is required to enable this setting. Alternatively, contact your host to enable this setting.

1. **Select Host⇨Host Settings from the site menu.**

   This takes you to the page where settings for all Web sites within this DNN installation are maintained.

2. **Click the Maximize button beside the Advanced Settings section**

3. **Click the Maximize button beside the Other Settings section.**

    4. **Deselect the Disable UsersOnline? check box.**

    5. **Click the <u>Update</u> link.**

       Any UsersOnline modules that you add to your Web site, or that are already on your Web site, are now capable of displaying all Membership, People Online, and Online Now information.

Ensuring that UsersOnline information is up-to-date

The great thing about the UsersOnline information module is that the information is always current. The module is alive! The DNN Scheduler manages the frequency with which certain tasks are performed on the DNN database. One of these tasks is a process that controls how frequently user information is updated with this module.

Here's how to ensure that UsersOnline information is up-to-date:

    1. **Select Host ⇨Schedule from the site menu.**

       This takes you to the Schedule page, where a summary of any tasks that have already been created is displayed.

    2. **Click the Edit button beside DotNetNuke.Entities.Users.Purge UsersOnline, DOTNETNUKE.**

       This takes you to a window where you can set how frequently the information is refreshed (updated) in the UsersOnline module.

    3. **Select the check box next to the Schedule Enabled field.**

       This turns on scheduled purging of old information and the display of current information.

    4. **Select 1 Minutes at the Time Lapse field.**

       This sets the schedule to update information each minute.

    5. **Select 5 Minutes at the Retry Frequency field.**

       This sets the schedule to retry updating user information every five minutes following a failed attempt. Skip the remaining fields.

    6. **Click the <u>Update</u> link.**

       A message informing you that your changes have been saved is displayed.

    7. **Click the <u>Cancel</u> link to return to the Schedule page or navigate to any other page.**

Setting the user information to be displayed on the UsersOnline module

The UsersOnline module can be set to display one of three types of information about registered users of the Web site. Here's how to set what information is displayed on the UsersOnline module:

1. **Select Settings from the module menu.**

   This takes you the Module settings page of the UsersOnline module.

2. **Click the Maximize button beside UsersOnline Settings section.**

   This displays the three different types of information you can choose to display in this instance of the UsersOnline module.

3. **Select one, two, or all three check boxes to display the related information, or deselect them to hide that information. Here are the options:**

   • **Show Membership:** This section displays information regarding the number of users registering on your Web site. This section displays the username of the last member to register, how many members registered today, how many registered yesterday, and the total number of registered users.

   • **Show People Online:** This section displays information about current Web site users. It displays the current number of visitors on your Web site, the current number of members logged in to your Web site, and the total number of people visiting your Web site.

   • **Show Online Now:** This section displays a list of the registered users who are currently logged in to the Web site. These users are listed by their usernames.

4. **Click the <u>Update</u> link.**

   The UsersOnline module now displays only the options you selected in Step 3.

Part III

Jumping to Light Speed with DotNetNuke

The 5th Wave   By Rich Tennant

YOU KIDDING!! TRUE INTERACTIVE CONTENT?! ME CAN'T WAIT, PULL LEVER, OPEN SCREEN!

In This Part . . .

*T*his Part kicks Web site administration up a notch. It covers the more advanced content modules that enable your Web site users to interact with the Web site by submitting their feedback, participating in forums, subscribing to newsletters, and more.

Chapter 7

Getting Interactive with DotNetNuke

. . . .

In This Chapter

▶ Find out about the Feedback modules

▶ Blogging with DNN

▶ Working with forums

▶ Sending newsletters

. . . .

*A*fter you have created a Web site by using the modules covered in Chapters 5 and 6, you're ready to tackle some of the more interactive modules that let people get involved with your site, have their say, and hear what others have to say.

The best Web sites have something new and interesting to read or do each time you visit them. An out-of-date Web site is a bit like visiting good old Uncle Bill: Everyone loves his storytelling, but he's told the same story the last ten times you've visited. But unless you're planning to dedicate your days and nights to writing new content, you need to enlist the help of people with knowledge and interest in topics relevant to your site. Who could be a better helper than your site's users? Everyone likes to have their say, so letting users contribute to your site gives them a sense of belonging to the community, as well as stimulating interest and debate. In return, you get free content, find out what's topical, and end up with more site content as a result.

Getting to Know the Feedback Modules

The simplest way to find out what people want from your site is by encouraging them to tell you. DNN comes with a feedback system of two modules that receive and share user feedback.

The first module, shown in Figure 7-1, is called the Feedback module and it enables users to send a message to the Administrator. This module is great because it allows you to receive feedback without revealing your e-mail address on the site, and it's very easy to use. This module can be used either by itself or with the Feedback Comments module. The Feedback Comments module, also shown in Figure 7-1, displays details of the feedback you have received.

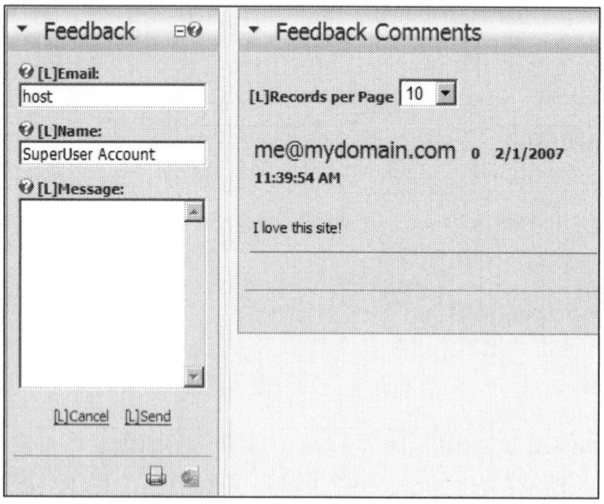

Figure 7-1:
The Feedback module lets people send you feedback, and the Feedback Comments module lets you share this feedback with others.

▼ Feedback ⊟❷	▼ Feedback Comments
❷ [L]Email: host ❷ [L]Name: SuperUser Account ❷ [L]Message: [L]Cancel [L]Send	[L]Records per Page 10 ▼ me@mydomain.com 0 2/1/2007 11:39:54 AM I love this site!

Receiving feedback in a flash

The Feedback module doesn't require any setup; you just add it to a page the same way you added the modules from Chapters 5 and 6. It works like a form: Users enter the details and click Send. To use the Feedback module, you simply need to add it to a page.

All roles that can view the module are able to send feedback, so you don't have to give users module edit permissions.

The Administrator who receives the feedback is the person specified under Advanced Settings on the Admin⇨Site Settings page.

Sending feedback

After you've added the Feedback module to a page, visitors to your Web site can use it to send messages to the Administrator. The user just completes the blank fields and clicks Send. Help buttons are displayed to everyone, making the form simple to complete.

To send feedback to the Administrator, users just need to complete these steps:

1. **Complete all fields.**

   Users don't need to register or log in to send feedback, but if they are logged in, the name and e-mail fields are prefilled for them.

2. **If you don't want a copy of the feedback sent to you, deselect Send Copy. The Send Copy option can be set in the Settings of the module to show or not show.**

   This option sends a copy of the feedback message to the e-mail address given.

3. **Click Send.**

   A confirmation message is displayed telling the sender whether the feedback was sent successfully.

Your host needs to enable your site to send messages. You can test if this has been set up by sending a test message to yourself.

Sharing the feedback workload

If your visitors have a lot to say, you might find yourself answering oodles of e-mails and not doing much else. To lighten the workload, you can add more than one Feedback module to your site and set them to send the feedback to different people. For example, you could add one Feedback module on a Sales Enquiry page that sends e-mail to your sales team, and another Feedback module on the Contact Us page that sends to your main contact person.

Here's how you can set a Feedback module to send messages to an e-mail address other than the Administrator:

1. **Select Settings from the module menu.**

2. **Expand the Feedback Settings section.**

3. **Enter the e-mail address to which you want the feedback to be sent in the Send To field.**

   The e-mail address you add here will receive feedback from this module now. The Administrator will no longer receive e-mails.

If you want the feedback to go to more than one person, create a distribution list by using your e-mail program, such as Microsoft Outlook. (Check the help system of your e-mail program on how to create a distribution list.) For example, you can create a distribution list called `salesteam@domain.com` that forwards any e-mails send to this address to all your sales team members. Simply enter the distribution list e-mail address into the Send To field.

4. Click Update.

This module is now set to send all feedback to the set e-mail address.

Sharing and moderating feedback comments

The Feedback Comments module lets you share feedback comments with others. If the feedback you're getting is all good, you will want to share it with everyone. If it's all bad, you should probably only share it with your staff! If it's some good and some bad, which is probably the most likely scenario, you can use moderation to choose what feedback you share and what you don't. Either way, you have full control over who sees what comments.

Here's how to share feedback comments with others:

1. Add the Feedback module to a page.

2. Select Settings from the Feedback Comments module menu.

This will take you to the Module Settings page.

3. At Permissions to View Module, select each of the security roles that can view comments.

You will need to deselect the Inherit View Permissions check box to do this.

4. Click Update.

The Feedback Comments module is now displayed to only the roles you selected. If you are happy for these users to see all feedback comments, you can skip these last steps, which add moderation to the module.

5. Select Settings from the Feedback module menu.

6. Select Moderated.

This sets the module to send a notification e-mail to the Administrator, or the address entered in the Send To field, whenever feedback is received. The e-mail includes a link to the feedback where the Administrator can choose to approve or delete the feedback.

7. Click Update.

Your Feedback Comments module is now ready to share comments with others.

Modifying the layout and fields of the Feedback module

The Feedback module has a number of settings that alter the fields displayed on the module and affect how it works. Here's how to change the standard Feedback module:

1. **Select Settings from the module menu.**

2. **Expand the Feedback Settings section below.**

3. **Enter the width (in number of pixels) for the message box in the Width field.**

   This lets you make the message box wider. The standard size of the message field is 150 pixels.

4. **Enter the number of lines long you want the Message box to be in the Rows field.**

   This lets you make the message box longer. The standard number of rows for the message field is ten lines.

   These two settings only control how big the message box is, not the length of the message your user can enter.

5. **Select the Send Copy field to send the user a copy of their feedback.**

   If this option is selected, the user is e-mailed a copy of their feedback message. Users generally like to receive a copy of their feedback as it confirms that the message was successfully sent and lets them review their comments. Skip to Step 7 if you did not select this option.

6. **Select Optout to give users the option to opt out of receiving feedback.**

   If this option is selected, a Send Copy selection box is displayed to the user on the Feedback module. This gives users the option to choose whether to receive a copy of their feedback.

7. **Enter a Subject for the feedback.**

   This will be the subject used in any e-mail notifications. The subject will also be displayed in the Feedback Comments module. Skip to Step 9 if you did not select this option.

8. **Select Can Select Subject to give users the option to edit your subject or add their own.**

   If this option is selected, the Subject field is displayed on the Feedback module. If you added a subject at Step 7, users will be able to modify it. If you didn't add a subject, users can enter their own.

9. **If you don't want to be notified when feedback is received, deselect the Notify option.**

   The notify option is selected by default so you know when feedback is received. If you deselect this option, you must have the Feedback Comments module displayed so any feedback is captured.

10. **Click Update.**

    The feedback module is now displayed with your new settings.

There is the option to add categories to Feedback modules and display a different category of feedback in different Feedback Comment modules. Unfortunately, categories can only be added by your host.

Getting Familiar with This Blogging Business

Since the late 1990s, one of the fastest growing areas of the Internet has been blogging. A *blog* (short for Weblog) is a personal online journal or diary where a blogger (a person who keeps a blog) shares their thoughts, ideas, knowledge (or lack thereof), and anything else they have to say. Blogs are written in a personal and informal way, so it's kind of like peeking at someone's diary — without the guilt.

Virtually everyone is blogging these days, including celebrities. Check out Moby's popular blog at www.moby.com/journal, or Shaun Walker's at www.dotnetnuke.com/Community/BlogsDotNetNuke/tabid/825/BlogID/1/Default.aspx. (Shaun Walker is the inventor of DotNetNuke.)

Blogging isn't just for celebrities. Individuals who know a lot about a particular subject also attract a huge following. Check out this techie blog from Robert Scoble: http://scobleizer.com/.

Getting to know the DNN Blog module

DNN includes a Blog module, which enables you manage one or more blogs for one or more people. Start by adding a Blog module to a page (like we did in Chapters 5 and 6) and looking at it. The first thing you notice is that it isn't really a single module, but five modules that work together, as shown in Figure 7-2. I discuss these five modules in the upcoming sections.

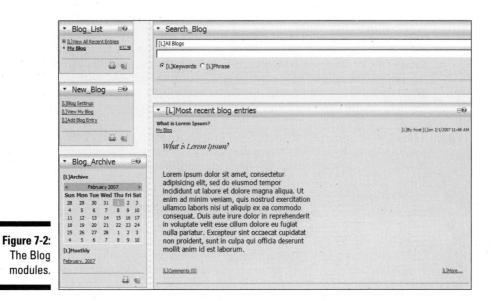

Figure 7-2:
The Blog
modules.

Most Recent Blog Entries

The Most Recent Blog Entries module is the main blog module that displays blog entries. When you first add the module, the title reads Most Recent Blog Entries; however, the module title changes depending on what entries are being displayed.

The Most Recent Blog Entries module displays the most recent entries from all public blogs by default. It can display a single blog if the user selects one from the Blog List module or clicks the Go to My Blog link on the New Blog module. This changes the module title to the name of the selected blog. The module also displays search results for the Search Blog module. Performing a search changes the module title to Search Results.

This module has an Administration page called Module Options located on the module menu. Here you can change the layout of blogs in this module and manage settings to enable bloggers to add attachments and images to their entries. (See "Setting Options for the Most Recent Blog Entries Module" later in this chapter for more information on these settings.)

Blog Archive

The Blog Archive module displays a monthly calendar where any days with a blog entry are highlighted. Click on a highlighted day to view entries for that day. Below the calendar is a list of all months that have an entry. Clicking on a month displays all entries for that month in the Most Recent Blog Entries module.

New Blog

The New Blog module gives authorized users the ability to add one or more blogs. After a user has added their first blog, the module displays links enabling them to add entries, change the settings applied to their blog, and go to their blog. Users can also create child blogs of their main blog, enabling them to create different blogs for different information.

This module provides access to the Edit Blog Settings page. This page enables users to manage the settings for each of their blogs. Settings include the title and description of the blog, blog options such as commenting and trackback, syndication, date settings management, and the ability to create child blogs.

A message that reads "You must be logged in and have permission to create or edit a blog" is displayed to unauthenticated users. If you don't want users to see this warning message, change the permissions for View Module to Registered Users only. This means the module won't show until people log in.

All roles that have permission to edit this module (under Module Settings) can create one or more blogs. Restrict who can create a blog by setting the Edit Module permissions accordingly. You can do this by clicking Settings from the module menu and then ticking the check boxes for the roles that you want to be able to create a blog.

Blog List

The Blog List module lists all public blogs on the site. Click on a blog to view it in the Most Recent Blog Entries module and to access the Edit Blog Settings page for that blog via the module menu.

Search Blog

The Search Blog module lets users search the title and content of public blogs by keywords or phrase. They can choose to search All Blogs, or select a parent blog from the drop-down list. Searching a parent blog also searches any child blogs it has.

This module doesn't have an Administration page, but there are three search-related settings on the Most Recent Blog Entries module. (See the section "Setting Options for the Most Recent Blog Entries Module" later in this chapter for more.)

Creating a public blog

Start by setting up your blog:

1. **Click Create My Blog on the New Blog module.**

   This takes you to the Create New Blog page.

2. **In the Title and Description fields, enter a title and description for your blog, as shown in Figure 7-3.**

   The description is displayed on your blog. It should accurately describe your blog's content so that users know what to expect.

3. **Under Blog Options, select the Make This Blog Public check box.**

   If you don't select this option, the blog is private, meaning only you can see it.

4. **Click Update.**

After you have created your blog, you may notice the following changes:

- ✔ Your blog is listed in the Blog List and in the Search module.
- ✔ The description is displayed on the Most Recent Blog Entries module.

Figure 7-3:
Creating a
public blog.

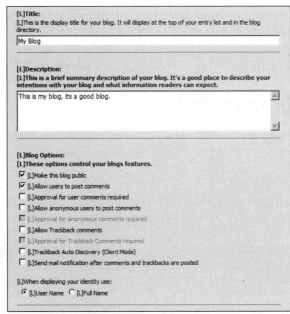

Creating child blogs

If you have a lot to say, you can create more than just one blog for yourself. For example, you might like to have one for your friends and family, as well as one for work stuff. Your first blog is known as your *parent blog*; all of your additional blogs are known as *child blogs*. Each child blog you create is listed and indented below the parent blog.

1. **Click Blog Settings on the New Blog module, which takes you to the Edit Blog page.**

2. **Scroll down to the bottom of the Edit Blog page.**

3. **Click the Add button beside the Child Blogs field.**

   This takes you to the Create New Child Blog page. This page looks just like the last page, so don't worry if nothing seems to change.

4. **Complete all the fields, just as you did when you created your first blog.**

5. **Click Add.**

   The child blog is now listed in the Child Blog field. You can also edit or delete Child Blogs from here.

6. **Click Update.**

Making blog entries

The best blogs are ones that are updated frequently or even daily, so don't be shy about sharing your thoughts. Here's how to add your first blog entry:

1. **Click Add Blog Entry on the New Blog module.**

   The date and time will be shown in the Entry Date field. You can change the date of your entry by editing it here, but you need to keep to the same format.

   Note: The date format can be changed under Blog Settings. (See "Setting date and time options" for more on date formats.)

2. **Select the parent blog.**

   This enables you to choose which of your blogs you want to add the entry to. If you don't have any child blogs, you don't need to select anything here.

3. **Add your entry.**

Enter the title and the blog. The Description field is optional as one is created from the first few lines of the blog if you don't enter one.

Note: The Description field can be made mandatory (See "Blog Settings for All Bloggers: Advanced Settings for Your Blog" to find out how to set this field as mandatory.)

4. **Set the entry options.**

If you select the Copyright Notice option, wait a moment while a new field is displayed. This shows the standard copyright notice. You can edit the notice, but it won't save your edits for next time. The standard message is Copyright (c)2006, followed by either your username or your first and last name (for example, Copyright (c)2006 John Black). (See "Blog Settings for All Bloggers: Advanced Settings for Your Blog" later in this chapter for more on the settings available here.)

See the section "Using trackback URLs" later in this chapter for more on the entry options.

5. **Click Update.**

Congratulations, you are now a blogger!

Viewing, editing, or deleting blog entries

Here's how to edit or delete a blog entry:

1. **Click View My Blog on the New Blog module.**

Your blog is now displayed in the Most Recent Blog Entries module.

2. **Click the entry title or the More link.**

The entry will now be displayed.

3. **Click the Edit Entry link to edit or delete the entry, or change the parent or child blog that it is listed under. Perform any of the following steps to do this:**

   • To edit the blog, change the text and click Update below the editor.

   • To delete the blog, click the Delete link below the editor.

   • To change the parent blog, select the blog name from the Parent Blog list above the editor and click Update below.

Setting Options for the Most Recent Blog Entries Module

The Most Recent Blog Entries module has a number of settings that control the presentation of blogs in the module, such as how many recent entries are displayed, the length of the blog summary, and so on. This section also includes miscellaneous settings, such as those that allow bloggers to upload images and enable the module to display only one blog.

To access the Administrator settings of the Most Recent Blog Entries module, select Module Options from the menu of the Most Recent Blog Entries module. The Module Options page is displayed, as shown in Figure 7-4.

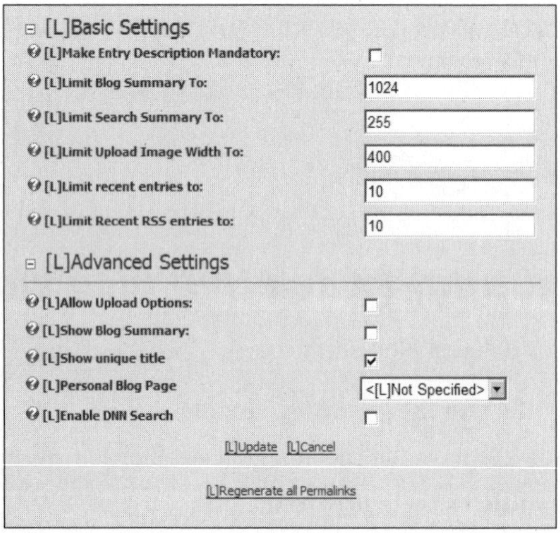

Figure 7-4:
The Module Options page lets you change the layout of the blog and allow bloggers to upload images.

```
⊟ [L]Basic Settings
  ❷ [L]Make Entry Description Mandatory:      ☐
  ❷ [L]Limit Blog Summary To:                 [1024      ]
  ❷ [L]Limit Search Summary To:               [255       ]
  ❷ [L]Limit Upload Image Width To:           [400       ]
  ❷ [L]Limit recent entries to:               [10        ]
  ❷ [L]Limit Recent RSS entries to:           [10        ]
⊟ [L]Advanced Settings
  ❷ [L]Allow Upload Options:                  ☐
  ❷ [L]Show Blog Summary:                     ☐
  ❷ [L]Show unique title                      ☑
  ❷ [L]Personal Blog Page                     [<[L]Not Specified> ▼]
  ❷ [L]Enable DNN Search                      ☐
                    [L]Update  [L]Cancel
                [L]Regenerate all Permalinks
```

Most fields are sufficiently explained under their respective help icons, so, in the next sections, we just cover the trickier ones.

Allow bloggers to add images and attachments

The Allow Upload Options check box enables bloggers to upload images and attachments while adding an entry. Uploaded images are displayed in the Rich Text Editor (RTE) and attachments are added as a link to the RTE. The

Module Options page also has a setting called Limit Upload Image Width To, where you can set the maximum pixel width for images. This doesn't prevent users from adding an image that exceeds the maximum; it just resizes it as it is added to the Rich Text Editor.

Setting a personal blog page

The Personal Blog Page drop-down list lets you choose a parent blog for this page. When you select one, the other blogs are no longer displayed on the site unless you add another Most Recent Blog Entries module to the page. This lets you display a different blog on different pages.

Search options

The Limit Search Summary To field lets you limit the length of the entry summaries in your search results to ensure quick and short results.

The Enable DNN Search option lets you enable the DNN search. Doing this means that your blog entries are also searchable from the DNN Search system.

Don't enable DNN search for more than one Most Recent Blog Entries module on your site: It will create duplicate results.

Show Blog Summary

This shows a summary above the entry. If the summary field is not mandatory, this information is a repeat of the beginning of the blog and therefore not of much use.

Blog Settings for All Bloggers: Advanced Settings for Your Blog

You may have noticed that we skipped a bucketload of settings when we created your first blog. These settings are available to the blogger for their own blog. Now take a moment to go back and look at these settings.

Select Edit Blog Settings from the Blog List module menu, or select Blog Settings from the New Blog module. This takes you to the Edit Blog page. If you want to edit the settings for a child blog, scroll down to the Child Blog field and click the Edit button to edit it now. This gives you these same options:

- ✔ **Public or private blog:** The Make This Blog Public option controls the visibility of your blog to others. Public blogs can be viewed by everyone authorized to see the Most Recent Blog Entries module. If you deselect this option, your blog won't be listed in the Most Recent Blog Entries module under Most Recent Blog Entries; it won't be listed in the Blog List module; and it won't be included in search results. In this case, you need to use the New Blog module to view your blog.

- ✔ **Let people add comments to entries:** You can enable people to add a comment to entries. This adds a comment box below each entry. If you set the blog to require approval for comments, the comments are not displayed until they are approved.

    Here are your options for comment settings:

    - **Allow Users to Post Comments:** Enables comments to be added to posts.

    - **Approval for User Comments Required:** Select this option if you want to approve user comments before they appear online. This gives you the chance to read the comment and either approve, edit, or delete it.

    - **Let Anonymous Users to Comment:** Select this option if you want to let unauthenticated users post comments. If this option is deselected, users must be logged in to post comments.

    - **Approval for Anonymous Comments Required:** Select this option if you want to approve anonymous comments before they appear online.

    - **Send Mail Notification After Comments and Trackbacks Are Posted:** If you have set approval for any comments (or trackbacks), this option lets you receive e-mail notification. If you don't select this option, you need to open each entry to see if it has a comment requiring approval, which is time consuming.

If comments are disabled, the blogger can override this setting for an individual entry when they are adding it by ticking the Allow users to comment on this entry (overrides Blog Setting) option.

Setting date and time options

This setting enables bloggers to display their own time and date information. This means that if you add a post from Australia to a site in the United States, when you're adding it, you see the Aussie time and date rather than those of the site.

At the time of this writing, changing the time zone resets the date format field to standard U.S. format such as 1/20/2007. Get around this by setting the time zone before the date.

Using trackback URLs

Trackbacks are a simple way of properly referencing other people's blogs. Say you are writing a blog entry about how you bought a new house. While you were making the decision about which street to buy on, you read a really good blog entry on someone else's blog that helped you make your choice. You want to say thank you to that person by referencing their blog in yours.

You can do this by adding a trackback to your blog entry. A *trackback* is a special URL that lets other blogs know they have been referenced. To find the trackback URL of the blog you want to reference, look for a link called <u>Trackback</u> on the entry. Most blogs display a URL that you can then copy and paste into your blog entry. Then when you add your entry, a message is sent to the other blog.

In DNN, these trackback *pings* are shown as comments next to your blog entry. This means that if someone adds a trackback to your blog on their site, it adds a comment to your blog.

The following options are provided to enable and set trackbacks:

- ✔ **Allow Trackback Comments:** If you select this option, when another blog adds your blog entry as a trackback, those comments from the trackback pings are shown on your site as comments.

- ✔ **Approval for Trackback Comments Required:** If you select this option, it marks the pings you receive from trackbacks as needing approval. This option can help reduce the amount of spam you receive on your blog comments. These comments are approved as usual.

- ✔ **Trackback Auto Discovery (Client Mode):** When this option is enabled, the Most Recent Blog Entries module searches for any links in your blog post and determines if those links are trackback-enabled. If they are, a trackback ping is automatically sent to those sites.

- ✔ **Send Mail Notification After Comments and Trackbacks Are Posted:** This option sends you an e-mail each time someone adds a comment or a trackback to your blog so you can either approve it or read it.

Syndicate this blog

Syndicating a blog means that you can display a summary of the blog on another page by using the News Feeds module, or others can display a summary of your blog on their Web site with a link to read it on your site. Selecting a blog for syndication adds the XML icon beside that blog on both the Most Recent Blog Entries module and the Blog List module. Syndication of blogs works the same as for the News Feeds module: You simply click on the XML button, copy the URL from your Web browser into the News Feed Source field of the News Feed module, select a style sheet, and you can display a summary of the blog anywhere on your portal.

Here's how to set a blog as syndicated:

1. **Select the blog from the Blog List module.**

2. **Select Edit Blog Settings from the module menu.**

3. **Scroll down to the Syndication section.**

4. **Select the Syndicate this blog option.**

   This adds the XML button beside the module.

5. **Enter an e-mail address in the Use This E-mail for the Managing Editor RSS field.**

   When a blog is syndicated, the XML file references an e-mail address for the Webmaster and Managing Editor of the blog. Depending on the style sheet applied, the e-mail address may be displayed in the syndicated feed. By entering an e-mail address here, you can control the e-mail referenced for this syndication. If no e-mail is entered, the Administrator e-mail (as set on the Site Settings page) is used instead.

6. **Click Update.**

Creating permalinks to your blog

A permalink (or permanent link) is a link that doesn't change for a long time. The purpose of a permalink is to let bloggers, and other interested people, generate a link to an entry and then quote that link in their own blog or Web site.

To get the permalink of an entry, do the following:

1. **Search for or navigate to the entry.**

2. **Click the <u>Permalink</u> link.**

   The permalink will now be displayed in the address bar of your browser.

3. **Copy the link from the address bar.**

   You can now add the link to a new blog entry, or wherever you want to reference this entry.

Getting to Know Forums

A *forum* is a place where people go to participate in online discussions. Forums have taken the place of bulletin boards and news groups, which were common in the earlier days of the Web. The Web has forums on nearly any topic you can think of, and forums are the places to go to ask questions, share thoughts, show off your expertise, or just have a bit of a rant.

Forums are great for building communities because they give people a real sense of belonging. They are also great for your site because you can let people join in and they end up writing lots of content for your site and help inspire you for new topics.

The DNN Forum module

The DNN Forum module, shown in Figure 7-5, gives you everything you need to manage forums for either small or very large groups. Start by adding a Forum module to a new page and we'll give you the grand tour.

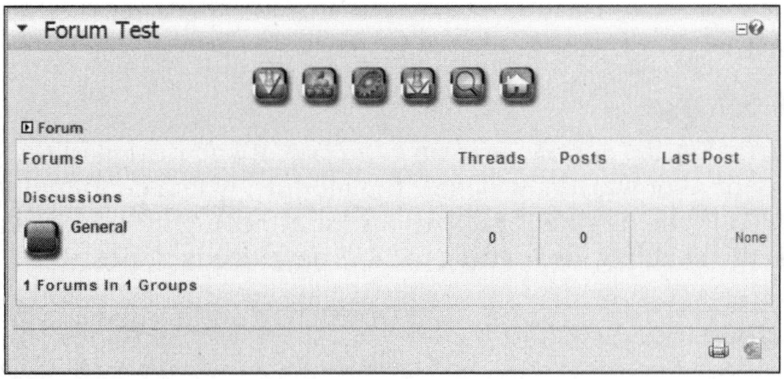

Figure 7-5:
The Forum module's initial view.

The module displays a table listing of all the forums, a summary of how many threads and posts are in each forum, and when a forum was last posted to. If you haven't edited the forums yet, you will see a sample Forum Group (called Discussions) and a sample Forum (called General).

In the top area of the module are four buttons (My Settings, My Posts, Search, and Forum Home) that all users can see. There is also a Moderate button, which is visible only to Administrators and moderators and also an Admin button which is available only to site and forum administrators. (See "Creating a moderated forum" for more information on what a moderated forum is and how to create one.)

Depending on the module container, these buttons might also be displayed to the Administrator in the bottomleft corner as hyperlinks.

The Forum Administration page

All administration tasks are managed from one handy control panel, called the Forum Administration page, shown in Figure 7-6. This page is accessed via the module menu.

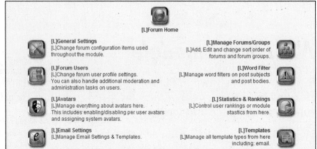

Figure 7-6:
The Forum Administration page.

General Settings

The General Setting section manages the layout and design of the module, the behavior of how users will view the module, which community features are enabled in the module, and settings for attaching files. This section also manages the enabling and setting for RSS news feeds of posts.

Forum Users

The Forum Users section provides you with a searchable list of forum users and manages profiles of each person. Information includes basic details from their DNN User Account maintained under Admin⇨Site Settings as well as additional profile information such as hobbies and occupation. Both the user and Administrators can maintain all information that isn't part of their DNN user account. Users are able to access this page via the My Settings page.

Administrators have some additional options at the bottom of each user account where they can set a user as trusted to post responsibly to a moderated forum, or make them a moderator of a moderated forum.

Avatars

The user avatar section allows users to associate a picture with their user profile. This option can be turned on or off depending on the Administrator's preferences. When users upload avatars, a thumbnail is generated based on the dimensions set in this section. Users are also restricted to the file size listed as the user image size limit.

If the Administrator configures the module to use an avatar image pool, users will not be permitted to upload their own images but instead will be allowed to select from a list of images uploaded by the site or module Administrator.

The system avatars behave similarly to the user avatars in terms of how they are uploaded, but also work in a similar manner as the user avatar image pool. These system avatars are uploaded by module Administrators just like the pool ones explained previously, but the main difference here is these avatars can only be assigned to users by module or site Administrators instead of the user selecting one themselves. One final important note here is that a user can only have one User avatar, but may have an infinite number of system avatars.

Manage Forums/Groups

The Manage Forums/Groups section enables you to add, edit, and manage groups and forums. If you want to take a forum offline for a while, you do it here by editing a forum.

The Manage Forums/Groups section enables you to add new forums and groups, edit forum and group settings, as well as delete or make a forum inactive. This section also lets you change the order that forums are listed, edit, and manage forum groups and forums. Forum settings include the ability to restrict the roles that can view and edit a forum and the ability to set a forum as moderated.

Word Filter

This section lets you add any words or phrases you don't want posted to your forums and replaces them with a word of your choice. For example, you might like to filter out the phrase "Builders Nightmare" and replace it with "Renovators Delight." More likely, you will use the filter to replace obscenities with a more polite phrase/word or a filter such as ****. You can filter both the subject and body.

Statistics & Ranking

This area lets you set the forum to rank forum users by the number of posts they have added. Users that contribute a set number of posts have a 1–10 star icon added beside their user details on their posts. This section lets you set the number of posts required to rank.

Creating a public forum

A public forum is available for all your site users to view. Public forums don't let people add posts anonymously. If an unauthenticated user attempts to add a post, they receive an Access Denied message, although no buttons are shown to them which mislead them to believe that they can do this.

Here's how to create a forum that all site visitors can view, but to which only registered users can add a post:

1. **Add a new page called Forums.**
2. **Add the Forum module to the page.**
3. **Click Settings in the module menu.**

   Role access is managed the same way as with other modules. View Module sets which roles can view the module and any posts, whereas Edit Module sets which roles are Administrators of this module.

4. **Set permissions to View Module to All Users and click Update.**
5. **Select Forum Administration from the module menu.**
6. **Click Manage Forums/Groups.**
7. **Here you can edit, add, and delete Groups and Forums.**
8. **Expand the group by clicking the plus icon.**

   Expanding the group displays any existing forums and the Add Forum link is now displayed. If this is your first time configuring the module after placing it on the page, you will see a group called Discussions. Note: You cannot add a post to a group, only to a forum; for example, you can't add a post to the Group called Discussions, only to the forum called General.

9. **Click Add Forum.**

   You must complete the Forum Name field when adding a new forum, as well as select a Group that this forum will belong to. If you want to add a description, you can do so at this time by typing information you expect to be discussed in your forum in the description field.

10. **Click Update.**

    To see the new forum, click the Forum Home link.

Turning a forum off

If you don't want one of your forums to be visible on your site, you can do so without deleting it:

1. **Select Forum Administration from the module menu.**

2. **Click Manage Forums/Groups.**

3. **Expand the group and click the Edit button beside the required forum.**

4. **Deselect the Enable Forum option.**

5. **Click Update.**

Posting to a forum

Having your say in a forum is known as making a post. Starting a new topic is called a starting a new thread. Here's how to start a new thread:

1. **Click Forum Home and click on the name of the forum you want to post to.**

   This takes you to the page of the selected forum. If any posts have been made to the forum, they are listed here. Remember, you can't post to a group, only to a forum.

2. **Click the New Thread button.**

   This takes you to the Add/Edit page, which is shown in Figure 7-7.

3. **In the Subject box, type a subject that best describes the content and purpose of the post. This will be the title of the post as it appears on the site.**

4. **Enter the content of your post in the large text box.**

5. **(Optional.) Click the Insert Image or Insert Smiley buttons if you want from within the text editor.**

6. **(Optional.) Upload an attachment.**

   Attachments must be enabled in order for you to be allowed to upload them. If attachments are not enabled, you will not see this as an option. However, if they are enabled and you want to add an attachment to your post, simply click the Browse button and select your attachment from your local file system. Click Upload File. After you do this, the file you just uploaded will be selected in the drop-down list.

7. **(Optional.) Select Pinned to have the thread listed first in this forum.**

   Pin important threads that you want to be prominent to everyone. When new threads are added, they are listed below any pinned ones. Only Administrators, Page Editors, and Moderators of forums have the right to pin a post.

8. **Select Notification to receive e-mail notification wherever someone replies to your post.**

   This is great if you are looking for answers or if it's a hot topic for you. You will not see this option if you are already subscribed to notifications for the forum you are posting this message in.

9. **Select Locked to prevent others from replying to this post.**

   Not everyone who is authorized to post to a forum has the ability to lock their post from replies. The settings for this are controlled by the Administrators from the Forum Edit section of the module outlined in Chapter 14. Locking a post keeps the thread from being replied to by other users.

10. **Click Update.**

    The post is now displayed.

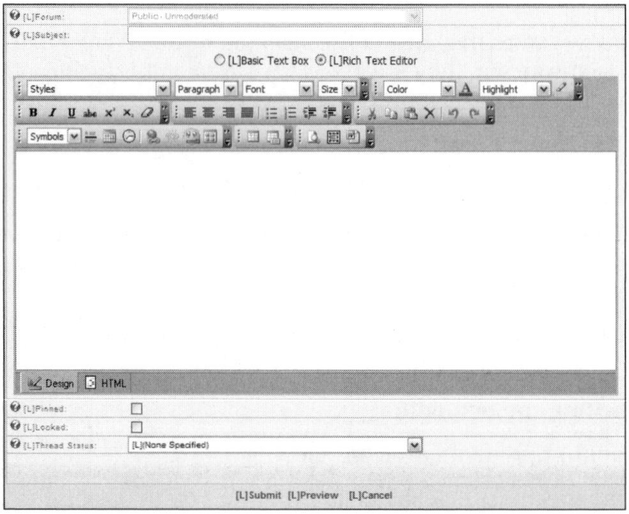

Figure 7-7:
The
Add/Edit
page, where
you can
add, edit,
and delete
forum posts.

Replying to forums is pretty easy too. Here's all you have to do:

1. **Click Forum Home and click on the name of the forum you want to reply in.**

   This takes you to the forum. The post you want to reply to should be listed. If there are lots of posts, you may need to do a search to find it.

2. **Click the Reply button.**

   Do your thing again.

3. **Click Update.**

Sometimes your reply will be relevant to only one part of a post and you want to make it easy for people to know what you're talking about. At other times, the thread you are replying to might already have ten posts and your reply is targeted at one reply in particular. By selecting Quote instead of Reply, the body of the original post is added inside the editor. This helps others understand the point of your post.

The Forums module has its own search function, although the standard DNN search works just fine. The search is simple to use, so we won't take you through it in detail. To use the Forum Search, simply click the Search button, which is shown by a magnifying glass, and you will be navigated to a screen that allows you to search by who posted it, what the subject is you are looking for, the date range during which the post was posted, which forums it may be in, and what is the content of the post you are searching for. Please note that leaving any of these blank will search for anything matching all the criteria you input on this screen.

Creating a role-restricted (private) forum

Say you've created a public forum where all of your registered users are having their say. The forum is so popular, in fact, that you have decided to create a second forum called Property Management just for your Property Managers. You don't, however, want your customers or your competitors looking at this forum because it includes some great ideas you want to keep under wraps. What you need is a role-restricted or private forum.

This is how you can control which roles can view and post to a forum:

1. **Select Forum Administration from the module menu.**

2. **Click Manage Forums/Groups.**

3. **Expand the group and click the Edit button beside the forum to be edited.**

4. **Expand the General Settings section.**

5. **At the very bottom, deselect the Inherit View permissions from Module checkbox.**

    This changes what items you can select in the permissions grid View Forum column.

6. **To set which roles can view the forum, select the View Forum column check box next to each role that you want to see this forum.**

7. **To control which roles can post in this forum, uncheck the Inherit Posting Restrictions permissions from Module View.**

   This allows you to select the Start Threads and Post Replies columns for the roles that you would like to be able to post in that forum. Please note that the difference here is that Start Threads means users can create new threads, and Post Replies refers to users being able to only respond to existing threads.

8. **Click Update when finished.**

Filtering out the bad words

The Word Filter located on the Forum Administration page lets you filter out undesirable words and phrases. To turn it on, select the Enable Bad Word Filter option, select Include Subject if you want to filter words in the Subject line as well.

Moderating what people say in forums

Is replacing the naughty words with the Word Filter not quite enough? Would you like to read people's posts before they appear on the site? Would you like the chance to edit poor spelling or to delete undesirable posts? All this is possible: It's called moderating. You can set which forums are moderated and can be notified by e-mail when you have a post that's awaiting moderation. The people who are able to moderate forums are called Moderators.

Creating a moderated forum

Administrators can set any forum as moderated as well as select which users have the ability to moderate posts to that forum:

1. **Select Forum Administration from the module menu.**

2. **Click Manage Groups/Forums.**

3. **Expand a forum group and click the Edit button beside the forum you want to moderate.**

4. **Expand the General Settings section.**

5. **Select Forum Is Moderated.**

Choosing the Moderated option means new posts must be approved before they go live. The only people whose posts don't need approval are Administrators, moderators of any moderated forums, and trusted users.

A new option is now displayed that enables you to choose the moderators for this forum. Choose the moderators for this forum by looking up there user-names one at a time and click Add Moderator.

You can also assign moderators by role by selecting the check box for each role that you desire to be a moderator of the forum. Remember, Administrators, Global Moderators, and Forum Admin, which are assigned in the module settings, are moderators of all forums, including nonmoderated ones.

Selecting a moderator

Moderators are the people you trust to approve or reject posts in moderated forums. Choose people who know what is okay to say, who understand the political climate, and who get what you are trying to achieve in this forum. Moderators are the trustees of their community, so think carefully and get the best person for the job.

Moderators and Administrators also have the ability to edit a post and move it to another forum. Moderators can only edit and move posts in forums they can moderate, whereas Administrators can do this for all forums.

Consider putting together some guidelines for your moderators so they understand exactly what you expect of them. Also, using the Word Filter makes life easier for your moderators as the replacement happens before the post is presented for moderation. That way, they don't have to scan the text for those undesirable words.

Moderators can choose to receive e-mail notification when new posts require moderation. This option is called Enable Moderator E-mails and is located inside the Tracking/Subscription section on each user's settings page.

Moderating forum posts

Moderating forum posts lets you choose the way to handle the post, whether it is adding it to the page, editing the post before adding it, or deleting the post. Moderation also includes e-mailing information back to the poster on how their post was handled.

To try out moderation, you might like to log in as a registered user and add a few posts to a moderated forum. To moderate a forum post, click the Moderate button. This returns a list of any posts that you have permission to moderate. You have a few different moderation options to choose from:

- ✔ **Approve:** This approves the post and notifies the poster of the approval.
- ✔ **Approve and Reply:** This approves the post, notifies the poster of the approval and lets you add a reply. This is the best way to moderate because moderators add their expertise on the fly and posts are responded to quickly.

✔ **Approve and Edit:** This approves the post, notifies the poster of the approval, and adds the post to the editor for you to edit.

 All Approve options add the post to the site regardless of whether you then reply or edit it. Make sure you have read the post before clicking any of the Approve options.

 ✔ **Delete:** This deletes the post and notifies the poster of the reason it was deleted, which you must supply.

You can also do post moderation when you are reading through posts. This is great for a bit of on-the-fly additional moderation.

Do you trust me?

If you trust some people to say only the right stuff, you can set it so that their posts aren't moderated. This saves you moderation time and their posts are still automatically filtered for naughty words if you are using the Word Filter.

One important note about this is that you can automatically trust all new users for your forum. To make this happen, you need to go into the Forum Administration, General Settings section and select the Trust New Users check box.

1. **Select Forum Administration from the module menu.**

2. **Click Forum Users.**

3. **Click on the first letter of the user's first name in the alphabet list, or click <u>All</u> to view all users.**

   Clicking the first letter or the <u>All</u> link returns a list of all matching users.

4. **Click the Edit button beside the required user.**

5. **Expand the Admin Settings section.**

6. **Select Is Trusted.**

7. **Click Update.**

Changing the layout and design

There are a number of options to modify the appearance of the module on the page and the skins or themes applied to it. The following settings can be managed by selecting Forum Administration from the module menu and clicking on General Settings.

Change the forum name

You can change the name of the forum, which is the link located in the top-left corner of the module below the module title, by changing the Forum Name text.

Change the theme/skin

The Forums module comes with a few themes to choose from. Themes change design elements like images, buttons, colors, fonts, and so on. A theme is like a skin that goes inside the module container. Depending on which themes you have installed, your options will vary. To select a theme, select any item from the Theme drop-down list that you want to use.

Change page layout

Set the standard layout of forum pages by setting the number of threads and posts that are displayed per page. This only affects users who are not logged in and the users who are new. A logged-in user can override this based on their own settings from My Settings screen.

Changing Member Name Display

The Member Name Display determines how all users will appear to other users throughout your forum. Select an item in this drop-down list such as username, or display name. Username, for example, displays the registered users' username to all users who are authorized to see posts by this user.

Enabling Thread Status

Thread status allows your users to select a thread status when posting a new thread in a forum. This allows other users to quickly associate what type of topic this is. For example, a user may post a question and set the thread status as Unresolved. All users will see an icon associated with the thread, which signifies that the thread is unresolved. After the user who originally posted the thread receives an acceptable answer, they can change the status of the thread to Resolved. The other option available here is Informative.

Enabling Private Messaging

This is within the next section entitled Community. Selecting this will allow users to communicate with one another outside of the public and private forums. Private Messaging is a conversation between only two users that nobody else will have access to.

Enabling Member List

When the Member List is enabled, users can view other users' profiles and send them private messages by using a convenient search option available in the Member List.

Going Public with Newsletters

When you have exciting news, you probably just can't want to share it with your Web site users. And why should you? DNN comes with a Newsletter module that lets you send an e-mail newsletter to your users in a flash.

Located on the Admin⇨Newsletters page, the Newsletter module lets you create either an HTML message by using the RTE, or a plain text message. Newsletters can be sent to one or more security roles at a time and can include an attachment.

To send a newsletter to one or more security roles, follow these steps:

1. Go to Admin⇨Newsletters.

The Newsletters window opens, as shown in Figure 7-8.

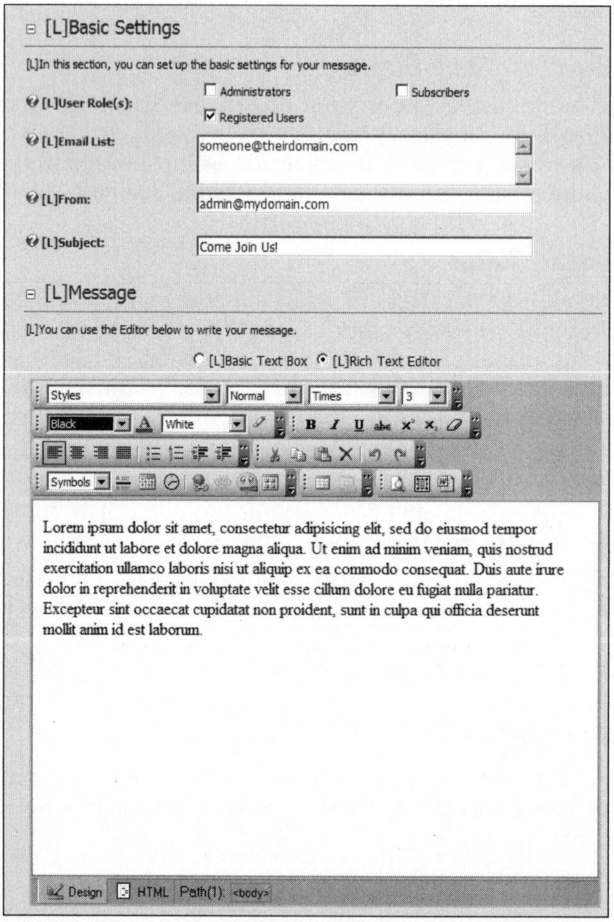

Figure 7-8:
Sending a
newsletter
by using the
Newsletters
module.

2. **In the User Role(s) area, select each role that you want to send a message to.**

   If someone belongs to more than one security role, they will still only receive one newsletter. Skip this step if you only want to send the newsletter to individual e-mail addresses rather than to security roles.

3. **Enter any e-mail addresses that you want to send the e-mail to in the Email List field.**

   Skip this step if you only want to send the newsletter to the security roles selected in Step 2.

4. **Enter a subject for the e-mail in the Subject field.**

5. **Enter your message in the Rich Text Editor, which is selected by default.**

   You can add images, links, and format your text as usual.

6. **Expand the Advanced Settings section.**

7. **(Optional.) Select an attachment in the Attachment drop-down list. If you don't see a file you want to attach, you can select Upload New File and then select it from the drop-down list.**

   This field displays all the files in your File Manager and lets you add new files. You can only attach one file to the newsletter. If you want to send more than one file, zip them into one file first.

8. **Select a Send Method from the drop-down box.**

   This field lets you change the way the e-mail is sent. The To: One Message Per E-mail address (Personalized) option is selected by default. This option sends one e-mail to each person and adds the word Dear followed by their first and last name to the beginning of the e-mail.

   For any individual e-mail addresses entered at Step 3, the To option adds their e-mail address to the beginning of the newsletter because their first and last name isn't known. (For example, Dear `lorraine@domain.com`.)

   The second option is the Bcc: One E-mail to Blind Distribution List (Not Personalized) option. This option adds all the e-mail addresses to a blind distribution list. This option doesn't personalize the e-mail, meaning it will not make each outgoing e-mail unique to the person receiving it. This option requires a lot less bandwidth and processing because it only creates one e-mail. Consider this option if you are sending to lots of people.

9. Click Send E-mail.

A Message Sent message is displayed at the top of the Newsletter module. This lets you know that processing and sending of the newsletter has started. DNN batches the e-mails into small groups and sends one group at a time. This means it won't try to send a thousand e-mails all at once and overload your e-mail system. When the sending is complete, the Administrator receives a Bulk E-mail Confirmation e-mail message, shown in Figure 7-9, that details when the newsletters began and finished sending, how many people the e-mail was sent to, and how many messages were sent.

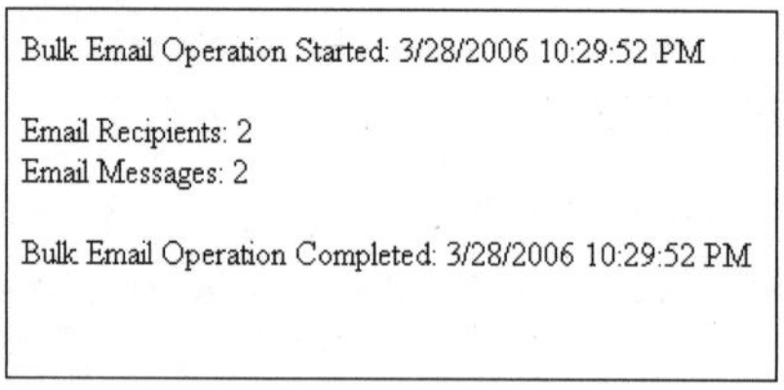

Figure 7-9:
The Administrator receives an e-mail reporting on the sent Newsletter.

Bulk Email Operation Started: 3/28/2006 10:29:52 PM

Email Recipients: 2
Email Messages: 2

Bulk Email Operation Completed: 3/28/2006 10:29:52 PM

Chapter 8

Collaborating and Selling with DNN

In This Chapter

▶ Showcase and share with the Repository module

▶ Sell it with the Store module

▶ Collaborate with Wiki

*I*n this chapter, we cover how to use more of the standard DNN modules. The first two modules detailed in this chapter are Repository and Store. Both are included with your DNN installation. The third module covered here is the Wiki module, which isn't included with your DNN installation but is available for free download from the DotNetNuke Web site. If any of these modules are not displayed in the module drop-down list on the Control Panel, you or your host will need to install them. See Chapter 3 for more on installing modules.

Showcase and Share with the Repository Module

The Repository is a very flexible module that has a number of unique uses. Some of the ways in which you might use the Repository are to store and display a list of documents; as a Web site directory of your favorite sites; or as an image library where users can upload and share images with each other. The Repository module also has an optional companion module called the Repository Dashboard. This module can be set a number of different ways to display links to repository categories and files.

A common use of the Repository module, shown in Figure 8-1, is to manage the upload and storage of a range of file types. A detailed listing of each item is displayed in the module, or users can filter items by category or search for an item. Each item can display all or some of this information: an image of the file, a URL, a description of the file, the size of the file, the number of times the file has been downloaded, the date and time when the item was uploaded or last edited, and the name and e-mail address of the person who uploaded it.

The Repository module is designed to be used as a community module whereby your Web site users can participate at different levels to maintain and access the content. Depending on the rights assigned by Administrators, users can upload files, moderate newly uploaded files, download files, rate files, and add comments and ratings to the item.

Repository skins control the type of information managed by each Repository module. Changing the repository skin can change it from a simple blog to a media library in moments.

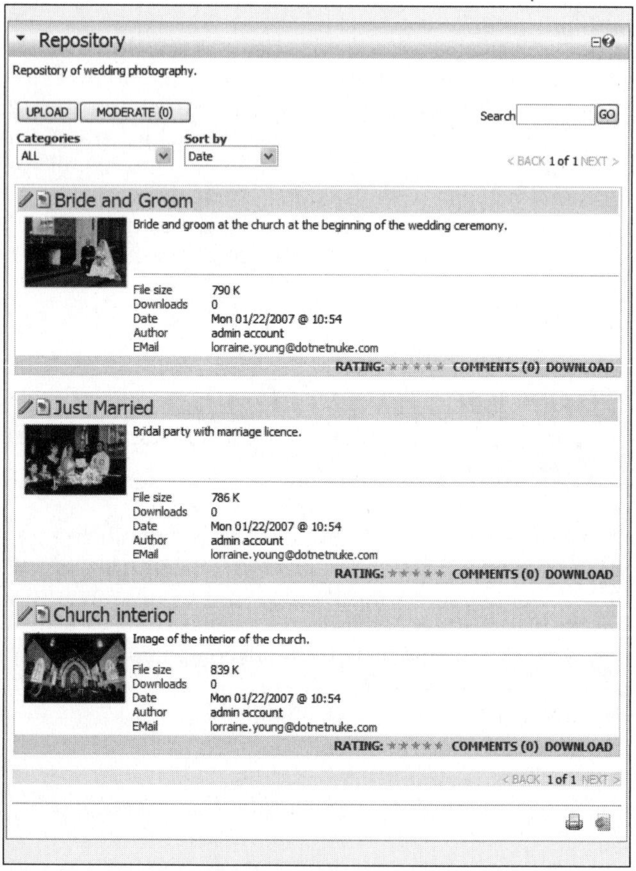

Repository ☐❷

Repository of wedding photography.

[UPLOAD] [MODERATE (0)]   Search [_____] [GO]

Categories   **Sort by**
[ALL ▾]   [Date ▾]   ‹ BACK **1 of 1** NEXT ›

✏🖻 Bride and Groom

Bride and groom at the church at the beginning of the wedding ceremony.

File size	790 K
Downloads	0
Date	Mon 01/22/2007 @ 10:54
Author	admin account
EMail	lorraine.young@dotnetnuke.com

RATING: ☆ ☆ ☆ ☆ ☆   COMMENTS (0)   DOWNLOAD

✏🖻 Just Married

Bridal party with marriage licence.

File size	786 K
Downloads	0
Date	Mon 01/22/2007 @ 10:54
Author	admin account
EMail	lorraine.young@dotnetnuke.com

RATING: ☆ ☆ ☆ ☆ ☆   COMMENTS (0)   DOWNLOAD

✏🖻 Church interior

Image of the interior of the church.

File size	839 K
Downloads	0
Date	Mon 01/22/2007 @ 10:54
Author	admin account
EMail	lorraine.young@dotnetnuke.com

RATING: ☆ ☆ ☆ ☆ ☆   COMMENTS (0)   DOWNLOAD

‹ BACK **1 of 1** NEXT ›

🖨 📧

Figure 8-1:
The Repository module with the Default skin.

The skin that controls the purpose of the Repository module is different from the container applied to the module or the skin applied to the page. Repository skins are specially developed for this module and are not managed by using the Admin Skins area. The skin applied to the Repository module is set under the Repository Settings section on the Module Settings page of the module. A number of skins are provided with the Repository module, each creating a different layout and displaying different information.

Setting Up the Repository

All administrative settings for the Repository module are managed from the module menu. Here you are able to configure the page layout of the module, the repository skin, and security role access to perform tasks such as file upload and moderation. You can also add new categories that people can use to filter items.

The fastest setup this side of Texas

To achieve a basic setup for the Repository module, you only have to set a couple of fields and it's ready to go. This setup creates a Repository that permits Administrators to upload files and permits anyone who can view the module to download it.

Here's how to set up a basic repository module:

1. **Select Settings from the module menu.**

   This takes you to the Module Settings page. Go to the last section called Repository Settings.

2. **Click the Maximize button to open the Repository Settings section.**

   This section enables you to set and modify the settings and Repository skin for this module.

3. **Enter a description of the module in the Rich Text Editor (RTE) below Repository Description.**

   The description appears between the module title and any files added to the Repository. Choose a description that best describes the content you will be adding to the module. (For example: "Feel free to browse our photo gallery and download any of our royalty-free photographs. You can also add your own photos to our gallery by clicking the Upload button below.")

4. **Go to the Security Roles setting and select the All Users check box below Download Roles.**

   This enables everyone who is able to view the module to download files.

5. **Below the No Image field, select or upload a default image by using the Link Type tool.**

   Depending on the repository skin selected, items added to the repository may display an image. If you don't upload an image when adding the item, the image selected here will be used.

6. **Click the Update link.**

   You have created a basic Repository where Administrators can upload and manage files and all users can download files.

Adding more categories

The Repository has a drop-down box that lets people filter items by categories, making it easy for them to browse through the listed items. The Repository comes with only one default category called All, so you have the task of adding others to suit your needs.

1. **Select Settings from the module menu.**

   This takes you to the Module Settings page. Go to the Repository Settings.

2. **Click the Maximize button to open the Repository Settings section.**

   This section enables you to set and modify the settings and Repository skin for this module.

3. **Enter a name for the category into the text box below the Categories field.**

4. **Click the Add Category link.**

   The new category is now added to the list of categories in the below box. Repeat Steps 3 and 4 to add more categories. When you are finished, either click the Cancel link below or navigate back to the page.

An All category is created by default. You can delete or edit the All category; however, you must always have at least one category in the list. If you delete all the categories, a new All category is created automatically.

You can also change the order in which the categories are displayed by selecting a category and using the up- and down-arrow icons to move it. If no categories are selected when a file is uploaded, it will automatically be assigned to the first category in the category list.

Setting the unique Repository security roles

The Repository has been designed with community participation in mind, so a variety of additional security settings are available to enable users to participate at different levels.

Earlier in this chapter (see "The fastest setup this side of Texas"), we create a basic security scheme where only Administrators can upload and maintain files, but where all users can view and download files. There are, however, five different security roles specific to the Repository.

Here's how to set the Repository security role access:

1. **Select Settings from the module menu.**

   This takes you to the Module Settings page.

2. **In the Basic Settings section under Module Settings, set the View Module Permissions for the module.**

   Under View Module, you can set which roles will be able to see the module. Do not change the Edit Module settings, as they are managed at Step 4 below.

3. **Click the Maximize button to open the Repository Settings section.**

4. **At Security Roles, select the DNN security roles assigned to the Repository roles. You can allow either All Users, Administrators, Registered Users, or Subscribers access to each role.**

   Here is a summary of each repository role:

   • **Moderation Roles:** Members of this role are able to moderate (that is, approve or reject) new items. See "Moderating new items" later in this chapter for details on how to moderate.

   • **Download Roles:** Members of this role are able to download files by clicking the Download button.

   • **Upload Roles:** Members of this role are able to upload new items by clicking the Upload button.

   • **Rating Roles:** Members of this role are able to rate files by clicking on the rating bar.

   • **Comment Roles:** Members of this role are able to add comments to a listing by clicking the Upload button.

5. **At View User Comments, select who can view comments added to listings.**

   Choose between All Users, which lets anyone who can view the Repository also view any comments, or Authorized Users Only, which only allows those set at Comment Roles in Step 4 to view comments.

6. **At View User Ratings, select who can view ratings given to listings.**

   Choose between All Users, which lets anyone who can view the Repository also view the ratings, or Authorized Users Only, which only allows those set at Rating Roles in Step 4 to view ratings.

7. **Click the <u>Update</u> link.**

The Administrator role is mandatory for all Repository security roles. If you deselect Administrators for any role, it will be automatically reselected when you update your settings.

Changing the Function of the Repository

The default skin for the Repository, (refer to Figure 8-1), lets people view and download files, as well as rate and comment on each listing. But the Repository can be used for endless purposes, depending on the skin applied to the module.

Setting the skin

You can change the skin applied to the Repository at any time; however, it is best to choose the purpose of your Repository and apply the best skin before you begin adding files. Each skin gives you different fields to complete when adding listings, so choosing a skin before you start ensures that the content remains relevant to the skin. The FileList skin, shown in Figure 8-2, transforms the Repository into a compact list of download files.

Here is how to set a skin:

1. **Select Settings from the module menu.**

   This takes you to the Module Settings page of this module.

2. **Click the Maximize button to open the Repository Settings section.**

3. **Select a skin from the Repository Skin drop-down box.**

   Listings are sorted by the selected field in the Repository.

4. **Click the <u>Update</u> link.**

   You are now returned to the Repository and the new skin is applied.

There are two types of Repository skins: global and portal. Global skins are stored in the \DesktopModules\Repository\Templates folder of your Web site and are available to all Repository modules on all portals that are on your Web site.

Portal skins are stored in the \Portals\#\RepositoryTemplates folder and are only available to Repository modules that are on pages for that particular child portal number.

Both global and portal skins are included in the Repository Skins drop-down box; however, portal skins are prefixed with an asterisk for identification.

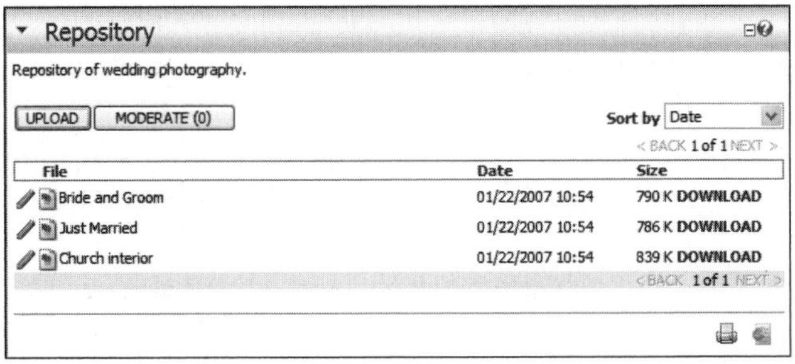

Figure 8-2:
The FileList skin transforms the Repository into a compact list of download files.

File	Date	Size
Bride and Groom	01/22/2007 10:54	790 K DOWNLOAD
Just Married	01/22/2007 10:54	786 K DOWNLOAD
Church interior	01/22/2007 10:54	839 K DOWNLOAD

Repository of wedding photography.

UPLOAD MODERATE (0) Sort by Date

< BACK 1 of 1 NEXT >

< BACK 1 of 1 NEXT >

Choosing a skin to suit

At the time of writing, twelve different skins were included with the Repository. Each skin provides a different layout, has different fields, and changes the purpose of the Repository.

Here is a summary of these different skins:

- **Articles:** Transforms the Repository into an article list. Each listing requires an article title, categories, a downloadable version of the article, a summary of the article and the article text. Displaying a picture of the author and her e-mail address are optional. The date and time when an entry was last updated is automatically displayed on each listing, as is the name of the user who uploaded the item. Comments and Ratings can be added.

- **Blog:** Transforms the Repository into a simple blog, as shown in Figure 8-3. Each entry requires a subject title, a category, and blog text. The date and time when an entry was last updated is automatically displayed on each listing. Displaying the blogger's e-mail address is optional. Comments can be added.

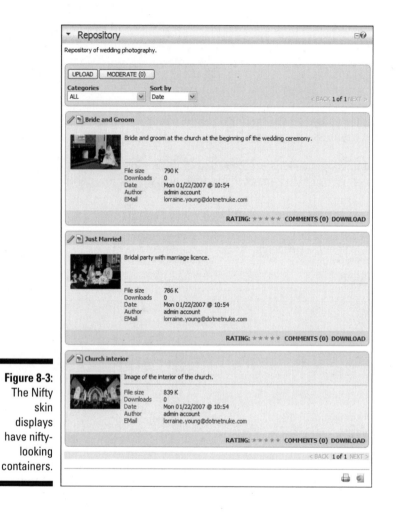

Figure 8-3:
The Nifty
skin
displays
have nifty-
looking
containers.

✔ **Business Cards:** Transforms the Repository into a Business Card directory. Each entry requires the company name, company logo, categories, optional attributes, company address and other contact details, and a company tagline. The date when an entry was last updated is automatically displayed on each listing. This skin also works well as a contacts list if you change the logo to a person's photograph.

✔ **Default:** The default skin, (refer to Figure 8-1), is a file repository. Each listing requires a title, a file to download, an image, categories, optional attributes, and a description of the file. Each listing automatically displays the name of the user who uploaded the item, the file size, and the date and time when the item was last updated, as well as the number of times the file has been downloaded. Ratings and comments can be added.

- ✔ **Directory:** Transforms the Repository into a Web site resource directory. This skin can also be used as a compact alternative to the default skin. Each listing requires a title, the resource URL (for example, `www.domain.com/sample.doc`), categories, and a description of the URL. An image can be added, but it is not displayed. Each listing displays the title, number of hits, date and time the listing was last updated, description, and a <u>Visit</u> link which opens the resource URL in a new browser.

- ✔ **File List:** Transforms the Repository into a basic and file list. This skin displays items in the most compact format of all skins and each listing is only a single line. Listings consist of only the file title, date and time it was last updated, the file size, and a link to download the file. No images or icons are displayed. Comments and ratings are not available.

- ✔ **Nifty:** This skin offers the same information as the default skin, but it has a "nifty" layout and design. (Well, somebody thinks it's nifty, anyway.)

- ✔ **Nifty Toggle:** This skin offers the same information as the default skin and the same layout and design as the Nifty skin. The difference is that a Show Details button is displayed rather than the description. Clicking on the button displays the description. This is handy when the descriptions are long as it keeps the page compact.

- ✔ **Portfolio:** Transforms the Repository into an images or photo gallery. Each listing requires a title, image, categories, and a description of the image. Listing automatically displays the date and time when the item was last updated. Ratings and comments are available.

- ✔ **Slides:** Transform the Repository into a photo gallery, as shown in Figure 8-4. This skin has a crisp design and each image is displayed as a slide. Each listing requires a title, image, categories, optional attributes, name and e-mail address of the person who uploaded the image, and a description of the file. Listings automatically display the date and time the image was last updated and a copyright notice. Ratings and comments are available.

- ✔ **Video Library:** Transform the Repository into a video library. Each listing requires a title, URL to the Video, a splash image, categories, and a description. Listings automatically display the file size and the date and time the entry was last updated. Ratings and comments can be added.

Create custom attributes in the same way you create categories. An attributes field is provided on several of the skins; however, these attributes are not displayed on any of them. If you want to display custom attributes, you need to have a custom skin created. To find out how to create new Repository skins or add attributes to existing Repository skins, go to the Repository Project page on the DotNetNuke Web site (`www.dotnetnuke.com/DotNetNuke Projects/ModuleRepository/tabid/830/Default.aspx`). Click the <u>Project Downloads</u> link and download the latest users' guide.

Figure 8-4:
The Slides
skin trans-
forms the
Repository
into a photo
gallery.

Changing the page layout

The Administrator can modify the layout of Repository pages by changing
the default sort order of listings, the number of listings per page, and a
default image to be displayed when one isn't uploaded to the listing.

Here's how to change the page layout:

1. **Select Settings from the module menu.**

   This takes you to the Module Settings page of this module.

2. **Click the Maximize button to open the Repository Settings section.**

3. **Select an option from the Default Sort drop-down box.**

   Choose the field that you want listings to be sorted by when displayed in the Repository. Choose from Date, Downloads, User Rating, Title, or Author Name.

4. **Change the number in the Enter the Number Of Items Per Page text box.**

   This setting controls the number of items displayed on each page. Next and Back links are displayed above and below listings to enable people to access other listings. You might like to change the number of items per page according to the Skin selected. For example, if you are using the FileList skin, each listing is only one line; therefore, it would be reasonable to display up to 20 items per page.

   RATING: ★★★★★
   RATING: ▬▬▬▬▬▬▭▭▭▭

5. **Select an option from the Image Set To Use for Ratings drop-down box.**

   Choose Default to display a five-star rating scale or Dashes to display a ten-bar rating scale.

6. **Click the Update link.**

   You are now returned to the Repository and your changes are applied.

Working with Repository Files

After you have set up the Repository, you can begin adding files. File upload is available to members of any security roles selected as Upload Roles under Repository Settings. See "Setting the unique Repository security roles" to find out how to set File Upload roles. Note that the fields to be completed vary, depending on the skin.

Here is how to upload a file and add a new listing for the Default skin:

UPLOAD

1. **Click the Upload button.**

   This takes you to the Upload a File page, as shown in Figure 8-5.

2. **Enter a title into the Title text box.**

   The title will be the name of the listing.

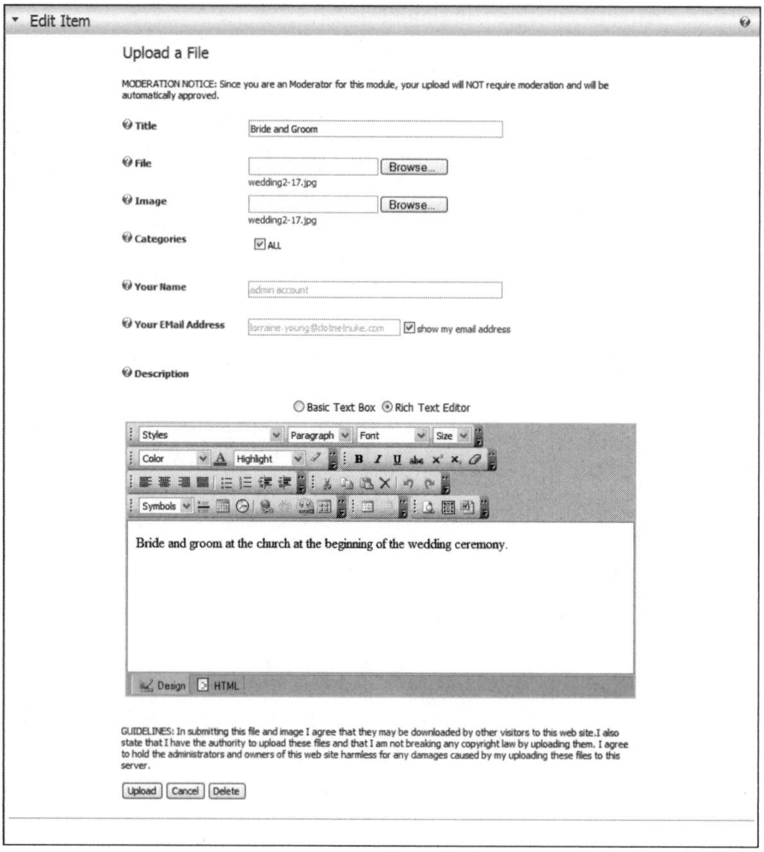

Figure 8-5:
The
Repository
file upload
page for
the Default
skin. The
fields vary,
depending
on the skin
used.

3. **Click the Browse button beside File and select the file from your computer.**

   This is the download file associated with this item.

4. **Click the Browse button beside Image and select an image.**

   This is the image is displayed for this listing. If you don't choose an image, the default image is displayed instead; see "The fastest setup this side of Texas" for more information.

5. **Select one or more Categories.**

   Select each category this listing should be listed under. You must select the All category if you want it to be listed under All.

6. **Deselect the Show My Email Address check box beside the E-Mail Address fields to hide your e-mail address.**

This option allows the uploader to request that his or her e-mail address not be displayed. The Your Name and Your EMail Address fields are prefilled with your details. When All Users can upload files and the user isn't logged in to the Web Site, these fields are blank and will need to be completed.

7. **Enter a description into the RTE Description field.**

   The description is displayed on the listing for this skin.

8. **Click the Upload button.**

   As an Administrator, you are automatically a member of the Moderation role, so the listing is added to the Repository.

If the uploader isn't a member of the Moderation role, the item is added to moderation queue. See "Setting the unique Repository security roles" to find out how to set Moderation roles. After the upload is approved the uploader is e-mailed a message confirming that the item is approved. See "Moderating new items" to find out how to moderate unapproved items.

If you are having problems uploading a file, check the maximum size of file uploads and verify with your host which file types can be uploaded.

Editing and deleting items

Administrators can edit any item uploaded to the Repository. Other users who are authorized to upload items can edit only the items that they uploaded and can't edit other people's uploads.

Here's how to edit or delete an item:

To access the page where you can edit or delete a listing, click on the Edit button located in the top left corner of any listing.

1. **Locate the item to be edited or deleted.**

   Use Categories or search if required.

2. **Click the Edit button beside the item.**

   This displays the Edit Item page for this item.

3. **Edit the item if required and click the Upload button; alternatively, click the Delete button and then OK to delete the item.**

Downloading a file

Files can be downloaded by members of any security roles selected in the Download Roles setting. See "Setting the unique Repository security roles" to find out how to set File Download roles.

To download a file, click the Download button or link for that item.

Searching the Repository

No setup is required for the search tool, which is available to all users with View Module permissions.

To search for a listing, enter all or part of the title of the listing, a word in the description, the author's name or the author's e-mail address. For example, searching on the word *Richard* also returns results for the words *Richards* and *Richardson*.

Moderating new items

Moderation is an approval process for new items. Moderation is available to any security roles selected in the Moderation Roles setting. See "Setting the unique Repository security roles" to find out how to set Moderation roles.

Here's how to moderate an upload:

1. **Click the Moderate button.**

   The number of uploads awaiting moderation is displayed on the Moderate button.

2. **Click the <u>View File</u> link to view a file to be moderated.**

   Open the file to view it. If the file is an image, you can either skip this step or click on the thumbnail of the image to view a larger image.

3. **Click either the <u>Approve</u> or the <u>Reject</u> Link.**

   If you choose to approve the item, it is added to the Repository and a confirmation notice is sent to the author. If you choose to reject the item, a text box is displayed that enables you to compose and send a rejection note to the author.

Adding a comment to an item

Many Repository skins enable people to add comments to items and read other people's comments. See "Setting the unique Repository security roles" to find out how to set the comment roles.

Here's how to add a comment to an item:

1. **Click the <u>Comments (0)</u> link.**

   In the default skin, this is located in the bottom-right corner of each listing. This displays any existing comments and provides a text box to add your comments.

2. **Enter a comment into the Your Comment text box and click the Post Your Comments button.**

   Your comment is added to the item and can be viewed by clicking on the <u>Comments</u> link again. Note that the number of comments for that item increases accordingly. For example, the link now reads <u>Comments (1)</u>.

Viewing, editing, and deleting comments

Administrators can edit or delete any comment; however, other users can only edit or delete their own comments.

Here's how to view, edit, or delete a comment:

1. **Click the <u>Comments (1)</u> link.**

   You can now view any existing comments.

2. **Click the Edit button beside a comment to edit or delete it.**

   This displays the comment for editing or deleting.

3. **Edit the comment and click Update to save your changes or Delete to delete the comment.**

   You are now returned to the Repository.

Rating files

Most Repository skins enable people to add ratings to items and see the average rating. See "Setting the unique Repository security roles" to find out how to set the rating roles.

Here's how to add a rating to an item:

1. **Click on the stars or dashes located between Rating and Comments.**

   This displays the number of votes cast for this item and the average rating. You are also provided with a series of radio buttons to add your rating.

2. **Select a radio button to rate the item and click the Post Your Rating button.**

   Your rating is added to the running total and the rating image changes to display the new total. Ratings cannot be edited; however, you can add more than one rating per item to change the results.

TIP

See "Changing the page layout" earlier in this chapter to find out how to change the five-star rating scale to a ten-bar rating scale.

Displaying quick links by using the dashboard

The Repository module has a companion module called the Repository Dashboard module. This module can display different information relating to the Repository module such as a list of categories, the latest uploads, the top downloads, and the top rated item.

Here's how to set up the Repository Dashboard module:

1. **Add the Repository Dashboard module to a page.**

   You can add the dashboard to any page on your Web site.

2. **Select Settings from the module menu.**

   This displays the Module Settings page of this module.

3. **Select the page/title of a Repository module from the Select Repository drop-down box.**

   This setting lets you select which Repository module on your Web site you want this dashboard to be associated with.

4. **Choose a radio button to set the information to be displayed from the Dashboard Module field. Your options are**

   • **Categories (single-column):** Display the categories in a single column of links

   • **Categories (multi-column):** Display the categories in multiple columns of links

- **Latest Uploads:** Displays links to the latest uploads
- **Top Downloads:** Displays links to the most frequently downloaded items
- **Top Rated:** Display links to items with the highest ratings

5. **Enter a number to set the maximum number of links for non-category modes into the Indicate the Number of Items to Be Displayed text box.**

   For example, enter **10** to display ten links. Category modes will ignore any value entered here.

6. **Click the <u>Update</u> link.**

   This returns you to the page, and the dashboard now displays your selection. You can add multiple dashboards for each repository.

Selling Stuff with a Store

One of the greatest benefits of having a Web site is the ability to create an online marketplace where people can browse and buy your wares 24 hours a day. Online stores are cheap to set up, cheap to run, and they give you a global presence that would be difficult to achieve with a physical shop at your local mall.

The DNN Store consists of five modules that work together to create a full online shopping experience. Your Web site visitors can browse your products, add them to a virtual shopping cart, and purchase them by using a secure online payment gateway. Administrators can manage products, manage product reviews, and manage customer orders as well as provide authorized roles with the ability to also manage products. In the upcoming section, we describe each of the five Store modules.

The Store Menu (Categories) module

The Store Menu module (which is titled Categories after you add it to a page, so that's what we call it in this chapter) enables customers to browse products by selecting a category. This module works with the Catalog module, which displays the description of the selected category and its products.

Categories can be managed by using either this module or the Store Admin module. Administrators, and other authorized roles, can add, edit, archive, and delete categories by using the Categories module menu. See Figure 8-6 to check out the Categories module in action.

The Store Catalog module

The Store Catalog module (which is titled Catalog after you add it to a page, so that's what we call it in this chapter) displays results from the Categories module. When a category is selected, the Catalog module displays the category description and a summary listing of all products within the selected category. Each listing includes a linked product title that goes to a detailed product description, and an <u>Add to Cart</u> link. Look at Figure 8-6 to see the Catalog module in action.

The Store Mini Cart module

The Store Mini Cart module displays a brief listing of any products in a customer's cart. This module provides customers with quick way of seeing how many products they have added to their cart and the total cost. Customers can adjust product quantities or delete items from their cart. A View Cart Details link takes customers to the Store Account module, which provides a detailed view of their shopping cart. See Figure 8-6 to see the Store Mini Cart module in action.

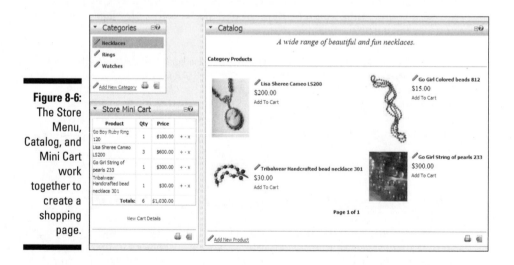

Figure 8-6:
The Store Menu, Catalog, and Mini Cart work together to create a shopping page.

The Store Account module

The Store Account module, shown in Figure 8-7, provides each customer with a place to manage their shopping account. The module consists of three screens: Customer Cart, Profile, and Order History. Customer Cart is the default screen, which enables customers to manage any products in their shopping cart. This screen includes a <u>Checkout</u> link, enabling the customer to proceed to the Checkout to complete their order. The Profile screen lets customers add and manage their shipping and billing addresses. The Order History screen enables customers to view details of their previous orders.

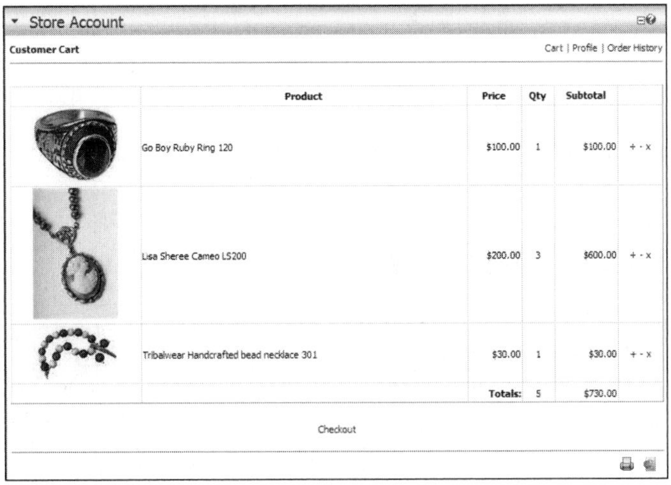

Figure 8-7:
The Store
Account
module
shows
customers
what's in
their cart. It
also enables
customers
to manage
their
addresses
and view
previous
orders.

▼ Store Account						
Customer Cart				Cart | Profile | Order History		
	Product		**Price**	**Qty**	**Subtotal**	
	Go Boy Ruby Ring 120		$100.00	1	$100.00	+ - x
	Lisa Sheree Cameo LS200		$200.00	3	$600.00	+ - x
	Tribalwear Handcrafted bead necklace 301		$30.00	1	$30.00	+ - x
			Totals:	5	$730.00	
	Checkout					

The Store Admin module

The Store Admin module enables Administrators to configure and manage all store settings. The module has five administrative sections: Store Info, Categories, Product, Customers, and Reviews. The Store Info section is required to configure the store and includes setup of your preferred payment gateway. The Store Info section is shown in Figure 8-8. The Categories and Products sections manages adding, editing, archiving, and deletion of categories and products. The Customer section displays a list of existing store customers and a summary of their previous orders. The Reviews section manages the approval, editing, and deletion of customer reviews.

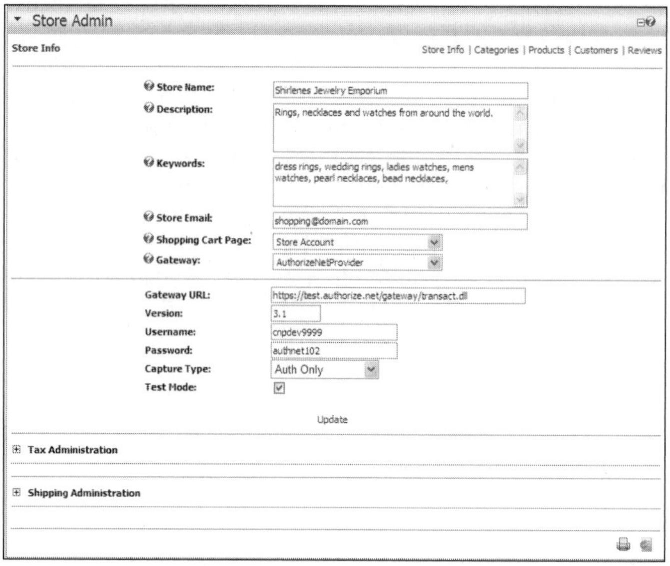

Figure 8-8:
The Store
Admin
page lets
Administrat-
ors set up
the store
and manage
categories,
products,
orders, and
reviews.

Laying Out Your Store

The Store modules must be arranged on different pages and have different
security roles set to create a shopping experience. As is typical with DNN,
you have full control over which security roles can view pages and modules.
The following example shows how to set up a store that lets all visitors
browse and select products before registering or logging in to their account.

Creating the Store page

Here's how to set up the page where customers come to browse and buy:

1. **Add a page titled Store.**

   At Permissions for View Page, select All Users.

2. **Add the Store Menu (Categories) module to the Store page.**

   Use all the default options when adding the module. This module looks
   good in either the left or right pane.

3. **Add the Store Catalog (Catalog) module to the Store page.**

   Use all the default options when adding the module.

4. **Add the Store Mini Cart module to the Store page.**

   Use all the default options when adding the module. This module looks good in either the left or right pane or below the Catalog.

   The setup of the Store page is now complete. Refer to Figure 8-8 for an example of the Store page with categories and products.

Creating the Store Account page

Here's how to set up a page where customers can review their current order, manage their profile, and view their order history:

1. **Add a page titled Store Account.**

   At Permissions for View Page, select All Users. This enables visitors who have been browsing and adding items to their Mini Cart to view more details about what's in their cart before they need to create an account.

2. **Add the Store Account module to the Store Account page.**

   Use all the default options when adding the module. The setup of your Store Account page is now complete.

Creating the Store Admin page

Here's how to set up the Store Administration module:

1. **Add a page titled Store Admin.**

   This is an administration-only page, so use the default page Permissions settings.

2. **Add the Store Admin module to the Store Admin page.**

   Use all the default options when adding the module. Your Store Admin page is now ready to be configured. See "Configuring the Store Admin Module" later in this chapter for details.

Choosing a Payment Provider

Before you can begin selling your products online, you need a method of receiving payment for your goods. DNN Store has been integrated with two well-known payment processing companies: PayPal and AuthorizeNet. Both companies can provide you with an account that enables your store to accept credit card payments and have these funds paid into an account.

Both of these companies provide an immediate and low-cost solution to processing online transactions. Visit the Web sites for both companies (at www.paypay.com and www.authorizenet.com) to see which company best suits your requirements. After you have made your choice, sign up for an account with your preferred company. Your account details are required before you can complete your Store Admin configuration.

AuthorizeNet provides a free test account service, which enables you to test out the full customer experience of buying from your store. I suggest you create a test account and use these details for the Gateway Provider setting until you are ready to go live with your Store.

Configuring the Store Admin Module

To configure the Store Admin module, you first have to complete the Store Info page:

1. **Go to the Store Admin page.**

   The Store Info page of the Store Admin module is displayed.

2. **Complete the Store Name, Description, and Keywords fields.**

   These fields are used to identify your store in search engines.

3. **Enter an e-mail address for the store into the Store Email text box.**

   This field is used as the e-mail address used by the store.

4. **Select Store Account as the Shopping Cart Page.**

   This field must be set to go to the page where the Store Account module is added.

5. **Select the Update link.**

   The Store setup is almost complete. The final step is to select and set your payment gateway.

Setting the payment gateway as PayPal

You must have a current PayPal account to complete this step. Make sure your account details are handy.

Here is how to complete the payment gateway settings for PayPal:

1. **Go to the Store Admin page.**

   The Store Info page is displayed.

2. **Select PayPal Provider from the Gateway drop-down box.**

   This displays the required PayPal fields.

3. **Enter the e-mail address in the PayPal ID field.**

   This is the e-mail address you used when you created your PayPal account.

4. **Enter your store name into the Cart Name text box.**

   This is the store name you entered in the first field on this page.

5. **Leave the Button URL field as it is.**

   This field contains the URL to the PayPal Buy Now button. You can check out the button by pasting the address into a new browser. If you want to use your own button, enter the URL in this field.

6. **Leave the Currency Type as USD.**

   This sets the currency of your store as U.S. dollars (USD). Although PayPal accepts money of different currencies, your Store will receive and process its funds as U.S. dollars.

7. **Click the <u>Update</u> link.**

   Your store is now ready to receive online payments.

Setting the payment gateway as AuthorizeNet

You must have a current AuthorizeNet account to complete this step. Make sure your account details are handy.

Here is how to complete the payment gateway settings for AuthorizeNet:

1. **Go to the Store Admin page.**

   The Store Info page is displayed.

2. **Select AuthorizeNetProvider from the Gateway drop-down box.**

   This displays the required AuthorizeNet fields.

3. **Enter the Transaction POST URL into the Gateway URL text box.**

   This URL is supplied by AuthorizeNet when you sign up.

4. **Enter 3.1 in the Version text box.**

   This is the latest version of AuthorizeNet.

5. **Enter your Login ID in the Username text box.**

   AuthorizeNet supplies the Login ID when you sign up.

6. **Enter your password in the Password text box.**

   AuthorizeNet supplies a password when you sign up.

7. **Select Auth and Capture in the Capture Type drop-down box.**

   This sets the transaction type for the Store. Authorize and Capture (Auth and Capture) sends a request to authorize and receive the funds for a purchase.

   The second option, Authorization Only (Auth Only), sends a request to authorize funds, but doesn't put the money into your account. AuthorizeNet provides this as an alternative method so that you can upload and process a large batch of mail order/telephone order (MOTO) sales. See Virtual Terminal/Batch Upload on the AuthorizeNet Web site (www.authorizenet.com) if you are interested in finding out more about this.

8. **Select the Test Mode check box if you want to test receiving payments before launching the store to the pubic.**

   AuthorizeNet enables you to test your Store before you begin to accept real transactions. You will need to deselect this option when you are ready to go live.

9. **Click the <u>Update</u> link.**

   Your store is now configured to receive online payments.

You must go back and deselect the Test Mode check box that you selected in Step 8 and then update the page before you can start accepting real transactions from customers.

Adding tax rates for each state

The store enables you to add a different taxation rate for each U.S. state. The tax rate is added to the Item Price of each product and is displayed to the customer when they go to their cart. The amount of taxation paid is also displayed on the confirmation e-mail sent to the customer when they complete an order.

Squishing bugs

At the time of writing, the Store Admin module contained a minor bug. It won't cause any real problems, but it is a bit frustrating. The bug causes the Shipping Fee value to incorrectly be saved as 0, rather than in the required format of 0.00.

This bug means that you have to readd the zeros to the end of the shipping fee each time you click the Categories, Products, Customers, or Review links on the Store Info page, or update the tax rates. To reduce the need to do this, you may prefer to use the Category and Catalog module menus to manage these items.

Here's how to work around this bug:

1. Whenever you see a warning box that says "The shipping fee must be in the format #.##", click OK on the warning box.

2. Click the Maximize button beside the Shipping Administration section.

   This displays the shipping fee for an order.

3. Enter 0.00 into the Shipping Fee text box.

   You can now continue with the task.

Here's how to set your taxation rates:

1. **Go to the Store Admin page.**

   The Store Info page is displayed.

2. **Click the Maximize button beside the Tax Administration section.**

   This displays an abbreviation of each tax code and the rate applied for that state. For example, the first box is AL for Alabama. The box below it displays the current tax rate for Alabama. The default value for each state is zero (0.00).

3. **Edit the tax rate for each state as required.**

   Tax rates are displayed as a percentage of 1.00, where 1.00 equals 100% tax. For example, to set the tax rate for Alabama to 10%, change the value in the text box below the AL text box to 0.10. Values of 1 or more are not accepted.

4. **Click the Update Tax Rates link.**

   The tax rates are now updated.

Adding a shipping fee

The Store provides you with an option to charge a shipping fee that is a percentage of the total order. Here is how to add your shipping fee:

1. **Go to the Store Admin page.**

   The Store Info page is displayed.

2. **Click the Maximize button beside the Shipping Administration section.**

   This displays the current shipping fee. The default setting is zero (0.00).

3. **Enter the shipping fee.**

   Shipping fees are displayed as a percentage of 1.00, where 1.00 equals a 100% shipping fee. For example, to add a shipping fee of 10%, change the value to 0.10. Values greater than 1 are not accepted.

4. **Click the <u>Update Shipping Fee</u> link.**

   The shipping fee is now updated.

Adding Products to the Store

Administrators handle product management by using the Store Admin module.

You can enable roles other than Administrators to add products by giving them Edit Module permissions to the Catalog module. This lets them manage products without being able to change store settings, or manage reviews and customer accounts. Similarly, you can provide Edit Module permissions on the Categories module to enable roles to manage product categories.

Creating and managing categories

Here's how to add a category:

1. **Go to the Store Admin page.**

   This displays the Store Info page of the Store Admin module.

2. **Click the <u>Categories</u> link.**

   It takes you to the Categories management screen, as shown in Figure 8-9. Any existing categories are listed here.

3. **Click the <u>Add Category</u> link.**

   This takes you to the Add Category screen.

4. **Enter a category name into the Category Name text box.**

   The category name is displayed in the category module to customers to help them browse through your products.

5. Enter a short description into the Description text box.

The category description is not displayed to customers and is for your records only.

6. Leave the Archived check box deselected.

7. Enter category details of the category into the Message text box.

When a customer clicks on a category to view its products, this message is displayed above the products in the Catalog module.

8. Click the <u>Update</u> link.

The new category is now listed on the Categories page of the Store Admin module, as well as in the Categories module. Repeat Steps 3 through 8 to add more categories.

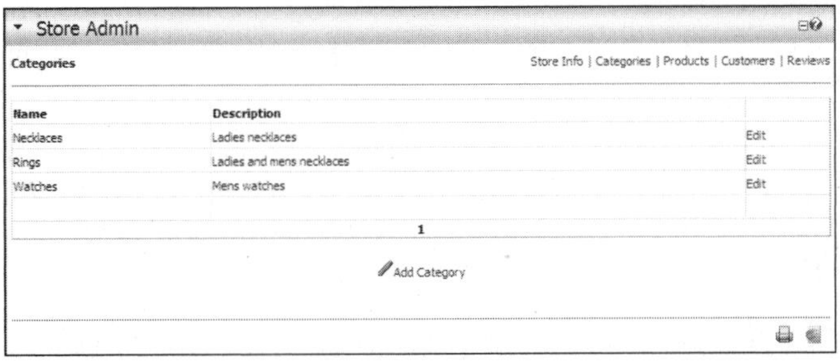

Figure 8-9:
The
Categories
page of the
Store Admin
module.

Here's how to edit a category:

1. Go to the Store Admin page.

This page has the Store Admin module on it.

2. Click the <u>Categories</u> link.

This link is one of five located in the top-right corner of the module. It takes you to the Categories management screen. Any existing categories are listed here.

3. Click the <u>Edit</u> link beside the category to be edited.

This takes you to the Edit Category screen.

4. Edit the category fields as required.

5. Click the <u>Update</u> link.

Archiving a category hides that category from customers in the Categories module. This stops customers from being able to browse any products associated with that category.

Here's how to archive a category:

1. **Go to the Store Admin page.**

2. **Click the <u>Categories</u> link.**

   This takes you to the Categories management screen. Any existing categories are listed here.

3. **Click the <u>Edit</u> link beside the category to be archived.**

   This takes you to the Edit Category screen.

4. **Select the Archived check box.**

   This hides the category and its products from customers, but doesn't delete any of the information. You can remove archiving at any time by deselecting this option.

5. **Click the <u>Update</u> link.**

   The category is no longer displayed to customers on the Categories module.

Deleting a category is permanent. You cannot delete a category that has any products listed in it. If the category to be deleted does have products listed for it, you must first either delete the products or move them to a different category.

Here's how to delete a category:

1. **Go to the Store Admin page.**

2. **Click the <u>Categories</u> link.**

   This takes you to the Categories management screen. All existing categories are listed here.

3. **Click the <u>Edit</u> link beside the category to be deleted.**

   This takes you to the Edit Category screen.

4. **Click the <u>Delete</u> link.**

   A message box appears asking if you are sure you want to delete the item.

5. **Click the OK button to confirm.**

   The category is now deleted.

Creating and managing products

You must add at least one category before you can add products. Each product listing displays an image.

Create a separate folder in your File Manager to keep your store images. If you are enabling roles other than Administrators to add products, remember to give those roles access to view and/or edit the folder. Uploading your product images before you begin adding products saves you time.

Here's how to add a product:

1. **Go to the Store Admin module.**

2. **Click the <u>Products</u> link.**

   This takes you to the Products screen, as shown in Figure 8-10. Any products belonging to the Category displayed in the drop-down box will be listed.

3. **Click the <u>Add Product</u> link.**

4. **Complete the first four fields, which relate to product details.**

   The Manufacturer, Model Name, and Model Number fields are displayed as the summary listing of the product in the Catalog module. This information along with the Summary is displayed on the detailed product page.

5. **Enter the cost of the product into the Unit Price text box.**

   Unit price must be either a whole or a decimal number. The unit price appears both in the summary listing and full listing pages for this product.

6. **Select the product category from the Category drop-down box.**

7. **Don't select the Archived check box.**

8. **Choose if you want to select the Featured check box.**

   Featured products are displayed first in the Featured category, as well as being listed below with all other products. You can change this setting at any time.

9. **Upload and/or select the product image by using the Link Type tool displayed at the Image field.**

   The image is displayed on the detailed listing of the product. The summary listing creates and displays a thumbnail of this image.

10. **Enter a description of the product into the RTE below the Description field.**

    The description is only displayed on the full listing page of this product and not in the summary listing displayed in the Catalog module.

11. **Click the <u>Update</u> link.**

    This returns you to the Products screen of the Store Admin module. The new product is displayed below.

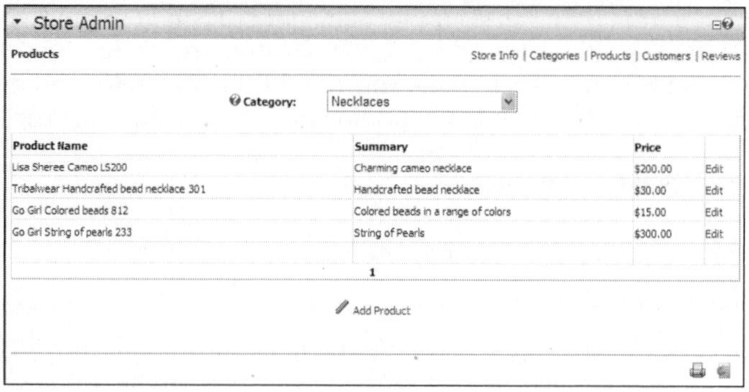

Store Admin

Products   Store Info | Categories | Products | Customers | Reviews

Category: Necklaces

Product Name	Summary	Price	
Lisa Sheree Cameo LS200	Charming cameo necklace	$200.00	Edit
Tribalwear Handcrafted bead necklace 301	Handcrafted bead necklace	$30.00	Edit
Go Girl Colored beads 812	Colored beads in a range of colors	$15.00	Edit
Go Girl String of pearls 233	String of Pearls	$300.00	Edit

1

Add Product

Figure 8-10:
The
Products
page of the
Store Admin
module.

Here's how to view a detailed description of a product:

1. **Click on a category in the Categories module.**

   This displays a summary listing of the products related to this category in the Catalog module.

2. **Click on the product link in the Catalog module.**

   The product link is a combination of the manufacturer, module name, and model name. This link displays the full product details and enables reviews to be added to the product.

Here's how to edit a product:

1. **Go to the Store Admin page.**

2. **Click the <u>Products</u> link.**

   This takes you to the Products screen. Any products belonging to the Category displayed in the drop-down box will be listed.

3. **Select the Category of the product to be edited.**

   This displays the products associated with this category.

4. **Click the <u>Edit</u> link beside the product to be edited.**

5. **Edit the product details as required.**

6. **Click the <u>Update</u> link.**

You are now returned to the Products screen where a summary of the edited product is displayed.

Products can also be edited by using the Catalog module. To delete a product by using the Catalog module, you must first select the relevant category from the Category module.

Deleting a product permanently removes all details of that product from your store.

Here's how to delete a product:

1. **Go to the Store Admin page.**

   The Store Admin page has the Store Admin module on it.

2. **Click the <u>Products</u> link.**

   This takes you to the Products management screen. Any products belonging to the Category displayed in the drop-down box will be listed.

3. **Select the Category of the product to be deleted.**

   This displays the resulting products below.

4. **Click the <u>Edit</u> link beside the product to be deleted.**

   This takes you to the Products screen.

5. **Click the <u>Delete</u> link.**

   A message box appears, asking if you are sure you want to delete this item.

6. **Click OK to delete the product.**

   The product is now deleted.

Approving and Editing Product Reviews

Anyone who can view the Store can add a product review by clicking the <u>Add Review</u> link located in the bottom-right corner of each detailed product page. Reviews consist of a rating of between one and five stars and an optional comment. An Administrator must approve reviews before they appear on the Web site.

Here's how to approve and edit reviews:

1. **Go to the Store Admin page.**

2. **Click the <u>Reviews</u> link.**

   This takes you to the Reviews screen, as shown in Figure 8-11. All reviews, including both authorized and nonauthorized reviews, will be displayed.

3. **Select Not Approved from the Status drop-down box.**

   This displays the reviews that are awaiting approval.

4. **Click the <u>Edit</u> link beside a review.**

   This takes you to an editing screen for this review. If required, you can edit the comments but not the rating or the username.

5. **Select the Authorized check box to approve the review.**

6. **Click the <u>Update</u> link.**

   This takes you back to the Reviews page. The approved review is now displayed on the full listing of that product page. Repeat Steps 4 through 6 to approve more reviews.

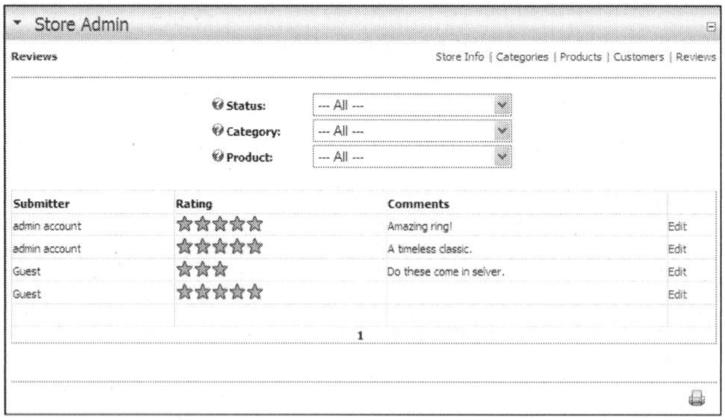

Figure 8-11:
The
Reviews
page of the
Store Admin
module lets
Administrat-
ors edit,
approve,
and delete
product
reviews.

▾ Store Admin					⊟
Reviews			Store Info | Categories | Products | Customers | Reviews		
	🕖 **Status:**	--- All --- ⌄			
	🕖 **Category:**	--- All --- ⌄			
	🕖 **Product:**	--- All --- ⌄			
Submitter	**Rating**		**Comments**		
admin account	☆☆☆☆☆		Amazing ring!		Edit
admin account	☆☆☆☆☆		A timeless classic.		Edit
Guest	☆☆☆		Do these come in seiver.		Edit
Guest	☆☆☆☆☆				Edit
		1			

Deleting a Product Review

Reviews must be deleted by using the Store Admin module. They can't be deleted via the Catalog module. Note: Deleting a review is permanent, so you may prefer to change it to Not Authorized for later consideration. Making a review Not Authorized removes the review from the product page but not from your records.

1. **Go to the Store Admin page.**

2. **Click the <u>Reviews</u> link.**

   This takes you to the Reviews screen. All reviews are displayed.

3. **Click the <u>Edit</u> link beside the review to be deleted.**

   This takes you to an editing screen for this review.

4. **Click the <u>Delete</u> link.**

   A message box appears, asking you if you're sure you want to delete this item.

5. Click OK to confirm deletions.

The review is now permanently deleted and you are returned to the Reviews page. Repeat Steps 3 through 5 to delete additional reviews.

Shopping 'til You Drop

After you have configured the store modules and added categories and products, you can launch your Store on the Web.

You must go back and deselect the Test Mode check box and then click Update before you can start accepting real transactions from customers.

Adding a product to the cart

Here's how to add a product to the store shopping cart:

1. Click on a category in the Categories module.

This displays a summary listing of the products related to this category in the Catalog module.

2. Click the Add To Cart link.

This link is also displayed on the detailed product page.

Going to the checkout

Here's how to proceed to the checkout, create a customer account, and place the order.

1. Log in to the Web site.

The user can either log in now or after Step 3.

2. Click on the View Cart Details link in the Mini Cart module, or go to the Store Account module.

This displays a summary listing of the products added to the cart.

3. (Optional.) Modify the quantities of any product.

Use the + and x buttons beside any product to increase or decrease the quantity.

4. **Click the <u>Checkout</u> link.**

   You are taken to the Checkout page. Details of the products being purchased are listed at the top of this page, along with the tax, shipping, and total amount payable.

5. **Complete the billing details in the Billing Address section.**

   This is where you enter the name, address, and contact details related to the billing of this order.

6. **Complete the shipping details in the Shipping Address section.**

   This is where you enter the name, address, and contact details related to the shipping of this order. If these details are the same as the billing details above, simply select the Ship the Order to the Billing Address radio button.

7. **Enter your payment details into the Payment Information fields.**

8. **Click the <u>Process Order</u> link.**

   This takes you to the Checkout page. Details of the products being purchased are listed at the top of this page, along with the tax, shipping, and total amount payable.

Viewing previous customer orders

Here's how the Administrator can view a summary of previous orders:

1. **Go to the Store Admin page.**

2. **Click the <u>Customers</u> link.**

   This takes you to the Order History screen of the Store Admin module.

3. **Select a customer name from the Customers drop-down box.**

   This displays a summary of orders placed by this customer.

4. **Click the <u>Back</u> link to return to the Order History page.**

Collaborating with Wiki

A *Wiki,* shown in Figure 8-12, is a type of Web site where all visitors can add, edit, and remove HTML content from HTML pages. Popular Wikis include `www.wikipedia.org`, which is a Wiki encyclopedia, and `www.wikitravel.org`, which is an online travel guide.

The DNN Wiki module lets Administrators create and manage multiple Wiki Web sites within the one DNN Web site. The DNN Wiki has a number of tools that enable users to quickly view the latest changes to a page and view the differences between each version. This makes it easy to revert to a previous version of that page. This can be important for a Wiki because they carry the risk of containing false information.

The ease of reinstating previous copy combined with a simple method of adding content without registration makes a Wiki ideally suited to collaborative writing.

While the traditional setup of a Wiki enables everyone to contribute to its content, at the time of writing, the DNN Wiki permitted contributions from logged-in users only.

The Wiki module isn't included with your DNN installation, but is available for free download from the DotNetNuke Web site by going to the Wiki Project page (www.dotnetnuke.com/DotNetNukeProjects/ModuleWiki/tabid/848/Default.aspx) and clicking the Project Downloads link. See Chapter 3 to find out how to install modules.

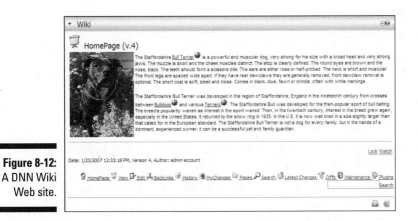

Figure 8-12:
A DNN Wiki
Web site.

Creating a Wiki Site

The Wiki module lets Administrators build one or more Wiki Web sites; however, you can only display one Wiki Web site per module at a time. For example, if you create a Canine Breeds Wiki site and a Canine Terminology Wiki site, you need to use two Wiki modules and select which module displays which Wiki Web site.

Configuring Wiki sites and choosing editors

Here's how to create a Wiki site:

1. **Add the Wiki module to a page.**

   If the security roles that have permission to view the module are the same as to view the page, skip to Step 6.

2. **Select Settings from the module menu.**

   This takes you to the Module Settings page for this module.

3. **Deselect the Inherit View Permissions from Page check box under the Permissions fields.**

4. **Select each role that is permitted to view the module.**

5. **Leave the Edit Module Permissions as they are.**

   Permissions to edit the Wiki are controlled on a different page. This is a nonstandard setup.

6. **Click the Update link.**

   This returns you to the page.

7. **Select Configure Wiki Sites from the module menu.**

   This takes you to the Configure Wiki Sites page.

8. **Click the Add New Site link.**

9. **Enter a name for the new Wiki.**

10. **At Editor Roles, select the check box beside each role that can contribute to the Wiki.**

    The Administrator role is mandatory and can't be deleted.

11. **At Moderator Roles, select the check box beside each role that can moderate Wiki content.**

    Moderators can add new pages without moderation.

12. **Click the Update link.**

    This saves your settings.

13. **Click the Back link.**

    This returns you to the main page of the Wiki. To complete the setup, you must also choose a Home page for the Wiki.

Choose the Wiki Web site for this module

Each Wiki module can manage multiple Wiki Web sites, but the module can only display one Wiki Web site at a time. The Choose Site and Door setting lets you choose the Wiki Web site to be displayed in this module and the start page of that site.

Here's how to choose the landing page of your Wiki:

1. **Select Choose Site and Door from the module menu.**

   This takes you to the Choose the Home Page page.

2. **Select the Wiki Web site for this module in the Connect to a Wiki Site list.**

   This displays all pages within this Wiki Web site in the Start Page box below.

3. **Select a page name in the Start Page window to select it as the start page of this Wiki Web site.**

   A page called Home Page is automatically created for all new Wiki Web sites. As more pages are added to the Wiki, they are displayed here. You can change the start page at any time.

4. **Click the <u>Back</u> link.**

   This takes you to the start page of the selected Wiki Web site, as shown in Figure 8-13. See "Editing Wiki Pages" later in this chapter for information on how to edit the description of the Wiki start page.

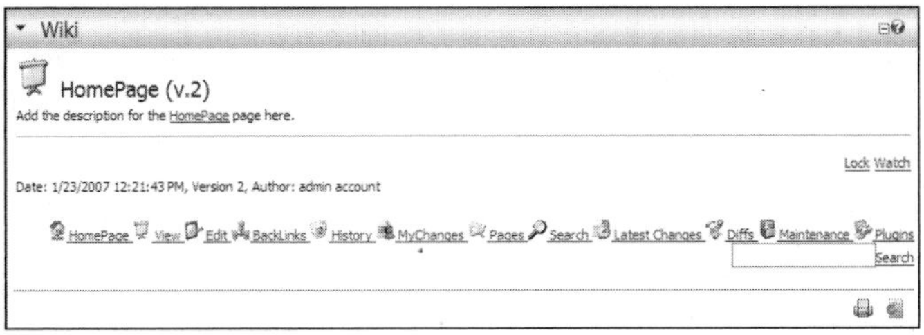

Figure 8-13:
The start
page of a
newly
created
Wiki.

Getting to Know Your Wiki

The Wiki displays the Wiki Landing Page and a row of links at the bottom that enables people to navigate, search, and edit the Wiki, view previous versions of the content, and more. Access to some links is role-based.

These buttons are displayed to everyone who can view the module:

- ✔ The Home Page button goes to the start page set for this Wiki.

- ✔ The View button takes people back to the last page they visited.

- ✔ The BackLinks button displays a list of any pages that link to the current page.

- ✔ The History button displays a list of major changes to the current page. By selecting Show Minor Changes, people can also view any minor changes. A View button beside each version displays the text of that version.

- ✔ The MyChanges button displays to the user a list of their changes to the current page. A View button beside each version displays the text of that version.

    Although the MyChanges button is displayed to everyone, people must log in to view changes.

- ✔ The Pages button gives you three options:

    - • All Pages displays a list of all pages in this Wiki Web site.

    - • Orphaned Pages displays a list of any pages that aren't linked to any other page in this Wiki Web site. This happens when the pages linking to this page are deleted.

    - • Strongest Pages displays the list of pages that are linked to the most.

- ✔ The Search button lets people search on all or part of a page name. For example, if you searched on the word *Canine*, the search would return all pages which contained that word, such as *Canines*, *Canine Teeth*, and so on.

- ✔ The Latest Changes button displays the ten latest changes to this Wiki Web site and lets you view any of these versions.

- ✔ The Diffs button lets people compare two versions of the Wiki content.

- ✔ The Plugins button goes to a page that displays all these buttons.

These buttons are only displayed to Editors and/or Administrators:

✔ The Edit button takes Editors to the edit screen of the current page.

✔ The Delete button is located on the History page and the Pages page. On the History page, it enables Editors to delete a page version. On the Pages page, it enables Editors to delete a page.

✔ The Maintenance button lets Administrators refresh the Wiki page records and create exportable versions of the content.

Editing Wiki Pages

Both Administrators and Editors can edit the content of any page. Here's how to edit a Wiki page, using the Wiki HomePage as an example:

1. Click the Home Page button.

This is the leftmost link along the bottom of the Wiki.

2. Click the Edit button.

This takes you to the Edit page. The name of the page you are editing is displayed above the editing box.

3. Edit the text displayed and add your description of the page.

The text that reads *[[HomePage]]* is included as an example of how to create a link to another page in this Wiki. You do not need to keep this or any of the text.

4. Deselect the Minor Change check box.

Most changes to a page will be minor; however, adding the initial description of the page is considered a major change. Defining each revision as either major or minor makes it easy to track major changes on the History and MyChanges pages.

5. Click Save.

You are returned to the landing page and the new description is visible.

Linking to New or Existing Wiki Pages

When you look at the links displayed across the bottom of the Wiki, you may notice the absence of an Add link. This is because you can only add a new page by editing an existing page. New pages are added whenever you choose to link to a Wiki page that doesn't exist. This ensures that new pages aren't created without being relevant to an existing page.

Here's how to add a new page to the Wiki:

1. **Go to a Wiki page that should be linked to the new page.**

2. **Click the Edit button located along the bottom of the module.**

3. **Create a page link or a new page by writing the name of the page inside double square brackets in the window.**

   Any word or phrase enclosed in double square brackets [[]] becomes a page title. For example, entering the text [[**Page Name**]] creates a new page named Page Name or a link to an existing page named Page Name.

4. **(Optional.) Deselect the Minor Change box located below the editor if you have made a major change to page content.**

5. **Click the Save button.**

   You are now returned to the page you have just edited. The new description and any links will be visible. A Bomb icon denotes any link that has created a new page. For example, Figure 8-12 shows three pages called Bull Terrier, Bulldogs, and Terriers, which do not have text on them. This lets users know that there is no description on that page as yet.

You can display a page link as a description rather than the page name. Do this by entering the link name and page name in square brackets, with a pipe symbol, as follows: [[**the link name | PageName**]]. For example, [[**a person who is selling their home | Vendor**]] will display as <u>a person who is selling their home</u> on the Wiki page and links to a page called Vendor.

Performing Maintenance on Your Wiki

Administrators can perform some database administrative tasks on their Wiki to keep the files in order. Here's how to perform maintenance on your Wiki:

1. **Click the Maintenance button.**

2. **Click the Refresh Links button.**

   This updates the records with the latest link information such as newly orphaned pages.

3. **Click the Clean Database button.**

   This ensures that all the database records are up-to-date.

Your database is now clean, refreshed, and is feeling great!

Exporting and Importing Wiki Web Sites

You can create as many Wiki Web Sites as you like by repeating the steps in the "Creating a Wiki Site" section, earlier in this chapter. Each new Wiki requires a new Wiki module to be set to display it. To kick-start a new Wiki, you can export data from an existing Wiki and import it into your new Wiki.

Here's how to perform an export and import of Wiki content:

1. **Go to the Wiki that you want to export content from.**

2. **Click the Maintenance button.**

   It is best to perform maintenance on your Wiki before continuing to Step 2. This ensures that you have an optimum database for importing. See the preceding section for details.

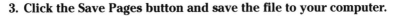

3. **Click the Save Pages button and save the file to your computer.**

   This creates and displays the wikidata.ZIP file for you to save.

4. **Go to the Wiki that you want to import content to.**

5. **Click the Maintenance button.**

6. **Click the Browse button and select the wikidata.ZIP file.**

7. **Click the Load Pages button.**

   This loads the saved pages into this Wiki.

8. **(Optional.) Click the Rake Versions button if you want to use only the current version of the imported Wiki content.**

   This optional step deletes all prior versions of the Wiki in the new Wiki.

Part IV
Getting Under the Hood

The 5th Wave   By Rich Tennant

"Before the Internet, we were only bustin' chops locally. But now, with our Web site, we're bustin' chops all over the world."

In This Part . . .

This Part is for readers who want to delve deeper into customizing, personalizing, and improving the experience of users. It explains how to customize the wording of automated e-mail messages sent out by DNN, how to enable users to change the language of some site content, and ways to customize the registration and login experience. This Part also demonstrates how to undertake routine maintenance and support activities for your Web site.

Chapter 9

Standard Stuff You Can Customize

· ·

· ·

*I*n this chapter, you find out how to customize some of the features of DNN. This includes setting up how you want your users to be able to search your site. You can do things like limit the size of the words they can search for and allow them to search for numbers. We also talk about the Language Editor and how you can use it to modify all sorts of messages and e-mails.

DNN has a huge worldwide following and a large number of non-English–speaking users, so DNN developed a system that allows the users to see some parts of DNN sites in their own language. Any piece of text that is part of DNN and not "content" can be switched to one of about 50 languages. Let's get down to it and see how to customize your DNN Web site!

Finding Things with Search Input and Search Results

Internet surfers are an impatient bunch. They want information and answers, and they want them now. If they can't find things easily on your Web site, they will probably go elsewhere for them. These quick clickers appreciate having access to an intelligent search function to hunt out what they seek. Aren't you lucky that DNN includes just what you need to provide easy searching?

DNN has a built-in search function that searches all the content of your Web site. This is a skin element that is included in most site skins. The standard DNN skin displays a search box in the top-right corner of all pages, as shown in Figure 9-1.

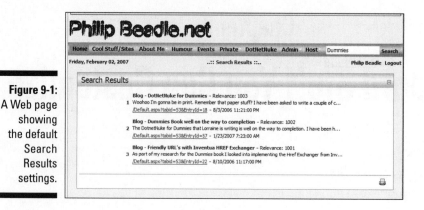

Figure 9-1:
A Web page
showing
the default
Search
Results
settings.

Setting up Search

You must have host access to set up the search options for your Web site. If you only have Administrator access, your host should have already done this for you.

Here's how to set up the search function on your Web site:

1. **Navigate to the Host⇨Search Admin page.**

   This displays the different settings for Search results. The Host has the ability to change these default settings for all Web sites in this DNN installation. The Administrator can, however, manage these settings on their Web site without needing host access. See "Changing the format of Search results" for more details.

2. **Set the Maximum Word Length.**

   This option allows you to set how long a word can be that is searched on. If you only want your users to be able to search on words with less than 7 characters, enter **7** here. The default is no maximum if you leave this empty.

3. **Set the Minimum Word Length.**

   This value is usually set to 3 or 4. If you set it to 1 or 2, your users can search on words like *a*, *I*, or *is* and will not generate meaningful results. Setting it to a higher value allows you to help them get a better search result. Doing this also makes the searching a lot more efficient. Your search indexing, which we discuss later in this chapter, will have fewer results, thus will work faster and give better search results.

4. **Include Common Words.**

   This value is set to False by default, which prevents words like "the," "was," and other common words from being included in the search indexing process. Again, this makes your search results more relevant and efficient.

5. **Include Numbers.**

   For the same reasons as that for not including common words, the option to exclude numbers from the search indexing process is available.

6. **Click the Update link.**

   Save your settings by clicking the Update link.

7. **Click the Re-Index Content link.**

   This does some magic that enables all the content on your Web site to be found when you use the Search box.

   DNN is scheduled to reindex the content on your Web site for searching every thirty minutes. You can manage this scheduled task under Host⇨ Schedule, as discussed in Chapter 6.

Adding more Search Input and Search Results modules

As well as the global search that can be included in the skin of your Web site, DNN also has Search Input and Search Results modules that you can add to any page of your Web site. By adding these modules to a page, you can add searching to your Web site if the skin you're using doesn't have the search box included.

Here's how to add more Search Input and Search Results modules to your Web site:

1. **Add a Search Input module to a page.**

   This module is now ready to use. Results are displayed on the default Search Results page and have the same format as is set on this page. Read on to find out how to set results to appear in a different search results page. You can see how to add a module in Chapter 3.

2. **Add a Search Results module to the page.**

3. **Select Settings from the Search Input module menu.**

   This displays the Module Settings for this Search Input module.

4. **Click the Maximize button beside Search Input Settings.**

   This displays the Search Input settings for this module.

5. **Select the page name where the Search Results module is located from the Search Results Module drop-down box.**

   This field lists the location of all Search Results modules on the Web site. The default search results page is named Search Results.

6. **Click Update.**

   Searches made with this Search Input module are displayed in the selected Search Results module.

Changing the format of Search results

The Administrator can modify search result settings such as the length of the title, the number of results, and more. Here's how to change the search results:

1. **Enter search text into a Search text box and then click the <u>Search</u> link or the Go button.**

   This displays the Search Results page associated with the Search Input module you used.

2. **Select Settings from the Search Results module menu.**

   This displays the module settings for the Search Results module.

3. **Click the Maximize button beside Search Results Settings.**

   This displays the search results settings that you can change.

4. **Enter the maximum number of results to be displayed in the Maximum Search Results text box, as shown in Figure 9-2.**

   The most relevant results are displayed first, so limiting results to, say, ten displays the ten most relevant results. Leave this field blank if all results should be displayed.

5. **Enter the number of results to be displayed on one page in the Results Per Page text box.**

   DNN automatically adds page navigation to search results. This means if you set this field to 20 and a search returns 30 results, links to get to the other 10 results are displayed. Leave this field blank to use the default setting, which is 10.

6. **Enter the maximum number of characters for each title length into the Maximum Title Length text box.**

   The module title is displayed as the title on each result. Leave this field blank to have no maximum title length, which is the default setting.

7. **Enter the maximum number of characters for each description into the Maximum Description Length text box.**

   The module content is displayed as the description on each result. Leave this field blank to have no maximum description length, which is the default setting.

8. **Check the Show Description check box to display a description for each result.**

   Alternatively, uncheck this option to hide the description.

9. **Click the <u>Update</u> link to save the settings.**

   Do a test search to see how the new settings have changed the results.

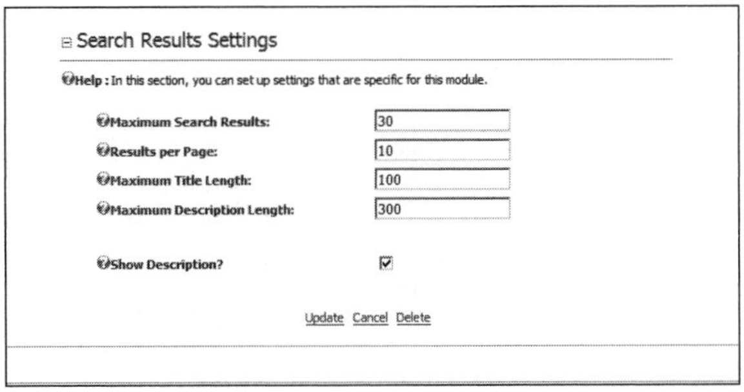

Figure 9-2:
This page
enables you
to modify
the format
of Search
Results.

```
⊟ Search Results Settings

ⓘHelp : In this section, you can set up settings that are specific for this module.

    ⓘMaximum Search Results:            [30      ]
    ⓘResults per Page:                  [10      ]
    ⓘMaximum Title Length:              [100     ]
    ⓘMaximum Description Length:        [300     ]

    ⓘShow Description?                  ☑

                        Update  Cancel  Delete
```

Inviting Authentication with Account Login

The standard method of logging in to a DNN Web site involves the user clicking the <u>Login</u> link that is standard in most DNN skins, and then entering their username and password. But DNN also offers a number of quick and easy ways for an Administrator to change this standard procedure to make it more enticing to log in, which we cover in this section.

Adding an Account Login module

Encourage users to log in by adding an Account Login module to a page. Having the Account Login module on a page reminds existing users to log in and can encourage new visitors to register on your Web site. Simply add an Account Login module to any page, and it is ready to use without any configuration.

Here are three simple ideas to customize your account Login module:

✔ Add a module header or module footer to an Account Login module to communicate a login message to users.

✔ Set the module to appear on all pages to really drive the login message home.

✔ Change the View Permissions module setting to be viewable only to Unauthenticated users. This means the module disappears when they are logged in. This is a nice personal touch that gives you back valuable page space.

Creating a unique login page

Most DNN skins include a <u>Login</u> link that displays the default User Login page for the Web site. This page displays an Account Login module and nothing else. You can't add other modules to this page; however, if you do want to jazz up the login page, you can create your own login page and set it as the login page for your Web site.

Here's how to create your own login page:

1. **Add a new page, setting the permissions to View Page to All Users.**

   Name the page title something easy to remember, like Login or Account Login.

2. **Add an Account Login module to this page, as shown in Figure 9-3.**

   This step is really, really important! If you don't add an Account Login module to this page or don't have one that is available to unauthenticated users on another page, nobody will be able to log in to the Web site, including you!

3. **Pretty the page up however you like.**

   Add friendly instructions, nice pictures, and any other stuff to jazz the page up the way you like it.

4. **Navigate to the Admin⇨Site Settings page.**

   This takes you to the settings page for this Web site.

5. **Click the Maximize button beside Advanced Settings.**

   This displays the advanced settings for this Web site.

6. **Select the name of the page you created in Step 1 from the Login Page drop-down box.**

   This changes the login page from the default one to your page. Selecting <None Specified> switches it back to the default page.

7. **Click the Update link.**

   The new page is now displayed when the Login link is clicked.

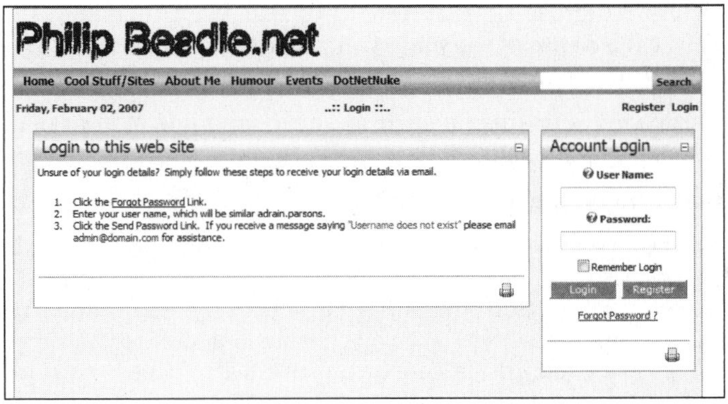

Figure 9-3:
Create a login page and set it for use on the site. Don't forget to add an Account Login module to the login page!

Personalizing with User Account

The standard method of registering as a member on a DNN Web site involves the user clicking on the Register link, which is standard in most DNN skins, entering their preferred user information, and then clicking the Register link. They are then able to log in to your Web site and access content that is only available to registered users. As the Administrator, you can modify this process by changing a few simple settings.

The User Account page accessed by the Register link has only a User Account module on it and nothing else. You can't add other modules to this page, but you can create your own User Account page and set it as the User page for the Web site.

Here's how to create your own user account page:

1. **Add a new page.**

   Name the page title something easy to remember, such as User Account.

2. **Add a User Account module to this page.**

3. **Pretty the page up however you like.**

   Add text and images to customize this page. Information such as why they should register, what they will have access to as a member, or some pictures of happy people is a good start.

4. **Navigate to the Admin⇨Site Settings page.**

   This takes you to the settings page for this Web site.

5. **Click the Maximize button beside Advanced Settings.**

   This displays the advanced settings for this Web site.

6. **Select the name of the page you created at Step 1 from the User page drop-down box.**

   This changes the user page from the default one to your new page. Selecting <None Specified> switches it back to the default page.

7. **Click the Update link.**

   The new page will now be displayed when the Register link is clicked.

Information that you add to this page that is designed to entice users to Register should have their View Page permissions set to Unauthenticated Users. This is a good idea because your users also access this page when they want to update their information by clicking on their name after they have logged in. If they are already registered users, you don't need to encourage them to register! Try it out and see what happens.

Personalizing Your E-Mail Notifications

When new and existing users undertake certain activities such as registration, requesting a password reminder, or updating their account, DNN automatically sends a notification message to their e-mail address. Similarly, when an Administrator performs certain administrative tasks such as adding a user to a security role or unregistering a user, they can choose to send a notification e-mail to that person. DNN comes with standard e-mail messages that save you from having to write them yourself; however, you can change the wording of any of these messages if you like and also add logos and other personal touches, as shown in Figure 9-4.

You can change e-mail notifications and other messages under either the Admin or Host areas. Changing a message under Host updates the default message for all Web sites. Changing a message under Admin updates the message for that Web site only. Changing a message under Host won't override changes made by the Admin, so you don't have to worry about losing changes.

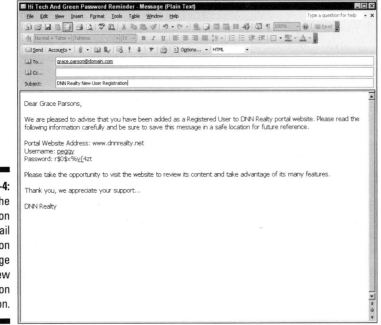

Figure 9-4:
The
Registration
e-mail
notification
message
sent to new
users upon
registration.

Changing the Registration e-mail message

As discussed in Chapter 4, DNN offers three different ways you can set up your user registration: Public, Private, or Verified. Each has a different e-mail message, so you need to verify how you have set up your registration to ensure that you change the correct registration e-mail message.

Here's how to change the e-mail message sent to users who register on your Web site:

1. **Navigate to the Admin⇨Languages page.**

   As well as managing the languages used on your Web site, which we discuss in the upcoming section, "Changing Your Default Language," this area gives you access to manage all the notification e-mail messages for your Web site.

2. **Select Language Editor from the Languages module menu.**

   This takes you to the Language Editor where you can view the notification messages.

3. **If your registration is set up as Public, locate the User Registration message titled Resource Name: EMAIL_USER_REGISTRATION_PUBLIC_ BODY.Text in the list of Resources on the right side of the page.**

   The user registration e-mail messages are located about halfway down the list. If your user registration isn't set for public registration, you will need to change either the Resource Name: EMAIL_USER_REGISTRATION_ PRIVATE_BODY.Text, or the Resource Name: EMAIL_USER_REGISTRATION_ VERIFIED_BODY.Text messages instead.

   The Resource Names of e-mail notifications and other messages are capitalized to make them easier to find.

4. **Click the Maximize button beside Default Value, shown in Figure 9-5, to view the current message.**

   The message includes text inside square brackets ([ ]). When the message is sent, these are replaced with the correct information for that user. For example, [User:FullName] is replaced with the user's full name.

5. **Click the arrow button beside Default Value to edit the current message.**

   This displays a message saying that all unsaved changes will be lost if you continue, and asking if you're sure you want to continue. The only date you will lose is anything you have typed into the text boxes on this page. If you have, click the <u>Update</u> link at the bottom on the page first.

6. **Click OK.**

   This displays the name of the message you are about to edit, the current text of the message, and an RTE to create the new message.

7. **Click the Basic Text Box option above the RTE.**

   Now you can copy the current message without copying any unwanted text formatting.

8. **Copy the existing message into the Basic Text Copy.**

   Copying the existing message and editing it ensures that the new message includes the important word replacement tags.

9. **Click the Rich Text Editor option above the RTE.**

   This switches you back to the rich text editor so you can edit the text, insert images, and add other fancy formatting.

10. **Edit the message.**

11. **Click the <u>Update</u> link.**

    You are now taken back to the Languages page. To check your new message, repeat Steps 1 through 4. You might also like to register a make-believe user with your e-mail address to experience receiving the message.

Changing other e-mail notifications

DNN offers 16 standard e-mail notifications and you can change them at any time. Here's the full list of e-mail notifications available:

- ✔ **Affiliate Notification:** This message can be sent from the Administrator to a Vendor with an affiliate referral account. It provides the affiliate referral URL.

- ✔ **Banner Notification:** This message can be sent to a Vendor from the Administrator and provides an activity report for one of their banners. See Chapter 6 for more details.

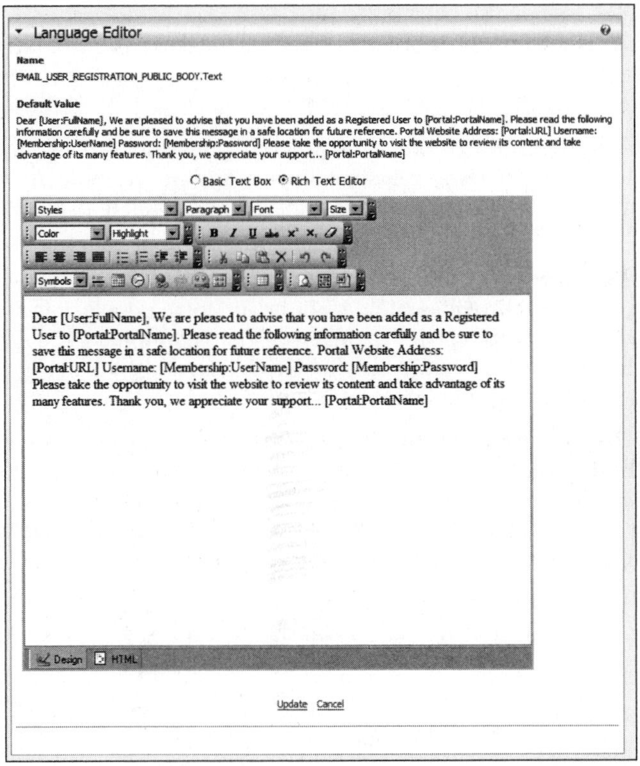

Figure 9-5:
Editing the
Registration
message for
new users.

- ✔ **Password Reminder:** This message automatically is sent to users who request a password reminder when using the Account Login module. It includes their login details.

- ✔ **Portal Signup:** This welcome message is sent by the host to the Administrator of a newly created portal. It provides account and login details.

- ✔ **Profile Updated:** This message is sent automatically to users when they update their profile.

- ✔ **Role Assignment:** This message is automatically sent to users when they subscribe to a security role. The Administrator can choose to send this message when they add a user to a new role.

- ✔ **Role Unassignment:** This message is automatically sent to users when they unsubscribe from a service (security role). When the Administrator removes a user from a role, they can choose to send this message.

- ✔ **SMTP Test:** This message automatically is sent to the host when they test their SMTP e-mail settings.

- ✔ **User Lockout:** This warning message automatically is sent to the Administrator when someone attempts to log in to a locked-out user account.

- ✔ **User Registration (Administrator):** This message is automatically sent to the Administrator when a new user account is created. It provides a summary of the user's account details.

- ✔ **User Registration Private:** This welcome message can be sent by the Administrator to newly registered users and provides account and login details. This version of the user registration e-mail is used when the portal is set for private registration.

- ✔ **User Registration Public:** This welcome message is sent to newly registered users and provides their account and login details. It is sent automatically to users who register themselves, but is optional if the Administrator registers them. This version of the user registration e-mail is used when the portal is set for public registration.

- ✔ **User Registration Verified:** This welcome message is sent to newly registered users and provides account and login details. It is sent automatically to users who register themselves, but is optional if the Administrator registers them. This version of the user registration e-mail is used when the portal is set for verified registration, and includes a verification code.

- ✔ **User Unregister:** This message automatically is sent to users when they unregister their user account from the portal.

✔ **Vendor Registration (Administrator):** This message automatically is sent to the Administrator when a new vendor account is created. It provides a summary of the vendors account details.

✔ **Vendor Registration:** This welcome message automatically is sent to new vendors and provides account and login details.

Whenever you edit a message, don't forget to include the word replacement tags that are enclosed in square brackets like this [User:FullName]. These tags not only personalize the message but also ensure that the person receives the vital information for the message, such as their password.

Changing Your Terms of Use Policy

Depending on the skin used on your Web site, it may provide links enabling visitors to view the Terms of Use and Privacy policy for the Web site. DNN comes with standard Terms and Privacy messages; however, you need to update these to reflect your true policy.

Here's how to change the Terms of Use message on your Web site:

1. **Navigate to the Admin⇨Languages page.**

   As well as managing the languages used on your Web site, which we discuss in the section, "Changing Your Default Language," this area gives you access to managing all the notification e-mail messages for your Web site.

2. **Select Language Editor from the Languages module menu.**

   This takes you to the Language Editor, where you can view the notification messages.

3. **Locate the User Registration message titled Resource Name: MESSAGE_ PORTAL_TERMS.Text in the list of Resources on the right side of the page.**

4. **Click the Maximize button beside Default Value to view the current message.**

   The message includes text inside square brackets ([]). When the message is sent, the brackets are replaced with the correct information for that user. For example, [Portal:PortalName] is replaced with the name of your Web site.

5. **Click the arrow button beside Default Value to edit the current message.**

   This displays a message saying that all unsaved changes will be lost if you continue, and asking you if you sure you want to continue. The only changes you will lose are those you have typed in to the text boxes on this page. If you have done so, you should click the Update link at the bottom on the page.

6. **Click OK.**

   This displays the name of the message you are about to edit, the current text of the message, and an RTE to create the new message.

7. **Click the Basic Text Box option above the RTE.**

   Now you can copy the current message without copying any unwanted text formatting.

8. **Copy the existing message into the Basic Text Copy.**

   Copying the existing message and editing it ensures that the new message includes the important word replacement tags.

9. **Click the Rich Text Editor option above the RTE.**

   This switches you back to the rich text editor so you can edit the text, insert images, and do other fancy formatting.

10. **Edit the message.**

11. **Click the Update link.**

    This takes you back to the Languages page. To check the new message, click the Terms of Use link on your Web site. It is usually located at the bottom of all pages.

Here's the full list of messages:

- **Login Instructions:** Create a message to be displayed on the Login page below the login fields.

- **Portal Privacy:** This message is displayed when a visitor clicks on the Privacy link. This link is displayed at the base of each page in the standard skin.

- **Portal Terms:** This message is displayed when a visitor clicks on the Terms of Use link that is usually displayed at the bottom of each page in the standard skin.

- **Registration Instructions:** Create a message to be displayed on the Register page above the registration fields.

- **Retrieve Password:** This message is displayed on the Retrieve Password page if your Web site has been configured with a question-and-answer format to receive a password.

Changing Your Default Language

Modifying the languages on a DNN Web site does not interpret all the content within the modules on your Web site into the chosen language. It's a fabulous idea, but it's not what you should expect.

What you *can* do is to make your Web site more accessible and user friendly by enabling users to read certain Web site information in their preferred language, as shown in Figure 9-6. The information that changes is everything apart from the content you add. This includes skin tokens such as Date and Terms of Use, the field names on the Admin and Host page, and the field names on the Add and Edit pages for modules and pages. (Big thanks to the DNN community members who have voluntarily produced and shared language interpretations for DNN!)

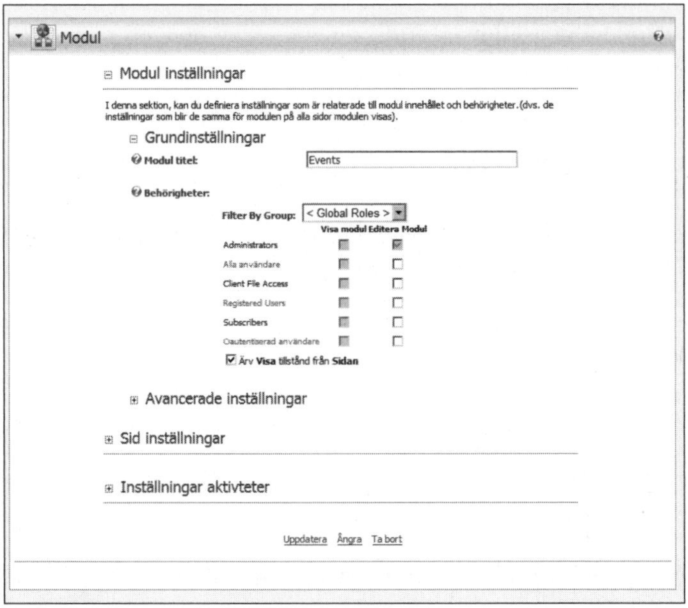

Figure 9-6:
Changing
the Web site
language
shows the
common
field names
on the
Module
Settings
Page in the
selected
language.

Adding a language

Before you can add a language to your Web site, you need to find an interpretation for the language you want. The best place to find interpretations is on the DotNetNuke Web site. Look under Community➪Languages. Here you will find a list of Language Packs. Download the language you require and then you are ready to add it to your Web site.

Here's how to add a new language to your Web site:

1. **Log in as the Host.**

   Host access is required to add a new language to a Web site.

2. **Navigate to the Host⇨Languages page.**

   This takes you to the Languages page, where you can add languages that will then be available on all Web sites.

3. **Select <u>Install Language Pack</u> from the Languages module menu.**

   This takes you to the Upload Language Pack page and lets you upload the Language pack to this Web site.

4. **Click the Browse button and select a Language Pack that you have downloaded.**

   The name of the Language Pack will be something like ResourcePack. Full.03.01.01.en-AU.zip. If you don't have a Language Pack, read the introduction to this tutorial.

5. **Click the <u>Save File</u> link.**

   This decompresses the file and uploads it to the Web site.

6. **Click the <u>Return</u> link.**

   This takes you back to the Languages page. The new language is listed as Enabled in the Supported Locales list. You can Enable or Disable a language here at any time.

Now that you have more than one language installed on your site, you may decide to disable the other language. Disabling a language means that your users can no longer select that language as their preferred language in their profile.

To disable a language follow these steps:

1. **Log in as the Admin.**

2. **Navigate to the Admin⇨Languages page.**

   This takes you to the Languages page for your site where you can disable a language.

3. **Click the <u>Disable</u> link.**

   This makes the language unavailable to your users. You can re-enable by clicking the <u>Enable</u> link.

See the next section, "Changing your preferred language," to find out how to set the default language to be used on your Web site.

Changing your preferred language

All registered users have the option to select which language is displayed to them when they are logged in to the Web site. This is a personal setting for this user only and doesn't affect any other user or the settings applied to the whole Web site.

1. **Click the <u>Login</u> link and enter your login details.**

2. **Click on your Display Name.**

   This link is located where the <u>Register</u> link is on your Web site. This goes to the User Account module.

3. **Click the <u>Manage Profile</u> link.**

   This takes you to the profile page.

4. **Scroll down to the bottom of this page and select a language from the Preferred Locale drop-down box, as shown in Figure 9-7.**

   This selects the language for this user.

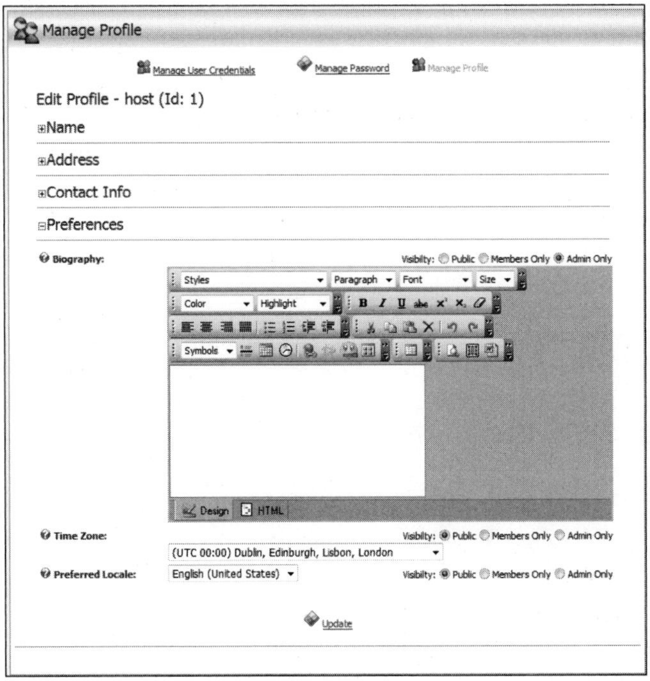

Figure 9-7: Changing your preferred language.

5. Click the <u>Update</u> link.

Check out the Admin and Host pages and the module and page edit screens. They are now translated to the chosen language.

As an Administrator, you can set the preferred language on any user's account by editing their profile under the Admin⇨User Account page.

Chapter 10

Keeping Tabs with the Site Log and Log Viewer

● ●

In This Chapter

▶ Checking your stats with the Site Log

▶ See what's happening with the Log Viewer

▶ Emptying your Recycle Bin

▶ Automating stuff with scheduled tasks

● ●

As part of the upkeep and maintenance of your Web site, you should make use of the instruments in DotNetNuke that let you keep your finger on the pulse. These simple-to-use tools let you know who is visiting your site, keep you in touch with what's happening behind the scenes, and allow you to clean up after accidents.

As with anything in life, a little bit of maintenance on a regular basis prevents bigger problems later on. For example, when was the last time you emptied the Recycle Bin on your computer? If it's been a while, you'll find that if you try to find a file that needs to be recovered, you have mountains of files to look through. A regular cleanup of the Recycle Bin makes it easy to find that file. It's the same with your Web site. The monitoring tools in DotNetNuke make it very simple to find out what's going on with your site and whether there are any problems that need your attention.

Getting to Know Your Site Log

One of the main things you should know about your site is how many people are looking at it and what pages they are looking at. This information can easily be found by looking at the reports the Site Log gives you. See Chapter 3 for how to set the history for your Site Log.

The Site Log has 12 reports that can tell you all sorts of interesting statistics about your site, such as which pages are the most popular, or how many pages are being viewed by the hour, day, day of the week, and month. You can also find out which search engines and affiliates are referring users to your site, how often individual users use your site, and where people are coming from. There is even a very detailed report that gives you information on every page that has been viewed! We discuss each of the reports in more detail in the following sections.

Creating a report is simple. Choose Admin➪Site Log, which shows you the Site Log report page, as shown in Figure 10-1. Here you can see how many days of history a superuser has allowed for your site and the options for creating the different reports.

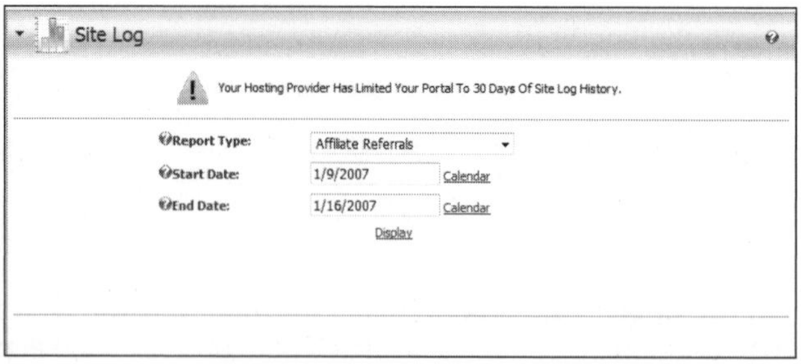

Figure 10-1:
The Site Log allows you to create reports easily.

Site Log	
⚠ Your Hosting Provider Has Limited Your Portal To 30 Days Of Site Log History.	
Report Type:	Affiliate Referrals
Start Date:	1/9/2007 Calendar
End Date:	1/16/2007 Calendar
	Display

To create a report, just compete these steps:

1. **Select the report you want to see from the Report Type drop-down list.**

2. **Click the Calendar button next to the Start Date.**

3. **Select the Start Date from the calendar that pops up.**

4. **Click the Calendar button next to the End Date.**

5. **Select the End Date from the calendar that pops up and click the Display button.**

You can copy and paste the results of these reports into a spreadsheet application like Microsoft Excel to manipulate and analyze the data.

The Page Popularity report

The Page Popularity report, shown in Figure 10-2, shows you in descending order how many times pages in your site have been viewed and when they were last viewed. This is a very important report because it gives you a great feel for which parts of your site your users find the most interesting. From this report, you can easily assess which parts of your site your users are most interested in, which enables you to concentrate your efforts there. It is also a great way for you to know on which pages you should advertise or tell people about the new parts of your site.

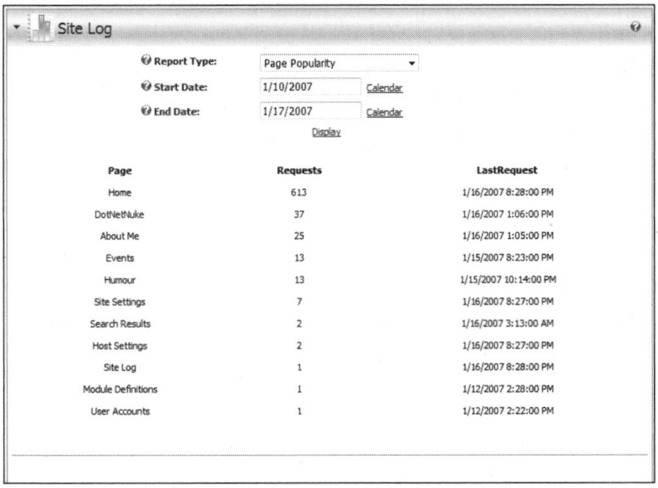

Figure 10-2:
The Page Popularity report gives an instant snapshot of where your site is hot and where it's not.

Site Log		
Report Type:	Page Popularity ▼	
Start Date:	1/10/2007	Calendar
End Date:	1/17/2007	Calendar
	Display	

Page	Requests	LastRequest
Home	613	1/16/2007 8:28:00 PM
DotNetNuke	37	1/16/2007 1:06:00 PM
About Me	25	1/16/2007 1:05:00 PM
Events	13	1/15/2007 8:23:00 PM
Humour	13	1/15/2007 10:14:00 PM
Site Settings	7	1/16/2007 8:27:00 PM
Search Results	2	1/16/2007 3:13:00 AM
Host Settings	2	1/16/2007 8:27:00 PM
Site Log	1	1/16/2007 8:28:00 PM
Module Definitions	1	1/12/2007 2:28:00 PM
User Accounts	1	1/12/2007 2:22:00 PM

The Page Views reports

DNN offers four Page Views reports, which tell you how many times your page was viewed between the dates you select in the Start and End Date fields, broken up into the selected time periods. If you run the Page Views by Day report, for example, the report shows you how many pages were viewed, how many users viewed them, and how many visitors viewed them on each day. (A *user* has a user account on the site and has logged in, so the site knows who the user is. A *visitor,* on the other hand, is an anonymous user who is not logged in, and therefore the site does not know who the visitor is.) Figure 10-3 shows the Page Views by Day report. This report is a great way for you to find out which days of the week your sites gets viewed the most. You can then use this information to schedule maintenance on your site's slow days, which will keep your users happy.

DNN offers three other reports of this type: Page Views by Day of Week, Page Views by Hour, and Page Views by Month. Each of these reports can tell you a bit more about how and when your site is used.

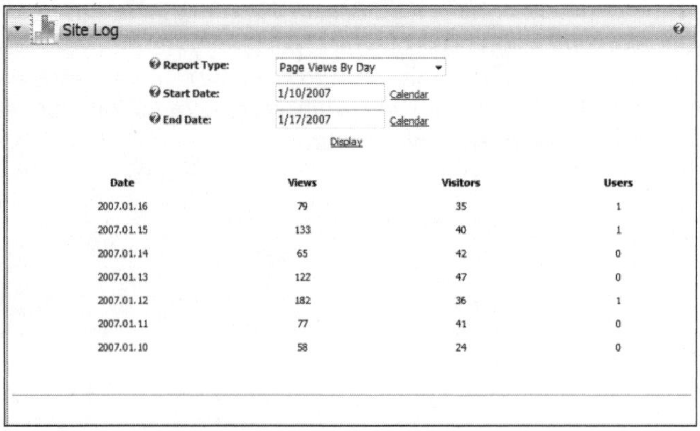

Figure 10-3:
The Page
Views by
Day report
tells you
when
people are
viewing
your site.

The User Registrations reports

The two User Registrations reports give you information on which countries your registered users come from and when they are signing up. The User Registrations by Country Report tells you the full name and country of origin for your users: This information tells you where the content of your site is most appreciated. For example, if you start to see a lot of users signing up from Australia, you might consider linking your site to other Australian sites to generate more traffic to your site.

The User Registrations by Date report, shown in Figure 10-4, shows when a user registers on your site. You can cross-check this against your advertising to see how an advertising campaign on a particular date affected the rate of registrations on your site.

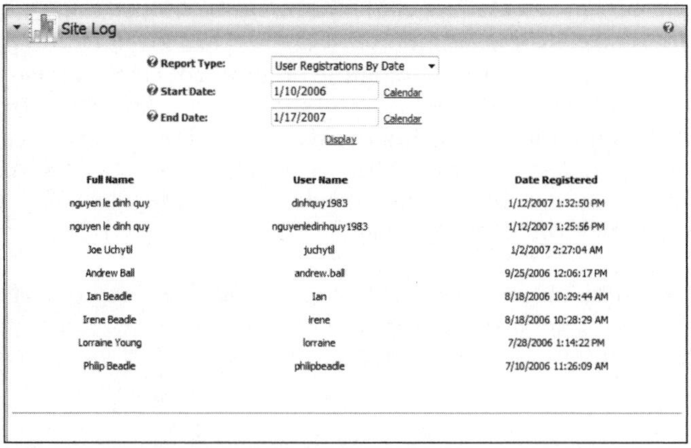

Figure 10-4:
The User
Registra-
tions
by Date
report tells
you when
people are
registering
on your site.

The User Frequency report

The User Frequency report is useful for finding out which users are frequenting your site the most. It gives a list of names, the number of times they have viewed the site, and the last time they viewed it. You can use this information to see if people keep coming back to your site, or if they get bored, view a few pages, and then never return. If your site is *sticky* (in other words, it provides new information on a regular basis), you will see long-term users accumulating large numbers of views and having a recent Last Request date. If your site is not sticky, you will see many users with similar numbers of views and Last Request dates that are old.

The Site Referrals report

Each time someone uses a search engine like Google and clicks on a result to be taken to your site, it is called a *site referral*. DNN records the URL of the page that the user who lands on your site has just come from. You can use this information, shown in Figure 10-5, to find out which of your advertising campaigns is working.

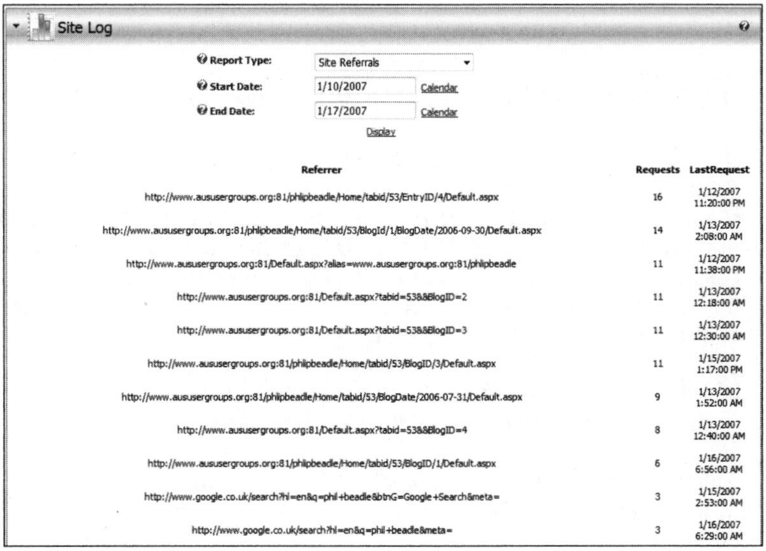

Figure 10-5:
The Site Referrals report shows you which links on other sites your users are coming from.

The Affiliate Referrals report

DotNetNuke contains a Vendor Management module that allows you to manage advertising campaigns on your own site. One of the options you have available is to create affiliates for your Web site and reward the sites sending you lots of new customers. DNN allows you to easily track when one of your affiliates sends a user your way to sign up. Each time a user signs up and has their AffiliateID recorded, it shows up in the Affiliate Referrals report, as shown in Figure 10-6.

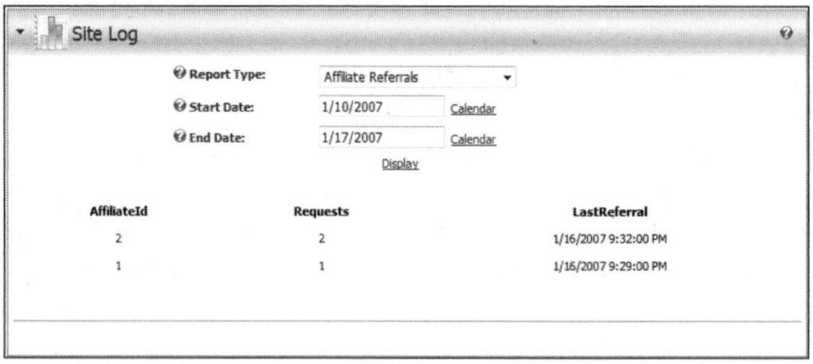

Figure 10-6:
The Affiliate Referrals report shows you which of your affiliates is sending you new users.

Site Log			❓
❓ Report Type:	Affiliate Referrals ▾		
❓ Start Date:	1/10/2007	Calendar	
❓ End Date:	1/17/2007	Calendar	
	Display		
AffiliateId	**Requests**		**LastReferral**
2	2		1/16/2007 9:32:00 PM
1	1		1/16/2007 9:29:00 PM

The Detailed Site Log report

If you want to know exact details about every page that has been viewed on your Web site, who viewed it, when they viewed it, what browser they viewed it with, and how they got referred to that page, the Detailed Site Log is for you. This report, shown in Figure 10-7, gives you all this information and even tells you the IP address of the user's Internet connection. This information is useful for situations where you need to know detailed information about your traffic during specific time periods. For example, if you believe someone is trying to hack into your site, or you are getting unusually high traffic, you can analyze this data to pinpoint what IP address they are using, which you can then use to track down any evildoers.

This report may take a long time to generate if you select more than one day in the Start and End Date fields: It shows every page view during the selected dates.

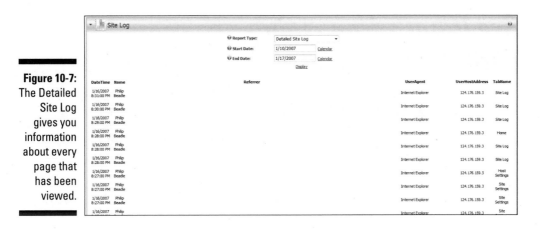

Figure 10-7:
The Detailed
Site Log
gives you
information
about every
page that
has been
viewed.

The User Agents report

Millions of people are surfing the Internet at any given time. These people use Web browsers such as Internet Explorer (IE), which comes in lots of versions, including 4, 5, 6, and now 7. They also use browsers such as Firefox, Opera, Netscape, and a host of others. Knowing what browser your visitors are using is helpful to you as a Web site owner because each browser works slightly differently: A Web site viewed in IE doesn't look exactly the same as one viewed in Firefox. One of the things that Web site designers try to do is to create "cross-browser" designs that look equally good in all browsers. This is not always economically viable, so it is good to know which browsers people are using to access your site. For example, if less than a half of a percent of your visitors are using Netscape, you probably don't want to spend money trying to make your site work properly in Netscape. The User Agents report tells you what browser your visitors are using. Figure 10-8 shows a typical User Agents report from `www.philipbeadle.net`.

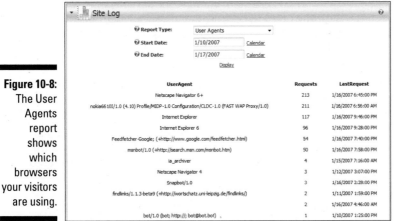

Figure 10-8:
The User
Agents
report
shows
which
browsers
your visitors
are using.

See What's Happening with the Log Viewer

The Log Viewer is your window to the soul of DotNetNuke. You get to it by selecting Admin⇨Log Viewer. This page lets you see what is happening behind the scenes and gives you an understanding of the health of your Web site as well as the activities going on. There are many different types of events you can monitor with the Log Viewer, ranging from when users logged in to when a new page was added to the site.

The Log Viewer also records when things are going wrong. For example, if one of the modules on your site has something wrong with it, the error that occurred will be recorded in the Log Viewer. You can then use this informa-tion to get it fixed, providing all the details the person fixing it needs. For example, if you have a module on your site that has not been configured properly and keeps failing with the same error, you can send those items in the Log Viewer to your support person. Your tech support person can ascer-tain that the reason for the module failing is because a setting has been missed. You can then log in to your site and use this information to correct the issue. The Log Viewer even helps you out with this task as well by provid-ing a built-in way for you set the threshold of when you want these messages sent to a particular e-mail address! How cool is that?

There is color-coding on each of the events that the Log Viewer records to help you gain insight into your Web site at a quick glance. Errors and failures are colored red and security issues are black. If you see these colors in your Log Viewer, you should either investigate further to find the cause or send those events to your technical support person. In Figure 10-9, you can see the color-coded legend for all the types of exceptions.

The Log Viewer is available to site Administrators to view the log entries and for them to send selected entries to an e-mail address. Superusers can also configure the Log Viewer by adding or removing the types of logs the Log Viewer records. With the Log Viewer, you can do a thorough health check on your Web site and ensure that your support team monitors it so that they can keep an eye on your site in real time.

Using the Log Viewer

The Log Viewer is configured by default to record whenever a particular event happens in your Web site. When you go to the Log Viewer, you will see a list of ten events most recently recorded. Lots of events get recorded by the

Log Viewer and you can look through them by clicking the page number buttons on the bottom right of the screen (refer to Figure 10-9). As a regular maintenance task, you should delete unneeded events to keep the log size down. You can delete selected items by clicking the Delete Selected Exceptions button or you can delete them all by clicking Clear Log.

Another way to look quickly through the Log Viewer is to change the number in the Records Per Page text box to a higher value. If you select 100, you will see 100 records per page. If you do this, be aware that the page will take longer to load depending on your Internet connection speed.

If you are logged in as a superuser, you will also see a drop-down list called Portal. Superusers are allowed to see the events created by any of the Web sites that have been set up by any user, and the Portal drop-down list allows you to select the events from a specific Web site. The default selection is All, which shows you the exceptions from all the Web sites at once. Simply select the name of the site from the drop-down list to narrow down the list of events.

Figure 10-9:
The Log Viewer gives you an easy way to do a health check on your site.

Whereas the Site Log lets you see who is on your Web site and where they went and when they went there, the Log Viewer gives you even more details. With the Log Viewer, you can see when a user logged in successfully and also when they tried to log in but failed. This is useful for spotting when users are trying to hack into your Web site because it records the IP address of the computer making the attempt, which you can later use to track the offender if need be. To easily see the failed login attempts, simply select Login Failure from the Type drop-down list.

One of the great things about DotNetNuke is that it enables you to do many tasks that would normally require a system Administrator. In the Dark Ages before DotNetNuke, if something went wrong with your site, your users would get a nasty error page with some cryptic message that was of no use to you. They would ring you up to tell you your site was broken, but when you asked them what was wrong, they could only repeat a cryptic message that told you nothing. With DotNetNuke, on the other hand, your site is still displayed, and only the one module that has a problem shows an error message saying that the module is not available. Now for the extra-cool part: Not only did DotNetNuke fail gracefully, but it also recorded everything about the failure that the technical support person will need to fix it. If the failure is from a module, DNN creates a Module Load Exception in the Log Viewer. You don't need to write anything down when your user rings you up and says that one of the modules on your site is showing an error: Simply say "Thanks," and go to the Log Viewer to look for any Module Load Exceptions. After you've found the list of exceptions (or errors), you can send them to your technical support person.

In Figure 10-10, you can see the message window that makes it very easy for you to get help with technical problems. To see this window, click the plus sign next to Send Exceptions. To send the exceptions to your technical support person, simply select the check box next to each of the items you want to send, enter the tech support e-mail address, and write a friendly message about the problems you are experiencing. Click Send Selected Exceptions and you're done. Your support team will now have all the information they need to solve the problem and get your site running perfectly again.

Configuring the Log Viewer

Superusers have the extra capability to change which events are recorded by the Log Viewer. A default set of events captures the most commonly used events and you should probably leave these as they are. You can add extra events to the list by selecting Edit Log Configurations from the module menu. This takes you the list of current events that are being recorded; if the word *True* appears in the Active column, they are being recorded now. If you click the Edit link you can also see for which Web sites the events are being recorded and if the events are being recorded in the standard event log or a specific event log file. You may want to use a different event log file if you need to keep a specific event's log in a separate file. This can be useful for your technical support team if they are having trouble diagnosing a problem.

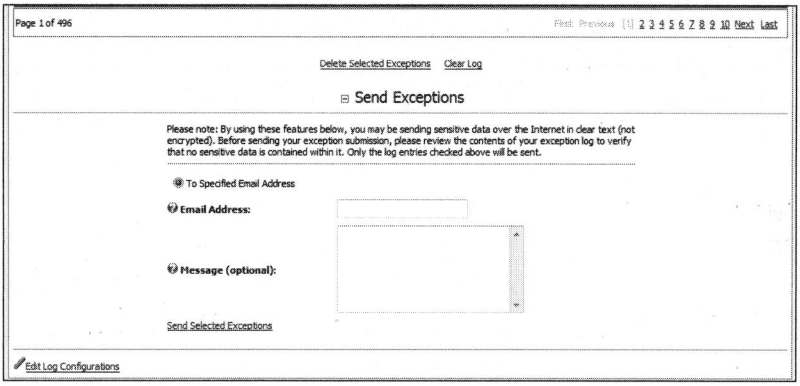

Figure 10-10: The Log Viewer Send Exceptions window makes it easy for you to get technical help with your site.

To add a new event to be recorded, select Add Log Configuration from the module menu. The edit page for adding and editing log configurations is shown in Figure 10-11. To get to this screen, click the Edit Log Configurations to show the list of current events and then either click the pencil next to any of the current items or click Add Log Configurations from the module menu.

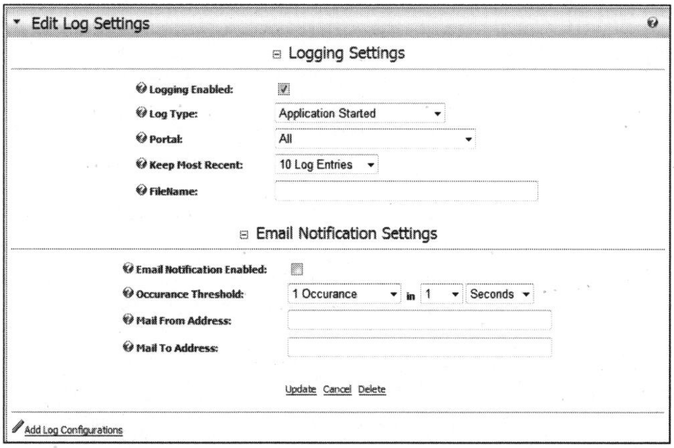

Figure 10-11: In the Log Viewer Edit Log Settings window, you can add, edit, and remove log configurations.

To add the new event, follow these steps:

1. **Select the Logging Enabled check box.**

   You can turn this on and off to decide which events are recorded.

2. **Select from the Log Type drop-down list which event you want to record.**

   You can record 47 different events in DotNetNuke!

3. **Select which Web site you want to record for in the Portal drop-down list.**

   If you select All, every time that event occurs, it will be recorded.

4. **From the Keep Most Recent drop-down list, select how many records of this type of event you want to keep.**

   After that limit is reached, the oldest events will be deleted and the new ones recorded. This stops the Log Viewer from getting too big.

5. **If you want to keep your Log Viewer records for this log type in a separate file, specify the filename here.**

   Log Viewer records its events in XML format, so the file you specify must be an XML file.

DotNetNuke automates as much of the management of your Web site as possible. To make your life even easier and to make sure that you don't miss out on important event notifications, you can set up your event to e-mail you or your technical support team when it occurs. You can see this at the bottom of the screen for editing an Event Log Setting.

To do this, follow these steps:

1. **Select the E-mail Event Notification Enabled check box.**

   This activates the e-mail sending feature for your event.

2. **In the Occurrence Threshold drop-down lists, enter when you want to be notified.**

   For example, if you want to be notified when the Login Failed event has occurred 25 times in 1 minute, which could indicate an attack, select 25 Occurrences and 1 Minutes from the drop-down lists.

3. **In the Mail From Address field, enter the address you want the person who receives the e-mail to reply to.**

4. **In the Mail To Address field, enter the address of the person who should receive the e-mail.**

   This will often be you or the technical support team, depending on the type of event.

5. **Click Update.**

Checking Out the Recycle Bin

DotNetNuke now has a handy utility called the Recycle Bin, which you can access from Admin⇨Recycle Bin. In the early days of DotNetNuke, if you deleted an item, it was gone. (Ahem: This caused all sorts of problems when one of the authors of this book was trying to show another of its authors how to use a computer.) Thus the Recycle Bin was born. The Recycle Bin is exactly what you would expect it to be: A place where you can go to restore modules and pages that you deleted from your Web site. Figure 10-12 shows the Recycle Bin with items in the Pages and Modules lists. As your Web site starts to mature and you and your site Administrators add and modify more and more content, the Recycle Bin will fill up with items. You should make cleaning up the Recycle Bin a part of your regular maintenance of your Web site so that when the time comes that you want to restore a module, you don't have to scroll through hundreds of deleted items.

Figure 10-12:
The Recycle Bin is where you can restore deleted modules and pages.

Restoring a page

When you delete a page in DotNetNuke, it is not permanently deleted, but is only marked ready for deletion. This makes it possible to restore the page back to its former glory in one easy step. Simply click the page name you want to restore in the list of deleted pages and click the Restore button. Your page is now ready for you to edit and add more content to.

Permanently deleting a page

To keep your Recycle Bin nice and tidy, you should regularly delete the items you know you will never need again. After you permanently delete an item, you are no longer able to restore the page and it will not show up in the Recycle Bin Page List. To permanently delete a page, click the name of the page in the list and click the Delete button. Now your Recycle Bin is getting tidy!

Restoring a module

The same process you followed for restoring a page works for modules as well. The only difference is that, with a module, you need to specify which page you want it to be restored to. Follow these steps to restore a module:

1. **Select the module to restore in the list of delete modules.**

2. **Select the page to restore the module to by selecting it from the Restore to Page drop-down list.**

3. **Click the Restore button.**

Permanently deleting a module

You will find as you use DotNetNuke that the module list in the Recycle Bin will fill up quite quickly, so it is a good idea to check it regularly and permanently delete any modules you no longer need. The process is exactly the same as for deleting a page. Simply click the module you want to delete and click the Delete button.

Emptying the Recycle Bin

A handy tool on the Recycle Bin allows you to permanently delete the contents of both the Deleted Pages list and the Deleted Modules list in one go. All you need to do is click the Empty Recycle Bin button and your Recycle Bin will be emptied for you. You may need to click it twice to completely empty the Recycle Bin. Remember that clicking this button will *permanently* delete all items in the Recycle Bin.

Checking on Scheduled Tasks

In a standard DotNetNuke Web site, some tasks automatically occur in the background. Operations that occur periodically on a regular schedule are listed here, such as indexing the content of your site for the search facility. You can view the schedule by going to Host⇨Schedule, where you will see a list of scheduled events, as shown in Figure 10-13. The list shows you which tasks are running in the background, how often they run, when they are scheduled to run again, and the history of when they have run recently.

Figure 10-13: The list of scheduled tasks lets you see what's going on in the background.

Type	Enabled	Frequency	Retry Time Lapse	Next Start	
DotNetNuke.Entities.Users.PurgeUsersOnline, DOTNETNUKE		Every 1 Minute	Every 5 Minutes		History
DotNetNuke.Services.Log.SiteLog.PurgeSiteLog, DOTNETNUKE		Every 1 Day	Every 2 Hours		History
DotNetNuke.Services.Scheduling.PurgeScheduleHistory, DOTNETNUKE	☑	Every 1 Day	Every 2 Days	1/17/2007 3:15:44 PM	History
DotNetNuke.Services.Log.EventLog.PurgeLogBuffer, DOTNETNUKE	☑	Every 1 Minute	Every 5 Minutes	1/16/2007 8:47:40 PM	History
DotNetNuke.Services.Log.EventLog.SendLogNotifications, DOTNETNUKE		Every 5 Minutes	Every 10 Minutes		History
DotNetNuke.Services.Search.SearchEngineScheduler, DOTNETNUKE	☑	Every 30 Minutes	Every 60 Minutes	1/16/2007 8:47:21 PM	History
DotNetNuke.Modules.Admin.ResourceInstaller.InstallResources, DOTNETNUKE		Every 30 Minutes	Every 60 Minutes		History
DotNetNuke.Services.FileSystem.SynchronizeFileSystem, DOTNETNUKE		Every 1 Hour	Every 2 Hours		History
DotNetNuke.Services.Cache.PurgeCache, DOTNETNUKE		Every 2 Hours	Every 30 Minutes		History
DotNetNuke.Modules.Events.EventNotification, DotNetNuke.Modules.Events		Every 30 Minutes	Every 30 Minutes		History

Add Item to Schedule

Clicking the History button next to each item lets you see when the tasks have run, how long they took to run, and if they were successful when they ran. It is important for the superusers to check this history on a regular basis so they can spot if anything has gone wrong recently and get an overall understanding of the health of the Web site. For example, if your Web site gets a lot of traffic and you have the Site Log set to 60 days, you should also set the PurgeSiteLog scheduled task to run at least once a month. This purges old stuff out of the Site Log, ensuring that it never gets too full, which may slow down your site. As part of your regular maintenance of your site, you should check the history of the task. If the history is regular, you can be assured that the Site Log has not become too large. If, however, the PurgeSiteLog task is failing, the Site Log may become too large for you to be able to view reports.

To set the PurgeSiteLog task to occur once a month, follow these steps:

1. **In the Schedule pane, click the Edit blue pencil icon next to DotNetNuke.Services.Log.SiteLog.PurgeSiteLog, DOTNETNUKE.**

   This opens the Edit Schedule Screen.

2. **Select the Schedule Enabled check box.**

3. **Set the Time Lapse to 30 Days.**

4. **Set the Retry Frequency to 1 Days.**

5. **Leave the rest of the fields as they are and click <u>Update</u>.**

In the history of a task, you should take a look at the time to execute the task, which is shown as Duration in milliseconds, and whether the task executed correctly. Most tasks should only take a few milliseconds to execute and, if they take longer, will quite likely fail. So when you are checking this list, first look for True in the Succeeded column, and then check for items over 250 milliseconds. Items with a Duration longer than 250 milliseconds may indicate a problem that your technical support team needs to be made aware of.

Chapter 11

Customizing the Look of Your Site with Components

● ●

In This Chapter

▶ Understanding components

▶ Installing the telerik r.a.d.editor

▶ Replacing the DNN editor with FCKeditor

▶ Adding HTTP compression

▶ Enabling Friendly URLs

▶ Customizing site navigation with a telerik skin object

● ●

When you build a Web site with DotNetNuke, you add modules to pages to create the site. This is very similar to how DotNetNuke itself was designed. The DotNetNuke application was designed as a series of individual components that all work together to create the application you use to build your Web sites. This design makes DotNetNuke very flexible, and means that, with a little bit of skill, you can easily change different aspects of the application without having to write any code yourself.

Take for example the Text/HTML module: You can edit the content of your page by using a WYSIWYG (What You See Is What You Get) editor. The WYSIWYG editor is actually a component of DotNetNuke and you will see it in lots of different modules, such as the Announcements module. Now say that you want to use a different WYSIWYG editor that has some other features, such as a spell checker. The component architecture of DotNetNuke means that you can switch which type of editor you use for editing rich text just by following a few simple steps, as you see a bit later in this chapter.

There are three types of components that make up DotNetNuke: providers, HTTP modules, and skin objects. We discuss each of these and show you how to change them to suit your situation.

Discovering Providers

In its early days, DotNetNuke stored its data in a Microsoft product called SQL Server 2000 and there was no other choice: To use DotNetNuke, you had to have SQL Server 2000. Many people in the DotNetNuke community wanted to be able to use other databases such as MySQL and Oracle, but couldn't do it without major changes to the code that DotNetNuke was written in. The code that DotNetNuke was written in was specific to SQL Server; therefore, DotNetNuke was tightly coupled with SQL Server. The people who created DNN wanted to find a way to be able to change which database was used without having to change DotNetNuke, and this is how the component idea was born.

DotNetNuke should behave the same way and give you the same features and experience no matter what database is being used behind the scenes. If the code that is specific to a particular database was in its own component and completely separate from DotNetNuke, you could swap it out and change databases without affecting the code in DotNetNuke. This is called the *provider pattern*.

To be able to change which provider your installation of DotNetNuke uses, you need access to the Web server to transfer files to it and you must be able to edit the web.config file. The web.config file contains all the configuration information for your installation. Most hosting companies allow you to have File Transfer Protocol (FTP) rights, which enable you to edit the web.config file and transfer it to your hosting server.

Working with HTTP Modules

When you click a link on a Web page, lots of things happen in the background before you see the next page. The Web server that the site is running on gets a request and then starts to process that request to produce the HTML that is then shown to you in your Web browser. Processing the request involves the HTTP pipeline, which consists of a number of steps, one of which is invoking any HTTP modules that are configured for the site.

HTTP modules are components that get executed each time someone makes a request to the Web server by clicking a link or pushing a button. The great thing about HTTP modules is that they get executed every time. They have events that fire both before the request is serviced and after. DotNetNuke takes advantage of this by rewriting the URL of each page so that it is search engine–friendly.

HTTP modules are similar to providers in that they are separate components from DotNetNuke that can be swapped in and out to change the behavior of DotNetNuke without actually changing any code in DotNetNuke.

You will need the same level of access to change HTTP modules as you need for providers: FTP access from your host should be sufficient.

Getting to Know Skin Objects

Skin objects are another type of component that allows siteAdministrators to easily modify the behavior of their Web sites. Skin objects are exactly the same as the modules you use to construct your site with the exception that you cannot add them from the Add Module drop-down list. They can only be added as part of a skin.

The skin of your Web site is made up of lots of skin objects. If you look at a standard DotNetNuke Web page, you see the date, the menu, the login and register links, the privacy statement, and a bunch of other objects. Each of these is a *skin object* and can be installed on your Web site in exactly the same way as you install a normal module.

Using skin objects to make up the various parts of your skin means that if, for example, you want to change the type of menu system you are using, you simply have to install the new skin object, change the token in your skin, and then reload your skin. We discuss how to do this very shortly.

Replacing the Standard DNN Editor with the telerik r.a.d.editor

The telerik r.a.d.editor is a WYSIWYG HTML editor that has extra features beyond what the standard Free Text Box editor that comes with DotNetNuke typically offers. The r.a.d.editor has several features that the standard DNN editor does not, such as

- Excellent support for tables.
- Compliance-checking of your content via tools like the W3C compliance-checker.
- Dockable toolbars, which means that you can move them around like you can in Microsoft Word.

✔ Undo and Redo buttons that allow you to undo specific actions rather than just the last actions.

✔ Great support for pasting content from Word. The r.a.d.editor has seven different ways of stripping the Word markup and converting it into properly formed HTML.

✔ Right-click context menus that make it easier for you to create your content.

✔ A statistics view that gives you information on the number of words and characters in the HTML you are working on.

✔ A spell checker.

Replace the standard DNN editor with the r.a.d.editor by following the steps outlined in the next several sections.

Installing the editor

The telerik r.a.d.editor is a commercial product, so you will either need to buy a copy or try it out with a trial version. These steps show you how to use the trial version:

1. **To get the trial version, first go to `www.telerik.com/client.net` and follow the instructions for logging in.**

2. **After you have logged in, go to the My Free Trials section, where you will see a list of telerik products on the right side of the page.**

   There are quite a few, and you can try them all out now that you are registered.

3. **Locate the r.a.d.editor section and download the r.a.d.editor Trial.EXE file.**

   At the time of writing, the current version was 6.6.0, which means the file was called RadEditor_6_6_0_trial.EXE.

   If you don't want to actually install the editor but instead just want to get the required files for DNN, you can download the RadEditor_6_6_0_trial.ZIP.

4. **Next copy two files into your DNN project: the RadEditor.Net2.DLL and the RadSpell.NET2.DLL files.**

   • If you installed the .EXE file, the files are located at C:\Program Files\telerik\r.a.d.editor6.5\NET2\bin.

   • If you downloaded the .ZIP file, unzip it onto your local hard drive and locate the files inside the net2/bin folder.

5. If you are running your DotNetNuke site on your local machine, copy the files and paste them into the bin folder of your local DNN site.

6. If you are doing this on a hosted Web server, use your FTP program to transfer the files to the Bin folder of your Web site.

7. You now also need to copy the RadControls folder from the same location you copied the two DLL files from.

8. If you are running your DotNetNuke site on your local machine, copy the folder and paste it into the "controls" folder of your local DNN site.

9. If you are doing this on a hosted Web server, use your FTP program to transfer the folder to the "controls" folder of your Web site.

Installing the DNN provider

After you have the files for the editor sorted out, you need to install the DNN provider for the r.a.d.editor so you can use it on your site:

1. Go to `www.telerik.com/client.net`, log in, and go to the My Free Trials section to download the provider, which, for version 6.6.0, is called RadEditor_6.60_DNN(2006_10_06).ZIP.

2. Unzip the file to your local hard drive.

3. If you are running your DotNetNuke site on your local machine, copy the Bin and Providers folders into the root directory of your site.

4. If you are doing this on a hosted Web server, use your FTP program to transfer the folders to the root of your Web site.

Configuring the web.config file

The last step is to configure the web.config file to use the r.a.d.editor on your DNN site. To modify the web.config file, follow these steps:

1. Open the web.config file that is in the root of your Web site.

   If you are doing this on a remote Web site, use your FTP program to download the file first.

2. Locate the <dotnetnuke> node in the web.config file.

3. Inside this section, locate the <htmlEditor defaultProvider= "Ftb3HtmlEditorProvider"> node.

4. **Change the `defaultProvider` value to `RadHtmlEditorProvider` so that it looks like this**

```
<htmlEditor defaultProvider="RadHtmlEditorProvider">
```

5. **Enter this into the web.config file:**

```
<add name="RadHtmlEditorProvider"
type="Telerik.DNN.Providers.RadHtmlEditorProvider,
        Telerik.DNN.Providers.RadHtmlEditorProvider"
providerPath="~\Providers\HtmlEditorProviders\
RadHtmlEditorProvider\"
AutoCreatePaths="true"
/>
```

6. **Save the web.config file and, if you are working on a remote Web site, use FTP to transfer it to your Web site.**

Now when you log in to your Web site to edit text, the editor you will see is the new r.a.d.editor, as shown in Figure 11-1. Included in the download is a file called Overview of RadHtmlEditorProvider. This file contains a list of all the properties you can set on the r.a.d.editor in the web.config file. Try some of them out and see how it affects the r.a.d.editor.

Figure 11-1:
The
Text/HTML
module
with the
r.a.d.editor.

Replacing the Standard DNN Editor with the FCKeditor Provider

The FCKeditor is a rich text WYSIWYG editor that has extra features not included in the standard Free Text Box editor that comes with DotNetNuke. And unlike the r.a.d.editor, it's free! It has many of the same features as the r.a.d.editor and many more than the standard WYSIWYG editor.

To replace the standard editor with the FCKeditor, follow these steps, which are very similar to the way you install the telerik r.a.d.editor:

1. **Download the .ZIP file by going to `dotnetnuke.com/DotNetNukeProjects/ProviderFCKeditor0153/Downloads/tabid/936/Default.aspx` and clicking the <u>Download</u> link.**

    This takes you to a site called Source Forge, where all the DotNetNuke files are stored for download.

2. **Unzip the file to your local hard drive.**

3. **If you are running your DotNetNuke site on your local machine, copy the Bin and Providers folders into the root directory of your site.**

4. **If you are working on a hosted Web server, use your FTP program to transfer the folders to the root of your Web site.**

Now that you have the appropriate files on the Web server, we need to modify the web.config file so that DotNetNuke knows to use the new FCKeditor. To modify the web.config file, follow these steps:

1. **Open the web.config file that is in the root of your Web site.**

    If you are working on a remote Web site, use your FTP program to download the file first.

2. **Locate the `<dotnetnuke>` node in the web.config file.**

3. **Inside this section, locate the `<htmlEditor defaultProvider="Ftb3HtmlEditorProvider">` node.**

4. **Change the `defaultProvider` value to `FckHtmlEditorProvider` so that it looks like this:**

    ```
    <htmlEditor defaultProvider=" FckHtmlEditorProvider">
    ```

5. **Open the file called Install.txt from the unzipped files.**

6. **Copy the section between `<add name="FckHtmlEditorProvider"` and `</providers>` and paste it into the web.config file underneath the node `<add name="Ftb3HtmlEditorProvider"`.**

7. **Make sure that your result looks like the install.TXT file.**

8. **Save the web.config file and use FTP to transfer it to your Web site.**

Now when you log in to your Web site to edit text, the editor you will see is the new FCKeditor, as shown in Figure 11-2.

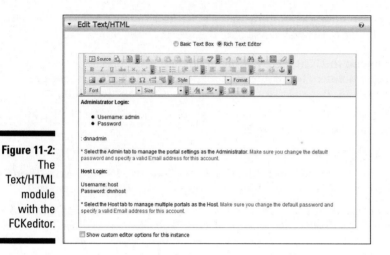

Figure 11-2:
The
Text/HTML
module
with the
FCKeditor.

In Figure 11-2, you can see a check box that says Show Custom Editor Options for This Instance. Selecting this check box brings up a new settings page, shown in Figure 11-3, for the FCK Editor that allows you customize the look and feel and functionality of the editor without having to edit the web.config file again.

Figure 11-3:
Customizing
the
FCKeditor by
using the
Custom
Editor
options.

Enabling Friendly URLs

DotNetNuke makes it easy for Web site Administrators to add as many pages as they like to their sites. Each new page that is added is stored as a record in the underlying database and is displayed when DNN retrieves the TabID from the URL to work out which page to show. For example, the URL `www.dnnangel.com/Default.aspx?TabID=xxx` will show you a featured real estate listing on the site. The problem with this URL is that it is not human-friendly (that is, easily remembered by a human), nor does this convoluted URL look good in printed materials.

DotNetNuke has an option to turn on Friendly URLs, which turns the above URL from `www.dnnangel.com/Default.aspx?TabID=336` to `www.dnnangel.com/xxxxxxxx/Default.aspx`. The second URL works really well for search engines, but is still not very useful for humans, and it's still way too long to put in the marketing material for your site. What you really want is a URL like `www.dnnrealty.com/FeaturedListing.aspx`, which is great for search engines and easy to remember.

To make Friendly URLs, install a new component called the Inventua HrefExchanger. You can download everything you need from `www.inventua.com/dnn-hrefexchanger.content`. HrefExchanger uses the name of the page to create the human-friendly URLs. This means that your page names must be unique within each portal, or HrefExchanger will not be able to differentiate between pages. If you have multiple Web sites in your DotNetNuke installation, you can have the same page name in each of the separate sites. For example, each separate site can have a page called Home Page without causing any conflict.

If your page name contains spaces, HrefExchanger replaces them with plus signs. The plus sign is the default replacement for the space character. (The HrefExchanger has a "replace-spaces-with" option that you can use to specify which character to use.) If your page name contains an ampersand (&), plus sign (+), dot (.), forward slash (/), backward slash (\) or question mark (?), the URL will not be rewritten because these characters are reserved characters for URLs. You don't have to use the friendly name for every page: Its main purpose is to give you a human-friendly URL to reference in writing, such as blog posts, and to have a page name that is easy to remember.

To install the HrefExchanger, follow these steps:

1. **Unzip the file you downloaded from the Inventua Web site.**

2. **If you are running your DotNetNuke site on your local machine, copy the Inventua.HrefExchanger.DLL file into the bin folder of your Web site.**

3. **If you are doing this on a hosted Web server, use your FTP program to transfer the Inventua.HrefExchanger.DLL file to the bin folder of your Web site.**

After you have the component in the correct location on your Web server, you need to modify the web.config file that holds your configuration information so that the site knows to use the new component. Follow these steps to update your web.config file:

1. **Open the web.config file that is in the root of your Web site.**

   If you are working on a remote Web site, use your FTP program to download the file first.

2. **Locate the < configSections> node in the web.config file.**

3. **Inside this section, paste this code:**

```
<section name="hrefExchanger"
        type="Inventua.HrefExchanger.ConfigurationHand
        ler, Inventua.HrefExchanger" />
```

Make sure you pasted the line containing <section name= "hrefExchanger" directly under the "configSections" section. It does not go inside the sectionGroup name="dotnetnuke" section.

4. **Locate the <httpModules> node inside the <system.web> node in the web.config file.**

5. **Paste the following line directly under the httpModules node so it is at the top of the list of httpModules:**

```
<add name="HrefHttpModule" type=
        "Inventua.HrefExchanger.HrefHttpModule,Inventu
        a.HrefExchanger"/>
```

6. **Now locate the last </system.web> node and paste this line directly underneath it:**

```
<hrefExchanger extension=".aspx" />
```

7. **If you want to use a character other than a plus sign + for spaces, you can set that inside this node. For example, to use an underscore, type this code:**

```
<hrefExchanger extension=".aspx" replace-spaces-
        with="_" />
```

8. **Save the web.config file and use FTP to transfer it to your Web site.**

You need to take one last step to make this component work properly.

1. **Log in as a superuser and go to the Host Settings page.**

2. **Open the Advanced Settings section.**

3. **Open the Friendly URLs section.**

4. **Deselect the check box, wait for the page to refresh, and click Update.**

You will notice that the URLs still display as TabIDs; for example, ?TabID=336. This is because, in Administration mode, the URLs aren't displayed in the friendly format. The reason for this is that some third-party modules may cause problems and you still need to be able to administer your site. If Administrators use normal DNN URLs, you will always be able to administer your site with this component installed.

To see your handiwork, log out of your Web site and have a look around. Click on a menu item and notice that the URL in the address bar is a nice, easy-to-remember, human-readable Friendly URL, as shown in Figure 11-4.

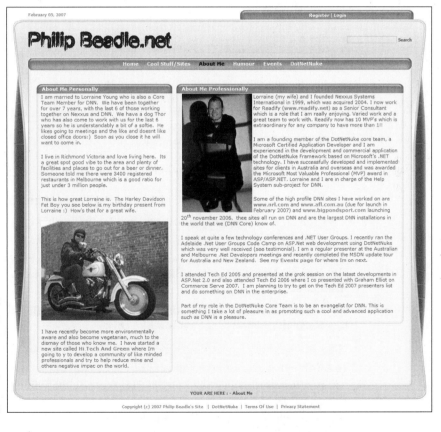

Figure 11-4:
A DNN Web site displaying a Friendly URL.

Replacing Standard DNN Navigation with a telerik Skin Object

DotNetNuke comes with two types of navigation options: the Tree view and the Solpart menu. Both of these menu systems are included on your Web site page as skin objects, which are special DNN modules that you can use to create customized DNN sites. As with most other aspects of DNN, you can install other types of skin objects to achieve the desired result. In this section, you see how easy it is to install a new skin object called the telerik r.a.d.menu skin object. The telerik r.a.d.menu is a commercial product that you can purchase from their Web site at www.telerik.com. They also have trial versions that you can download. After you have registered for the trial versions, you can download the r.a.d.menu skin object from www.telerik.com/dnn/Support/radmenuskinobject/tabid/50/Default.aspx.

The telerik r.a.d.menu has several features that make it an excellent replacement for the menus that come with DNN. The code uses Semantic Rendering to reduce the amount of HTML. It's tuned to be search engine–friendly but still remain 100 percent compliant. Also, the extensive use of the keyboard to control the menus is another factor that allows Web applications to behave more like Windows applications. The best feature, however, is that you can easily skin the telerik r.a.d.menu. The menu comes with a set of cool skins such as Windows XP, Office, and Visual Studio.

After you have downloaded the skin object, follow these steps to install it:

1. **Unzip the folder you have downloaded onto your computer.**

   After the file is unzipped, you will see two folders called net1 and net2 and a readme text file.

2. **Open the net2 folder and you will see a file called Telerik.DNN. SkinObjects.Menu.ZIP, one called RadMenu.ZIP and a skinning whitepaper.**

3. **If you purchased a license to the r.a.d.menu and installed the product, it will usually install to a location like this:**

   ```
   C:\Program Files\telerik\r.a.d.menu3.2.
   ```

   To be able to use your licensed version in the skin object, simply open the Telerik.SkinObjects.Menu.ZIP file and replace the RadMenu.DLL with your licensed version.

4. **Alternatively, if you have a license key for the trial edition, you need to edit the LicenseFile.XML found inside the .ZIP file in the Telerik. DNN.SkinObjects.Menu.zip\Resources.zip\RadControls folder. Simply edit the file and replace the license key with the one for the trial edition.**

If you just want to test the skin objects without buying a license, they will only be accessible from your machine (localhost).

5. **Go to your Web site and log in as a superuser.**

6. **Navigate to Host⇨Module Definitions.**

7. **Select Upload New Module from the module menu.**

8. **Find the Telerik.DNN.SkinObjects.Menu.ZIP file on your computer and click Open, and then click Upload New File.**

Your skin object is now installed on your site, ready to be used. To use the skin object, you need a skin that uses it. In the package, telerik includes a sample skin for you to try out:

1. **Go to the skins page (Admin⇨Skins or Host⇨Skins) and click on the <u>Upload Skin</u> link located near the bottom of the page.**

2. **Select the sample skin that comes with the RADMenu skinobject - RadMenu.ZIP.**

3. **Click Add and then click Upload New File.**

4. **After the skin installation is complete, go back to the Skins page and preview/apply the new skin.**

Now have a look around your site with the new skin. You can see the new menu skin object, shown in Figure 11-5, and how it behaves differently from the standard DNN menus.

Figure 11-5:
A Web site with the telerik sample skin and r.a.d.menu skin object installed.

Part V
The Part of Tens

The 5th Wave   By Rich Tennant

In This Part . . .

Chapters 12 and 13 are a sampler platter of the numerous content modules that you can add to your Web site. Chapter 13 lists really cheap or free modules, and Chapter 12 lists modules that cost a bit more money. Chapter 14 is a supplement to the Forum module and lists ten fun things for forum users.

Chapter 12

Ten Commercial Modules Worth a Look

*T*he World Wide Web is simply brimming with DotNetNuke modules that you can buy to enhance the functionality of your portal. In this chapter, we review ten commercial modules that we feel represent good value and interesting functionality. Our list doesn't claim to represent the best of every-thing on offer, but hopefully it will whet your appetite.

DotNetNuke recently launched a rapidly growing online module and skins store at `marketplace.dotnetnuke.com/default.aspx`. The products sold from this store have been tested and approved to work with DNN. Furthermore, the profits from this store go back to the project.

Another online store for DNN modules and skins is `www.snowcovered.com`. This is an independently owned store that does not offer any testing or verifi-cation of the items it sells. However, it currently has a large product offering.

Building Forms with Enterprise Forms

A major benefit of a Web site is that is reduces your workload by enabling people to access information without your involvement. One step better is the addition of forms to collect data and report on that data. Enabling people to complete forms to place orders, to register for events, and so on can save hours of administrative time that would be spent receiving and processing information.

Enterprise Forms is a highly advanced suite of four modules that interact to provide everything you need to collect and process data. Enterprise Forms comes with four modules that work together to enable you to design form templates, display forms in one or more places, process the data that is collected, and to view or export the collected data. Get these modules and more details at www.longnhi.com/Home/tabid/36/Default.aspx.

Here is a quick overview of these four modules:

✔ The Form Templates Manager module, shown in Figure 12-1, enables you to design any type of form you like. You can customize each of the form fields by adding text boxes, check lists, radio buttons, HTML text fields, file upload fields, mandatory fields, and more. After you have created a form, you must create and set up which security roles can view the form, edit the form, approve the form, and so on. These are called the different form *states*, and creating different security roles to manage different form states means that you can create complex workflow systems.

✔ After you have created a form template, the hard work is done: The other three modules are used to display, process, and report on data. Although the Form Templates Manager module can be a bit tricky the first couple of times you use it, after you get the hang of it, you can create complex and highly functional forms.

Figure 12-1:
The Form Templates Manager displays the form templates that have been created.

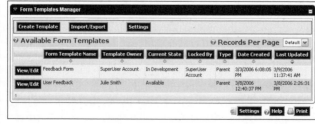

✔ The Data Collection Manager module, shown in Figure 12-2, displays a form that you have previously created by using the Form Template Manager. All you have to do is to select one of your templates from a drop-down list and your form is displayed for use.

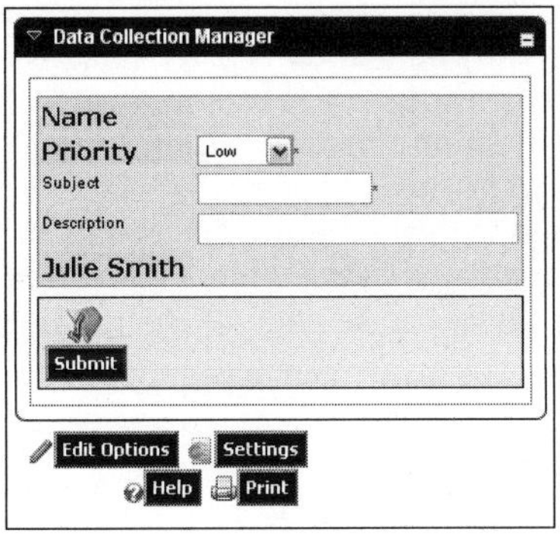

Figure 12-2: Example of a form displayed in the Data Collection Manager module.

✔ The Form Workflow Manager module, shown in Figure 12-3, enables the Administrator and any other roles with appropriate rights to approve, reject, edit, and so on, the information that has been submitted by using the Data Collection Manager.

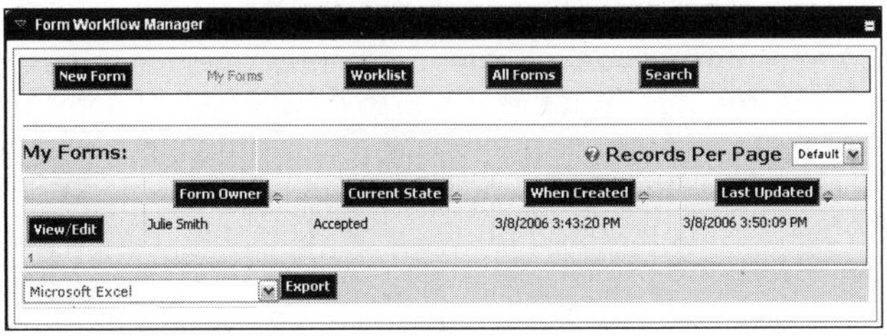

Figure 12-3: Collected data ready for processing in the Form Workflow Manager.

✔ The final module is the Report Manager, which lets you export the information collected in either a Comma Separated Values (CSV) or as a Microsoft Excel format. This module also enables you to design dynamic reports.

Here are some things you can do with this module:

✔ Create a form template once and use it in multiple places.

✔ Send a customized message to users after their form has been successfully submitted.

✔ Export collected information into Microsoft Excel or as Comma Separated Values (CSV).

✔ Create security roles to manage different stages of form workflow such as accepted or rejected.

✔ Ability to include submitted forms in e-mail notifications.

✔ Form approval can be managed by selected security roles.

Here are some resources for more help on this module:

✔ A compiled help file is supplied with the Enterprise Forms module. This includes a walk-through on creating a User Feedback form, which is a good place to start finding out how to use each of the modules

✔ Nearly all fields have a help button with a description.

✔ A support forum is located at `www.longnhi.com/Forums/tabid/138/Default.aspx`.

✔ A contact form can be submitted at `www.longnhi.com/ContactUs/tabid/144/Default.aspx`.

Managing Images with the DNN Photo Gallery

Whether you are running a commercial or a hobby Web site, chances are you will want to display photos. You might like to display your family photos, wedding photos, or pictures of other personal events with your friends and family. Alternatively, if you're running a commercial Web site, you might need to share libraries of corporate logos and branding with your staff, photos of your products with your users, and photos of current projects with your customers.

Regardless of the content, the DNN Photo Gallery module, shown in Figure 12-4, provides an effective way to display and manage large numbers of images.

The DNN Photo Gallery module lets you create one or more photo galleries that can be displayed in endless ways on your site. You can set the Gallery to display thumbnail images in any combination of rows or columns on the page. Get this module at `www.dnnphotogallery.com`.

Figure 12-4:
The standard layout of the DNN Gallery module.

Here are some features of this module:

✔ Create multiple galleries on the My Gallery page, shown in Figure 12-5, and assign the ability to manage galleries to different security roles.

✔ All Administration tasks are managed from the one page, making this module easy to work with.

✔ Import any of the gallery layouts you see on the dnnphotogallery.com Web site with just a few clicks from the Setting Catalog Web page. This saves you time spent discovering how to design layouts.

✔ Comes with language support for English, Portuguese, French, and German. Changing the selected language displays fields in the selected language. At the time of writing, there were also new files for Dutch and Russian, which can be obtained from the DNN Gallery Web site.

✔ Upload a compressed (zipped) folder of images and the DNN Photo Gallery module automatically extracts all the photos and places them in your chosen gallery. A great timesaver!

To get help using this module, download a quick start video demonstrating functionality from www.dnnphotogallery.com/QuickStartVideos/tabid/82/Default.aspx.

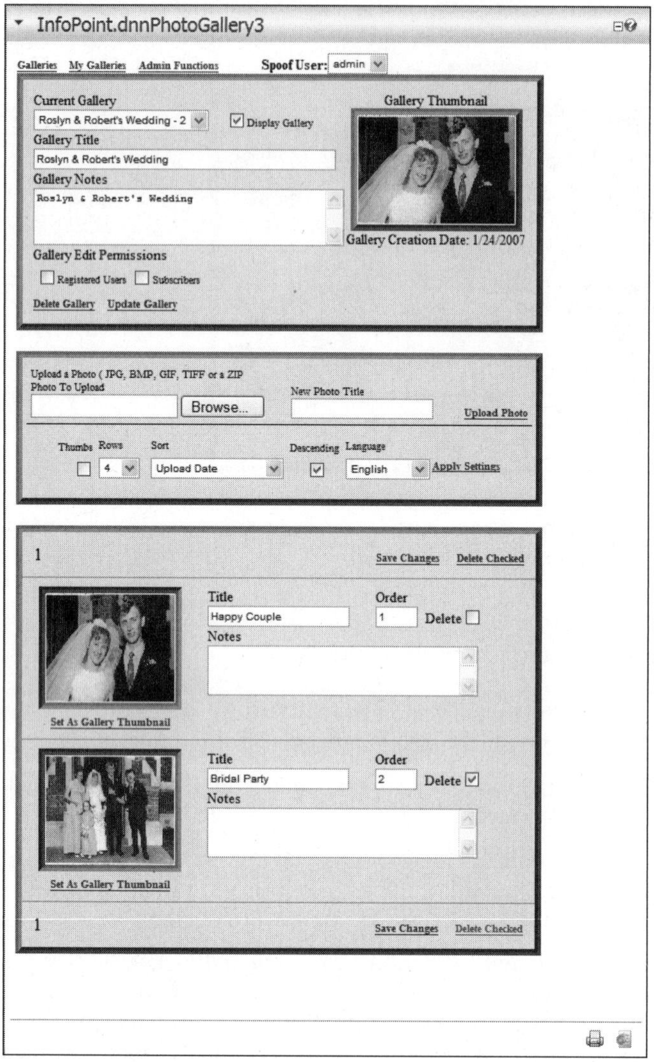

Figure 12-5:
The My
Gallery page
lets users
manage
images in
their
Gallery.

Skinning Shortcuts with the ZLDnn-Module Wrapper

Unless you discover a passion for designing skins or have a designer on standby, every now and then, you will find that the skin you are using just doesn't quite provide the unique layout you want. We used to simply make do with the existing pane layout because we just wanted to keep building our site and didn't want the interruption of designing a new skin. However, thanks to the ZLDnn-Module Wrapper module, shown in Figure 12-6, there is now a simple and slick solution to this problem.

The ZLDnn-Module Wrapper lets you create a table and display existing modules within that table, all within the same pane. For example, you could add the ZLDnn-Module Wrapper to the Content Pane of a page and set it to display two modules across and two modules down the pane. This gives you a unique page design in minutes without the hard work of designing a new skin for the task. Get the ZLDnn-Module Wrapper module at `www.zldnn.com/Modules/ModuleWrapper/tabid/51/Default.aspx`.

Here's a list of features for this module:

- ✔ The ZLDnn-Module Wrapper lets you design complex tables, shown in Figure 12-7, known as *nested* tables, that allow you to have one module in the top row, three in the next, two in the third, and so on.

- ✔ The table layout can also be changed at any time without losing any settings, making it a robust module.

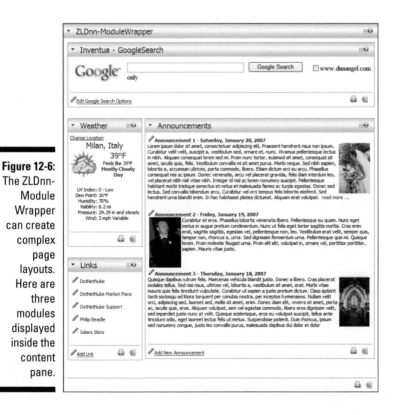

Figure 12-6: The ZLDnn-Module Wrapper can create complex page layouts. Here are three modules displayed inside the content pane.

✔ Another slick feature is the ability to set all the wrapped modules to scroll up or down or left or right within the ZLDnn-Module Wrapper. Alternatively, you can set just one or more modules to scroll. There are endless combinations available, and experimenting with different setting doesn't seem to bother the module at all.

✔ You can wrap modules that are located on a hidden page; for example, a page that is set as hidden in your Web site menu.

✔ Set the height value of the modules to keep the bottom of your page neatly aligned.

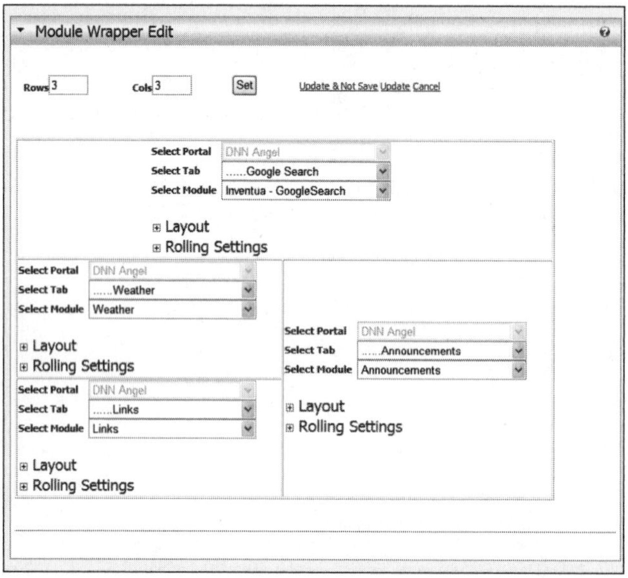

Figure 12-7:
The Edit page of the ZLDnn-Module Wrapper.

You can't choose the same module twice within the one instance of the ZLDnn-Module Wrapper.

Here's how to get help on this module:

✔ A comprehensive help document is supplied with this module or can be downloaded from `www.zldnn.com/Default.aspx?tabid=51`. This document provides an overview of how to use the module, as well as giving a good example of how to build a complex table.

✔ A user's manual can be downloaded from `www.zldnn.com/Download/tabid/233/Default.aspx`.

✔ Find answers to your questions or submit your question at `www.zldnn.com/FeedBack/tabid/195/Default.aspx`.

Online Chat and Support with SWIRL (AJAX-Based Chat)

Online chatting usually refers to either a one-on-one chat program or a group chat, also known as a chat room. Common chat programs include Window Messenger and ICQ. Online chatting lets your users communicate with you and each other. It's a great way to build a community, to create interest in topics, and to find out more about your users.

SWIRL is an online chat module for your portal. The module, shown in Figure 12-8, is dead easy to use and works exactly like other chat programs, so any of your users who have chatted online before will feel at home using the module. Get this module at `www.swirlhost.com/Default.aspx?alias= www.swirlhost.com/chatroom`.

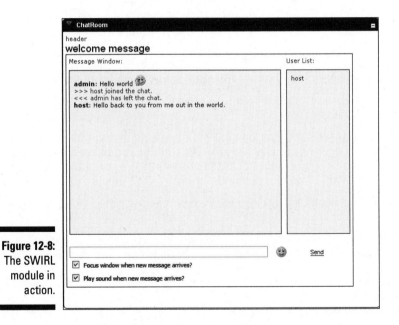

Figure 12-8: The SWIRL module in action.

As well as being used as a chat room, SWIRL can be used to provide online support for your users or customers by switching it to operator mode, asshown in Figure 12-9. This mode sends an e-mail to one or more security roles when a user enters the chat room. This means that you don't have to be logged in to the Web site all the time waiting for a support call.

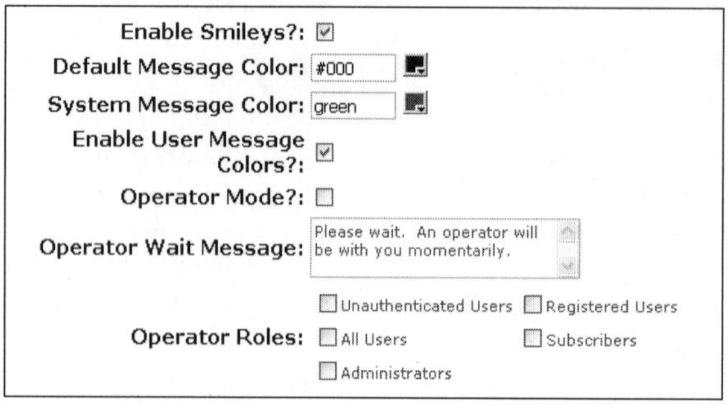

Figure 12-9:
This section
of the Chat
Room
Settings
page lets
you set the
module to
Operator
Mode for
online
support.

Here's a list of features for this module:

- A simple and fun color picker that enables you to change the color settings.

- Users can be enabled to choose their own text colors.

- A library containing 60 funny animated smileys can be enabled.

- The bad word filter can be set up to replace any word you choose with ****.

- Log the transcript of your chats. If you are using the module for support (that is, in operator mode), this feature enables you to record a support session by selecting and copying the transcript to a program such as Microsoft Word. You can delete the transcript whenever you like.

- If you send a full URL into the chat room, it is converted to a clickable link.

- An Optional Message Notification feature highlights the chat room window in your computer's taskbar each time a new message is received.

Here's a list of ways to get help on using this module:

- Watch a movie of this module in action at www.swirlhost.com/ chatroom/quickstart/Swirlchat_QuickStart.html.

- A user guide can be downloaded from www.swirlhost.com/ chatroom/Documentation/Guide/tabid/75/Default.aspx. It contains simple instructions on how to use and set up the module.

- An installation guide (for your host) can be downloaded from www. swirlhost.com/chatroom/Documentation/Installation/tabid/ 69/Default.aspx. It contains complete information detailing how to install the module and apply the module license to activate all the features of the chat room.

✔ A Change Log is located at `www.swirlhost.com/chatroom/Documentation/ChangeLog/tabid/73/Default.aspx`. This log outlines each major and minor release of the module, which features have been added, and what bug fixes have been applied for each release.

Designing Pages with the Aggregator 3.1

Aggregation can loosely be described as a way of gathering information from a number of places and organizing it by using a common interface, which is exactly what the Aggregator module does. The Aggregator module, shown in Figure 12-10, lets you aggregate modules into a single module interface and creates a menu of clickable tabs to select which module you would like to see. It's like having a second menu on the page that gives access to modules rather than to pages.

The Aggregator module provides both functional and design benefits. By aggregating multiple modules into one module, you can save space on your page and reduce the need to scroll down the page. This module also offers a new and attractive way to display information on your site without having to do any skinning. Get this module at `www.dnnstuff.com/Default.aspx?tabid=207`.

Here's a list of features for this module:

✔ The module comes with five different layouts that place the menu or tabs either above, below, left, right, or in line with module content.

✔ The module comes with two different color schemes.

✔ A range of free design themes can be downloaded from the company's Web site `www.dnnstuff.com`.

✔ You can add existing modules from other pages.

✔ You can set the module to hide module titles. This means that the title will only be displayed in the tab menu and not repeated again above the module content.

✔ By default, the title of the module becomes the text displayed on each tab. You can alternatively set the tab title to any text you like.

✔ You can enter a token (a placeholder) to any tab title that is replaced by real data on the page. For example, if you add the token [DNN:USER:FULLNAME] to a title, the token will be replaced with the user's full name, as shown in Figure 12-11. A list of tokens is included in the user manual.

✔ You can download free themes (like skins) from their Web site.

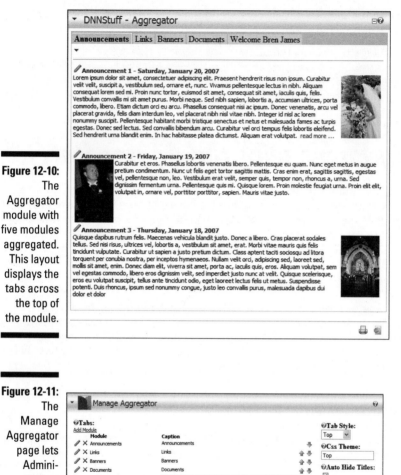

Figure 12-10:
The
Aggregator
module with
five modules
aggregated.
This layout
displays the
tabs across
the top of
the module.

Figure 12-11:
The
Manage
Aggregator
page lets
Admini-
strators
select the
modules
to be
aggregated.

Here's a list of ways to get help on using this module:

✔ A user guide is supplied with the module. It contains simple instructions on how to use and set up the module.

✔ User manual in PDF format is provided with the module.

✔ You can find a free online support forum at www.dnnstuff.com/ Forums/tabid/189/Default.aspx.

✔ An online FAQ is located at www.dnnstuff.com/Modules/
AggregatorTabbedModules/AggregatorFAQ/tabid/293/
Default.aspx.

✔ Find free e-mail support at support@dnnstuff.com.

✔ Free bug fixes and upgrades are available until the next major release.

✔ Field-level help is available.

ActiveForums

The beauty of DNN as an open-source project is that many different types of modules are developed commercially. Some of these module types are also later developed as core DNN projects. This parallel creates competition for commercial module developers, who must strive to maintain a superior product. ActiveForums, shown in Figure 12-12, is one such product. Despite a free forum module being available, this module holds its own and is an alternative worth considering. It is very simple to set up and offers several additional features to the core forum module. For more information on what a forum is and why you might want one, see Chapter 7. Get this module at www.
activemodules.com/Products/ActiveForums/tabid/58/Default.
aspx.

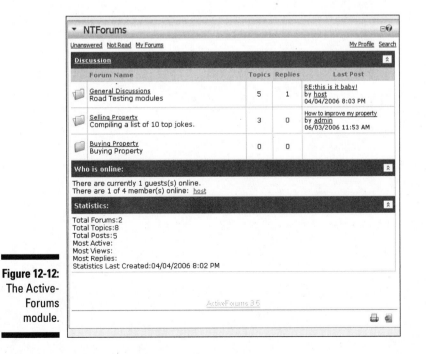

Figure 12-12:
The Active-
Forums
module.

Here are some of the features of this module:

- ✔ Setting up new forums is really easy, especially choosing different security settings for each one, which is just a matter of ticking check boxes, as shown in Figure 12-13.

- ✔ All forums within a forum group can inherit the security roles of that forum group, making it simple to manage.

- ✔ Choose from three different text editors for entering HTML posts. Some editors have fewer buttons than the standard DNN one, so they load quickly.

- ✔ An Alert button enables all users to alert forum moderators or Administrators of profanity, harassment, duplication, or spam in any post.

- ✔ Moderator options let you click a button to see who's read a post and who's subscribed to a post.

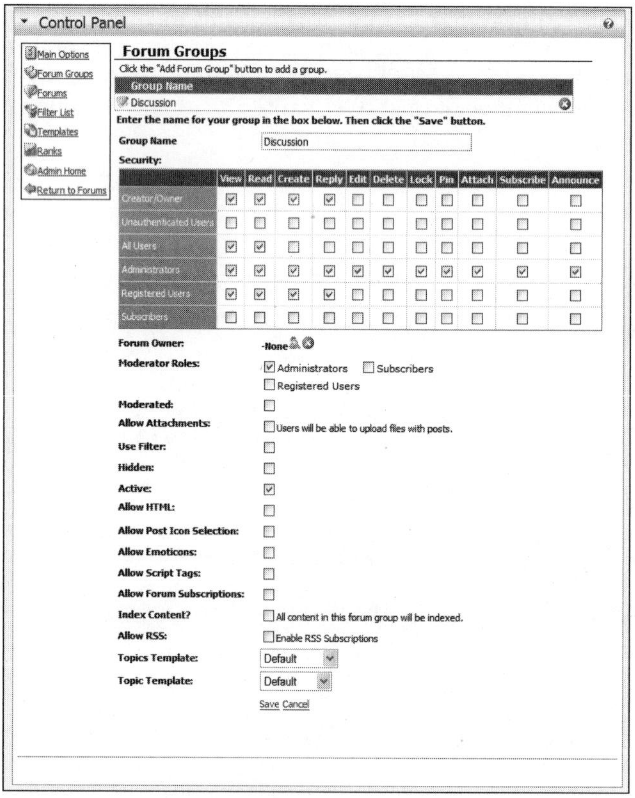

Figure 12-13:
Controlling security settings for forums is a breeze.

✔ The Unanswered Posts button provides a quick list of any posts that don't have a reply. This helps Administrators and moderators to ensure that feedback is given to all posts.

✔ The Not Read button provides a quick list of any posts the user hasn't read yet. This makes it easy for users to keep up-to-date with posts without having to trawl through the different forums.

✔ The module uses e-mail templates for actions like accepting or rejecting posts. This saves moderators time and ensures uniformity of responses. The text of the templates can be changed.

✔ Details of the number of forum users and forum guests, as well as the number of forum users currently online, can be displayed on the module.

Here's a list of ways to get help using this module:

✔ Field-level help is included for most fields on the forum.

✔ A user manual is provided with the module.

✔ A list of frequently asked questions is available at `http://www.activemodules.com/Support/CommonQuestions/tabid/77/Default.aspx`.

✔ An online help desk is also provided for registered users at `www.activemodules.com/Support/SupportDesk/tabid/78/Default.aspx`.

✔ Good old-fashioned e-mail support is available from `support@activemodules.com`.

Streamlining Content Approval with Content Manager

Content Manager is a suite of two modules that provides an approval system for new content added to your Web site. This is a great tool if you have several people contributing content to your Web site and want to add a final check before the new content is displayed to the world.

The first module is called Content Manager and it lets you create new content by using the RTE. After the new content is updated, it is added to the Content Approval module, shown in Figure 12-14, which displays a list of content requiring approval. People in the approval group can then choose to approve, edit, or delete the changes.

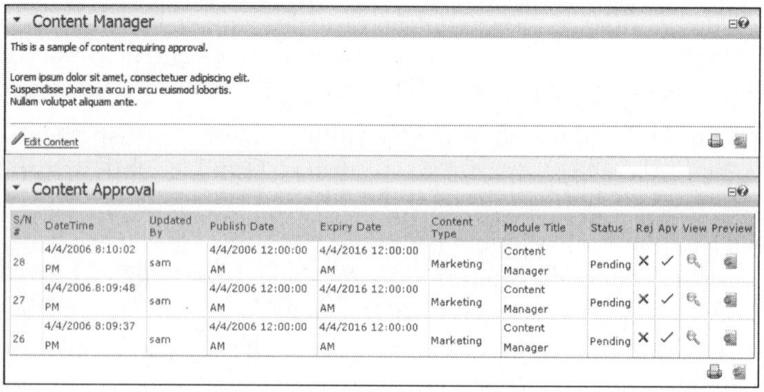

Figure 12-14:
The Content Approval module displays a list of content awaiting approval.

The Content Manager module lets the Administrator create different workflow schemes, shown in Figure 12-15, for the approval of content. For example, you might create an approval workflow for your marketing department that requires all new marketing content to be approved by a marketing person. You might also create an approval workflow for shareholder information that must be approved by an Administrator.

Each Content Manager module you add to your Web site can then be set to undertake one of these approval workflows. This means you can really break down the workload as well as track accountability for your content.

Try out and purchase this module from `www.invenmanager.com/contentmanager`.

Here are some features of this module:

- ✔ Set a publication and expiration date for new content. This lets people create one or more future versions of content which will be displayed in the module as scheduled, as shown in Figure 12-16. This means you can create and approve multiple versions of content in advance.

- ✔ A one-click approval model that ensures a fast and usable approval system. E-mail notification is sent when content requires approval and when content approval has been given. The recipients of these e-mails are set by security roles and you can easily change the text of the notifications.

- ✔ A list of tokens (placeholders) that can be added to e-mail notifications is included. These include adding a link to go to new content awaiting approval.

- ✔ Set the system to save as many versions of each content as you like — see details like which role approved it and when.

A user manual is provided with the module or can be downloaded from `dev.hyperresources.com/portals/10/contentmanager4.0.pdf`.

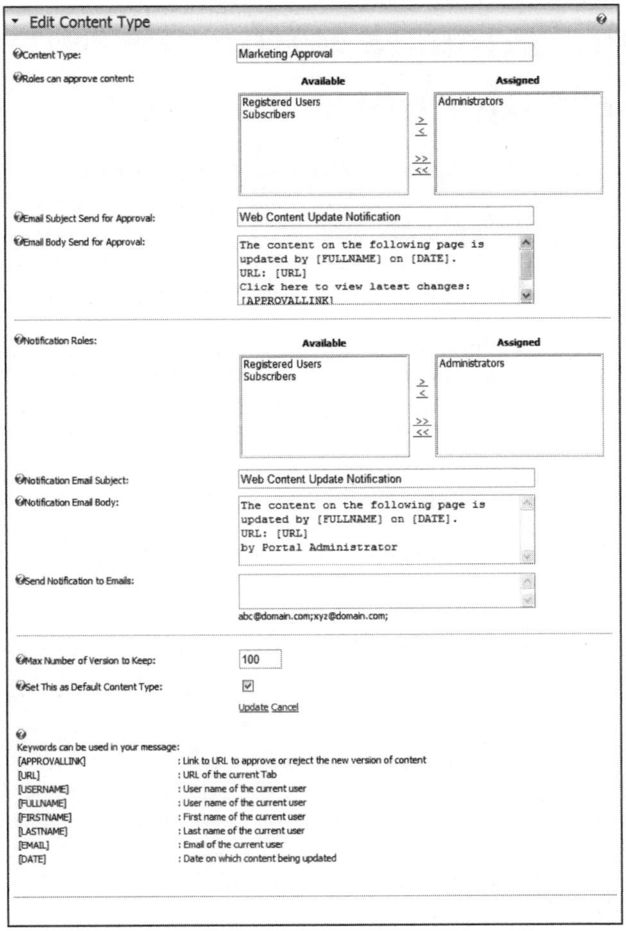

Figure 12-15:
The Edit
Content
Type page
lets Admini-
strators
create one
or more
workflow
processes
for the
approval
of new
content.

Figure 12-15:
The Edit
Content
Type page
lets Admini-
strators
create one
or more
workflow
processes
for the
approval
of new
content.

Figure 12-16:
The Version
Manager
page
displays a
detailed
history of
previous
versions.

Distributing Podcasts with the Podcaster Module

A *podcast* is generally an audio or video file that you can subscribe to online, although it can also be another file format such as a PDF. The cool thing about a podcast is that after you have subscribed to it, updates automatically appear in your podcast reader. Podcast information is downloaded to your computer or your mobile device so you can view it at your leisure.

For example, Scott Willhite, one of the authors of this book, might decide to write a six-episode series on how to sell your home. Scott creates his series in MP3 format and releases one episode a week for six weeks. You think it sounds like good stuff, so you go to his Web site and click on the Podcast icon. A complicated page is displayed, but all you need to do is copy and paste the address of this page into your podcast reader and you're done. For the next six weeks, you don't have to go to his Web site to locate the episodes: They are automatically downloaded into your podcast reader for you to view whenever you get a chance.

For more information on podcasts and to download podcast readers, go to www.microsoft.com/windowsmobile/articles/podcasts.mspx.

The Podcaster module, shown in Figure 12-17, enables your users to subscribe to a single or multiple episode podcast. The main page of the module displays any marketing information about the podcast that you enter by using a Rich Text Editor. Below this, a link to subscribe to the podcast is displayed. To subscribe to your podcast, users need to click on this button and copy and paste the URL into their podcast reader. You add a new Podcaster module for each podcast you create.

The module has one page where you add general information about the podcast and another where you upload one or more podcast episodes and add details for each podcast. Try out, read more, and purchase this module from www.arrownuke.com/Modules/Podcaster/tabid/114/Default.aspx.

Here's a list of features for this module:

- Create single or multiple episode podcasts, as shown in Figure 12-18.
- Create podcasts of MP3, MOV, MP4, P4U, P4A, and PDF file types.
- List or block your podcasts at iTunes. Listed podcasts will be searchable at iTunes.
- Podcast categories are based on the categories maintained by iTunes. When iTunes adds a new category, it is also added to the category list in the module.

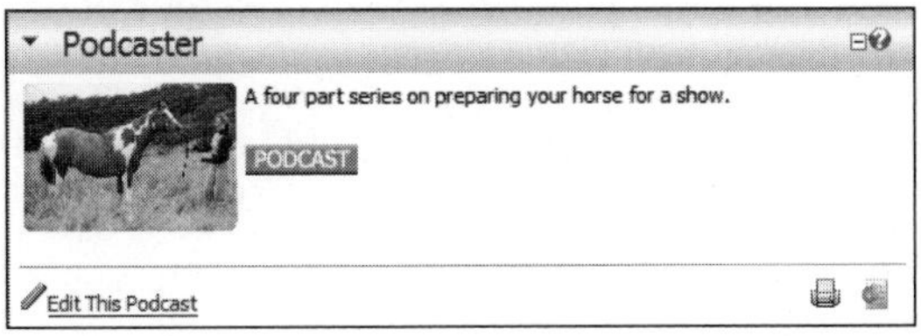

Figure 12-17:
The
Podcaster
module
displays any
information
you want
to use to
market your
podcast
above the
Podcast
button.

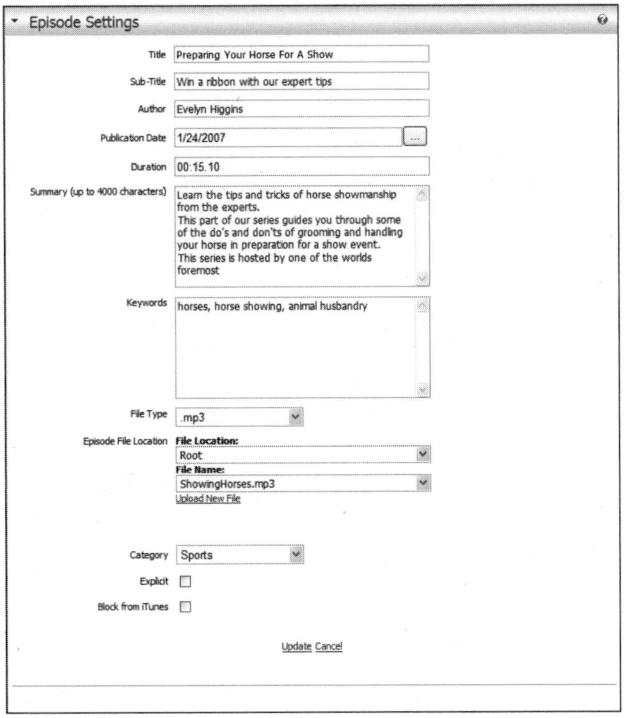

Figure 12-18:
The Episode
Settings
page, where
you add
episodes
to your
podcast.

Here's a list of ways to get help using this module:

- ✔ This module has an extensive easy-to-understand online user manual at `www.arrownuke.com/Modules/Podcaster/Documentation/tabid/241/Default.aspx`. It takes you through all the steps of creating your podcast as well as listing it on iTunes.
- ✔ A support forum is provided at `www.arrownuke.com/Support/tabid/313/Default.aspx`.
- ✔ Free bug fixes for life.
- ✔ Free access to upgrades for new versions of iTunes and new specifications for iTunes podcasting.

Interacting with Page Options

Page Options is a great module that is a piece of cake to set up and use. The Page Options module, shown in Figure 12-19, displays a range of links that enable users to print or e-mail the page, add the page to their favorites list, and display a counter of page views as well as an inquiry form. This module offers an easy way to encourage feedback from your users, as well as making it easy for them to print or e-mail the page content.

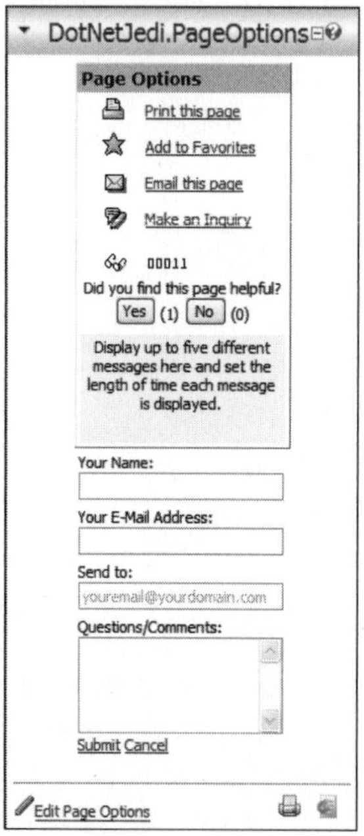

Figure 12-19: The Page Options module.

The Edit Page Options page, shown in Figure 12-20, has a wide range of settings that enable you to turn different options on or off, as well as control the design of the module.

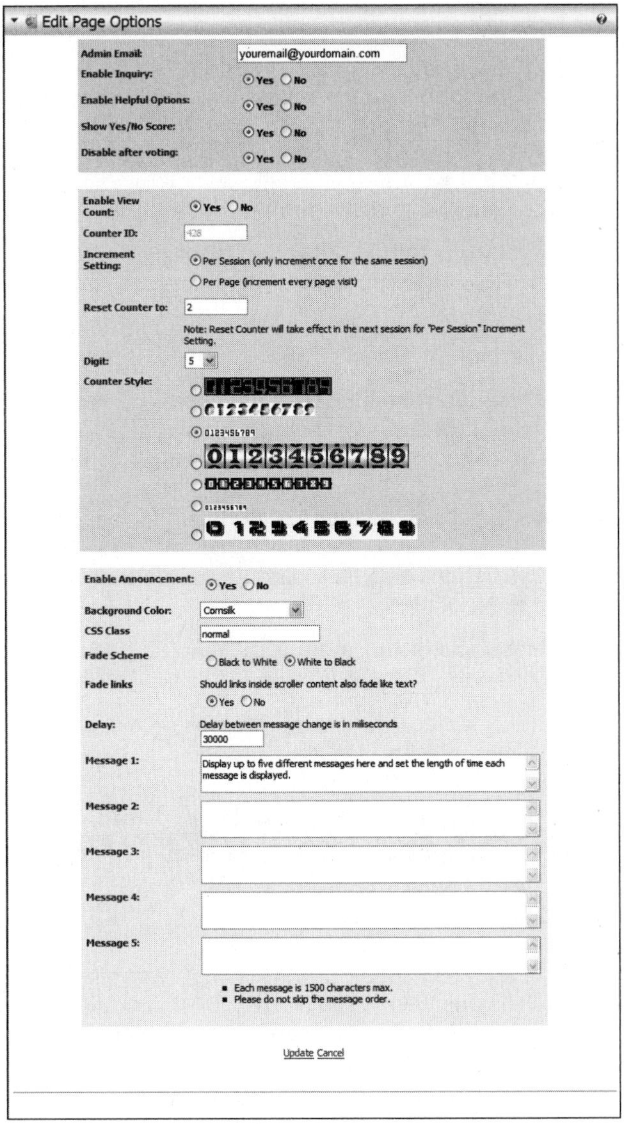

Figure 12-20:
The settings
page for
the Page
Options
module.

Get this module and more details at `dotnetjedi.com/Default.aspx?ItemID=24&TabID=53&uc=info&mode=dir`.

Here's a list of features this module offers:

- Print This Page link.

- Add to Favorites link.

- E-mail this Page link.

- Make an Inquiry link, which displays a simple feedback form.

- Configurable e-mail message for submitted inquiries.

- Voting Yes/No buttons to find out if the user found this page useful. Vote buttons can be disabled after a user votes. Results can be kept private.

- Optional page view counter with a variety of counter styles to choose from and a reset option.

- Display up to five different announcement messages and set the frequency with which the messages change. The background color of the message can be configured as well.

Here's a list of ways to get help using this module:

- Installation instructions as well as set-up instructions are included when you purchase the module.

- Watch an online demo of this module at `demo.dotnetjedi.com/PortalEnhancements/PageOptions/tabid/70/Default.aspx`.

- Contact `dotnetjedi@dotnetjedi.com` for support.

Managing Online Issues Ticketing with Help Desk

A popular way to manage customer inquiries or support requests is by adding a help desk to your Web site. The Help Desk module enables users to submit questions or requests to your Web site and receive a ticket number for the inquiry. Having a ticket number gives your users a warm, fuzzy feeling because they have a reference to quote if they don't get a response. They can also go back to your Web site and review the status of their inquiry at their leisure.

Administrators or other security roles can then process the inquiry and keep the user informed along the way through the use of e-mail updates.

Using a help desk is far better than playing e-mail tag back and forth with your users. All support tickets are located in one central place, shown in Figure 12-21, and all comments and activities are recorded beside that ticket. This makes it easy to retrace the history of the item and manage the status of a ticket, as shown in Figure 12-22.

Figure 12-21: A list of the current tickets.

Using a help desk also ensures that all authorized persons can provide support instead of a support request sitting impatiently in someone's e-mail box while they are away on holidays for the week. Get this module at `www.dnntoolset.com/DotNetNuke/Modules/HelpDesk/tabid/62/Default.aspx`.

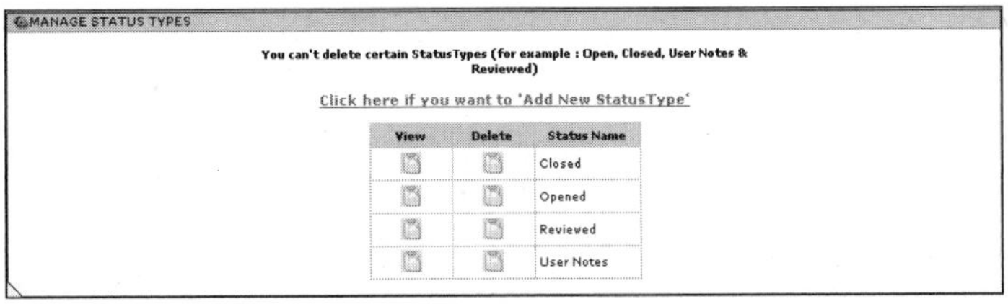

Figure 12-22: Manage Status Types available for tickets.

Here's a list of features for this module:

- ✔ Users can create new tickets, edit, or add notes to existing tickets as well as monitor the status of their tickets.

- ✔ Quick-find links to view all tickets, all tickets that have not been claimed for processing by an Administrator, as well as any tickets you have claimed to process.

✔ Advanced searching feature lets Administrators search tickets by more than ten different fields, including category, priority, date, and status.

✔ Create categories for tickets; for example, Property Valuation, Property Maintenance, and so on.

✔ Create ticket status types; for example, High, Medium, or Low priority.

✔ Each time an action is taken on a ticket, the Administrators can add the time taken to do that action. All times are added up to provide an overall total of time taken to resolve the ticket.

✔ E-mail notification is sent when an Administrator claims a ticket, when a ticket is created, or when a ticket is resolved.

✔ Optional e-mail notifications can be sent each time a ticket has a status update.

Here's a list of ways to get help on how to use this module:

✔ A support forum is provided for registered users at `www.dnntoolset.com/Support/tabid/56/Default.aspx`.

✔ A brief but clear user manual is supplied with the module.

✔ E-mails with support requests can be sent to `support@dnntoolset.com`.

Chapter 13

Ten Free (Or Really Cheap) Modules You Shouldn't Pass Up

• •

• •

*T*he open-source community tends to breed a devoted and charitable culture. As a DNN user, you benefit from the large number of highly skilled people who willingly share their modules and other resources for free, for a small donation, or for a nominal fee. The modules covered in this chapter represent only a drop in the ocean of the many freebies waiting out there, so get on the Internet and start hunting!

We don't want to rain on this free parade, but here are just a few words of warning: Free modules are wonderful gifts from generous people, but they don't come with a guarantee. If a free module doesn't work the way you expect it to, don't complain too loudly! The best thing to do is to visit the Web site where you acquired the module and see if there is a support forum or information on how to manage the problem. If not, contact the developer and, after thanking them repeatedly for their kindness, let them know the problem. You will usually find people that are very willing to help you.

You can even step up and get involved by testing the module or by offering suggestions on good features for the next version. Remember, it's your community: The more you give, the more you get.

To get you started, check out the Web site of DNN Core Team member Cathal Connolly at `www.cathal.co.uk/Default.aspx?tabid=80`. Cathal's Web site lists more than 100 freebies!

GoMap

No doubt you will have heard of Google and their fantastic search engine of the same name. Google recently came up with another great tool called Google Maps, which lets people view detailed maps of most places in the world.

Hot on Google's development trail, a DNN company called Bi4ce has developed the GoMap module, shown in Figure 13-1, which integrates the functionality of Google Maps with your Web site. Google Maps have lots of great and fun features that are available through the GoMap module. Users can zoom in and out of maps, going from a global map to street level in very little time. Maps can be displayed as a satellite image or as a street map, or a hybrid of both.

To display Google Maps on your Web site, you must sign up for a Google Map API. This is a free service and the sign-up process is quick and easy. You will be given the API information via a Web page, so remember to record it somewhere safe so you can find it again.

The GoMap module has been set up to display a map plotted with a complete list of your users by country or by name. This information is drawn from your user accounts and plotted on the map. Plotted points are links to information related to that point. For example, when the GoMap displays Country Online information, each point displays the region, country, and the number of users plotted at that point. Alternatively, when GoMap displays People Online information, each point displays the region, country, and a list of the people (first name and last name) in that region, as shown in Figure 13-2.

Of course, you may not want to display user online information on your Web site, but this is only an example of how the module can be used. By enlisting the help of a DNN developer, you can set the module to display any type of information on the map. For example, your DNN developer could integrate GoMap with the Real Estate module to plot any of the listed properties on the global map. Pretty cool, huh?

Figure 13-1:
The GoMap
module set
to display
people
online.
Clicking on
a plotted
point
displays
information
about that
point.

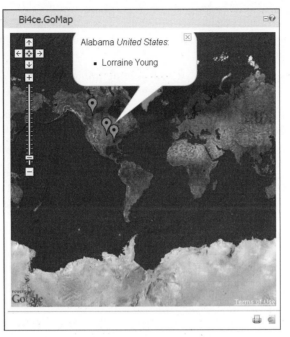

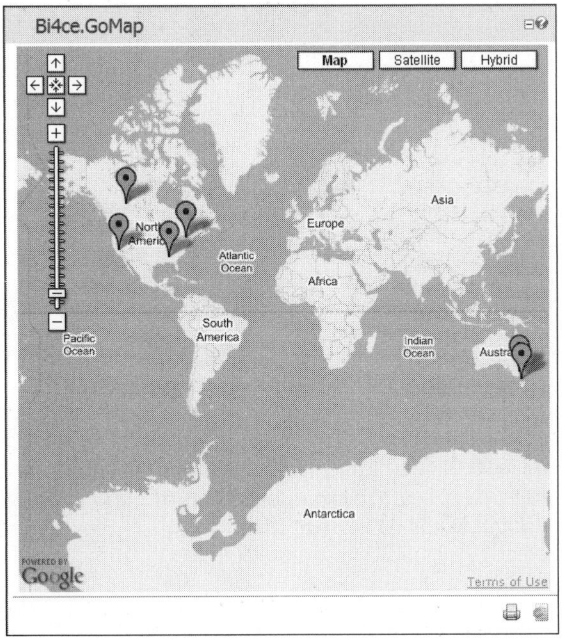

Figure 13-2:
The GoMap
can be
displayed as
a satellite
image, a
map (used
here), or a
hybrid.

Here are some features of GoMap:

- Visitors can move to a map of nearly any location in the world and zoom in to street level.

- The map can be set to display as a satellite image, a map, or a hybrid of the two. Visitors can change their view.

- Administrators can set the midpoint of the map and maintain information for that point. By default, this is set to Bi4ce's company details.

- The setup wizard, shown in Figure 13-3, keeps this complex module easy for beginners. Just keep clicking the Next button and you'll be right.

- Administrators can add, edit, and delete points. This doesn't include those automatically rendered from people online or countries online.

- The wizard includes a Find Address tool that provides the longitude and latitude for a given address.

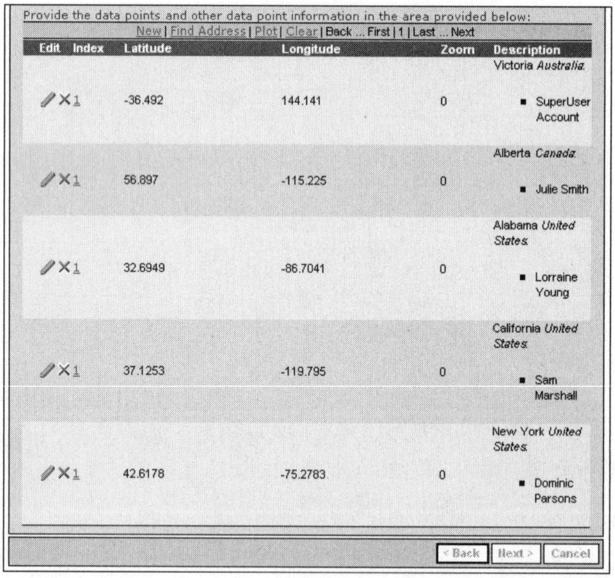

Provide the data points and other data point information in the area provided below:
New | Find Address | Plot | Clear | Back ... First | 1 | Last ... Next

Edit	Index	Latitude	Longitude	Zoom	Description
					Victoria *Australia*
✏×1		-36.492	144.141	0	▪ SuperUser Account
					Alberta *Canada*
✏×1		56.897	-115.225	0	▪ Julie Smith
					Alabama *United States*
✏×1		32.6949	-86.7041	0	▪ Lorraine Young
					California *United States*
✏×1		37.1253	-119.795	0	▪ Sam Marshall
					New York *United States*
✏×1		42.6178	-75.2783	0	▪ Dominic Parsons

< Back | Next > | Cancel

Figure 13-3:
The GoMap Wizard lets you manage any plotted points.

To get started with GoMap, read about and download the module from `dnn. bi4ce.com/Default.aspx?tabid=264`. Read more about Google Maps and sign up for a Google Maps API key at `www.google.com/apis/maps`.

GoogleSearch

Another Google-based module is the GoogleSearch module, which integrates the search engine capabilities of Google with your Web site. This means people can search from your Web site and get the same results as if they had searched using the Google Web site. The results are displayed in a separate Web browser and Google Search results are a free Google service, so there are no hidden costs.

The module can be set to search the entire Web for results, or just your Web site. Alternatively, you can give your users the option to choose.

Developed by Anthony Glenwright for the Australian-based company Inventua, the GoogleSearch module, shown in Figure 13-4, is one of a dozen freebies available from their Web site. Inventua provides their modules on a try-before-you-buy basis, so you can freely download modules and use them for as long as you like before deciding if you want to buy them.

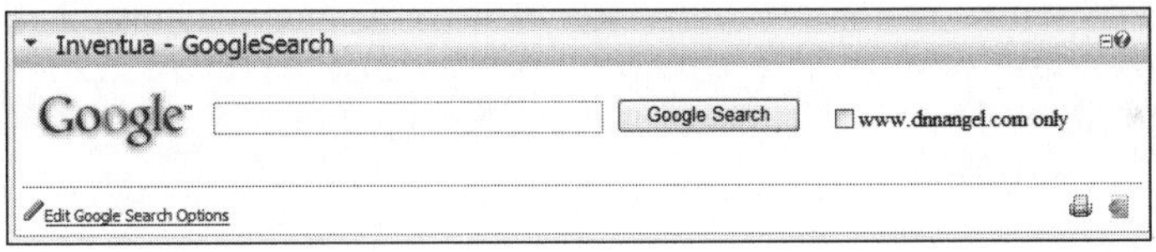

Figure 13-4:
The Google-
Search
module lets
users
search
either your
Web site or
the entire
Web.

Here are some options of the GoogleSearch module that you can customize, as shown in Figure 13-5:

✔ Choose from three different sizes for the Google logo.

✔ Choose the background color of the Google logo to be white, black, or gray.

✔ Modify the Search button to display any text you like.

✔ Modify the size of the text box where people enter their search.

✔ Choose a regional Google Web site for the results. For example, if you are in the United Kingdom, you enter www.google.co.uk; in Australia, you enter www.google.com.au. This is set to www.google.com by default.

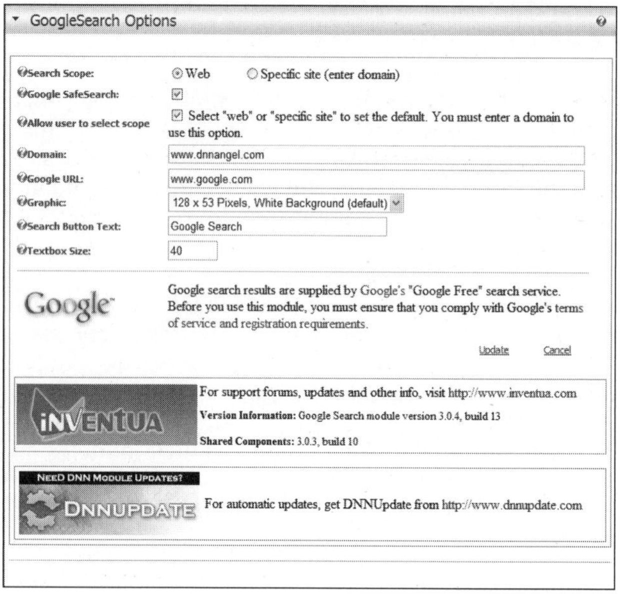

Figure 13-5:
The Google-
Search
Options
page lets
you set
whether to
search the
entire Web,
just one
domain, or
both.

To get started, download the GoogleSearch module from `www.inventua.com/dnn-googlesearch.content`. This page has instructions on how to configure the module. These instructions are also included in the download. A support and feature request forum is provided at `www.inventua.com/forums.content`.

MMLinks

The MMLinks module, shown in Figure 13-6, offers two major benefits over the standard Links module, plus a range of other funky tools. The first major benefit is the ability to restrict viewing of each link to one or more security roles. Role access is typically managed at page and module levels; however, the MMLinks module manages role access to view each link individually. This means one MMLinks module can be set as viewable by all visitors, but each user sees different links depending on their security roles. This saves you time because you don't need to add multiple Links modules that have many of the same links, except for a couple of links only available to a different role.

The other major benefit of the MMLinks module is the ability to display the content to each user in their preferred language as set under Preferences on their User Account. Unfortunately, this doesn't mean that the module will translate the content for you, but it does give you somewhere to manage content for each language.

Figure 13-6:
The
MMLinks
module with
the default
template.

Module titles can also be localized, enabling you to create a different module title for each language used on your Web site. For example, when a user from Israel looks at the module, the title might be *Shalom*; however, for an Australian user, the title might read *G'day*.

Here are some features of the MMLinks module:

✔ The module comes with nine different template designs that alter the layout of links.

✔ You can create your own layout templates and include replacement tags for fields such as username, full name, or portal name.

✔ The module uses the RTE to add link descriptions, as shown in Figure 13-7. This means you can add a long description, images, links, and other formatting.

✔ Includes the usual link options to display links vertically, horizontally, or in a drop-down list.

✔ Optionally displays an image beside each link.

To get started, download the module and a user manual from `dnn.tiendaboliviana.com/Web/Default.aspx?tabid=77`.

Daily Comic

Among all these serious and practical modules, we just can't resist slipping in a fun module. The Daily Comic module, shown in Figure 13-8, displays a new comic on your Web site each day. There are over 100 different comics to choose from, ranging from classic comic strips such as *Andy Capp*, *Marmaduke*, and *Dilbert*, to popular editorial cartoonists Ed Stein and Larry Wright.

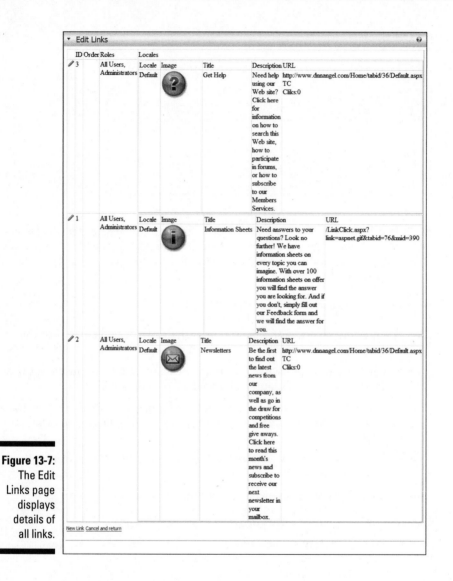

Figure 13-7:
The Edit Links page displays details of all links.

The comics are provided at no cost from the www.comics.com Web site. The module has been set up to access these comics without requiring any sign-up process to Comics.com.

There are no guidelines on configuring the module. When you first add it to your page, it displays a technical message that is really daunting. Please don't be put off: All you need to do is select the Edit option and Update to start displaying a comic.

Figure 13-8:
The Daily
Comic
module can
be set to
let your
registered
users
choose their
favorite
comic and
save it to be
displayed
next time.

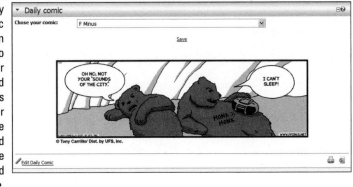

This module is provided to you by Mike Horton, based on previous versions created by Francis Noël and David Kafrissen.

Here are some features of the Daily Comic module, which you can access on the settings page in Figure 13-9:

✔ Choose from more than 80 comic strips and 30 editorial comics. Many comics are in full color.

✔ Choose to enable your registered users to browse through the full list of available comics and select their preferred comic. This comic is displayed to them when they are logged in to the Web site.

✔ Set the width and height properties of a comic. These override the default size of each comic but may skew the size of the comic. You should avoid this setting if users are able to select their own comic as the size and shape of comics vary greatly.

✔ Choose to display a link to the comic's home page on the Comics.com Web site. The Web site includes information about the comic, the characters, and the artist.

✔ Choose to display the name of the comic as a tooltip when the user places their mouse over the comic.

The module can be downloaded from dnn.gmss.org. This page includes some information about the module and its history.

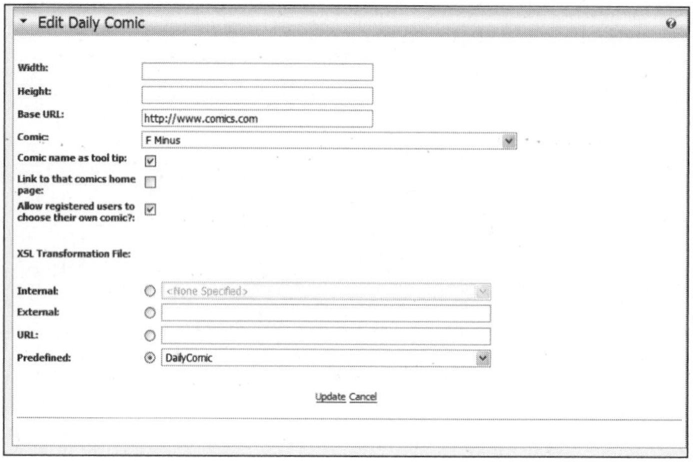

Figure 13-9:
The Edit
Daily Comic
page.

Multi Page Content

Despite all the fancy modules that you can use on your Web site, it seems the one that you just can't live without is the simple Text/HTML module: that is, until you discover the Multi Page Content module, shown in Figure 13-10, which is a kind of souped-up version of Text/HTML.

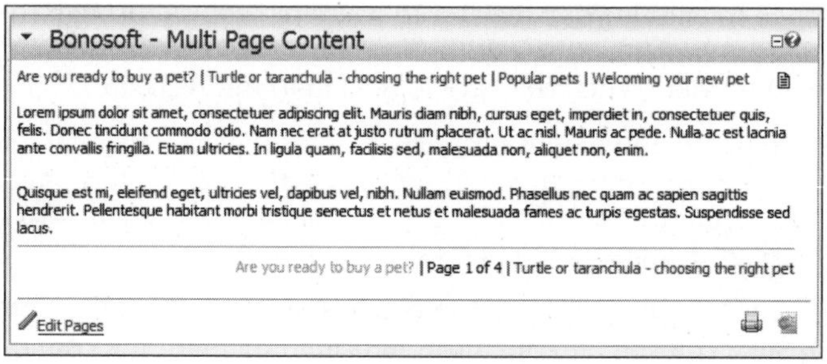

Figure 13-10:
The Multi
Page
Content
module with
a left-side
page index.

The Multi Page Content module lets you create and manage multiple pages of content all within one module and one interface.

Each time a content page is created, the title of that page is added to a page index. The page index is displayed on the module and works like a menu, enabling people to click on the content they want to view. The use of a page index on the module means you can manage large amounts of content on one page without having to scroll down a lengthy page.

Developed by Bo Norgaard of BonoSoft in Denmark, the Multi Page Content module is one of a small number of freebies they offer.

Here are some of the customizable features of the Multi Page Content module, as shown in Figure 13-11:

- ✔ The module uses the RTE, so you are able to format content, add links, images, and more.

- ✔ Choose to display an icon on the module that enables people to switch between viewing one page at a time or all pages at once.

- ✔ Choose to display the page index to the left, right, above, or below the page content.

- ✔ Configure design elements such the width of the page menu, the type of rule displayed between menu items, and the font properties of the page index links.

- ✔ The module displays a page index and current page location summary below module content; for example, Page 1 of 5.

- ✔ The module displays a link to the next page below the current page content.

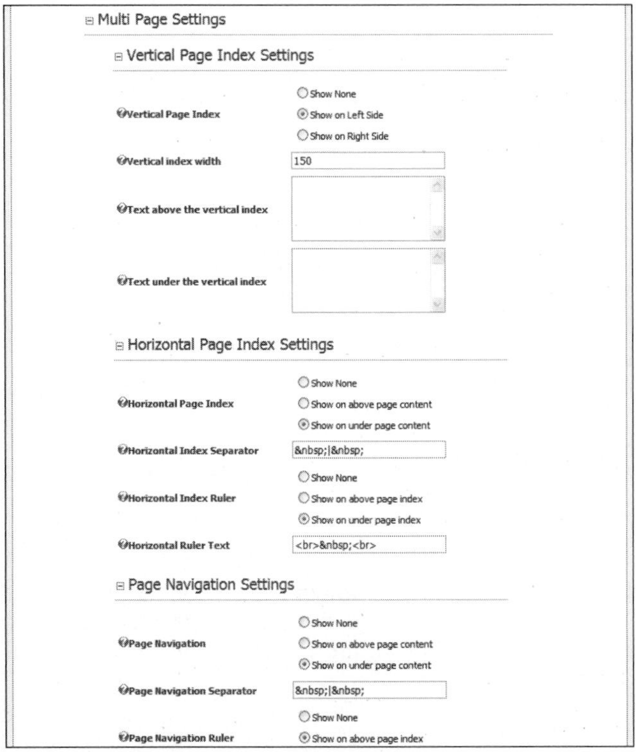

Figure 13-11:
Some of the settings available to customize the look of the Multi Page Content module.

Download the module from www.dotnetnuke.dk/Default.aspx?tabid= 181. Go to www.dotnetnuke.dk/Default.aspx?tabid=58 for full details on this module.

TemplatePrint Skin Object

The TemplatePrint skin object isn't really a module but, as the name suggests, is a skin object that can be used as an alternative to the standard DNN [PRINTMODULE] skin object.

The standard DNN [PRINTMODULE] skin object for module containers displays the standard DNN print icon on the module. This enables people to view a print-friendly version of the module content, as shown in Figure 13-12.

One limitation of the [PRINTMODULE] skin object is that the content is displayed for printing without the module title. This means the information can lose its context.

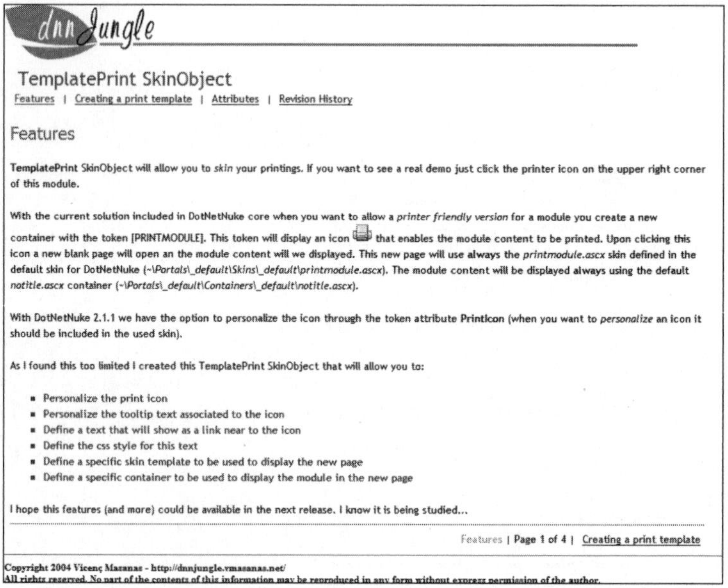

Figure 13-12:
A print-friendly page from the Template-Print Web site. The text is the module content and the rest is the template.

The Template Print alternate skin object not only includes the title of the module in the print-friendly version, but also lets the Administrator create a template to display the content within. This means you can ensure that valuable information such as copyright notices, the URL of your Web site, your company logo, or your company details are printed along with the content.

Developed by Vicenç Masanas, a DNN Core Team member based in Spain, this is one of a small selection of modules and skin objects freely available from Vicenç's Web site.

Here are some things you can do with the TemplatePrint skin object:

- ✔ Use your own print icon or the standard DNN Print icon.
- ✔ Choose a tooltip for the Print icon.
- ✔ Display text of your choice as a link beside the Print icon.
- ✔ Define a specific skin template to be used to display the new page.
- ✔ Define a specific container to be used to display the module in the new page.

Download and read about the skin object at `dnnjungle.vmasanas.net/MyModules/SkinObjects/TemplatePrint/tabid/41/Default.aspx`.

Weather

The Weather module displays a daily weather forecast and is a simple way to add up-to-date and interesting content on your Web site with very little effort.

Weather reports are supplied for most countries, including Europe and the United Kingdom, as shown in Figure 13-13. Administrators can choose the city for the weather forecast, enable visitors to search for weather forecasts, or display the user's local weather report.

Each weather forecast displays the forecasted temperature, what the temperature "feels like," a two- or three-word description (such as sunny, clear night, partly cloudy, and so on), and an image of the description. The module can be set to display up to ten days of extended weather forecast, as well as additional weather information such as wind speed and UV index.

To access the weather forecasts, you must sign up for a free account with `www.weather.com`. The sign-up process is quick and easy, and you can expect to receive partner login and license key details via e-mail within seconds. Developed by Oliver Hine, this module and an alternative HTML Editor are available for free download.

Figure 13-13:
The
Weather
module
displaying
optional
settings:
location,
detailed
daily
forecast,
and
extended
forecast.

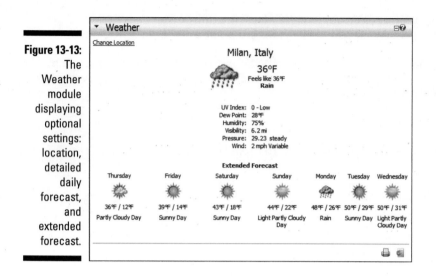

Here are some options of the Weather module, as shown in Figure 13-14:

- ✓ Worldwide weather retrieval for almost any location.

- ✓ Set the module to display today's forecast only, today's forecast and up to ten days extended forecast, or the extended forecast only.

- ✓ Choose to enable users to select the location for the weather forecast. This information is stored as a cookie, so that forecast is displayed next time they visit the page.

- ✓ Simple search tool for discovering the correct code required to display a forecast. By entering the ZIP code or name of a city, the Administrator (and user, if enabled) can search for and select a forecast.

- ✓ The module can be set to display a local weather report to each user based on the ZIP code recorded in their user account. This means that when they are logged in to the Web site, they will see their local weather report instead of the default report. This service is only available in the United States.

- ✓ A detailed forecast can be displayed for today's weather. This displays the UV index, dew point, humidity, visibility, pressure, and wind speed.

- ✓ Hide or show the city name above the forecast or display the observatory location instead.

- ✓ Choose to display the weather icons in one of three different sizes.

- ✓ Weather temperature can be set to display as either Celsius or Fahrenheit.

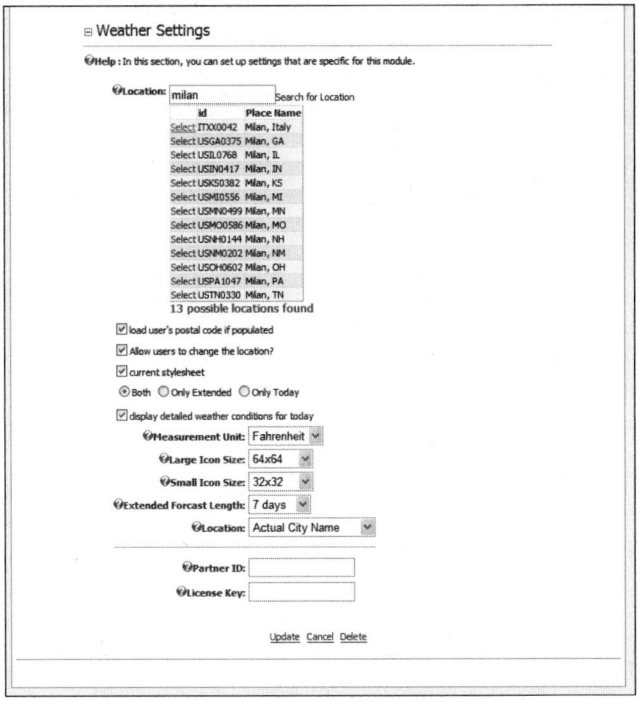

Figure 13-14:
The
Weather
Settings
page
includes a
simple
location
search
tool. This
example
displays the
results of a
search on
Milan.

Here are some tips on getting started:

- ✔ Download the module from www.oliverhine.com/?tabid=615. **This page includes information about the module and examples of it in use.**

- ✔ The settings page of the module includes help for each field as well as a Help link that explains how to sign up.

- ✔ Support requests and feedback can be submitted at www.oliverhine.com/?tabid=617.

Child Links

Child Links is one of those simple little modules that you don't need until you have it, and then you wonder how you ever got along without it! This module displays a list of any child pages belonging to the page on which the module is placed, as shown in Figure 13-15. For example: Say you have a page called Rental Services, which has four child pages called Tenant Services, Owner Services, Inspection Times, and Document Downloads, respectively. If you add the Child Links module to the Rental Services page, it will display a list of links to each of the child pages in the order they are listed.

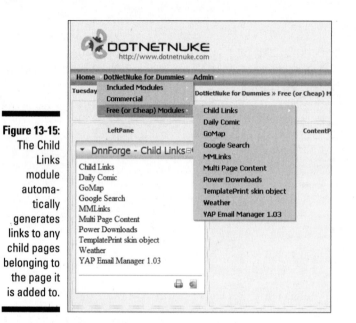

Figure 13-15:
The Child
Links
module
automa-
tically
generates
links to any
child pages
belonging to
the page it
is added to.

The Child Links module is one of nine modules available for a small cost from the www.ventrian.com Web site. Developed by DNN Core Team member Scott McCulloch, these modules plus a number of skins are available to sub-scribers for as low as $20. This includes a full year's access to download the modules and any updates. At about $2 for a module or a skin, it's not a bad value!

Other modules available from Ventrian are the Feedback Center, News Articles, Quotes, Shout Box, Simple Gallery, Subscription Tools, and two modules that integrate with the Users Online module: Private Messages and Where Are They. The Private Messages module enables users to send and receive pri-vate online messages to users that are online. The Where Are They module displays a list of who is currently on the Web site and a link to the page they are viewing.

Some things that you can do with the Child Links module include

✔ Add a header and footer above and below links.

✔ Enter a separator to be displayed before each link.

✔ Customize links by adding HTML styles to the content.

✔ Choose to hide or display any hidden pages.

Here's how to get started:

- ✔ Read more about this module at `www.ventrian.com/Products/ Modules/ChildLinks/tabid/194/Default.aspx`. Members can download the module from this page.

- ✔ The module is provided with field-level help and a walk-through on using the module is available from `www.ventrian.com/Products/Modules/ ChildLinks/Walkthrough/tabid/226/Default.aspx`.

- ✔ A support forum for all modules is located at `www.ventrian.com/ Support/ProductForums/tabid/118/Default.aspx`.

- ✔ Subscription information is available from `www.ventrian.com/`.

YAP Email Manager 1.03

YAP Email Manager is an advanced alternative to the core Newsletters module. The YAP Email Manager offers three major benefits above the standard Newsletter module: the ability to simplify the management of newsletter subscriptions, the ability to create dynamic content, and the ability to create unique mailing lists.

In the standard DNN setup, users must be logged in to the Web site and go to their user account and subscribe or unsubscribe to a newsletter (security role) under Members Services. This isn't very hard, but people expecting things to work a certain way are easily frustrated when they don't. What people expect is to see an Unsubscribe link at the bottom of e-mails, which they can click on to unsubscribe. This is exactly what the YAP Email Manager does! An Unsubscribe link is included in the footer of the newsletters, which will automatically unsubscribe the related e-mail address from that mailing list. Newsletters also have a Subscribe link, shown in Figure 13-16, that goes to a Subscribe page for your mailing lists.

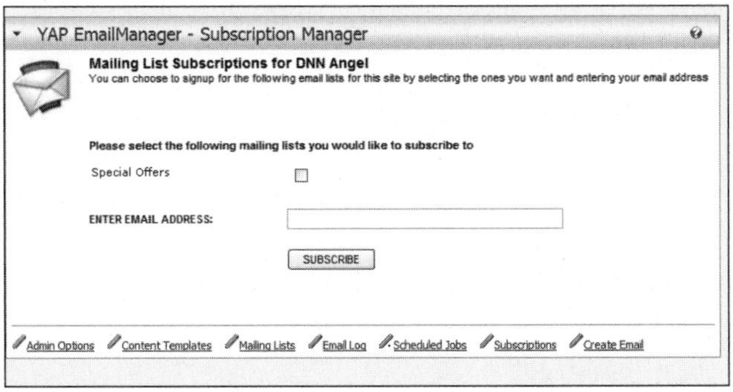

Figure 13-16: Users can subscribe to any mailing list that you create.

Another great feature of the YAP Email Manager is the ability to create unique mailing lists. The current Newsletter module lets you send e-mails to one or more security roles; however, if you want to manage multiple Newsletters or other types of e-mail not related to access to the Web site, it seems unnecessary to create a security role just to define that group of users. This is where the ability to create unique mailing lists is great. You can simply add a role as a mailing group, or you can create your own mailing list, shown in Figure 13-17, by adding one or more e-mails to it.

Last but not least, this module will (almost) write the newsletters for you! Newsletter templates mean that the content will be copied from your Web site and inserted into your newsletter. For example, you might have a module where you add the latest company news and another module that lists products currently on special. By creating a newsletter template that includes the content of these two modules, you can automatically send a monthly newsletter that includes your latest news and product specials, as shown in Figure 13-18. You will need a DNN developer to set up newsletters for you; however, it's a great time-and-money saver to not have to copy, paste, and format your content to create a newsletter each month. What's more, if you combine this with the DNN Scheduler, you can schedule newsletters to be sent automatically at a regular interval. Look, Mom: No hands!

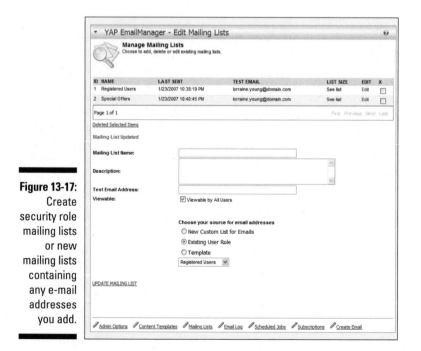

Figure 13-17:
Create security role mailing lists or new mailing lists containing any e-mail addresses you add.

This module has been developed by Jason Koskimaki of YAP Club and is available for free download without any Web site registration required.

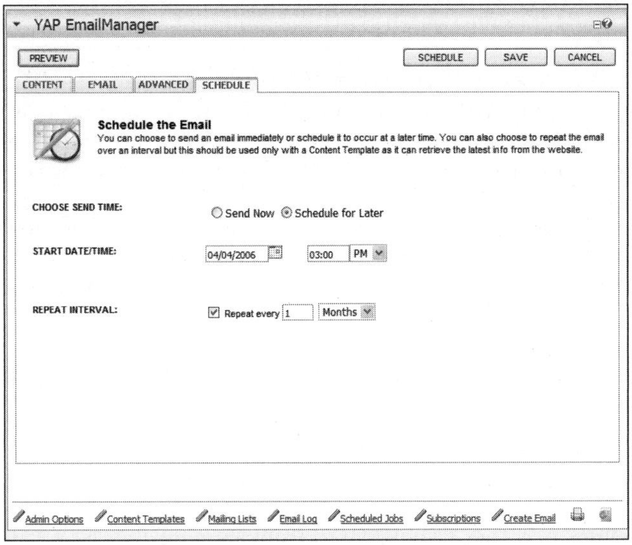

Figure 13-18:
Schedule
e-mails to
be sent out
at regular
intervals.

Here are some features of YAP Email Manager:

✔ Choose a test e-mail address that is displayed as the sender of newsletters.

✔ Schedule any e-mails to be sent immediately or at a later time or date.

✔ Schedule an e-mail that is sent out at regular intervals. Choose a schedule of any number of minutes, hours, days, weeks, or months. Combined with content templates, this creates an ongoing automated newsletter process.

✔ View a log of scheduled e-mails and choose to edit or delete any scheduled e-mail.

✔ View a complete log of previously sent e-mails.

✔ Preview e-mails before they are sent.

To get started, download the module from www.yapclub.com/dnn/ DOWNLOADS/tabid/2786/Default.aspx.

Power Downloads

Power Downloads, shown in Figure 13-19, is a souped-up version of the standard Downloads module, which offers a handful of additional features.

The module looks great thanks to DNN Core Team member Leigh Pointer, who is both a DNN developer and designer. Each download record includes an attractive download button, an image that changes transparency levels when someone mouses over it, and an animated New icon for recent listings.

The second feature that makes this module great is that you can control viewing of each listing by roles. Role access is typically managed at page and module levels; however, as does MMLinks, this module manages role access to view each download individually.

Here are some things you can do with the Power Downloads module:

- ✔ Set the number of items displayed on each page.
- ✔ Display the number of times each item is downloaded.

Download this and other free modules from `www.subzero-solutions.net/Default.aspx?tabid=79`. Registration to this Web site is required to access downloads.

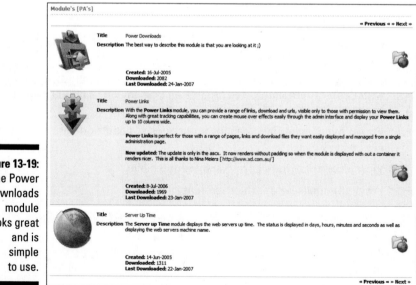

Figure 13-19: The Power Downloads module looks great and is simple to use.

Chapter 14

Ten Fun Things for Your Forum Users

In This Chapter

- Ranking your most active users
- Displaying user-specific time zones
- Showing the poster's location

In this chapter, we cover ten fun things to keep in mind for your forum users: everything from updating profiles to letting users rank their favorite posts. Enjoy!

Maintaining Their Profiles

Your users are free to share as much information as they like about themselves with you and other forum users by clicking the My Settings button, which has a gear symbol on it, as shown in Figure 14-1. Some of the interesting options here are the ability to choose an alias and the ability to create a signature that will appear under all of their posts.

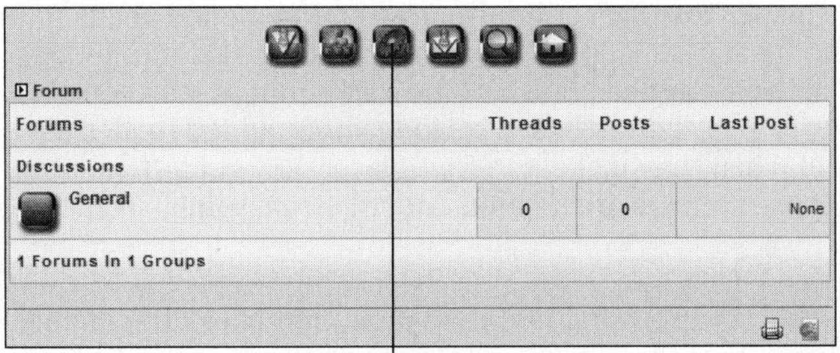
Forum
Forums
Threads
Posts
Last Post
Discussions
General
0
0
None
1 Forums In 1 Groups

The My Settings button

Figure 14-1: The My Settings button allows users to change their profile preferences.

Administrators can see also these settings for all users and more under Forum Administration⇨User Settings, where they can look up a user and edit their profile.

Subscribing to Favorite Forums and Getting Notification of Posts

Users can track all forums that they want to receive an e-mail notification each time someone replies or adds a new thread. For users to do this, they simply need to expand the Tracking/Subscriptions section from within My Settings and expand the Tracking Forum section. After this section is expanded, users can select the check boxes next to each forum they want to subscribe to, as shown in Figure 14-2.

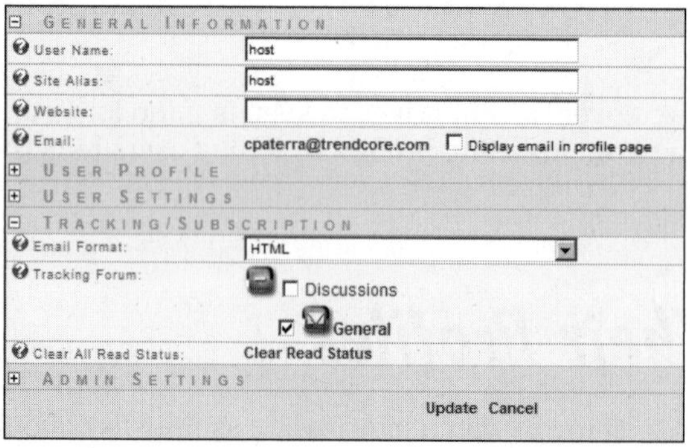

Figure 14-2:
Subscribing
to a forum.

Ranking Your Most Active Users

Acknowledge your most active users by ranking them on the number of posts they have made. You can set how many times someone needs to make a post to win a first-place ranking, second-place ranking, down to tenth-place ranking. Then when a user has reached the number of posts needed to be in fifth place, they will get a stars-based ranking image added to all their posts below their name. When they make it to first place, they get a "ten out of ten stars" ranking. These settings are located under Forum Administration⇨Statistics & Rankings.

To enable this feature, administrators must first check the Enable Rankings check box, as shown in Figure 14-3. Another item that can be set here is the number of posts required to achieve a specific ranking status.

Figure 14-3:
Configuring
statistics
and
rankings.

Giving Users Additional Avatars

Create a special logo for your trusted users and one for your moderators.
These logos will become status symbols of leadership and bring kudos to
these people within their community. Here's how:

1. **Select Forum Administration from the module menu.**

2. **Click User Settings.**

3. **Find the user and click the Edit button.**

   Find the user by clicking on the letter in the alphabet that is the first
   letter in their first name.

4. **Maximize the Admin Settings section.**

5. **Select one or move avatars.**

   You will see a drop-down list that contains images already uploaded,
   available for you to choose from. If you would like to select an image
   that is already in the drop-down list, simply click the Add button. If you
   want to add an image not already available, click the Browse button and
   then select Upload New File, as shown in Figure 14-4. After uploading the
   image, you need to select the image in the drop-down list and click the
   Add button.

6. **Click Update.**

Figure 14-4:
Adding
more
avatars.

One important thing to keep in mind is that you must click the update button in order for these settings to take effect. If you do not, the images you uploaded will still remain available to you but the avatars will not be applied to this user. At any time you can also delete an avatar assignment by clicking the red X next to each avatar image shown in that user's profile. As with the assigning of an avatar image to a user, you must click the update button when deleting, or the avatar image will not be removed from the user's profile.

Enabling Time Zones Specific to Each User

Users often like to see dates of forum post information relative to their own time zone settings. This is managed under Forum Administration➪General Settings under General Settings. When on this page, administrators simply need to select the Enable User Time Zones check box. After this is done, users can change their time zone preference by editing their site user profile, available when clicking their username in the portal.

Letting Users Rate Their Favorite Posts

Let your forum users rate their favorite threads. Here's how:

1. **Select Forum Administration from the module menu.**

2. **Click Statistics & Ranking.**

3. **Expand Ratings and select Enable Forums Rating.**

4. **Click Update to apply the changes.**

Displaying the Poster's Location

Share the country of all forum users with each other by doing the following:

1. **Select Forum Administration from the module menu.**

2. **Click General Setting.**

3. **Select either All Users or Administrators from Display Poster's Location.**

4. **Click Update to apply the changes.**

Displaying a Forum Group on a Different Page

You can add a second Forum module to your site and set it to display forums from a single group. This means that you don't have to add and set up a new forum module each time, which would mean managing forum settings and users in two modules, which would lead to a decent headache! Here's how to display forums from a single group:

1. **Add a new page for the new Forum module.**

2. **Add Existing Forum Module by using the Control Panel.**

   You need to select the page the existing module is located on and then select the Forum module. This adds the existing Forum module to this new page. The module displays all the existing forums and works just like the other one.

3. **Select Module Settings from the module menu.**

4. **Expand the Forum Settings section.**

5. **Select the forum you want to be displayed from the drop-down list.**

6. **Choose to enable or disable the footer.**

   The footer refers to the Statistics pane and the What's New pane. If you plan to add more than one group to this page (by repeating this whole tutorial again), disabling the footer means you can compactly display more than one group without having multiple Statistics and What's New panes.

7. **Click Update.**

Index

• S •

• T •

• U •

Notes

Notes

Notes

BUSINESS, CAREERS & PERSONAL FINANCE

0-7645-9847-3

0-7645-2431-3

Also available:
- Business Plans Kit For Dummies
  0-7645-9794-9
- Economics For Dummies
  0-7645-5726-2
- Grant Writing For Dummies
  0-7645-8416-2
- Home Buying For Dummies
  0-7645-5331-3
- Managing For Dummies
  0-7645-1771-6
- Marketing For Dummies
  0-7645-5600-2

- Personal Finance For Dummies
  0-7645-2590-5*
- Resumes For Dummies
  0-7645-5471-9
- Selling For Dummies
  0-7645-5363-1
- Six Sigma For Dummies
  0-7645-6798-5
- Small Business Kit For Dummies
  0-7645-5984-2
- Starting an eBay Business For Dummies
  0-7645-6924-4
- Your Dream Career For Dummies
  0-7645-9795-7

HOME & BUSINESS COMPUTER BASICS

0-470-05432-8

0-471-75421-8

Also available:
- Cleaning Windows Vista For Dummies
  0-471-78293-9
- Excel 2007 For Dummies
  0-470-03737-7
- Mac OS X Tiger For Dummies
  0-7645-7675-5
- MacBook For Dummies
  0-470-04859-X
- Macs For Dummies
  0-470-04849-2
- Office 2007 For Dummies
  0-470-00923-3

- Outlook 2007 For Dummies
  0-470-03830-6
- PCs For Dummies
  0-7645-8958-X
- Salesforce.com For Dummies
  0-470-04893-X
- Upgrading & Fixing Laptops For Dummies
  0-7645-8959-8
- Word 2007 For Dummies
  0-470-03658-3
- Quicken 2007 For Dummies
  0-470-04600-7

FOOD, HOME, GARDEN, HOBBIES, MUSIC & PETS

0-7645-8404-9

0-7645-9904-6

Also available:
- Candy Making For Dummies
  0-7645-9734-5
- Card Games For Dummies
  0-7645-9910-0
- Crocheting For Dummies
  0-7645-4151-X
- Dog Training For Dummies
  0-7645-8418-9
- Healthy Carb Cookbook For Dummies
  0-7645-8476-6
- Home Maintenance For Dummies
  0-7645-5215-5

- Horses For Dummies
  0-7645-9797-3
- Jewelry Making & Beading For Dummies
  0-7645-2571-9
- Orchids For Dummies
  0-7645-6759-4
- Puppies For Dummies
  0-7645-5255-4
- Rock Guitar For Dummies
  0-7645-5356-9
- Sewing For Dummies
  0-7645-6847-7
- Singing For Dummies
  0-7645-2475-5

INTERNET & DIGITAL MEDIA

0-470-04529-9

0-470-04894-8

Also available:
- Blogging For Dummies
  0-471-77084-1
- Digital Photography For Dummies
  0-7645-9802-3
- Digital Photography All-in-One Desk Reference For Dummies
  0-470-03743-1
- Digital SLR Cameras and Photography For Dummies
  0-7645-9803-1
- eBay Business All-in-One Desk Reference For Dummies
  0-7645-8438-3
- HDTV For Dummies
  0-470-09673-X

- Home Entertainment PCs For Dummies
  0-470-05523-5
- MySpace For Dummies
  0-470-09529-6
- Search Engine Optimization For Dummies
  0-471-97998-8
- Skype For Dummies
  0-470-04891-3
- The Internet For Dummies
  0-7645-8996-2
- Wiring Your Digital Home For Dummies
  0-471-91830-X

* Separate Canadian edition also available
† Separate U.K. edition also available

Available wherever books are sold. For more information or to order direct: U.S. customers visit www.dummies.com or call 1-877-762-2974.
U.K. customers visit www.wileyeurope.com or call 0800 243407. Canadian customers visit www.wiley.ca or call 1-800-567-4797.

SPORTS, FITNESS, PARENTING, RELIGION & SPIRITUALITY

0-471-76871-5

0-7645-7841-3

Also available:
- Catholicism For Dummies
  0-7645-5391-7
- Exercise Balls For Dummies
  0-7645-5623-1
- Fitness For Dummies
  0-7645-7851-0
- Football For Dummies
  0-7645-3936-1
- Judaism For Dummies
  0-7645-5299-6
- Potty Training For Dummies
  0-7645-5417-4
- Buddhism For Dummies
  0-7645-5359-3

- Pregnancy For Dummies
  0-7645-4483-7 †
- Ten Minute Tone-Ups For Dummies
  0-7645-7207-5
- NASCAR For Dummies
  0-7645-7681-X
- Religion For Dummies
  0-7645-5264-3
- Soccer For Dummies
  0-7645-5229-5
- Women in the Bible For Dummies
  0-7645-8475-8

TRAVEL

0-7645-7749-2

0-7645-6945-7

Also available:
- Alaska For Dummies
  0-7645-7746-8
- Cruise Vacations For Dummies
  0-7645-6941-4
- England For Dummies
  0-7645-4276-1
- Europe For Dummies
  0-7645-7529-5
- Germany For Dummies
  0-7645-7823-5
- Hawaii For Dummies
  0-7645-7402-7

- Italy For Dummies
  0-7645-7386-1
- Las Vegas For Dummies
  0-7645-7382-9
- London For Dummies
  0-7645-4277-X
- Paris For Dummies
  0-7645-7630-5
- RV Vacations For Dummies
  0-7645-4442-X
- Walt Disney World & Orlando
  For Dummies
  0-7645-9660-8

GRAPHICS, DESIGN & WEB DEVELOPMENT

0-7645-8815-X

0-7645-9571-7

Also available:
- 3D Game Animation For Dummies
  0-7645-8789-7
- AutoCAD 2006 For Dummies
  0-7645-8925-3
- Building a Web Site For Dummies
  0-7645-7144-3
- Creating Web Pages For Dummies
  0-470-08030-2
- Creating Web Pages All-in-One Desk
  Reference For Dummies
  0-7645-4345-8
- Dreamweaver 8 For Dummies
  0-7645-9649-7

- InDesign CS2 For Dummies
  0-7645-9572-5
- Macromedia Flash 8 For Dummies
  0-7645-9691-8
- Photoshop CS2 and Digital
  Photography For Dummies
  0-7645-9580-6
- Photoshop Elements 4 For Dummies
  0-471-77483-9
- Syndicating Web Sites with RSS Feeds
  For Dummies
  0-7645-8848-6
- Yahoo! SiteBuilder For Dummies
  0-7645-9800-7

NETWORKING, SECURITY, PROGRAMMING & DATABASES

0-7645-7728-X

0-471-74940-0

Also available:
- Access 2007 For Dummies
  0-470-04612-0
- ASP.NET 2 For Dummies
  0-7645-7907-X
- C# 2005 For Dummies
  0-7645-9704-3
- Hacking For Dummies
  0-470-05235-X
- Hacking Wireless Networks
  For Dummies
  0-7645-9730-2
- Java For Dummies
  0-470-08716-1

- Microsoft SQL Server 2005 For Dummies
  0-7645-7755-7
- Networking All-in-One Desk Reference
  For Dummies
  0-7645-9939-9
- Preventing Identity Theft For Dummies
  0-7645-7336-5
- Telecom For Dummies
  0-471-77085-X
- Visual Studio 2005 All-in-One Desk
  Reference For Dummies
  0-7645-9775-2
- XML For Dummies
  0-7645-8845-1

HEALTH & SELF-HELP

0-7645-8450-2

0-7645-4149-8

Also available:

- Bipolar Disorder For Dummies
  0-7645-8451-0
- Chemotherapy and Radiation
  For Dummies
  0-7645-7832-4
- Controlling Cholesterol For Dummies
  0-7645-5440-9
- Diabetes For Dummies
  0-7645-6820-5* †
- Divorce For Dummies
  0-7645-8417-0 †

- Fibromyalgia For Dummies
  0-7645-5441-7
- Low-Calorie Dieting For Dummies
  0-7645-9905-4
- Meditation For Dummies
  0-471-77774-9
- Osteoporosis For Dummies
  0-7645-7621-6
- Overcoming Anxiety For Dummies
  0-7645-5447-6
- Reiki For Dummies
  0-7645-9907-0
- Stress Management For Dummies
  0-7645-5144-2

EDUCATION, HISTORY, REFERENCE & TEST PREPARATION

0-7645-8381-6

0-7645-9554-7

Also available:

- The ACT For Dummies
  0-7645-9652-7
- Algebra For Dummies
  0-7645-5325-9
- Algebra Workbook For Dummies
  0-7645-8467-7
- Astronomy For Dummies
  0-7645-8465-0
- Calculus For Dummies
  0-7645-2498-4
- Chemistry For Dummies
  0-7645-5430-1
- Forensics For Dummies
  0-7645-5580-4

- Freemasons For Dummies
  0-7645-9796-5
- French For Dummies
  0-7645-5193-0
- Geometry For Dummies
  0-7645-5324-0
- Organic Chemistry I For Dummies
  0-7645-6902-3
- The SAT I For Dummies
  0-7645-7193-1
- Spanish For Dummies
  0-7645-5194-9
- Statistics For Dummies
  0-7645-5423-9

Get smart @ dummies.com®

- **Find a full list of Dummies titles**
- **Look into loads of FREE on-site articles**
- **Sign up for FREE eTips e-mailed to you weekly**
- **See what other products carry the Dummies name**
- **Shop directly from the Dummies bookstore**
- **Enter to win new prizes every month!**

* Separate Canadian edition also available
† Separate U.K. edition also available

Available wherever books are sold. For more information or to order direct: U.S. customers visit www.dummies.com or call 1-877-762-2974.
U.K. customers visit www.wileyeurope.com or call 0800 243407. Canadian customers visit www.wiley.ca or call 1-800-567-4797.